NATIONAL SERVICE RECRUITING

THE PRIME MINISTER TO BROADCAST

FROM OUR PARLIAMENTARY CORRESPONDENT

The Prime Minister is to broadcast an ddress to the nation from 10, Downing reet at 9.25 p.m. on Monday on the ...nis will mark ... recruiting ... for all

---

A.R.P. SHELTER FOR 900 PEOPLE

UNDERGROUND CHAMBERS ON GREAT WEST ROAD

Sir John Anderson's recent speech on air raid prec... sibility shelters difficulti... space, b... Fireston... are in a... factory t...

...rted in Danzig ...ember Is Feared

...DER
...TIMES.

Hitler's pact with Poland British guarantee to Poland e same: the maintenance of ...us quo in Danzig and the ...—in the case of the pact for ...rs—hence there is no con- ...tween Herr Hitler's recent ...nd Britain's.

...nzig itself could vote on its ...e, it probably would favor

---

BRITISH NOTE TO JAPAN

TWO VIEWS IN TOKYO

FEARS OF ECONOMIC PRESSURE

From Our Own Correspondent

TOKYO, JAN. 18

Officials here see no particular need of hastening the Japanese reply to the British

---

Books of the Day

THE FUTURE OF NAZISM

A NEW PHASE?

...EVOLUTION DES NIHILISMUS. By HERMANN RAUSCHNING. Europa ...ag, Zürich.

ITALY SENT SPAIN 100,000 IN 4 MONTHS

Rome Army-Navy Magazine Bares Submarine Attacks on Merchant Ships

MILITARY PACT FORESEEN

Visiting Spaniards Talk With Mussolini, Presumably on Paying Franco's Debt

By HERBERT L. MATTHEWS

CALM COURAGE IN BARCELONA

MYSTICAL FAITH IN VICTORY

PAUSE IN OPERATIONS

From Our Own Correspondent

BARCELONA, JAN. 18

Goebbels Paper Forbids Wirelessing of Cartoon

Wireless to THE NEW YORK TIMES.

BERLIN, March 9.—The An- griff, Propaganda Minister Jo- seph Goebbels's newspaper, de- clined today to release for radio transmission to THE NEW YORK TIMES a copy of one of the prize- winning cartoons selected to prove that there is such a thing as humor in Nazi Germany.

One cartoon that supposedly tickled Nazi ribs showed a fat pug dog accosting a lean, long dachs-

---

...E IS RENEWING ...PEACE EFFORTS, ...ES BRITISH ENVO...

See Hopes to Ascer'... ether There Is Basis f... ...ccord Among Powers

Y SUPPORTING MOV...

Who Are Experts... ... Meet With Pa... ...ary of State

E M. CIANFARR... THE NEW YORK TIMES. ...CITY, June 5.—Th... ...eption given to his ... ...le soundings with ... ...nks

---

NEW BRIBE OF $1,750 CHARGED TO MORAN BY TAXI OPERATOR

Accusation, Not in Indictment, Made by President of the Parmelee Company

HITLER HAILS DEEDS OF HIS MEN IN SPAIN AS LESSON TO FOES

Reviewing the Condor Legion of 15,000, He D... 'Encircling

—The 0,000

COUNTRY PROPERTIES

3 lines 7s. 6d. (minimum)

A.R.P.—Scottish Highlands, far from danger ...zones. COTTAGES are available to be ...LET from now onwards.—Write Box P.1346. The Times, E.C.4.

KEE, R.   The World we left
           behind.

ROLLE COLLEGE
EXMOUTH

THE WORLD WE LEFT BEHIND

Charles Seale-Hayne Library
University of Plymouth
(01752) 588 588
LibraryandITenquiries@plymouth.ac.uk

AT THE NEW YORK WORLD'S FAIR: *A Father of To-day Takes His Child to See the World of To-morrow*

He is an American. He is proud of his country, proud of New York, proud of the World's Fair—proudest of all of the son he is taking round with him. The theme of the Fair is the World of the Future. What does the future hold for this child—to live in poverty, to die in a war, or to enjoy peace and have a share in the world's riches and the world's happiness and beauty? If every statesman hung this picture in his office and looked at it every day, perhaps the world of to-morrow would be the world every father wants for his child to live in.

ROBERT KEE

THE WORLD WE LEFT BEHIND

A CHRONICLE OF THE YEAR
1939

WEIDENFELD & NICOLSON
LONDON

FOR SUE

CONTENTS

CONTENTS

CONTENTS

CONTENTS

PART III
3 SEPTEMBER–31 DECEMBER 1939

REMEMBERING

Erna Rosenthal, Wucherer Strasse 24, Halle an der Saale, Germany
Edith Kaufmann, Augsburger Strasse 16, Berlin W.50
Helene Gleich, Raupachstrasse 8, Berlin C.2
Erna Blass, Münchener Strasse 15, Berlin W.30
Lucie Kallmann, Nachodstrasse 28, Berlin W.
Meta Nussbaum, Brandenburgische Strasse 46, Berlin-Wilmersdorf
Hilda Löwenthal, Geberstrasse 4, Hanover
Else Reisman, Augustastrasse 16, Breslau
Margot Wolff, Gandystrasse 8, Berlin N.8
Hildegard Eppstein, Carmen Sylva Strasse 129, Berlin 113
Johanna Raphael, Wilmersdorfer Strasse 60, Berlin-Charlottenburg
Hesta Podolski, Berliner Strasse 147, Berlin-Tempelhof
'German girl, Jewess (18), still in Germany, able to do housework, good
    dressmaker, very fond of children. Turiner Strasse 5, Berlin'

all of whom advertised in the Domestic Situations Required column of
The Times on Saturday 7 January 1939 and who, together with many others
in similar plight throughout that year, long ago left such addresses

In little more than twenty-four hours we shall be entering upon a new year. I trust that it will not only be a peaceful one but a happy one for everybody, and I can assure you that the Government for which I am speaking will do its utmost to make it so.

NEVILLE CHAMBERLAIN
Swinton Hall, Masham,
Yorkshire
31 December 1938

The looming danger of war, imminent and inevitable, which seems to be spreading over the world prevents youth from being light-hearted and makes young men feel as though they were in a boat without oars being borne on a swift current towards a cataract and whirlpool.

HERBERT SAMUEL
Oxford
9 February 1939

When huge armaments are being piled up on every hand we cannot avoid a certain anxiety lest some incident, perhaps trifling in itself, should set in motion the machinery that would bring them into operation. We know that if that dread event should come to pass there would be none of those who are dearest to us who could count on escaping the consequences . . .

NEVILLE CHAMBERLAIN
Blackburn, Lancashire
22 February 1939

War was made on Germany but not war of a kind or a heat to compel her to bring back her airmen from Poland. This is a terrible episode in our history whatever the explanation may be.

Manchester Guardian
25 September 1939

We sneer at the press, but they give an extremely true picture of a great deal that is going on, a very much fuller and more detailed picture than we are able to receive from Ministers of the Crown . . .

WINSTON CHURCHILL
House of Commons
13 April 1939

INTRODUCTION

1939 was to see the outbreak in Europe of the most terrible war the world has yet known. This is an account of that year as it unfolded at the time.

Academic history can sometimes lose sight of one important element in both the experience and the shaping of great events, namely, the straightforward but exciting fact that no one at the time could ever say exactly what was going to happen next. This book tries to show as nearly as possible what it was like to follow the course of events in that year with the only public source of information available: daily newspapers and radio broadcasts.

Whether or not this adds anything useful to our knowledge of history depends on what you think history is for. There is a strict school which believes that the only meaningful historical fact is one which lends itself to some coherent interpretation of man's activities and his social organization. To such people there may seem little here but blind alleyways and leads that either take one nowhere or only to places where one has been before. A wealth of documents from the archives of many countries is now available, together with many politicians' memoirs, for study in depth of what actually happened behind the scenes in this year, and much historical analysis has been made of it. The text of this book takes no account of this, or indeed directly of anything that happened after the 31 December 1939. Indirectly an unavoidable knowledge of what did happen next lends, I hope, additional interest to the narrative.

The result of this approach is that emphases here are not always what they are in the history books. Many journalistic 'stories' momentarily emerge to reassume a significance of which 'history' has deprived them; words and actions similarly diminished by time reacquire ephemeral status and what, in the light of subsequent events, often turned out to be futile thinking can again sometimes seem quite reasonable.

My own view of history is that it has many different rôles; the one with which this book is concerned is uncomplicated, providing mainly only insights in eventful times into both the bright and the dark side of the human race, and a chance to contemplate the poignancy of both.

The use of newspapers as historical source material can justifiably be questioned with the familiar cry: 'You don't believe all you read in the newspapers, do you?' My own experience is that for all their periodic exaggerations and inaccuracies – which they themselves usually have to adjust over a period of time – newspapers do provide invaluable historical evidence not only of forgotten events but also of the way things looked before later events made them look different. And that is as much a part of history as the way things actually were.

1939 is a year which I lived through myself in a state of reasonable political awareness, between the ages of nineteen and twenty. But I have been continually surprised in writing this book to find that events did not evolve at the time quite as my memory, conditioned by later historical hindsight, has since led me to think. There is, for instance, the discovery that during the first two and a half months of the year it did not necessarily look at all as if the year would end the way it did. The detail of individual events has become equally distorted. Because we have known for over forty years that the Spanish Civil War ended in April 1939 with the collapse of the Republican Government, its end is virtually the only 1939 association we have for it. Chamberlain's appeasement visit to Mussolini in January of this year proved of no consequence whatsoever in history and as a result I find I have no memory of it at all, though I was then quite an avid newspaper reader. Chamberlain's initial reaction to the occupation of Prague in March 1939, later rather obscured by the fact that he was finally the Prime Minister who declared war on Nazi Germany, now seems almost unbelievable, though a majority of the House of Commons loyally supported him in it. Later memory of a more terrible event – the most appalling in all human history – has similarly conditioned forgetfulness of how the matter of Germany's treatment of the Jews appeared in that year.

It is for such reasons that I have concentrated much of the detailed narrative in the early part of the year's chronicle. But there is also, of course, another more general reason, the nature of which must be clear from some of the quotations with which I have prefaced the book. It is impossible to read of the year 1939 as it seemed at the time without being struck by disturbing pre-echoes of the way our own times seem to us.

Because this is primarily, though by no means exclusively, a European story, the evidence is drawn largely, though not exclusively, from newspapers on the European side of the Atlantic. Because, too, I am a British writer they are mainly British newspapers and the viewpoint is mainly one from Britain. But because it was a European story which was deeply to concern the other side of the Atlantic as well, the intermingling of viewpoints from both sides becomes one of its sub-themes. I am at the same time very much aware that on both continents, but particularly the American, many everyday aspects of the way the human race was faring have been eclipsed by concentration on the narrative of the main course of world events.

The newspapers from which this narrative has been taken represent a by no means totally comprehensive selection. However, the range is probably wider than all but the most obsessional watchers of current affairs at the time would have suscribed to. Like all newspaper readers I have found my preferences. In the United States I have relied almost entirely on the *New York Times*. In Britain I have made use primarily of *The Times*, the *Manchester Guardian*, the *News Chronicle*, the *Observer*, the *Daily Express*, the *Daily Telegraph* and the *Sunday Pictorial*. I am grateful particularly to these, but also to all other papers from which I have quoted and to the journalists who wrote for all of them.

My thanks are due, as often before, to the Trustees and the courteous and efficient staffs of the London Library and the British Library Newspaper Library at Colindale; and, for guidance, assistance and encouragement, to Gill Coleridge in particular but also to John Gross, Alex MacCormick, Ray Roberts, Tanya Schmoller and Topsy Levan, who was reputed to be the fastest typist in the Admiralty in 1939 and is surely the fastest and most efficient outside it today.

References are in many cases self-explanatory, but when not fairly immediately clear may be found in the Source Notes at the end of the book.

ROBERT KEE

PART I

1 JANUARY – 15 MARCH 1939

In whatever pertains to outdoor life—
be it motoring or sport—one name
is now predominant, and that is

DUNLOP

I

Every New Year allows mankind the momentary sensation that it is possible to do better than in the year before, or even to make some sort of fresh start. In this the year 1939 was like any other. To some extent the sensation was even stronger than usual, at least for many people in Europe and even in the United States, for they had just come through a traumatic experience. The fear of an imminent war, even more terrible than that Great War from which the world had emerged twenty years before, had receded only three months earlier.

The Munich Agreement between Britain, France, Germany and Italy in September 1938 had substantially re-drawn the frontiers of Czechoslovakia, to that small democratic republic's serious disadvantage but in such a way as to satisfy at the last moment the German Chancellor, Adolf Hitler, who had been about to march across them. What he had described as his last territorial ambition in Europe – the incorporation of the German-settled Sudetenland into the German Reich – was fulfilled. (He had incorporated Austria the year before.) A vicious officially organized pogrom against Jews in the German Reich some weeks after the Munich Agreement, in which synagogues were burned, Jewish houses broken into, Jews humiliated and beaten in the streets, and the Jews themselves made to pay for the vast amount of damage caused, had thereafter lost Herr Hitler much goodwill among those in the western democracies who were disposed to trust him; and this disapproval of the democracies had in turn excited much aggressive hostility in the German state-controlled press. But at least there no longer seemed immediate cause for fearful international concern.

Some concern did proceed from the stridency with which Herr Hitler's fellow dictator in Italy, Benito Mussolini, building on a triumph of his own a few years before in Ethiopia, was now urging Italian claims against France in the Mediterranean, particularly in Corsica and Tunisia. This was aggravated by the fact that some 10,000 Italian troops, engaged on the side of General Franco in the Spanish Civil War, were, at the turn of the year, fighting their way against the armies of the Spanish Republic Government towards the French frontier on the Pyrenees. But all this seemed of secondary importance beside the ending of 'the crisis' – which is what the English-speaking world still called it – of the previous September.

The year thus began under a sort of cloud of relief. It was a cloud inasmuch as those who felt relieved were uncertain as to how far their sense of relief was self-deluding; but it was not the storm which had momentarily seemed inevitable. And those who felt more anxiety than relief and those who felt more relief than anxiety had this in common: that neither knew, or could possibly know, which feeling would eventually prove to have been more justified. Such uncertainty could be, at this New Year, a source of hope.

The German Chancellor, Herr Hitler, issued his own message for the first day of the New Year from Berchtesgaden and this in itself could be read as quite encouraging. Though he defined future tasks as the education of the German people in National Socialist unity and the strengthening of Germany's armed forces, and emphasized that German policy was determined by the anti-Comintern Pact with Italy and Japan, he went on to say: 'We have but one wish: that in the coming year we may also be able to make our contribution to the general pacification of the world.' And the correspondent of the London *Times* in Berlin noted that 'the rockets which rose over German cities and the Bengal lights thrown on to the snow from so many windows were manifestations of a thankfulness and hope which have seldom welcomed the New Year since 1918'. The German paper, *Das Schwarze Korps*, however, the organ of the SS, had on its New Year front page a drawing of an SS man fastening on his steel helmet and it was captioned: 'Tighten Your Chinstrap!'

The editor of the London Sunday *Observer*, J.L. Garvin, a staunch supporter of the British Prime Minister, Neville Chamberlain, and his policy of trying to accommodate the dictators where reasonably possible, expressed on New Year's Day a qualified optimism, though in rather guarded terms. He faced up to the blow which the Munich settlement had delivered to the small democracy of Czechoslovakia and weighed things in the balance.

'On the one hand,' he wrote, 'seeing the choice of evils as the dire dilemma stood, Mr Chamberlain was a thousand times right in saving the world's peace at Munich even at the price exacted.' On the other hand, weaknesses in Britain's defences had been revealed and must be remedied. Provided this were done, though, 'there is more and not less need for pursuing the Prime Minister's policy of seeking agreement and appeasement by all reasonable means compatible with the real increase and not decrease of security'.

The next attempt at seeking such appeasement was to be made on 10 January, when Chamberlain was due to go to Rome with his Foreign Minister, Lord Halifax, for talks with Mussolini. Any possible risk that this visit might irritate France because of Mussolini's anti-French campaign in the Mediterranean would, the *Observer* said, have been 'cleared up through the diplomatic channel' beforehand.

On Monday, 2 January, the editor of the London *Times*, another strong supporter of Neville Chamberlain, also summed up the prospects. While conceding that 'the year that is now beginning cannot be entered upon in a mood of mere optimism', he thought that 'if its difficulties are faced with steadiness, energy and a readiness for self-sacrifice it is not an unreasonable hope that, before its close, firmness and good sense together will have found a constructive answer to some at least of the larger differences that threaten a troubled peace'.

Clashes of interest such as some of those between the dictatorships and the democracies were inevitable in a competing world, but 'it is common ground that there neither is nor should be the slightest reason for their making war upon each other, however great the contrast in outlook, merely on account of differing ideologies'.

It was true, the editor of *The Times* went on, that certain ideological repercussions of the dictatorships' notions of race and state, such as the treatment of the Jews 'not only affect the interests of other countries but challenge the general conscience of humanity. ... Yet the instinct is sound that there is in these differences of political creed alone no sane case for armed conflict.'

A column on a nearby page recorded factually that new anti-Jewish measures became effective in Germany with the New Year. No Jew could henceforth own or drive a car, or engage in the retail trade or any craft. (Jews were already forbidden to attend cinemas, theatres and concerts.) 'There is a fear', the report concluded, 'of even sterner measures in the next few days.'

The *New York Herald Tribune*, reporting these new German decrees, added that all Jews over three months old must now carry a special police identity card with photographs and fingerprints. It understood that this was in fact a substitute for a still harsher decree that had been under discussion, namely that all Jews should wear a yellow star. And a Philadelphia Quaker group working in Germany 'with every co-operation and courtesy of the German Government' said that the message from the 600,000 Jews still there was, 'Above all, get us out before something more awful happens.'

It was the fate of the unemployed, however, which principally concerned the British Labour Party paper, the *Daily Herald*, at the New Year. The official figure for Britain was 1,800,000 registered unemployed, but there must, said the paper, be at least another 200,000 unregistered. Parliament had recently acted in a number of good causes – such as the new Criminal Justice Bill which was to abolish flogging – but had done absolutely nothing to put even one hundred men to work.

> Yet what national problem compares in importance with unemployment? What evil comes near it in magnitude? ... We face an international crisis demanding of Britain that she should stand at the peak of efficiency and produce to the maximum. And we have over an eighth of our total labour force doing nothing. ... To-day the problem does not seem to touch the nation's heart. Yet the suffering goes on. ... Regrettable? Blush for shame at that word. It is intolerable and it shall not be tolerated.

H.G. Wells, writing a New Year forecast in the liberal *News Chronicle*, concentrated on the international outlook but struck a domestic radical note of his own. He castigated Chamberlain's efforts for peace as 'disastrous antics' and said that a reaction to them was gathering force 'with the effect of a national awakening'. People had been hissing Chamberlain when he appeared on the newsreels recently, and hissing was not something often heard in British cinemas.

9

John Bull was slowly 'realizing what sort of figure he has been made to cut in this world of men. . . . He is asking questions. He has been fed with the story that he is the brave wise master of a great Empire, and now he asks: "What have you been doing with this Empire of mine?" '

Wells saw a new wave of 'very patriotic radicalism' sweeping away the present British Government at a General Election by the middle of the year, together with 'maybe much of the existing class and party government, for good and all'. This new government would be Nationalist and Leftist and would include young Tories and 'competent outsiders'. He thought it essential that Britain and America should get together, but said he did not mean by that that the impending visit of the King and Queen to the United States, which had just been announced, would be of much use:

> These young people are, I believe, a very charming couple, constantly smiling and bowing, but they mean absolutely nothing in the problems of today. For a couple of centuries the British Royal Family has had no relationship whatever to the thought, literature, art and science and education of our community and its interventions in military and clerical promotions and political life have been of very questionable value. That visit is of very small importance in my horoscope. But what is of very great importance is the approach of daily transatlantic air services. This means a rapid development of mental assimilation.

In the United States themselves the New Year seemed to be welcomed with a greater revelry than for some years past. In New York the emphasis at nearly all the many private and public parties in hotels and restaurants was on the theme of the New York World Fair which was to open in May: 'Dawn of a New Day'. At midnight in most places the Fair's anthem of that name, the last composition of George Gershwin, was played and sung.

But from the United States there was only one New Year message that really counted and for that the world would have to wait until 4 January, when President Roosevelt, already half-way through a second term of office, was to address Congress. His address this year was particularly eagerly awaited, not only because of what he would say about the international situation but because this, the seventy-sixth Congress, was a newly-elected one and its members looked like being noticeably less compliant with the President's wishes than the previous one. In the mid-term elections opposition to Roosevelt's New Deal and the national spending it involved had been heavily augmented in both the Senate and the House of Representatives.

But of course for most people most of the time public affairs, even in awesome or interesting times, form only the background to life. And though a literary man with political interests like Harold Nicolson, Member of Parliament for West Leicester, might write, as he did, on the first page of his diary for 1939 the words 'The Year of Destiny', a minor headline in the New Year's Day *Observer*, '1939 Begins Well' was probably more in tune with the ordinary Briton's approach to the opening year. This preceded an article about the new Morris Ten (10 h.p.) car with 'its lively performance and lightweight highly efficient English engine': it could be bought with a fixed roof for £175 or with a sliding roof for £10 more. The same paper carried a letter from that London district said to be the home of English intellectuals, Bloomsbury, beginning: 'I am perhaps unduly exercised about the morning rasher' – the correspondent being unable to decide whether to fry his breakfast bacon fast (in which case he found it turned out 'a tasteless chip') or slowly (which made it 'equally tasteless but with a resemblance to wet flannel'). The following week there were more letters on this subject in the paper than on any other. An analogous American concern was expressed in a long January article in the *New York Times*, on the making of coffee, in which, after dealing scathingly with what among Europeans passed for coffee, it recommended traditional techniques such as the 'old-fashioned' method of putting the grounds in cold water and bringing them to the boil, 'sometimes mixing the grounds with a raw egg or dropping an eggshell into the coffee just before taking it off the fire'.

As well as the prospects for Chamberlain on his next journey of appeasement to Rome or for Roosevelt faced by his new Congress, people looked at the prospects for the theatre, the cinema and sport. (Joe Louis, for instance, was to meet John Henry Lewis, challenging him for the World Heavyweight Championship in New York on 25 January.)

In Britain, successful plays from 1938 which continued to run were Terence Rattigan's *French Without Tears* ('London's Longest Run') and Emlyn Williams's *The Corn is Green*. Another new Priestley, *Johnson Over Jordan*, was expected shortly. John Gielgud, who had had a highly successful classical season of Shakespeare, Sheridan and Chekhov at the Queen's Theatre in 1938, was now appearing there in *Dear Octopus* with Marie Tempest. In New York, Maurice Evans's uncut *Hamlet* still had another three weeks to run, and there were a number of musicals: *Hellzapoppin* ('the season's unchallenged smash hit' – *New York Times*), Rodgers and Hart's *The Boys From Syracuse* and Walter Huston in *Knickerbocker Holiday* by Maxwell Anderson and Kurt Weill. The British D'Oyly Carte company were to open on Broadway with *The Pirates of Penzance* in the first week of the year.

Altogether there was quite a strong British element in both the New York theatre and cinema. *Spring Meeting*, a play by the Anglo-Irish writer M.J. Farrell (Molly Keane) was running with Gladys Cooper and A.E. Matthews. Robert Morley was starring in *Oscar Wilde*. In what the *New York Herald Tribune* still called 'Picture Theaters', a number of British films were to be found: *The Citadel* with Robert Donat and Rosalind Russell, *Pygmalion* with Leslie Howard and Wendy Hiller, Hitchcock's *The Lady Vanishes* and *The Beachcomber* with Charles Laughton and Elsa Lanchester. In the first days of the year the New York Critics' Award went to *The Citadel* as the best film of the year and to Hitchcock as best director for *The Lady Vanishes*.

The American film industry was, however, in a healthy enough condition and the *New York Herald Tribune* found Hollywood with its 'veins running with new blood', citing Darryl F. Zanuck at 20th Century-Fox, Harry Cohn at Columbia, Walter Wanger at United Artists and Frank Capra. One question exercising Hollywood was when David Selznick would finally make his choice for the part of Scarlett O'Hara in *Gone With the Wind*. He had bought the film rights as early as 1936 and a number of stars including Norma Shearer and Greta Garbo had already been considered and turned down. His decision was expected soon.

Among foreign films in New York there were to be found Jean Gabin and Erich von Stroheim in *La Grande Illusion*, a prison-camp story of the Great War expressing a mood of Franco-German reconciliation. The talents of the German cinema had once been devoted to something analogous in Pabst's *Kameradschaft* but they were now at their most effective when harnessed to the energies of the new State, the Third Reich, and a film called *Pour le Mérite* about the resurrection of the German Air Force after its heroic demise before superior odds in 1918, was playing to packed houses in Berlin.

In Britain, where *The Times* also still called cinemas 'Picture Theatres', though with English spelling, Disney's *Snow-White and the Seven Dwarfs* was a success, as was *The Citadel*. But C.A. Lejeune, the critic of the *Observer*, noted that the British public was showing a certain sales resistance to new films as compared with a year ago. She put this down partly to competition from good radio shows such as *Monday Night at Seven* and *Band Waggon*. But television, for which Britain provided the only public service in the world, was also, said Lejeune, collecting 'a rapidly growing body of viewers'.

The term 'rapidly growing' has to be interpreted in the sense that public television transmission had only recently started. There were fewer than 20,000 sets altogether (standard size: eight inches by ten inches with a twelve-inch tube) with reception reaching only up to about forty miles from the transmitting station at Alexandra Palace in London, though some freak reception had been reported from as far away as Yorkshire and the Channel Islands. The Director-General of the BBC, Mr F.W. Ogilvie, who had just replaced Sir John Reith, made it clear however in this first week of the year that television was intended to be a national service and that the first official jump in transmission by relay would be to the Midlands, where the Corporation had an option on a site in Birmingham. The second play to be televised in its entirety from a London theatre went out in this first week, a Michel Saint-Denis production of *Twelfth Night* with Peggy Ashcroft and Michael Redgrave. The first had been J.B. Priestley's *When We Are Married*. *The Times* compared the two viewing experiences.

The Priestley, it judged, had been a success,

in spite of the unevenness which must necessarily appear when three cameras are

Ralph Richardson in a scene from J.B. Priestley's *Johnson Over Jordan*, New Theatre, London.

Sybil Thorndike and Emlyn Williams in his play *The Corn is Green* at London's Duchess Theatre.

trying to cover a spectacle too big for one. It did not matter that the spectacle was never or hardly ever complete. The joke was clear ... the wheeling cameras caught all its principal points. But *Twelfth Night* is more than a joke and its lyric beauty defies the vigilance of mechanical eyes which alter their range minute by minute.... The result was to falsify the fluid grace of the production and to tempt all viewers who were not preoccupied with the mechanical wonders of the apparatus to close their eyes and treat the affair as broadcast drama.

For the smaller television sets of 4 inches by 3¾ inches which were just beginning to come on to the market, *The Times* was recommending Mickey Mouse cartoons 'frequently shown to the delight of all ages'. The Director of Television at the BBC however made clear that there was every intention of continuing to televise material of high quality. He said that their ideal was to broadcast a play a day and revealed that there would be occasional 'horror plays' with, on the first Wednesday of the year (4 January), one by Edgar Allan Poe called *The Tell-Tale Heart*. 'In such cases', he added, 'we intend to give ample warning so that viewers can keep children from the home screen and refrain from looking themselves if they are at all sensitive.'

In the United States, where there was as yet no public television, a bizarre goad to competition appeared in the form of freak receptions at RCA's station at Riverhead New York of transmissions from Alexandra Palace, three thousand miles away. Joan Miller had been seen sitting at a desk introducing the BBC's *Picture Page*, though sometimes the picture was there without the sound and sometimes vice versa. Technical breakthroughs in television were in fact already occurring in the States and before the end of January television equipment installed experimentally in one of the nine operating rooms of the Israel Zion Hospital on Tenth Avenue and Broadway would be enabling medical students in the gallery to observe surgical techniques more closely than they could possibly have done otherwise – 'believed to be the first time television had been put to such use', wrote the *New York Times*. Also before the end of January, NBC was to announce in a special demonstration interview with Senator Lundeen of Minnesota transmitted to his colleagues in the National Press Club in Washington more than half a mile away, that in January 1941 it planned to televise the Presidential Inauguration (after the election of 1940), such a feat being 'only recently made possible by the development of mobile television stations'. RCA planned to market sets in April at 125 dollars each and would be applying to the Federal Communications Committee by the end of the year for permission to start regular television broadcasts.

France and Italy also hoped to start television services later in the year.

Thus technological innovation, mankind's salient achievement of the twentieth century, continued to hold out hope for the future, whatever the international outlook, suggesting that by such means if by no other the quality of life would be steadily improved.

Airline services, too, were as Wells suggested on the threshold of a new age.

A regular weekly transatlantic airmail service by British Imperial Airways was due to start in June with twenty-four-ton Cabot flying-boats between Southampton and Montreal, the forerunner of a twenty-one-hour England to New York pasenger service. Permission to land in New York had not yet been granted but negotiations were taking place. France and Germany (which already itself had an airmail service to South America) had similar plans for 1940, though Field Marshal Goering's newspaper, the *National Zeitung*, said that the inauguration of a North Atlantic service was being delayed by 'politics, propaganda and prestige' in the United States. In fact before January was over, Pan-Am announced that it would soon be starting its first transatlantic passenger service from New York to Marseilles via the Azores.

But there were also signs of hope of a less material sort – flickerings of that would-be progressive and idealistic part of mankind's nature as much alive in a material and turbulent age as in any other though less noticeable because seemingly less relevant. Some such even came from the dictatorships.

On 2 January it was learned from the USSR, where ruthless purges by Stalin had long been in full swing, that five NKVD (secret police) officials had been executed after being tried in Moldavia for arresting people on false charges and using criminal methods to extort confessions. The Public Prosecutor emphasized how important it was for the public to have faith in the political police, 'the flaming sword of the revolution', and said that this crime had been particularly heinous because 'it sullied the humble name of Chekist with contemptible deeds'.

The principal authoritarian régimes of the world were of course in themselves by origin the products of revolutionary idealism, an aspect that could be easily forgotten when, as now, at the height of their powers they could be often simply categorized as 'reactionary'. Mussolini, himself an old socialist, had stressed this aspect in his New Year message to Hitler, saying that 1938 had revealed to the world that the two revolutions were marching together. And whatever direction their revolutionary idealism might since have taken, a strange reminder of some of its origins in Germany came on 2 January when a treason trial was announced as opening in Berlin, of a forty-nine-year-old former school teacher, Ernst Niekisch. It was unusual in any case that the opening of a treason trial in Germany should be announced at all because normally the only indication that the People's Tribunal had done its work was the appearance in the street outside of the ominous red placards announcing that the accused had been guillotined. There were in fact six beheadings in the first six days of the year in Berlin. But the trial of Niekisch with other conspirators was to continue into the second week of the year. What made it particularly interesting was that Niekisch was an old Nationalist of the sort that had always put the emphasis on the socialism in National Socialism. In 1918 he had been imprisoned by the Weimar Republic for setting up a local Soviet in Bavaria. He had been an early admirer of Hitler but had become increasingly critical, reproaching the Nazis for being too bourgeois, and advocating a 'Fourth Reich' close to the USSR. He had more recently described Hitler as a German misfortune and he had been under arrest since 1937.

The administration of justice in any society provides a useful barometer of that society's character. In the United States a celebrated twenty-two-year-old case of alleged miscarriage of justice came up once again at the beginning of the year before the Governor of California, as it had been up before five previous State Governors already. The case was that of a prisoner in San Quentin, No. 31921 Thomas Mooney, a left-wing trade union activist who twenty-two years before had been sentenced to death, but subsequently reprieved to life imprisonment, for a bomb explosion at a San Francisco parade in 1916. Ten people had been killed and forty injured. Mooney had consistently maintained that he was innocent, saying he was elsewhere in the city at the time of the explosion, and there had been sufficient doubt about the evidence for the President of the day, Woodrow Wilson, to appeal for clemency over the death sentence. But after the reprieve the Supreme Court had refused to intervene to help change the verdict and the State Legislatures, like the five Governors and indeed Congress itself, had all turned down Mooney's appeals for a pardon. He had steadfastly refused parole as being tantamount to an admission of guilt. Now Governor Olson was taking his turn with the problem. His decision was expected shortly.

In Britain the police were congratulating themselves that 'the use of wireless communication and the motor-car' had enabled them 'to keep such offences as burglary, house-breaking and "smash and grab" robberies within limits ... while the crime of bag-snatching has almost disappeared'. But a public debate was still continuing over the new Criminal Justice Bill with its provision to abolish flogging except for certain offences committed against warders within prisons. Sir Reginald Coventry KC gave the old arguments a New Year impetus at Worcester Quarter Sessions on 2 January, when he complained in general that 'prison was no longer going to be a house of correction but a rest house where people can have comfort they would not enjoy in their own homes'. In attacking the abolition of corporal punishment he gave away in an unconscious slip of syntax the very case that he imagined himself to be defending. The professional garotters of Liverpool and Cardiff, he said, could look forward to being spared the only punishment which deterred them. They could 'ply their occupation without the slightest fear of being punished *in the only way which really appealed to them - the cat-o'-nine-tails.*' Supporters of the Bill made the most of the Cadogan Committee Report on whose recommendations it had been based, principally the evidence which showed that a higher proportion of men who had been flogged committed crimes again than did those who received less severe punishment. It was a debate which would continue in the press for months, with the wife of the former Prime Minister, Stanley Baldwin, entering the fray in public before long to remind people that 'all animals shun the lash'.

Thus opened a year which in its fears, hopes, plans, doubts, optimism, interest and bewilderment was not all that different from any other in the history of the world. The Archbishop of Canterbury expressed some of the bewilderment in endearingly human terms for a prelate, with a call to 'prepare for the worst and hope for the best'. No wonder, he began, it sometimes seemed as if the whole world was going mad. On the other hand: 'We must go forward into the New Year with hopefulness. . . . Enough of these cries and moans and fears.' Later he returned to his original theme. 'Are there not signs of a return to the Dark Ages?' he asked, concluding nevertheless: 'We cannot tell what changes and chances may befall this dear land of ours.' Making allowance for the patina of sonority in which the utterances of prelates have to appear, this probably represented as good a cross-section of the ordinary English-reading man-and-woman-at-the-breakfast-table's approach to the year as one would be likely to be able to identify.

A columnist in the *New York Times* wrote on 3 January: 'Even after such a year as 1938 which was once young and innocent as 1939 is now, there persists the unconquerable human conviction that the turn of the year is also the most auspicious moment in which to turn over a new leaf.'

A columnist in the London *Observer* two days before had felt comfortable enough to be facetious. 'Few years', he wrote, 'have been so disliked in advance as 1939. All the prophets look for a time of alarms and excursions with what Shakespeare calls "noises without". But we have been through anxious times before, for instance in AD 1000 when the end of the world was thought to be imminent.'

2

In the first days of 1939 it was by no means only stories about the dictatorships of Germany and Italy that took the headlines in the foreign news.

For eighteen months the Japanese had been waging a ruthless war in China against the Chinese Kuomintang leader, Marshall Chiang Kai-shek, and his co-belligerent the Communist leader Mao Tse-tung. The Japanese war aim had been declared to be 'the destruction of communism' and the establishment of 'a new order in East Asia', during the first phase of which it would be necessary for Japanese troops to be stationed in China as an anti-Communist precautionary measure. European and American economic activity in China, while not excluded, would have to be regulated. Just before the end of the old year, the United States had sent Japan a blunt note rejecting this 'new order' and reserving all American rights in China. But the appointment within a few days of a new Japanese Prime Minister, Baron Kiichiro Hiranuma, to replace the relatively liberal Prince Fumimaro Konoye did not augur well for an improvement in relations. The new Prime Minister was assessed by the *New York Times* as 'nearer than anyone else to a Japanese Hitler'.

In Palestine, administered by Britain under a League of Nations mandate, British military forces had for two years been in action against a major Arab revolt which aimed to prevent any further Jewish immigration into the territory. Some two thousand people had already been killed in the course of the fighting. On Saturday 7 January, the *New York Times* published a long report from a woman correspondent, Anne O'Hare McCormick, assessing the situation there. According to the British authorities, of all the problems harassing the British Empire Palestine was the most important, and a high official was quoted as saying: 'Things cannot go on as they are now. If there is no answer we must invent one.'

Lydda airport, she wrote, was a war zone in which soldiers in the uniforms of crack British regiments mingled with black-uniformed police all ostentatiously armed. Long lines of troop-filled lorries, with guns mounted, careered along the twisting Jaffa road. Arab Jerusalem was like a city of the dead in protest against the posting of soldiers in holy places. There were troops too encamped in the courtyard of the Church of the Nativity in Bethlehem which had only just been recaptured from the rebels.

Fervent Arab nationalists complained that Jewish colonization was preventing the Palestinians from being given independent status such as that which Iraq had achieved. They said they would never stop resisting this attempt by another people to overwhelm them and claimed to be speaking for every Arab in Palestine. Other Arabs, however, complained that the British were not tough enough with the rebels and were failing to arm the village chiefs.

Between five and six thousand Jews had been armed and enrolled in a super-numerary police force to patrol the roads and protect their 'colonies', these latter with their watchtowers and searchlights enclosing wooden stockades reminding the correspondent of early American settlements. 'Armed as they are, the re-straint of these people in the face of incessant attacks is truly extraordinary. Nobody looking at the fabric they are constructing can doubt that they are establishing a State and shaping a new form of society.' She concluded, however, that the British too were there to stay. Aerodromes, barracks and look-out posts were going up all over the country and were obviously not intended to be temporary structures.

But the longest-running foreign story of all and one which, as the first days of 1939 went by, began to dominate the foreign news in both Britain and America was the latest phase of the Civil War in Spain.

In Spain an army revolt led by a General Francisco Franco, co-ordinating forces of the political Right against a democratically-elected Government of the Re-public (itself an uneasy coalition of the Centre and Left), had been in progress since July 1936. In December 1938 the Republic, which had successfully halted Franco's forces in front of Madrid in the early days of the war, continued to hold just under half of Spain, but in two separated regions: the centre and the south-east of the peninsula including the embattled capital Madrid and the port of Valencia, and also Catalonia with its heavy industry and armament produc-tion and the largest city in Spain, Barcelona, to which the Republican Govern-ment had moved from Madrid.

A week before the start of the New Year Franco had launched a major new offensive against Catalonia. The London *Observer* on New Year's Day described what was going on as 'Europe's greatest battle since the World War'.

New Year's Eve itself had seen an air raid on Barcelona between 7 and 8 p.m., which the Republican Prime Minister, Negrín, described as the most terrible in terms of callous brutality that the city had yet suffered. The city had indeed suffered many air raids from the Italian and German bombers (mainly Savoias and Heinkels) sent by Mussolini and Hitler to help Franco. Thanks to deep air-raid shelters, casualties had been much reduced after the early raids and Barce-lona was the model to which many in the rest of Europe looked when discussing their plans for the 'Air-Raid Precautions' thought necessary since the Munich crisis. Casualties in Barcelona on this New Year's Eve were not particularly high but the raid had obviously been directed primarily at the civilian population on an occasion when they were most likely to be out in the streets. By a three-quarters moon which, according to the correspondent of the *New Chronicle*, William Forrest, who was there, 'made a mockery of the blackout' five Italian bombers flying in presumably from their base in Majorca dropped about sixty small high-fragmentation bombs on the Paseo de Gracia and the upper part of the city above the Plaza de Cataluña. This part of Barcelona had not been bombed since the previous March, after which raids had been concentrated on the harbour area. This evening therefore, while people living near the harbour had rushed to their shelters as usual, those living in the upper part stood, as had become their habit, in doorways watching the play of the searchlights and the red tracer of the anti-aircraft fire. Forty-four people were killed (seventeen in one doorway by a single bomb) and sixty-six seriously injured. The actual damage to buildings was slight and the relatively light casualties were due to the fact that those who had been prudent enough to take shelter had had about eight minutes after the sounding of the alarm in which to do so before the bombs started falling.

At Madrid, where Franco had now been held up for over two years, he celebrated the New Year with heavy shelling of the city which reached its climax about 1 a.m. on 1 January, this being the actual stroke of midnight for the Franco forces, whose clocks were kept one hour behind those of the Republic.

In Catalonia his army, said to number half a million men, was attacking on a hundred-mile front, and on Tuesday the 3rd, the *Manchester Guardian*, which strongly supported the Republican Government, assessed the military position.

It conceded that 'defeat in Catalonia would mean the defeat of Spain', but, despite the fact that it was now the eleventh day of the offensive and Franco had certainly made some gains all along the front, the paper maintained that he had still not made any gains of importance. 'Barcelona by Easter!' was said to be the cry of Franco's army but the Government, which held a line running roughly from the Pyrenees in the north down the river Segre and past Artesa to near Lérida, then through the Sierra de la Llena down the Ebro to the sea west of Tarragona, had defences in depth behind this line and two crack divisions in reserve.

Franco already held two bridgeheads on the Segre at Balaguer and Lérida and his new offensive had been gaining some ground both round Artesa and in the region east of the Ebro below Lérida. On New Year's Day itself his troops successfully stormed the hill village of Cubells on the Balaguer–Artesa road and Artesa de Segre itself thus appeared to be in some danger.

On the southern front, where the New Year opened with cloudless skies and brilliant sunshine allowing Franco to make full use of his superiority in aircraft and artillery, his army under General Solchaga edged forward through the foothills of the Sierra de la Llena though, according to *The Times* correspondent, the Republican defence had a natural strength here: 'each ridge is a new line of defence and each cottage a new redoubt, while the groves of fig trees and stunted olives facilitate the use of barbed-wire entanglements'. Where badly held up Solchaga was leaving fortified Republican positions behind and pushing on for Granadella.

However, a big attack by the heavily-mechanized Italian Littorio division

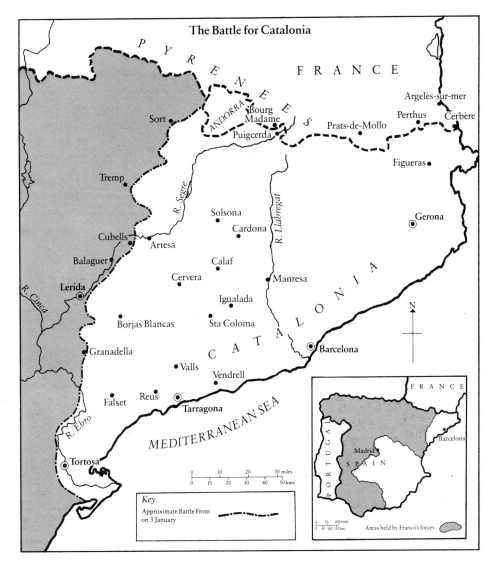

The Battle for Catalonia

FRANCE

Argelès-sur-mer

Sort
Bourg Madame
Perthus
Cerbère

ANDORRA
Prats-de-Mollo

Puigcerda

Figueras

Tremp

R. Segre

R. Llabregat

Solsona
Cardona

Gerona

Cubells
Artesa

Balaguer
Calaf

Lerida
Cervera
Manresa

C A T A L O N I A

R. Cinca

Igualada

N

Borjas Blancas
Sta Coloma

Granadella
Valls

C A T A L O N I A

Barcelona

Falset
Reus
Vendrell

R. Ebro
Tarragona

MEDITERRANEAN SEA

FRANCE

Madrid
Barcelona

PORTUGAL
SPAIN

Tortosa

0   10   20   30 miles
0   10   20   30   40   50 kms

Key
Approximate Battle Front
on 3 January

0   50   100 miles
0   50 100 150 km
Areas held by Franco's forces

against the major rail junction of Borjas Blancas to the north-east had just been driven back some eight miles with heavy losses (annihilating some thirty per cent of the Italian strength, Barcelona claimed). This check to the Italians (one of four divisions in General Gambara's Legionary Corps of which the other three included Italian officers) seemed to the *Manchester Guardian* to augur well for the Government, which claimed that their main defensive line had not yet been reached. There were rumours too that Mussolini was beginning to tire of his costly effort in Spain and there were said to be signs of unrest behind Franco's lines. With the chance of a Republican counter-attack in the offing, a failure by Franco to force his offensive home, let alone a defeat, might, in the *Manchester Guardian*'s view, be disastrous for him.

Vernon Bartlett, the distinguished correspondent of the *News Chronicle*, which also supported the Spanish Government, shared this view. He said that their General Staff, while admitting that they were fighting the fiercest battle of the war, were very calm and confident, and claimed that stiffening Republican resistance had already put the Franco rebels behind their timetable.

'Unless', wrote Bartlett, 'within the next few days rebel prospects brighten very considerably the whole offensive may turn out to be a strategic blunder.... Furthermore,' he continued, 'it is strongly suspected in London diplomatic circles that the rivalry between the different factions supporting General Franco is so intense that they will break out into open rebellion if the offensive against Barcelona fails.'

The Spanish Republican Premier Negrín broadcast to the United States: 'In spite of the bitter trials past and coming we shall emerge victorious from the struggle.' And William Forrest, the *News Chronicle* correspondent on the spot, found in these first days of the year the same spirit of confidence among rank-and-file Republican militia as he did in the presence of the General commanding all Government forces in Catalonia. Everyone paid generous tribute to the courage the Italians were showing in their attacks on Borjas Blancas on the Lérida–Tarragona road, returning again and again in an attempt to finish the war at a knock-out blow. But though Italian war correspondents had been claiming its capture a week before, it remained in Republican hands, 'proving once again', commented Forrest, 'that the pen is mightier than the sword'. Now the correspondent of *La Stampa*, writing of 'strenuous counter-attacks by the best of the Republican troops', said he was not optimistic about a quick result and that the fighting would have to continue probably for a long time.

On 3 January Forrest found himself coming back from the front through Borjas Blancas. He said this must now be added to the list of Spanish towns which after surviving wave after wave of invasion in the past have finally disappeared under the weight of totalitarian bombs. The whole place lay in ruins. Never had Franco employed such masses of planes as now. Though they couldn't be seen because of cloud cover, the air was filled with their droning and the earth trembled with the explosion of bombs.

On the same day in Britain a group of British public men and women published a New Year Greeting they had sent to the Republican Government, expressing admiration for its courage, sympathy and gratitude for its services to the cause of liberty. This was signed by, among others, Stafford Cripps, the Labour lawyer now pressing for a Popular Front against appeasement (to the strong disapproval of the Labour Party's leadership), the Duchess of Atholl, the extreme-leftist lawyer D.N. Pritt, the painter Muirhead Bone and the writer Storm Jameson. What was happening in Spain, said the signatories, was 'a lesson and example to ourselves. When we feel despondent at the temporary triumph of Fascism in Europe we turn our eyes to Republican Spain and take fresh courage.'

An advertisement appeared in *The Times* that day for 'Bombproof Air-Raid

Shelters' made to measure by a firm inappropriately named Glazier and Sons, in Savile Row. 'Properly-designed air-raid shelters', they said, 'had been found to give safety against bombs' and their own had been designed by 'a pre-eminent technical expert who has made a careful study of the actual conditions of aerial warfare in Barcelona'.

3

The United States Senate met for a short preliminary session on 3 January, the day before President Roosevelt was due to address Congress. The Republicans seemed 'rejuvenated' (*New York Times*) by the results of the recent mid-term elections, and celebrated their new feeling of independence of the President by throwing darts about the place before the formal session was adjourned. The next day they confronted him.

He began on a solemn uncontroversial note which broadened steadily into more and more positive concern for the European scene:

> A war which threatened to envelop the world in flames has been averted, but it has become increasingly clear that peace is not assured.... There comes a time in the affairs of men when they must prepare to defend not their laws alone but the tenets of faith and humanity on which their churches, their governments and their very civilization are founded. The defense of religion, of democracy and of good faith among nations is all the same fight. To save one we must save all.

He turned to the Neutrality Act which forbade arms sales and restricted the supply of other material help to any side in an international war. It had been further strengthened since the outbreak of the Civil War in Spain, to which the sale of arms was now specifically embargoed:

> It is time to reconsider whether an Act adopted in the Spring of 1931 now represents the opinion of, and promises to conserve the interests of, the American people. Americans are forced to ask themselves, in a moment of dreadful crisis, whether they would really wish to prevent the European democracies from acquiring in our industry the instruments of self-defence in case of a war of aggression were forced on them by the dictatorships.... They cannot forever let pass, without effective protest, acts of aggression against sister nations – acts which automatically undermine all of us.... Our neutrality laws may operate unevenly and unfairly – may actually give aid to an aggressor and deny it to his victim. The instinct of self-preservation should warn us that we ought not to let that happen any more.

However welcome such words might be to some quarters in Europe, Roosevelt knew well that much of Congress was wary of all such talk as likely to involve the United States in another European war. And since his arguments for supporting the democracies with arms were cleverly bound up with arguments for his own domestic and economic policies, he was careful to allay as far as possible any precipitate fears. America's own defence in any case required attention.

What in fact became unmistakably clear was that he was using the need for extensive rearmament by America for one reason or another as inspiration for further New Deal 'pump-priming', or spending to create employment without immediate concern for a balanced budget. The figure for unemployed in the United States was 11,000,000. Because, went Roosevelt's argument in an emotive phrase, America's net income was $60 billion it did not mean it had to remain a $60 billion nation; by putting men and resources to proper use by spending money, he said, it could be made into an $80 billion nation.

The *New York Times*, a paper favourable to Roosevelt, reported that during the speech, so long as the President remained on the theme of the defence of democracy, his audience was with him to a man. But when he used national defence as the basis for his spending programme the lines of difference with the Republicans emerged at once. And the *Kansas City Star* noticed that when during his speech he outlined the two alternative budget policies, one for strictly balancing the budget at all costs which he thought wrong, and the other for his own principle of pump-priming, it was what he had categorized as the wrong policy which got most applause from Congress.

Reaction in the States in fact run along predictably partisan lines, though all recognized that it had been something of an epoch-making speech.

'The President's message marks a new phase of the administration,' said the *Minneapolis Tribune*. 'Mr Roosevelt will find his chief preoccupation in the field of foreign affairs.' Senator Taft of Ohio commented with curt hostility: 'The logical conclusion is another war with American troops again sent across the ocean.'

Criticisms in the States centred round Roosevelt's linking of defence with economic policy. Senator Townsend of Delaware, for instance, remarked: 'I am in favour of a reasonable amount of armaments expenditure but not as a smokescreen for domestic issues.'

The *Buffalo Courier-Express* said Roosevelt was using the fraught international situation and the United States' need for adequate defence as justification for his domestic measures. 'Neither the American people nor Congress, we believe, will accept Mr Roosevelt's untenable assumption that a continued blank check policy will serve as a guarantee against dictatorship.' And the *Cleveland Plain Dealer* thought similarly that a $40,000 million national debt 'did not seem a particularly impressive rampart against invasion'.

The Republican *New York Herald Tribune*, picking up the President's remark that 'There had never been six years of such far-flung internal preparedness in our history', retorted: 'Alas! the only thing that has been far flung under the New Deal has been the tax-payer's money. Having brought the country to a state of financial unpreparedness unprecedented in its history, and having done everything possible to sow dissension among American people, the New Deal now calls upon the country to spend for a fight. The American people will refuse to do this.'

The *Washington Post* too was critical and even the *Pittsburgh Post Gazette* which praised the President highly for 'one of the most forceful speeches of his career' added a gentle corrective to its own enthusiasm with the advice that his 'eloquent analysis of the armament programme should not be permitted to create war hysteria or lead us into an excessive amount of expenditure'.

It was of course in the democracies of Europe and particularly in Britain that Roosevelt's address was most strongly welcomed.

The *Birmingham Post* declared that it was the biggest departure from isolationism that any American President had ever made and said that it would act as an encouragement to Chamberlain to take a strong line on his forthcoming visit to Rome, a viewpoint shared by the equally-pleased *Glasgow Herald* which, for a Conservative paper, was beginning to have some misgivings about the whole policy of appeasement. 'We must begin to ask ourselves', it said, 'whether the assumption on which we have hitherto based our foreign policy is going to hold good' (the assumption being that democracy and dictatorship could be harmonized). 'We cannot escape the suspicion that this process of harmony is not making as much progress as one could wish.'

The *Scotsman*'s comment on Roosevelt was that it was not clear whether the United States would insist on cash down for its aid.

The *Manchester Guardian* thought that most English men and women 'must have wished sadly that it was the head of their own Government who was saying these things. . . . They must have regretted that it has been left to an American President to state the British (as it is also the American) way of life without apologizing for it.' (Chamberlain had said he could not become very excited about different systems of government.) 'The contrast is painful and need not be pursued.'

Herbert Morrison, one of Britain's Labour Party leaders, echoed this thought. Roosevelt, he said, was the one statesman who could best speak the mood of the British people today. 'It is a thousand pities that among our Ministers we have none who approach President Roosevelt for drive, rallying power and idealism.'

A surprise reaction to Roosevelt's address, however, had been that of Chamberlain himself, who went out of his way to welcome it. This, commented the *New York Times* correspondent in London, was a fairly unprecedented sort of thing to do when Parliament was not sitting, and he wondered about the reason. He came up with this answer: 'The Government have just begun to realize the extent of the belief in the United States that Mr Chamberlain is a Fascist or at least in sympathy with the Fascist regimes in Europe.' The British Embassy in Washington, he went on, was known to be perturbed by what a large section of American opinion thought. Was there any chance of the Neutrality Act ever being revised if it were thought Chamberlain was a Fascist? Moreover, how would it have looked if Chamberlain had kept silent just before going off to see Mussolini?

But Chamberlain's approval of Roosevelt had actually dismayed at least one of the Prime Minister's supporters, who wrote to *The Times*: 'We should like to assume that the ideals after which Mr Chamberlain strives are of a different kind from those trumpeted abroad by Mr Roosevelt.'

In France it was the effect which the President's speech would have on the visit to Rome that seemed highly important to Geneviève Tabouis of *L'Œuvre*, and she thought it might alter considerably the terms of the Rome talks. She called the speech one of the greatest international events of the past six months. The Paris *Intransigeant* thought it was bound to cause a great stir in Germany and Italy and would make their leaders more cautious, concluding: 'This in itself is a great contribution to peace.'

In Germany the *Völkischer Beobachter* said that Roosevelt was trying by every trick and subterfuge to manoeuvre his people into an attitude hostile to Germany, which had not harmed America and did not dream of doing so, and the *Deutsche Allgemeine Zeitung* put the whole tone of the speech down to Roosevelt's dependence on Jewish interests.

The *Börsenzeitung* said that Roosevelt was nearly at his wits' end because of internal difficulties and wanted to provoke a world conflict, to which end he wished to do away with the neutrality laws. It said his aim was not only to prostrate Germany but also so to weaken Britain that she would be unable to hold on to her Empire and would have to let the United States take Canada.

The Italians, perhaps because Chamberlain had welcomed the speech so close to his Rome visit, played it down in their newspapers, relegating it to the inside pages. The *Popolo d'Italia* ran a headline: 'Usual Sermons and Threats', while *La Stampa* of Turin, like the *Deutsche Allgemeine*, ascribed it to the powerful influence of Jewish cliques.

In the States a secret joint meeting of the House and Senate Military Affairs Committee was to take place in a week, at which information was to be given in detail by the US Ambassadors in London and Berlin of just how dangerous the European situation looked. The meeting would more or less coincide with the President's request to Congress for $552 million for national defence.

Meanwhile a statement from William R. Castle, a former Under-Secretary to President Hoover, effectively summed up US critical doubts about Roosevelt's policies. The President, he said, was risking war by setting himself up as

prosecuting attorney and judge of the rest of the world. . . . We must all be sorry for the Chinese. We can be racked with regret and horror at what is happening to the Jews in Germany but we have enough to do to keep our own house in order, to see that the miseries brought on innocent people the world over do not fall on our citizens. . . . The New Deal is committed to the spending theory and as people all over the country begin to crack down on the extravagances and what appears to be graft in connection with the funnels through which public money pours, it has become essential to invent some new method of spending which will have popular support.

Anthony Eden, the former British Foreign Secretary who had resigned from Chamberlain's Cabinet, was in New York and addressed the American Chamber of Commerce. Roosevelt's message to Congress, he said, was 'a masterpiece of clarity and candour … a signpost which points the way along which all the liberty-loving nations of the world would wish to travel … it is difficult to exaggerate the tonic effects of that speech on the British people.'

A few days after Roosevelt had spoken, a wholly different story held the front pages of the American newspapers alongside the news from Europe. The Governor of California, Cuthbert L. Olson, had made his decision on the case of Thomas Mooney, the trades union activist who had been serving a life sentence for murder for the past twenty-two years in San Quentin prison. The decision was given on 7 January: Mooney had got his pardon. A man of fifty-six now, in good health, though with greying hair, he emerged from San Quentin having discarded his prison uniform and put on a neat, grey pin-stripe suit.

The main facts of the case had not been in dispute. A suitcase loaded with dynamite and fitted with a clock timing device had exploded on the corner of Stuart and Market Street, San Francisco, on 22 July 1916, while a Preparedness Day parade, and in particular a contingent of veterans from the Spanish–American war of 1898, had been marching past. Ten people had been killed and forty injured.

Thomas Mooney was the son of a coal-miner and had himself become an iron-moulder at the age of fifteen. In 1908 at the age of twenty-five he had joined the Socialist Party and had been a leading figure in a number of violent strikes. In the course of one of these he had had his leg broken when run down by a carload of strike-breakers. Earlier in 1916 he had been arrested for distributing inflammatory literature.

The police arrested him for the San Francisco bombing and found witnesses to identify him as the man who had planted the suitcase, though there had been some talk of this evidence being perjured. Mooney in his defence denied totally that he had been near the junction of Stuart and Market Street at the time and even produced a photograph of himself and his wife, which he said had been taken on that day, on the roof of the building where they lived, with clocks in the street below showing a time close to that of the explosion. Though convicted and sentenced to death, the fact that there had been some doubt about the reliability of the witnesses' evidence led to his reprieve. But his twenty-two-year fight to get the conviction quashed had had no success until now. Governor Olson however had come to the conclusion that Mooney had in fact been convicted solely because he was a convenient person for the police to accuse, being much hated by officialdom for his radical activities.

The interesting question then remained: who had done it? The bomb had, after all, gone off and ten people had been killed. Circumstantial evidence – and there was never now going to be anything else – seemed to suggest that it was the work of some Mexican terrorists. Mexicans had set off a suitcase-bomb on a train the month before. It was interesting too that Spanish war veterans appeared to be the special target. Moreover, Mexicans with suitcases had been seen by some witnesses near the scene of the explosion shortly beforehand. This last information had never been forwarded to be heard at the trial by the District Attorney.

Governor Olson was applauded for two minutes when publicly announcing his decision. Mooney on being released rewarded him by telling him that in his view 'the present economic system was in a state of decay'. It would be replaced, he hoped, 'by a new and better social order. To that end I pledge my efforts and to work for the common good.'

In reply Olson counselled Mooney to urge people 'not to plunge themselves into a futile and inhuman chaos of bloodshed and revolution'. In fact the whole thing had been too much for the Governor. He collapsed later at an election celebration barbecue and was found to be suffering from nervous exhaustion and overwork.

Mooney at his first public speech to a crowd of some three thousand people in Silberside Park declared: 'Capitalism is like a dying old man who is given shots of narcotics to ease the pain before he passes away. The present economic structure is on the edge of an abyss and may be plunged into eternity. Hitler and Mussolini are the doctors who are administering the shots to capitalism.'

Congratulations on his release arrived for him predictably from Earl Browder, General Secretary of the United States Communist Party, who spoke of this 'long-delayed justice to a magnificent fighter, one of the finest representatives the American working class has produced'. Mayor La Guardia of New York also sent congratulations, saying he had believed in Mooney's innocence for twenty years.

There was to be no pardon however for another famous convict in the news that week. Alphonse Capone had still a year to run of his eleven-year sentence for income tax evasions during his years of prosperity. He was suffering from paresis and was being transferred from Alcatraz to the Terminal Island prison of San Pedro. Convicts who had been released from Alcatraz reported that he had been unpopular there and that there had been several attempts to kill him.

With the ending of the Mooney case there were those who wondered again for a moment about Sacco and Vanzetti. But the fates of individuals, with only a few exceptions, count for little in the broad spectrum of history and it was the international scene and the way Roosevelt was likely to play it in relation to his political and economic problems at home that were to command the attention of the United States for the rest of the year.

4

In the week between Roosevelt's Congress speech and Chamberlain's arrival on his next round of appeasement in Rome, dramatic developments took place in the war in Spain. If Mussolini had hoped that the prospect of eventual victory for Franco would by the time of the visit be sufficiently assured for the whole awkward question of Italian intervention in Spain to be virtually off the agenda, he was to be disappointed.

In Catalonia itself Franco had made some important advances. The strategic road and rail junction of Artesa, on the Republican line of communication between north and south of the Catalan front, fell on 4 January after very heavy fighting in which the Government troops, though surrounded and called upon to surrender, had refused to do so. The trenches round the town were found piled high with dead. 'Come over to the side where you'll get enough food and be received as brothers!' and, 'If you have no murders on your conscience you have nothing to fear!' were the sort of messages that had been addressed to them. But there had also been much publicity given in Franco's zone to a card-index said to contain a million or – some said – two million names against whom charges had been laid, and the effect was to encourage resistance.

General Franco was now at the front himself and, according to the *New York Times*, 'in a position to begin his great mid-winter offensive in earnest'. But the paper's correspondent on the Government side, Herbert Matthews, pointed out that Franco's troops were still well short of the main Republican fortified line even at their most advanced point and that they would have to make a much greater effort than any they had made so far to get through that, always supposing that they even managed to reach it. He wrote that it would 'be a great mistake to suppose that the Loyalist troops are dispirited or weakening. I can guarantee that those with whom I have come into contact certainly are not.' The day Artesa fell, the Italians were still being held four miles from Borjas Blancas. And there was a report, said to have much disconcerted Franco's air command, to the effect that the Republicans had just received from over the French frontier thirty-five Curtiss aircraft sent by the Russians. These were said to be faster than anything so far seen in action and, although because of their speed they were difficult to handle, it was also reported that eighty-five Spanish pilots had recently returned to Barcelona after a long period of training in Russia.

Two days later came news that Borjas Blancas had at last fallen.

William Forrest of the *News Chronicle* wrote: 'The Battle of the Segre, first phase of the offensive against Catalonia, is approaching its climax after two weeks of titanic struggle overshadowing everything in the Spanish war.'

ABOVE General Francisco Franco: 1–2 million names on his death list?

BELOW Spanish refugees fleeing before Franco in Catalonia.

At Republican headquarters he found the same ultimate confidence as ever. 'Franco can win every battle except the last,' was what people were saying. The Barcelona call-up was increased to include all men between the ages of eighteen and thirty-eight. Forrest was reminded that Catalonia was not alone and that there were other regions of Spain loyal to the Republic which could be relied on to play their part. In confirmation of this the Republican Government announced the same day that it had launched a new offensive under General Miaja on the Estremadura front in central Spain. It claimed to have broken Franco's lines there and to be advancing victoriously. The *New York Times* reported that the Government troops there were 'travelling as fast as infantry can go'. The London *Times*, reporting the new offensive, nevertheless emphasized how dangerous the situation was for the Government in Catalonia, where their main defence system had now been broken at two points, and where, it said, they had lost 700 square miles and 29,000 prisoners in just over a fortnight.

It was in fact on the twin supports of the new Republican offensive in Estremadura and the conviction that the indomitable spirit of Madrid would be repeated in Barcelona that supporters of the Spanish Republican Government now rested their hopes. *The Times*, while asking if the disintegration of the entire first line of defence in Catalonia did not make one wonder if the army of the people really would prove equal to the task of defending Barcelona, ran on 9 January a headline 'War on Two Fronts'.

'The Spanish battlefield', it said, 'is extending and the impression that the Civil War is reaching a climax grows stronger.' The Republicans had taken four important towns on the Estremadura front, including Fuenteovejuna. And *The Times* concluded: 'Who can keep up the pace longest will win.'

William Forrest, driving up from Tarragona to the front the day before, had been astonished by the absence of any of the usual Franco planes attacking the roads, crowded, as usual, with troops, lorries and refugees. He concluded that they had been diverted to the Estremadura front where, as his paper pointed out elsewhere, the Republicans had pushed forward to a point relatively much closer to Franco's vital communications than he was to Barcelona; they were now as close to his important railway link between the north and south of his territory as he himself was to Tarragona. Forrest saw only one Franco plane all afternoon though he heard very distinctly the thunder of guns as the Italians pushed further down the road to Tarragona.

He said the Italians were fighting with greater spirit and determination than at any time in the Spanish war, but they were being answered by an unshakeable spirit of resistance among the Government militiamen. He found among the new recruits and battalions of volunteers he had seen drilling and marching just the same enthusiasm as he had found among the first militiamen two and a half years ago. 'Can anything possibly defeat these people?' he asked.

Nevertheless, by 10 January, the day on which Chamberlain left London for Rome, it was clear that the Republican Government's front on the Segre had collapsed and that their troops were now in full retreat in Catalonia. Franco's Aragonese Army Corps, commanded by General Moscardó, the man who had held out in the Alcázar in Toledo, had swept forward from the Balaguer bridgehead towards the Lérida–Barcelona road, capturing fourteen villages in one day and storming the defences at Mongay and Bellcaire, said by *The Times* to be 'the Gibraltar of Catalonia's defences'. The Government troops were having to pull back hurriedly from what was now a dangerously exposed Lérida salient.

On the other hand in Estremadura they were now only seventeen miles from the main railway line which linked Franco's headquarters at Burgos with Seville and Málaga. Forrest in the *News Chronicle* called the Catalonian retreat 'a straightening of the Government line' though he had to admit that the fighting to the south on the Lérida–Tarragona road was grim and bitter. But he now saw Estremadura as the important front. He quoted General Miaja, the Republican commander in Estremadura, in his Order of the Day: 'Our brothers in Catalonia are fighting heroically.... I am proud of your conduct in the offensive that has now begun. Your triumph is one that has been achieved by Spaniards alone, that we share with no one else. Forward to Victory! Long live Spain!'

Forrest said the swift success of the offensive threatened to transform the whole situation in Spain and was particularly inopportune for Franco on the eve of Chamberlain's visit to Mussolini, when the whole question of Italian intervention would be under discussion. Even the London *Daily Telegraph*, which always referred to Franco's troops as 'the Nationalists' or, at worst, 'the insurgents', rather than 'the rebels' of the liberal press, reported that the Estremadura front was assuming greater proportions daily, and judged that another week was needed before it could be said whether 'Franco's great effort to overcome Catalonia is going to succeed'.

Air-raids on Spanish cities by Italian bombers based in Majorca continued daily in the run-up to the Rome talks. On 3 January two passenger trains standing in Tarragona station had been hit and thirty people in them killed and forty injured; five planes dropped light bombs on the centre of Valencia on the afternoon of 8 January, killing thirty-five people and injuring fifty, and in a raid on Barcelona the day before Chamberlain left, the chief engineer of the British merchantman *Aylesford*, Victor Farthing, was killed while dashing for an air-raid shelter.

Mr Chamberlain and Lord Halifax, the Foreign Secretary, left Victoria Station for Paris and Rome on the morning of 10 January. There was a demonstration by the National Unemployed Workers' Movement carrying a black coffin to see them off. Though they were kept away from the platform by the police they could be seen and heard 'dancing about', as *The Times* put it, and shouting: 'Appease the Unemployed – not Mussolini!', while women chanted: 'Arms for Spain!' The coffin got smashed when the police tried to seize it and three men were arrested for obstructing them. The booing of Chamberlain, however, was drowned by cheers.

The demonstration plainly did not affect the Prime Minister's spirits for he was reported as walking jauntily along the quay at Dover a little later, 'swinging his famous umbrella by the ferrule for all the world like a niblick'.

His first stop was in Paris, where he arrived at 5.45 in the evening. At six o'clock he was at the Quai d'Orsay, where with the French Prime Minister, Daladier, and the Foreign Minister, Bonnet, he and Halifax took a 'thé diplomatique'.

It would have needed to be just that. For all the necessary 'smoothing-out through the diplomatic channel' of French fears to which Garvin's *Observer* had referred, the Italian newspapers were still suggesting that the British were sympathetic towards some of Italy's demands against France in the Mediterranean. Daladier had in fact only just come back from an apparently highly successful tour rallying support in Corsica and North Africa, where the warm reception he was given had brought tears to his eyes at one point. 'France', he said in Algiers, 'wishes all great problems to be settled, not by war, but by constructive effort. But if anyone interprets her attitude as a sign of weakness or abdication then I cry "Halt!"' In Tunis he declared: 'We are at a turning-point in the history of France. We enter upon the concept of an Empire of which Tunisia is an integral part. Woe to him who dares touch our country! We shall never yield either to violence or to guile.'

However it was reported after the diplomatic tea with Chamberlain that 'a general identity of views' was confirmed.

Nevertheless the Italian review *Relazioni Internazionali*, which often carried articles from the Italian Foreign Office, made clear how the Chamberlain visit was being seen in Rome: a means of welding relations between the Axis powers and Britain so that Britain would at least watch passively while France could be isolated and Italian demands be met for a special status for Italians in Tunisia, cession to Italy of the Addis Ababa and Jibuti railway, special privileges in Jibuti, seats on the board of the Suez Canal Company and eventually even the acquisition of Corsica itself. France must mend her ways, concluded *Relazioni Internazionali*, or there could be war.

Vernon Bartlett, the *News Chronicle* diplomatic correspondent, wrote that the French dislike of British mediation on their behalf, combined with Franco's failure to secure the final crushing military victory for which Mussolini had been hoping in Spain, meant that 'much more emphasis would have to be laid upon the social than upon the political side of the visit'.

But supporters of Chamberlain's policy saw the social side of the exercise as, in a way, the political point. Garvin in the *Observer* the previous Sunday had said that the Prime Minister was going in 'pursuance of appeasement' with the true good-will of Britain towards Italy and would be welcomed in Rome in the same spirit. What, he said, had earlier disturbed relations between the two countries was Britain's part in sanctions against Italy for her action in Abyssinia (in July 1936, before Chamberlain became Prime Minister), but that step – 'one of the most disastrous errors in British foreign policy' – had now been rectified by recognition of Italian sovereignty there. Of course there were differences on Spain, and 'indirect' differences over Italy's relations with France which were 'bristling'. If this had been the only matter for discussion, 'the doubt about the exact opportuneness of the Prime Minister's journey might seem a balanced question'. But, reckoned Garvin, the visit was 'vindicated because the only hope of improving the bedevilled international situation is through the possible moderation and mediation of Mussolini. Within certain limits he is the balance-holder and arbiter of Europe. . . . The main thing at present is . . . to promote a better human feeling.' He concluded by saying that even if mere consultations were all that took place, 'the searching and friendly enquiry cannot be other than enlightening and may yet lead to a turning-point for good'.

On one point, strangely, the liberal *Manchester Guardian* agreed with Garvin: 'The man whom Mr Chamberlain will meet in Rome', it wrote, 'is recognized as the most formidable statesman in Europe today – more formidable even than Hitler who is in some ways a smaller man in charge of a larger nation.'

The *News Chronicle* predictably said that Chamberlain 'would have done better to stay at home. . . . Mr Chamberlain's previous visits abroad have usually resulted in his giving something away – something belonging to other people.' Mussolini, said the paper, had obviously been hoping that in Spain by now General Franco would have smashed his way into Barcelona and that Chamberlain could thus have been brought to concede Franco belligerent rights. Not only should Chamberlain not do this but justice demanded that arms should be sent to the Spanish Government. As for France, 'Mr Chamberlain will be doing the worst day's work for the democracies that even he has yet done if he so much as hints that the British might bring pressure on the French to be more accommodating to the Italian demands'.

The Times, which deplored the manner and style of the Italian claims against France, said, 'the British Government cannot but fully sympathize with the French refusal to treat in circumstances such as these', but it consoled itself with the thought that Signor Mussolini and his Government had not formally identified themselves with the extreme pretensions of the Italian press, and therefore it thought 'the way may thus still be open for some modification here and there of the present position in Africa'.

This, of course, as the *News Chronicle* pointed out, was the sort of thing *The Times* had been saying about Czechoslovakia the previous September.

In general *The Times* saw the visit as 'primarily one of courtesy, made in response to the invitation of Signor Mussolini extended in the cordial atmosphere of the closing stages of the Munich meeting. . . . Mr Chamberlain goes to Rome bearing the greetings of one Imperial race to the leader of another and in the confident hope that a new and fuller understanding between them may be brought nearer.' The paper did not seem unduly troubled that 'the totalitarian racial doctrine is now being put into practice in Italy as well as in Germany – though with considerably greater regard for common humanity', and simply noted that 'Signor Mussolini is believed to have recently given the American Ambassador in Rome assurances that he wished to help to settle the consequent refugee problem in an orderly and practical manner'.

Three days before Chamberlain left there was a photograph in the *News Chronicle* of Jewish prisoners, numbered (1307, 1446, etc.), in striped pyjamas and with shaven heads, being paraded in an orderly and practical manner at Sachsenhausen Concentration Camp for the benefit of Professor Landra, leader of the Race-Political Department in the Italian Ministry of Culture.

Chamberlain and Halifax finally arrived in Rome from the French frontier at 4.20 on the afternoon of 11 January. They found the roofs and walls of the railway station festooned with Union Jacks and Italian flags. Two sets of rails had been covered in to broaden the arrival platform on which Mussolini, Ciano, Grandi, the Italian Ambassador in London, and Alfieri, the Minister of Popular Culture, stood ready to greet them. Mussolini came forward with a warm smile and vigorous handshake as Chamberlain got out of the train. Carrying a brown-handled umbrella with a gold ring at the top, which was seen to be much newer than the one he had taken to Munich, Chamberlain inspected the Fascist Guard of Honour in their black and silver uniforms.

After being driven through the streets of Rome past interested and friendly crowds to the Villa Madama where they were staying – a house designed by Raphael in gardens above the Tiber – Chamberlain and Halifax met Mussolini and Ciano again almost at once – at 6 p.m. at the Palazzo Venezia, for their first talks. These lasted an hour and a half and were described as having been full and frank, a general *'tour d'horizon'*. Mussolini apparently pleased Chamberlain by declaring repeatedly how much he desired peace for every reason and how ready he would be to throw his weight on the side of peace, should need arise.

At the state banquet for two hundred people later in the evening Chamberlain, in thanking Mussolini ('Your Excellency') for his welcome, said he was there because Britain wanted 'close, friendly and even intimate relations' with Italy. He said he was convinced that their interests in the Mediterranean 'need in no way conflict with each other'. He also said it was 'a real pleasure ... to see with our own eyes the new Italy, powerful and progressive which has arisen under Your Exellency's guidance and inspiration', and concluded, 'I raise my glass to His Majesty the King of Italy, Emperor of Ethiopia and to the continued welfare and prosperity of the people over whom he rules.'

The *Corriere della Sera* thought that because Chamberlain would in Paris have passed through the 'violent and artificial waves' of France's reaction to Italy's claims, the political and moral basis of these claims needed to be stressed

The Italian dictator, Benito Mussolini, greets the British Prime Minister, Neville Chamberlain, as he arrives in Rome in pursuance of appeasement, January 1939. BELOW A night at the Rome opera with British Foreign Secretary Lord Halifax and Count Ciano (*right*).

to him. 'They can be inserted, like the German demands, in the system of peace and order in Europe which has not been realized.'

Hints to Chamberlain from the German press were similar. The official *Diplomatisch-Politische Information* hoped that he, as representative of a nation which had been able to secure political and commercial advantage for itself in the Mediterranean in the past, would take account of 'the fact of the existence of a united Italian nation assured in the possession of strong friends and the legitimate requirements of that nation'.

However, the French paper *Le Temps* said the idea of Britain's acting as a mediator in the Franco-Italian difficulty was absolutely ruled out both in London and Paris. 'France and Great Britain are wholly in agreement on this matter as on all others.' Most of the French press was of the same opinion, though Mme Tabouis in *L'Œuvre* saw some danger that the atmosphere of the Rome visit and his welcome might soften Chamberlain up.

Chamberlain was certainly not short of advisers trying to keep him firm. The weekend before he left, the International Peace Campaign had tried to get him to receive a delegation including Rebecca West, Augustus John, R.H. Tawney and others who wanted to make clear to him their view that friendly relations with Italy could not be assured so long as Italian intervention in Spain continued. He replied that he did not think any useful purpose would be served by inter-rupting the holiday he was taking, to see them.

He had also been appealed to the previous week at a Conference of University Conservative and Unionist Association, in London by an Oxford undergraduate, a Mr Edward Heath, 'to give up the policy of appeasement and adopt a firmer policy'. And a new all-party group calling itself 'The Hundred Thousand' headed by Duncan Sandys and including Harold Macmillan, the cartoonist David Low, Randolph Churchill and many others had come into being in opposition to appeasement.

Duff Cooper, who had resigned from Chamberlain's Cabinet over Munich, was not, however, opposed to the talks. The journey to Rome, he wrote in the London *Evening Standard*, might prove to be as important in the history of the world as any that had ever taken place. But he did caution Chamberlain in one sense, namely that the British 'are a generous people and hesitate less than most to pay a high price [for peace], but the one thing they hate is to be done in the eye. They were promised peace on 30 September, but they are not sure that they got it.'

Even in Rome itself Chamberlain was not free from advice. He received a telegram there from the National Union of Seamen asking him to press on the Italian Government the need to withdraw all troops from Spain and to discon-tinue bombing attacks on British shipping, and the Captains of the British merchant ships in Barcelona sent him a telegram saying they had just buried Victor Farthing, the chief engineer of the *Aylesford* 'killed by a fascist bomb', and demanding protection for themselves.

There was no evidence of any of this weighing on Mr Chamberlain's mind in the course of his conversations with Mussolini, though he did develop a slight cold the day after his arrival. After laying a wreath at the Tomb of the Unknown Warrior that morning he lunched with King Victor Emmanuel and Mussolini and about fifty other guests, and in the afternoon watched a display of physical training and small arms drill by some four thousand Fascist youth, including members of the Fascist Academy, whom he had expressed a special interest to see. From there he drove through crowds gathering in groups several hundreds strong, hand-clapping and waving Union Jacks, to the second and last formal session of talks with Ciano and Mussolini. In the evening Chamberlain and Mussolini appeared together at a gala performance at the opera where they received round after round of enthusiastic applause. 'God Save the King' and the Fascist anthem 'Giovinezza' were played. The programme included the third act of Verdi's *Falstaff* (with Mariano Stabile singing the title rôle) and the ballet *La Boutique Fantasque*. The *New York Times* correspondent, Anne O'Hare McCormick – who had recently been reporting from Palestine – watched the two statesmen closely in their box. In the intervals it seemed to be Chamberlain who was doing most of the talking, leaning forward and earnestly addressing Mussolini. The Duce himself, though attentive, responded laconically and only once or twice took the initiative in the conversation. Chamberlain was smiling broadly as the lights went up after Falstaff's humiliation in Windsor Forest.

On Friday the official communiqué spoke only of 'the greatest cordiality', 'a frank and wide exchange of views' and a firm determination by both countries to 'pursue a policy which aims effectively at the maintenance of peace'.

This was the most his supporters had expected of the meeting. It had been the fear of his opponents that something positive might be given away. Thus the seemingly negative result could not be regarded as a failure, though it was difficult to hail it as a great success. With some ten thousand Italian troops actively engaged in the Catalan offensive it had been inconceivable that Mussolini would agree to withdraw from Spain. Casualties of the Littorio Division for the first seventeen days of the offensive were announced in Rome while Chamberlain was there: 27 officers killed, 1 missing and 141 wounded; 217 NCOs and men killed, 29 missing and 1,160 wounded. Conversely, with the offensive more seriously held up than Mussolini had plainly hoped would have been the case by then, and the Republican Government's counter-offensive in Estremadura in full swing, it had not been difficult for Chamberlain to continue to refuse Franco the belligerent rights he wanted. It seemed likely that Chamberlain had at least been able to accept an assurance from Mussolini, for what it was worth, that Italian troops would be withdrawn 'once the Spanish problem had been resolved'.

On the question of Italian claims against France in the Mediterranean, the fact that there had been no agreement by Chamberlain to act as mediator could itself be seen as a sort of achievement, and the fact that the Anglo-Italian accord of the previous April (which accepted the status quo in the Mediterranean) was held to be confirmed could be taken as suggesting that the claims were not to be vigorously pressed.

French newspapers indeed congratulated themselves that the Anglo-French entente had proved as strong as the Berlin–Rome axis and even referred to it as the London–Paris axis. Mme Tabouis in *L'Œuvre*, who had had reservations before the meeting, confirmed that all attempts to separate Britain from France had failed. There seemed general agreement that nothing positive had come out of it, a conclusion with which the German press was quite happy to agree, expressing satisfaction with the cordial and friendly atmosphere which had prevailed. The *Berliner Tageblatt* even commented that the climate had 'improved'.

In Britain on the whole Chamberlain's supporters shared a certain defensiveness about their approbation of the visit. 'No worse' was Garvin's comment in Sunday's *Observer*. 'The Prime Minister brings back neither sheaves nor sorrow.' The visit 'leaves the general situation no worse and does not exclude the hope of better', while *The Times* made a point of stressing 'the greatness and moderation of Mussolini'. (Garvin too spoke well of 'the Duce who when he pleases can be one of the most attractive men in the world'.) The *News Chronicle* predictably declared the visit pointless but it was the Labour opposition paper, the *Daily Herald*, which oddly managed to find one really quite positive aspect to the meeting. The Italians, it said, would now better be able to take into account that Anglo-French solidarity was a reality and that any rash policy would prove more dangerous than they thought. The *Daily Telegraph* was reduced to a rather lame eulogy of the Prime Minister. 'If', it wrote, 'the sowing of the greater international accord which Mr Chamberlain was trying to bring about does not produce the harvest he so strongly hopes for, it will decidedly not be his fault.'

This was really just a flattering and more optimistic way of putting what the lady from the *New York Times* who watched the two statesmen in the box at the opera thought about the visit. Chamberlain, she admitted, had got from Mussolini an assurance that Italy would not resort to force in her claims against France. But that was all. While not going so far as one of her colleagues on the paper who described the meeting as 'what in the United States might be termed a wash-out', she seemed to think that it had been the final test of the policy of appeasement. 'The Prime Minister came to Rome because he has the soul of a missionary and nothing could deter him from following his mission to the end. This is the end.' Her editor thought this too conclusive, running a leader the next day which summed up the meeting more soberly, saying it was 'an error to see the meeting as a failure. At least Chamberlain returns home with a clearer perception of what to expect, and what not to expect.' And this apparently was just about what Chamberlain himself made of it.

After staying on in Rome for an audience with the Pope he held a press conference at the Villa Madama on the day of his departure. At this he declared:

NAZIS PARADE VICTIMS FOR ITALIAN CULTURE CHIEF

Jewish prisoners in Sachsenhausen concentration camp paraded for Italian inspection shortly before Chamberlain and Halifax went to enjoy Mussolini's 'progressive' new Italy in Rome (*below*).

Everyone in Rome from His Majesty the King Emperor to the Head of the Government, from Ministers to the people in the streets, have accorded me a reception I shall never forget.... We are returning home more than ever convinced of the goodwill of the Italian Government ... certain ... our conversations will bear fruit in the future not only for the relations between our two countries but also for European collaboration.

Mussolini saw him off from a red carpet at Rome station just after midday. The two seemed on excellent terms. A section of the British community in Rome was there applauding and singing 'For He's a Jolly Good Fellow', which apparently puzzled the Duce for a moment because he was unable to recognize the tune.

The next day Chamberlain stepped jauntily off the train at Victoria Station in London with a pink carnation in his buttonhole which a Finnish girl on the Channel boat had given him, and clutching his umbrella in one hand while doffing his hat with the other. The *New York Times* man in London who observed him said he looked 'as jaunty as if he had been spending a holiday in the country'. The correspondent had himself given proof of some professional resilience in being there to witness the scene at all. For the police, anxious that scenes such as those organized by the National Union of the Unemployed for the Prime Minister's departure should not mar his arrival, had been falsely encouraging the crowds at the Continental Arrival platform in their belief that it was there the Prime Minister was expected to arrive, shepherding and controlling them as they waited. In fact Chamberlain's Pullman had been detached from the main train at Herne Hill and was brought in alone to the Continental *Departure* platform at the other end of the station.

On the very day that Chamberlain had set out for Rome the week before, there had taken place in Washington the expected secret joint meeting of the House and Senate Foreign Affairs Committees. Testimony had been heard from the US Ambassador to London, Joseph Kennedy, and the US Ambassador to Paris, William Bullitt. Although the House and Senate members had been pledged to secrecy it did not seem difficult for correspondents to discover what had been said. Evidence had been heard of the immense superiority in numbers of the German air force, now greater than that of Britain and France combined. One East Coast Republican, Senator Bridges, said he had been very much impressed by this. 'It changed the opinion I have held that England and France let Czechoslovakia down last autumn. It seems there is a grave danger of a major war in the spring.' The dominant impression was that such a war might well be set off by Mussolini's pressing his demands on France at that time.

In the light of informed views such as these, Chamberlain's pilgrimage to Rome assumed a reasonable significance.

On the other hand there were other Senators and Representatives (Senators Nye, Clark and Lee for example, and Representatives May, Snyder and Thomson) who voiced the suspicion that what they had been told was all just part of Roosevelt's propaganda for his armaments programme, which in turn was his way out of his economic difficulties. Their contention was that a US armaments programme should only be for the defence of the country's own shores. Senator Reynolds of North Carolina was even more forthright.

'Who is going to fight?' he asked. 'Hitler has all Eastern Europe under his thumb right now. France has become a second-rate power and England is in the tightest spot of her history; her life-line threatened at various spots by Italy and needing to import 50,000 to 60,000 tons of food to feed her people.'

By the light of that interpretation the Rome pilgrimage had been a thinly-disguised humiliation, with little but a carnation in the buttonhole to show for it.

5

While Chamberlain was away it had been reported that in Germany Jews were queueing up at consulates all over the country trying to get visas with which to emigrate. Four hundred daily had been queueing at the British Passport Control Office in Berlin. In Vienna there were reckoned 'at a conservative estimate', according to *The Times*, to be five hundred suicides among Jews a month, most of them 'finding sanctuary' in the Danube.

A journey from Britain in the same week as the Prime Minister's to Italy but which had commanded somewhat less attention had been that of an American to Germany. His name was George Rublee, and he was Director of the London office of the Evian Committee on Refugees which had been set up after a thirty-two nation conference on the Jewish refugee problems at Evian in 1938. Rublee was a Washington lawyer and friend both of the late President Wilson and of Roosevelt. He had arrived in Berlin on the morning of 11 January after an invitation from Goering to discuss with the Head of the German Reichsbank, Dr Schacht, the subject of Jewish emigration from Germany. The fact that it was Schacht with whom it was to be discussed (with Field Marshal Goering exercising an overseeing interest) and that the venue for their meeting that day was the Reichsbank was itself symptomatic of the German Government's approach to the matter.

Three weeks before, Germany had put forward a plan by which the 600,000 or so Jews then in Germany could be enabled to leave the country in two stages, the younger ones going first over a period of three years so that they could then send back remittances to their older relatives and dependants who would be allowed to join them later. This youthful emigration was to be financed, according to this plan, by a loan of £500 million which was to be raised by Jewish capitalists abroad to provide each Jew (whose money and property in Germany would all be confiscated) with £1,000 with which to emigrate. In this way, it was proposed, the chief obstacle to emigration would be removed, namely, the reluctance of other countries to receive destitute refugees. (The point of releasing Jews by stages was also intended to make it easier for other countries to absorb them.)

Difficulties in the negotiations had arisen largely over Germany's conditions for the loan. The security for it was to consist of the property confiscated from Jews in Germany and the interest was to be paid from new export facilities which Germany was to be granted by countries interested in the resettlement of Jews. But what this amounted to, as *The Times* pointed out, was that Jews would have to pay an enormous lump sum for the release of fellow-Jews while

Germany kept those fellow-Jews' property and at the same time received much-needed export facilities which might well be to the economic detriment of those countries receiving the refugees. Or, as the *Daily Express* more graphically put it: 'The Germans have a scheme by which they hope to get rid of the Jews and at the same time turn every Jew into a commercial traveller for Germany.'

Even were acceptable financial terms eventually to be worked out the basic problem always remained: there was nowhere available for the Jews to go to in any large numbers. The major Arab revolt in Palestine with which Britain was engaged placed obvious immediate limitations on further use of the traditional Jewish homeland; a German proposal that Alaska might be suitable had been turned down by the Americans and a proposal by Roosevelt that they might go to Ethiopia had been turned down both by Mussolini and by Jews who said they had no wish to go there. Mussolini himself, who the Americans said was 'helpful and co-operative in his attitude to the Jewish problem', apparently favoured Russia and Brazil and, pointedly, above all the United States. There had been some talk too of Manchuria but recent news of the virtual collapse of a Soviet settlement for Jews in Siberia which had been started on the Manchurian frontier in 1928 did not augur well for this. The plan there had been for a hundred thousand Jews to be settled by 1938, but though the area was raised to the status of an 'autonomous Jewish Republic' in 1934 and some Jews not only from the Soviet Union but Poland, Lithuania, the United States and even Palestine had gone there, few seemed to want to stay. The population was now said to be only about twenty thousand, most of them living in the town of Birobijan and not on the land as had originally been intended.

Five hundred Jews had arrived recently in Trinidad but the Governor and Executive Council of the island had banned all further Central European immigration after 15 January.

Some Jews were reaching South America, but their difficulties were by no means over when they got there. Five hundred from Germany and Italy who had obtained entrance papers to Paraguay found themselves stranded at Montevideo in Uruguay in the middle of January when Paraguay cancelled their papers on finding that they were not, after all, farmers. They had brought with them well over a thousand pieces of luggage filled with scent, cognac, cameras and musical instruments which they hoped to exchange for cash. The Uruguayan Government was prepared to let them stay for sixty days. Some of those stranded tried to get smuggled into Argentina but Argentina stepped up shore patrols to prevent this.

Refugee Jewish children were however coming in to Britain in increasing numbers. The first party to come by air – eighteen of them, all under the age of thirteen – landed at Croydon on the day Chamberlain set off for Rome. All had guaranteed homes, as did 115 who had arrived from Germany the day before by sea; a further three hundred were expected by sea later in that week. There were

BEFORE IT IS TOO LATE...

get them out!

HOMELESS, HATED, HOPELESS — 600,000 doomed to a living death in Germany unless you will rescue them soon. Christians as well as Jews, many of them children who once had no fear of life. What will you give to the Lord Baldwin Fund for Refugees, so that they may be removed to safety here while awaiting settlement overseas?

They will not be allowed to take the jobs of British workers here or receive unemployment benefit. The Trades Unions are satisfied about that.

Because we in this country are free to show our pity, will you not give yourself the joy of giving? Are not these lives worth saving? Then give — *before it is too late!*

★ **WHAT YOUR GIFT WILL DO**

1   *It will help to get the victims out of Germany and transport them to their temporary refuge.*

2   *There it will help to train them in agriculture etc., while they are awaiting emigration overseas.*

3   *It will help to settle them finally in a land where they can lead a new and useful life.*

TEAR OUT THIS FORM NOW

Here is my gift to the Lord Baldwin Fund for Refugees.

Name ....

Address ....

....

Amount	£	s.	d.

by cash/cheque/postal or money order.
(Please write in BLOCK CAPITALS and cross out the inapplicable words.)

YOU CAN HAND IN THIS FORM with your gift at any branch of any bank in the country, or post it with a cheque or postal order to Lord Baldwin, 32 Essex St., Strand, W.C.2. Cheques etc. should be crossed and made out as follows:—

LORD BALDWIN FUND FOR REFUGEES

The Executive Committee consists of representatives nominated by the Church of England, the Roman Catholic Church, the Federal Council of Free Churches, the Church of Scotland, the Jewish Community.

T.27.2.39

This advertisement is one of a series issued by the Committee of the Lord Baldwin Fund to tell the public about its aims and activities.

Unemployed appeal to Ernest
Brown, Minister of Labour,
from Trafalgar Square, London.

Sunday Pictorial cartoon.

2,244 Jewish child refugees in Britain by the middle of the month, and double that number by the end of February.

No refugees could stay in Britain unless they were sponsored or their livelihood was in some way assured. For this purpose a Fund under the patronage of Lord Baldwin to help refugees to Britain had been started just before Christmas and had reached over £350,000 in a month, collected largely from sums of £5 or less. The figure included contributions, for instance, from 'an old lady' of the Uttoxeter Rotary Club (ten guineas); 'Proceeds of a Nativity Play, Forest Row' (£7); *Daily Mail* Compositors and Readers Chapel, Manchester (£5); 'Thankful, Kings Lynn' (£1); Wamphray Girl Guides (10/6d); and many 'anonymous' (from £100 to 3/2d).

However, compassion for Jewish refugees was not universal. On Saturday 14 January, which had been declared 'Stage and Screen Day Appeal' for the Fund in London with many 'stars' furthering the Appeal and all cinemas giving ten per cent of their gross takings to it, a Fascist demonstration took place in Piccadilly with men marching round and round the Circus chanting 'Britain for the British' as the theatre and cinema audiences came out. Pamphlets were distributed, saying: 'Why a Relief Fund for Czechs, Austrians, Basques and Jews while British Unemployed are starving?' There was a counter-demonstration by the National Unemployed Workers' Movement with banners saying: 'The Unemployed are not enemies of Refugees. Help them both.'

Nevertheless ambivalent feelings about refugees coming to Britain were not confined to Fascists.

The *Sunday Pictorial* that weekend carried a headline 'Refugees get Jobs – Britons get Dole', and part of the accompanying text ran: 'European refugees are stealing jobs from Britons by the hundred every week ... disrupting labour conditions in the tailoring and garment trade by under-cutting.' And there was a leading article in the *Evening Standard* of 17 January which, having noted the success to date of the Baldwin Fund, contained a number of unsentimental observations:

> ... Yet those who have organized the public subscription would be the first to admit that financial assistance is not a remedy ...
>
> It is not possible, for instance, to contemplate permanent increased Jewish settlement in this country. British traders and those employed in the professions cannot be expected to view a large influx of competitors with equanimity. British workers, particularly the 1,800,000 unemployed, cannot be deprived of the prospect of earning their livelihood by unchecked immigration from the dictator countries ...
>
> Another and equally important side of the problem is raised by the belief which seems to have grown in the dictator countries that the democracies are willing to aid their policies of expulsion by unlimited financial support for the refugees. Such a miscalculation appears to underlie Dr Schacht's negotiations. We hope that illusion has been effectively dispelled ...
>
> It is not possible for the British Government to allow immigrants to pour into this

country. We can only allow harbourage here so long as provision is being made at the same time for refugees to move on elsewhere . . .

The *Standard* concluded by viewing with approval the code of conduct which the Board of Deputies of British Jews had drawn up for German-Jewish refugees. This gave a detailed list of 'the precautions which should be taken by Jewish immigrants against abusing the hospitality of the country which gives them refuge', particular emphasis being placed on the need to refrain from political activity and to obtain permission from the Aliens' Department of the Home Office before starting any new business or accepting any form of employment. A further recommendation went as follows: 'Do not make yourself conspicuous by speaking loudly, nor by your manner or dress. The Englishman greatly dislikes ostentation.'

Finally refugees were warned: 'Do not expect to be received into homes immediately because the Englishman takes some time before he opens up his home wide to strangers.'

If a certain bleakness thus pervaded conditions in the host country, these were plainly preferable to the conditions in their own from which with an increasing sense of urgency, Jews were feeling impelled to try to emigrate. While George Rublee talked with Schacht in Berlin the *New York Times* correspondent, stressing the importance of these negotiations, wrote: 'Today some eight million Jews living in Central and Eastern Europe are facing the dire choice of emigration or strangulation – economic strangulation at best, physical strangulation at worst . . .' His estimate of the number of Jews in Greater Germany itself was slightly higher than others' – he put it at 700,000 – but his main point was that the Central European countries were bound sooner or later to imitate Germany's example. 'The remainder of the world', he pondered grimly, 'can of course wash its hands of the whole matter. It can refuse to accept the migratory host and let Germany and the other countries inclined to follow her solve their problems in their own way irrespective of their victims' fate.'

That the Germans' chief consideration at this stage was to hasten emigration with the maximum possible financial and economic advantage to the Third Reich was emphasized yet again by Alfred Rosenberg, described as Nazi Cultural Director, speaking that week in Detmold. 'The League of Nations', he said, 'must deal with the Jewish problem. The Reich will not rest until the last Jew has left German soil.'

But the League of Nations was already in trouble with World Jewry for acquiescing in Jewish emigration. Jews were being forced to emigrate from Danzig, the Free City in Poland with a predominantly German population, and at a meeting of the Administrative Committee of the World Jewish Congress in Paris on 16 January, Nahum Goldmann, its Chairman, severely criticized the League for not withdrawing its Commissioner from that 'Free City' in protest. Goldmann further made it clear that as a general principle World Jewry was not in any case interested in solving its difficulties on the basis of charity and philanthropy. He said Jews should not allow the Jewish problem to be sunk to the level of charitable aid but should fight, win or lose, for equal rights. 'We must not let ourselves pay cash premiums to our oppressors,' he said, with unmistakable reference to the negotiations then going on between Rublee and Schacht, and added: 'I do not think I was as much hurt by Hitler's measures as by that attitude of the Washington Foreign Office and those of other democratic countries that our situation was one calling for philanthropy. We want equality, not treatment as second- or third-class citizens.'

An official of the Jewish Agency, David Ben-Gurion, made a harder-headed statement the same day, though in view of what was happening in Palestine it too struck an unrealistic note. Provision could be made, he said, for 100,000 German Jews to go and settle there, adding: 'Jewry wants peace with the Arabs, but on one issue it cannot yield a single inch – the right to immigrate to Palestine.'

The Arabs in that land continued to dispute such a right with rifles turned against Jews and British alike. A typical day at the beginning of the year, the 3rd of January, had seen five fatal casualties. At half past five in the morning a party of Jewish workers of the Potash Company, hitherto on good terms with its Arab neighbours, had been ambushed on their way to work with a police escort just south of the Dead Sea. Two Jews were killed and one of the police seriously wounded. Near Rishon le Zion the same day a Jew working in an orange grove was killed by an Arab sniper while two armed Arabs were killed by British troops searching villages in the Acre and Samaria districts. An official announcement gave the figure of 5,000 as the total number of Arabs so far detained by the British for interrogation in the course of the revolt, though no more than 2,100 had ever been held at one time.

Accusations of brutality towards the Arabs by British forces in Palestine were being broadcast by the German radio. There was talk of 'Ungeheure Grausamkeiten' (monstrous cruelties). Almost as if to help counter such unfortunate propaganda there started on 4 January a trial in Jaffa of four British constables of the Palestine police on a charge of murdering a handcuffed Arab prisoner there the previous October. They pleaded 'Not Guilty'.

Two Arab witnesses described how they had seen a car in which the prisoner was being taken to prison stop and the handcuffed prisoner get out of it. He had walked away a few yards, they said, when he was shot down by all four constables. The witnesses could neither describe how the prisoner was dressed, nor identify the constables but they were quite certain that the prisoner had not run from the car. A Jewish Civil Guard on the other hand, who had seen the incident from thirty yards away, said the prisoner had been running when fired at. A German woman described how she had seen one of the police without a hat come up behind the Arab as he lay on the ground and shoot him. An Arab doctor from the Government Hospital who had examined the body said he gained the impression that the shots had all been fired at short range. One of the accused police, Constable Wood, admitted that he had killed the prisoner but maintained that it had not been his intention. He said he had fired low at him while he was running but that the man must have been in the act of falling when he fired, which is why the shot hit him in the head.

On 11 January the Court gave its verdicts. Constable Wood was found guilty not of murder but of 'attempted manslaughter' and the other three police were found guilty of 'attempting to inflict grievous bodily harm'. The Court found that there had been no premeditated decision to kill the prisoner and that the car had stopped because it had broken down. The prisoner had been moving away from the car but had not been running. He was about twenty yards away when his action was detected. The question was whether or not the constables had been justified in firing at him. The Court decided that he should have been recaptured without the use of firearms. Since it could not be established beyond reasonable doubt that Wood's shot was the fatal one, he must have the benefit of the doubt and was therefore guilty only of the attempt to commit manslaughter. He was sentenced to three years' imprisonment, which it was expected he would serve in Britain.

Of the three others, one, Constable Mansell, was sentenced to a year's imprisonment, probably to be served in Palestine. The other two were only bound over 'in view of their youth and inexperience'.

The day before these verdicts were given the War Office issued a statement apparently designed to remove disquiet about the methods being used in Palestine. It pointed out that troops were having to deal with an armed rebellion but that there was no organized rebel army against which British troops could act to the exclusion of peaceful citizens; peaceful citizens were inextricably mixed up among the active rebels. The total number of the latter probably did not exceed fifteen hundred, split up in small bands under the command of various leaders, but they were reinforced from time to time by armed peasants from villages near which they were operating. Such bands tried as far as possible to avoid engagement with the troops and, except when surprised, offered little real fight.

While the general policy for the revolt was laid down by the Grand Mufti and the Higher Arab Committee, the local Arab leaders were acting very independently within their own areas. There were two principal such leaders: Abdul Rahim El Haj Mahomet, the titular commander-in-chief, and Aref Abdul Razzik, who was on bad terms with him. Rahim, according to the War Office, was a man of good family and a more honest and genuine patriot than many of the other leaders, and he had tried to conduct his campaign on decent lines, frequently refusing to carry out the Mufti's more ruthless orders. Razzik, a man of much lower origins and less education, had had no hesitation in doing so. Only twelve months before he had been a very minor leader and had achieved promotion by this implicit obedience to orders, pocketing in the process a large rake-off from compulsory subscriptions to rebel funds.

There were many other independent smaller leaders in the revolt, continued the War Office statement, and the only possible way of trying to identify these and their bands was by search-and-check operations in villages and towns, which was now the normal military operation in Palestine. Such operations necessarily had to be carried out in considerable force because they were frequently undertaken on information that an armed band was in the area.

'Since', said the War Office,

the innocent and guilty are completely mixed together and quite indistinguishable on sight there is no alternative to the collection of all males irrespective of excuse if wanted men are to be prevented from slipping through the net by giving false accounts of themselves. Inevitably the process involves a certain amount of hardship for the innocent, and the spectacle of weeping women watching their menfolk marched off for identification naturally offers opportunity for propaganda but in the present conditions no other course is possible.

In house-to-house searches every proper precaution was being taken to prevent looting or wanton damage and women were only searched when a policewoman was available; mosques were only entered and searched at the invitation of the local mukhtar. On the question of the demolition of houses by troops, which had attracted criticism, the statement had this to say: 'Critics fail to realize that the principle of the responsibility of a community for a crime or disorder committed within its boundaries is fully recognized and understood by the Palestinian Arab. Collective punishment is frequently the only method of impressing upon a peaceful and terrorized majority that failure to assist law and order may be more unpleasant than submitting to intimidation.'

Sefton Delmer gave an eye-witness description of British action in the *Daily Express* of 12 January.

'Yes, sir,' he wrote, 'there are concentration camps in Palestine, "Cages" they call them. ... The families of the men interned are expected to provide them with food and blankets. ... I saw the menfolk of three entire villages led off to the cage while I was up in Northern Palestine ... for having harboured the rebels in their villages.' He added:

All Arabs regard the anti-Jewish campaign as one of self-defence against the Jewish invaders who every time they buy land from one of the Arab landlords turn all Arabs off it and refuse for ever more to employ any Arabs on that land. Again and again the Arab leaders insisted in conversation that they bore no racial bias against the Jews and that they are willing to live side by side with the Jews if the Jews will renounce their ambition of driving the Arabs out of Palestine.

Meanwhile *The Times*, in a leader on the 11th, had reminded its readers of the other side of the picture. There was, it said, no time to lose in the task of finding permanent settlement somewhere for the vast mass of Jews whose sufferings had aroused such widespread pity. 'If the governments represented at the Evian conference do not translate professions into practice a very terrible chapter will have to be written into the history of human hypocrisy.'

6

On 11 January, the day Chamberlain arrived in Rome, it was still possible for supporters of the Spanish Government to believe that the opening of the new Estremadura front round Madrid might change the course of the war, though heavy reinforcements of Franco's troops were pouring into the area. 'Madrid army within five miles of Franco's life-line' had been the *Daily Express* headline of the day before. The Republicans could claim to have won back three hundred square miles of territory in the few days of the offensive. Recaptured lead mines in the area were already working again for the Government and their troops were in a key position dominating Peñarroya. But from Catalonia it was reported that Franco had broken through the iron ring round Montblanch, thus penetrating the Government's second line of defence there. William Forrest of the *News Chronicle*, visiting that front, 'watched lorry load after lorry load of reinforcements going up to man the new line now established after the timely withdrawal from the Lérida salient. . . . If this line can be held, the industrial heart of Catalonia will remain secure and continue to provide the Government with the sinews of war.'

By 15 January, the day on which Chamberlain got back to Victoria station, the only reports from Estremadura were of heavy rain. There was some news of another attempt by the Republican General Miaja to open a third diversionary front round Madrid but this was already eclipsed by Franco's spectacular victories in Catalonia. The new line did not hold. Montblanch, Falset and Tortosa fell on successive days on the way to Tarragona and on the 15th Tarragona itself fell, where only two days before the Government had said it was digging in for a strong stand. It fell in three hours almost without firing a shot. Barcelona, on the coast road, was only thirty-five miles away.

Forrest of the *News Chronicle*, who the day before had been able to write: 'Tortosa is lost to Catalonia but Catalonia is not yet lost to Spain' now wrote: 'Now it is backs to the wall for Barcelona, for Catalonia and for Spain.' It was 'the blackest day of the whole war' though 'leaders of the army of Catalonia are still confident of ultimate victory'. General Juan Hernández Saravia, the commander of the Republican forces in Catalonia, was looking tired but his face lit up when Forrest asked him about future prospects. 'The war', he said, 'will not be decided by the loss or gain of territory but by men. And we have the men. As long as there is one man in Catalonia able to handle a rifle the fight will go on.' A new line was being formed, running from the sea through a point on the main Balaguer road east of Cervera to the frontier at Andorra. Nor would it be the last. But Franco's superiority in war materials was massive. Forrest watched a battle that day for the village of Santa Coloma de Queralt. After the artillery had first pounded the Republican lines he saw Franco's bombers, Junkers and Heinkels, flying along them unchallenged and punishing them mercilessly while twenty-five Franco 'chasers' performed aerobatics overhead for fun.

The *New York Times* man with the Government forces, Herbert Matthews, had been experiencing some of this sort of thing at first hand, having been caught in the bombing and shelling of Valls just before the fall of that town near Tarragona. He described how, under the ceaseless shelling,

> soldiers walked about, but civilians ran desperately in short spurts hugging the lees of the houses, for the shells came from the sierra to the west. Shops were closed, women peeped from doors and asked anxiously of all passing – soldiers, friends or foreigners – what was happening, what was going to happen. But nobody knew. We did not hear any alarm; we just saw everybody scattering for refuges, and followed the nearest stream. It took us below a big ruined building with the usual passage hewn out of the hard ground – nothing to fear down there. A latecomer said he had spotted fourteen bombers. The ground shook under the impact. There were some gasps of dismay from women and swearing by men. Then we could hear the rattle of swift Oerlikon anti-aircraft machine-guns. It takes more than Oerlikons to bring down Junkers. There was no use staying in Valls.

Later that day he counted at least sixty of Franco's bombers and only ten Katiusha bombers and four Mosca fighters for the Government.

But for all Franco's material superiority and his Catalonian successes he himself was being cautious about the future. His spokesmen declared the Estremadura offensive was now immobilized and they were dismissive of the new front near Madrid, but Franco himself, pressed by the *New York Times* man on his side to say whether or not he thought the war would be over by May, refused to commit himself and even declined to reply when asked if he thought it would be over by the third anniversary of the war's outbreak on 18 July. All he would say was that this was the last winter campaign.

In Barcelona general mobilization had already been ordered even before the fall of Tarragona. Barcelona, according to *The Times*, was now preparing to emulate Madrid and by Tuesday 17 January, when Franco had made still further advances, leap-frogging his divisions so that each could spend two to three days at a time out of the line and capturing eighty-two villages since Sunday, the *Daily Telegraph* correspondent said the atmosphere in Barcelona was indeed reminiscent of that in Madrid in November 1936. The situation, he said, was actually worse, but not hopeless. The outcome was by no means a foregone conclusion; the army was intact and its discipline good.

From Hendaye the *New York Times* reported military observers as seeing 'little immediate danger' to the city. The orderly withdrawal of Government forces suggested that it might be part of a long-laid plan to make the most determined stand along the natural line of mountain defences that now lay ahead of Franco. There was, too, the hope that the French might reopen the frontier to allow arms and foreign volunteers in to the Government as they had done at the beginning of the Civil War. On this point, however, the Italian *Informazione Diplomatica* Bulletin issued a sharp warning, which it said merely confirmed what Mussolini had said in his talks with Chamberlain – that if in the near future there was intervention on a larger scale on the part of those Governments friendly to Negrín, Italy would resume her liberty of action because she would thus consider the non-intervention policy ended and a failure. (He meant, of course, the non-*further*-intervention policy. The Spanish Government had disbanded, it said, the 10,000 remaining foreign volunteers of the International Brigade but Mussolini did not accept this statement as either reliable or adequate and in any case said he would only send his own legionaries home if Franco were granted full belligerent rights. He was now threatening actually to increase their numbers should the French frontiers be opened.)

In Barcelona itself all males between eighteen and forty-four were now called directly to the colours; men up to fifty-five were called up for building fortifications and men over fifty-five told to hold themselves in readiness. Pamphlets were being distributed in the streets proclaiming: 'In the struggle against Napoleon, children of eleven took part in the defence of Gerona. The flesh of cats was a delicacy for the patrols of those days. And their resistance defeated Napoleon. The courage of Catalonia will once again save Spain.' Women were offering themselves for war work in their thousands and were parading through the streets shouting, '*Hombres al frente, mujeres al trabajo*' (Men to the front, women to work). A great banner spanned the central avenue of the city: 'We will yet win the war' and posters placarded the city: 'To the last man and the last shot'; 'Catalonia will never be Italian'. Girls of the Socialist Youth organization were distributing pamphlets saying, 'Even the stones of Catalonia have turned against the invader', and sometimes they invaded the cinemas, still playing to capacity, and addressed the audiences. Theatres too were crowded though gunfire from the front less than fifty miles away was becoming more and more audible. Newspapers were full of articles about cultural and sporting events as well as the war.

William Forrest now found he could visit the front comfortably between breakfast-time and tea-time, though he stressed the '-time' factor in the phrase because the meals themselves were becoming increasingly meagre. Food was short with thousands of refugees adding to the city's million and a half population. These refugees, homeless and utterly worn out after many days on the roads during which they had been bombed and machine-gunned, lay around in the open spaces of the city such as the garden strips of the broader avenues with their bundles and household goods all about them. Raids on the city itself continued, but so in a curious way did normal life side-by-side with a life that was not normal. Groups gathered at the shoe repairers; children walked about with shopping baskets on their arms; at an open-air shooting gallery people shot at ducks and drakes as Franco's troops drew closer, and now and again people were injured by bombs while standing in food queues.

There was a certain confidence in the air of the city. Writing on 16 January the *New York Times* man, Herbert Matthews, thought there were good possibilities of the offensive being stopped well short of it. The Government lines were shorter and its troops no longer so thinly spread out, and there must, he thought, surely be a limit in the end to Franco's supplies of men and material. The Communist paper *Frente Rojo* reported encouragingly that new material had just arrived for the Republic which, it said, should be enough to make all the difference. The Government, reported Matthews, was resenting pressure, particularly from London and Paris, to allow some form of mediation with Franco. It did not want mediation. What it wanted was the right to buy arms, and British and French insistence on the withdrawal of foreign aid to Franco.

On the other hand there were growing reports of traffic in the wrong direction across the French frontier. Government deserters were entering France in increasing numbers. One group of forty-four men armed with rifles and pistols was brought through the Pyrenees by a guide on 16 January. It was impossible to hold out any longer, they said.

7

Many other items in addition to the news from Spain caught the world's attention while Chamberlain was away in Rome, some trivial, some bizarre, some telling of natural disasters and some dependent for their final resolution only on the ultimate success or failure of that mission for peace on which he was engaged.

Thus the news that Lady Mary Dunn had broken a hand while hunting in Ireland was recorded on the centre page of *The Times* beside that of the Spanish Civil War, together with the latest report on the condition of George Robey, who was enjoying at last a fairly comfortable night after falling off the stage and breaking three ribs in *Robinson Crusoe* at Birmingham.

Vivien Leigh, the 5 foot 3 inches tall, twenty-five-year-old English actress with green eyes and brown hair, had got the part of Scarlett O'Hara in *Gone with the Wind* which Hollywood had been trying to fill for nearly three years. She was little known in the States; her three films to date had all been British, and a flood of anti-fan letters poured into Hollywood. A correspondent wrote to *Movie Mirror*: 'Why not cast Chiang Kai-shek and change the part to Gerald O'Hara?' The new star herself made matters worse by revealing that she had never heard of a June bug, the plant-destroying insect which infests the South, and the studios were swamped with every sort of June bug within hours of her statement. David Selznick himself replied to criticisms of his choice by saying that it was very much easier for an English woman to achieve a Southern accent than for a Yankee.

A titled employer in Northamptonshire, England, wrote an advertisement to appear in *The Times* for a head kitchen-maid to be paid sixty pounds a year 'if good', adding that there were two in the family and twenty servants.

A terrible fire had been sweeping the State of Victoria in Australia, blackening over a thousand square miles and killing over seventy people. H.G. Wells, who had been on a tour there, had been getting himself into trouble. 'Hitler and Mussolini', he was rash enough to say in public, 'are freaks enforcing a state of affairs similar to the days of the criminal Caesars.' Mr J.A. Lyons, the Prime Minister of Australia, took severe exception to this, saying that such personal insults were to be deplored and that he wished to make it clear that Wells's views were not those of the Government.

In Germany the Berlin 'paper' *Der S.A. Mann* had been attacking the popularity of the dance *The Lambeth Walk* in Germany as 'Jewish mischief and animalistic hopping'. The Nazi Governor of Tirol and Vorarberg had been reinforcing last March's Anschluss of Austria by forbidding people to play 'evil swing music'.

More serious local news from Germany was that the trial of Ernst Niekisch, the Nationalist Bolshevik who had for a time flirted with Nazism, had ended, though in a certain amount of mystery. Niekisch was not executed, as many expected he would be, but sentenced to penal servitude for life while two of his colleagues received lesser terms of imprisonment. Eighteen other people, however, who had originally been arraigned with him before the People's Court, were no longer mentioned and the authorities, who held the trial in secret, seemed to be at pains to minimize the nature of the conspiracy and play down the notion that treason was any sort of serious problem at all in the Reich. There had been, it was stated, only a few hundred cases since 1933. Nevertheless, on Saturday 14 January, the day on which Chamberlain left Rome, about 3,500 Germans in Dahlem, Berlin, packed the church of Pastor Niemöller, the former U-boat commander now in Sachsenhausen concentration camp, and overflowed onto the pavements outside to hear a sermon of protest on his behalf by Pastor Hans Gollwitzer. Seven other pastors who had been banned from their own pulpits by the State walked in, wearing full clerical garb, and stood by the altar throughout the service.

The internal state of affairs in Nazi Germany was something which by definition was not easy to judge. The *Times* correspondent had had a shot at it at the beginning of the year. He listed a number of areas of dissatisfaction with the regime in addition to the objection of Protestants and Catholics to the State's treatment of the Churches. There was, he said, resentment by intellectuals of the subordination of art and science to political considerations. There was resentment by employers of the increasingly complex and irksome system of controls being imposed on capitalism. There was working-class dissatisfaction at the destruction of the trades unions. Moreover, as memories of unemployment faded, the advantage of being employed at low wages for long hours seemed increasingly less attractive. A sixty-hour working week had been introduced in some cases and there were provisions for conscription of labour which could take workers at times away from their families and homes.

Some women who had taken temporary jobs in factories at Christmas had been forbidden to leave them. There was – all according to the *Times* man – general dissatisfaction about food shortages and the deteriorating quality of certain products such as clothing. There was a shortage of coffee (rationing was predicted) and also of coal, due it was said to the withdrawal of miners from the pits to work on the western fortifications. There was also resentment of the 'Party' men using their positions for personal gain. However, the *Times* correspondent conceded that the action against the Jews had probably stirred public opinion less in Germany than abroad and said that the amount of active opposition provoked could easily be exaggerated. Persecution of the Jews was not popular among 'decent people' but, he added: 'These people are beginning to adopt the attitude that one must not be surprised at anything these days.'

To the world at large Germany's foreign policy was a matter almost as opaque

Vivien Leigh signs up as
Scarlett O'Hara in *Gone
With The Wind*, watched
by director David O.
Selznick, Leslie Howard
and Olivia de Havilland

Margaret Lockwood,
Michael Redgrave and
Paul Lukas in Alfred
Hitchcock's film *The Lady
Vanishes* (New York
Critics Award).

as her domestic scene. There was an uneasy feeling, particularly in Britain, that in spite of Hitler's expansion of the Third Reich in 1938 to include both Austrians and Sudeten Germans he was not yet satisfied. The London correspondent of the *New York Times* wrote:

> There is no doubt here that Germany will 'push' somewhere in the Spring and the decision rests with one man. Every nation in Europe is doing what it can to shove Germany away from its own frontier in the direction of the other fellow. Colonel Beck [Foreign Minister of Poland] has just been to see Hitler and Ciano is about to see Beck and the Foreign Ministers of Yugoslavia and Hungary. These men will move heaven and earth to prevent Germany driving East – not of course by thinking to fight Germany but by encouraging Germany to go West in search of glory.

There was indeed plenty of evidence in the German Press and elsewhere of a psychological mood suggesting that Germany meant some sort of business somewhere. The new German battleship *Scharnhorst*, which Hitler himself had launched two years before, had been commissioned at Wilhelmshaven with ensign and pennant broken on board on the day the above article appeared. The ship's first commander, Captain Otto Ciliax, who had fought at Jutland and had bombarded the Spanish Republican port of Almería from the pocket-battleship *Admiral Scheer* in 1937, used this occasion to speak of 'a period of unprecedented political and historical importance that finds its external expression in the concept of Greater Germany ... at a time in which more than ever forces hostile to it sound a battle-call to the Third Reich'.

The pronouncement was very representative of the public voice of National Socialist Germany. Forces were seen as hostile not because of any active opposition to the Third Reich (though moral disapprobation of its attitude to the Jews was resented) but because of an apparently perverse failure to regard its further aspirations with much enthusiasm.

What precise form such further aspirations might take was still not clear. Hitler himself had said after Munich that he had no further territorial ambitions left in Europe. But in his New Year message he had reminded people that the anti-Comintern Pact was the cornerstone of the Third Reich's foreign policy and it was well known that he had ideas for an independent Greater Ukraine as part of some general concept of a *cordon sanitaire* against Bolshevism in Eastern Europe. Nevertheless the manœuvring required to achieve that ambition appeared a most laborious business which could involve adjustments with other States in the region.

Typical of the local difficulties he was likely to experience was the problem of adjusting, after Munich, Czechoslovakia's new eastern frontier in Ruthenia, or, as it was now to be called, Carpatho-Ukraine. Hungary and Poland both wanted to share a common frontier there. Germany, looking further eastwards and ahead towards an independent and presumably German-dominated Greater Ukraine, wanted to keep the gap open. The previous year's incursions by both

Poles and Hungarians into the Ruthenian part of Czechoslovakia had been ended by a so-called 'Vienna Award' made by Germany and Italy in November 1938, which ceded to Hungary and Poland sizeable parts of both the Slovak and Ruthenian territory of Czechoslovakia but really satisfied neither aggressor.

As for post-Munich Czechoslovakia itself, it was clearly increasingly difficult for it to preserve much of its national and democratic identity in its need to oblige Germany. Moreover it was pressured internally by increasingly assertive Slovak autonomy and thus was in little condition to exert effective will or independent authority, though still capable of occasional reflexes. One such reflex had occurred on 6 January and illustrated the complexity of the situation with which German policy in the area had to deal.

According to the Hungarians, at half past three in the morning on 6 January, Czech troops launched an attack with three armoured cars, mortars and machine-guns against Hungarian troops in Munkacs, a former Ruthenian (Carpatho-Ukrainian) town ceded to Hungary by the Vienna Award. Four Hungarians were killed and ten wounded, while one of the Czech armoured cars was knocked out and left behind with four Czech dead on Hungarian soil. An hour and a half later the Czechs started shelling the town, damaging houses, the theatre, a cinema and a hotel; and they repeated the shelling in the afternoon, severely wounding a child. The Hungarians said their own response to this was very restrained and that they did not return the artillery fire. Both the Czecho-slovak Government and the semi-autonomous internal Governments of Slovakia and Carpatho-Ukraine maintained that it had been Hungarian regulars and irregulars who had started the whole thing, attacking with such ferocity that artillery had to be used in reply. The Carpatho-Ukrainian Prime Minister, Father Voloshin, an Orthodox priest, declared in a broadcast: 'I want to establish with all emphasis that the Hungarians were the aggressors. Our soldiers have been provoked by them for a long time and only the discipline of our Army prevented clashes taking place earlier.' (He then went off at what seemed, from the Czechoslovak point of view, an unfortunate tangent, to say that Carpatho-Ukraine was interested in a Great Ukrainian State and that he had every confid-ence that Greater Ukraine would be created in the near future.)

Although at least one other violent incident immediately followed, the matter was amicably submitted to an enquiry by both sides within a few days. The goodwill shown by the Czech Government derived perhaps from recognition that it was hot-head Carpatho-Ukrainian elements in the State's army who were partly responsible. The incident, though soon closed, at least demonstrated the instability in one small corner of that Eastern Europe in which Germany had major strategic interests, however imprecise, and since the beginning of January Hitler had been taking steps to put some order into his consideration of those interests.

On 5 January he had had Colonel Beck, the Polish Foreign Minister, to see him in his 'Berghof' above Berchtesgaden and talked to him for three hours in the presence of Ribbentrop, his own Foreign Minister. The next day Beck, after visiting the Architectural Exhibition in the new House of German Art in Munich, lunched with Ribbentrop in the *Vier Jahreszeiten* hotel and had another long conversation with him before returning by train to Warsaw.

The brief communiqué issued afterwards gave nothing away but there was a good deal of speculation as to what might have gone on. Only five weeks before, Poland had renewed her Non-Aggression Pact with the Soviet Union; it seemed unrealistic to suppose that Hitler had been trying to get Beck to join the Anti-Comintern Pact, though presumably the exact significance of the Russo-Polish Non-Aggression Pact's renewal would have been discussed. As for the German hopes of a Greater Ukraine, Poland had a problem with her own Ukrainians so was unlikely to be interested in stirring up independent Ukrainian nationalism. There was of course a problem in Danzig, with its German population and its special Free City status while at the same time an important Polish port. There was also the question of a motor road, possibly to be under German sovereignty, crossing the Polish Corridor between the main block of Greater German territory and East Prussia. On the whole commentators seemed to think that what Germany wanted to ascertain was whether or not there had been any pro-Russian swing in Poland's inevitable policy of trying to maintain a balance for herself between her two powerful neighbours. It was thought interesting that Litvinov, the Soviet Foreign Minister, who had been scheduled to visit Warsaw later in the month, was now said not to be going. Certainly official circles in Warsaw, while saying little about the Berchtesgaden meeting, seemed to want to suggest that there had neither been any change of direction in Polish policy nor any insurmountable difficulty under discussion with Hitler.

A good part of the month was in fact to be spent in Germany in taking the pulse of Eastern Europe in this way. Count Czaky, the Hungarian Foreign Minister, went to Berlin on the 16th and in the course of a two-day visit had talks with Hitler, Ribbentrop, Goering and Hess – and also saw a good deal of the Italian and Japanese Ambassadors there, fellow-members of the Anti-Com-intern Pact, to which Hungary now adhered. Commentators assumed that Hungarian worries over the situation on the Slovak and Ruthenian borders of Czechoslovakia would have to be set at rest and the question of certain 'disturb-ing' and unsatisfactory elements in the Hungarian population consisting of radicals, Jews and reactionaries disposed of.

A few days later, on the evening of 20 January, the Foreign Minister of the new shrunken Czechoslovakia, Frantisek Chvalkovski, also went to Berlin. However, his rather different, even vassal status was signalled not only by the fact that he stayed less than twenty-four hours but by a certain displeasure voiced for instance by the *Berliner Tageblatt* over the incompetent work of the Czech censors in dealing with articles about Nazi Germany. 'It is not just the matter but the fact that the censors let it pass.' And the Czech Government's own paper *Venkow* was cited as being allowed to 'demand a return to Czech patriotism of an old type' (i.e. of Dr Beneš). 'Do they not realize in editorial offices in Prague what it means to make reactionary appeals to a mistaken past? ... When we see this attempt to raise old passions it is a clear hint that certain circles set no store by good-neighbourly relations.' Better economic cooperation, too, was wanted.

Some aspects of this latter were already in evidence. The Czechs had agreed to the building of an autobahn between Vienna, Brno and Breslau which was to run under German sovereignty right across some of the best farming land of Bohemia. (Symbolically, the first object it was due to destroy on reaching Czech territory was the Jewish cemetery at Jevičko.) The world-famous Skoda armament factory was now reported to have been taken over by Krupp, this, according to *The Times*, being urged by the Germans 'as only logical now that there is no point in making arms for the Czechoslovak army any more'. The reward for Czech good behaviour was to be consideration by Germany of that guarantee on her part of the country's frontiers which was promised at Munich four months before, but had so far not been forthcoming.

On Chvalkoski's return to Prague after his brief Berlin stay a plan was immediately drawn up for increased Czech economic cooperation with Germany, though he reported that there had in fact been no demand for any formal customs or economic union. The Czech-Soviet alliance was formally repudiated and twelve Communists were arrested in Prague for distributing leaflets.

For a precise indication of the direction which the German Government's thoughts on foreign policy were taking it was thought likely that the world would have to wait until 30 January, when Hitler was to address the Reichstag on the sixth anniversary of his accession to power. The speech was as eagerly awaited as had been Roosevelt's at the beginning of the month.

8

Chamberlain had returned from Rome to a Britain increasingly concerned that
he should implement the other half of his appeasement policy – namely, preparation for 'every eventuality' should the central tenet of that policy prove wrong.
But there were considerable doubts among his opponents as to whether the
Government was as enthusiastic about the second part of the policy as it was
about the first. Sir John Anderson, his Lord Privy Seal with responsibilities for
coordinating civilian defence against air-raids, had gone on a skating holiday to
Arosa in Switzerland at the beginning of January and came under much criticism
for doing so.

All that had really been decided on before he left was a 'short-term policy'
which he had outlined in the House of Commons just before Christmas to
provide as soon as possible individual steel shelters to householders to be
distributed by local authorities and erected by the householders themselves.
Meanwhile, to many, the deteriorating conditions of the shelters which had been
hastily dug for the Munich crisis the previous September appeared symbolic of
Government inertia. While Anderson was away people wrote to *The Times* and
to other papers urging attention to different aspects of 'air-raid precautions',
now generally abbreviated to ARP. Some were concerned with the need to
emulate Barcelona and build deep shelters, others with the impracticability of
this. The Air-Raid Protection Institute reckoned it would cost £500,000,000 to
do so, while it was pointed out that there might not actually be time for them to
be constructed – it had taken Barcelona eighteen months. The need to plan
evacuation preoccupied many people, as did the possibly false assumption on
which evacuation might be based, namely that the enemy would not want to
bomb civilians if he could help it. Others stressed the importance, whatever the
shelter provision, of having an efficient air-raid warning system. There were, as
one correspondent pointed out, roughly two schools of thought about shelters:
the 'deep' and the 'shallow' schools, though a retired Major-General writing to
The Times the day after Sir John Anderson returned from Arosa added a third,
the 'Trenchard', in reference to that Air Chief Marshal's theory that bombing
attack was ultimately the best method of aerial defence.

'Other nations', wrote the Major-General, 'are just as averse from being
bombed as we are, *conceivably more so*; for most of us can remember how in the
late War when London was raided crowds of aliens from the East End choked
the Tube stations, dislocating traffic while the stolid Briton went about his
business.'

Winston Churchill, out of office now for nearly ten years, also maintained that air-raid precautions alone were not enough. 'I cannot', he declared, 'subscribe to the idea that it might be possible to dig ourselves in and make no preparations for anything other than passive defence. It is the theory of the turtle which is disproved at every Lord Mayor's banquet.'

Sir John Anderson confronted criticism of muddle and delay in his department with equanimity, readily ascribing much of it to the visual effect on passers-by of those muddy and unsightly trenches in the London parks. The present plan, he insisted, bore no relation to what happened then. Certain short-term measures such as the steel shelters would soon be ready, he said, but the possible provision of deep bomb-proof shelters was quite separate from this, and he concluded, 'We are working on the assumption that there is a risk of war within a comparatively short time; but that does not mean that we expect war.'

This muted compromise between action and inaction seemed somehow symptomatic of a wider Government initiative now gathering a momentum of sorts in all aspects of possible war-time emergency. The Ministry of Health, on the day Anderson spoke, issued a list of evacuation areas (including all twenty-eight Metropolitan London Boroughs, Manchester, Hull, Birmingham and other big cities), neutral areas (Watford, Coventry, Bristol, Plymouth, etc.) and reception areas (the counties of Bedford, Berkshire, Cambridge, Dorset, etc.). Local authorities in the reception areas were being asked to produce lists of available accommodation.

It was widely recognized that there was much to be done. On 12 January Sir John Anderson took part in a conference with representatives of the London Boroughs at which he heard that the London County Council was forty per cent below its target for the number of auxiliary firemen. The National Federation of Building Trade Operatives, restless over those trenches in the parks which it called 'unsightly and waterlogged holes and mud-heaps ... scars upon the landscape, blots on the scenery, eyesores and impediments to recreation', demanded that they should be transformed at once into adequate shelters by the unemployed. The Air Ministry, however, revealed that it had found a type of shelter capable of protecting fifty people at a time against all but direct hits and which could easily be made gas-proof. It announced that it was adopting these for all Government aircraft factories (cost £95 with seats, £50-£60 without).

The Metropolitan Police had been testing different forms of air-raid siren, but the sounds eventually chosen did not altogether satisfy the public. A letter-writer to The Times suggested that the warbling warning was too depressing and miserable and that a more inspiring call should be substituted such as the old 'Prepare to receive cavalry' or even 'The Charge'. Another, writing later the same week, while agreeing with him, also asked for a happier note for the 'All Clear'. In the war, she said, Paris had used the merry note of the French army bugle-call 'Dismiss', a tune known as La Berloque.

The public also entered passionately into arguments about the appropriate type of shelter for the Government to provide. The deep shelter school had received something of a jolt from the secretary of Barcelona's ARP committee, who declared, 'The search for an absolutely bomb-proof shelter is futile.' The bomb always had the last word, he said, and added that it had been perfection of the warning system and evacuation which had most effectively reduced casualties in Barcelona (seventy-five per cent of the population had been evacuated from the port area). Twenty-one members of medical and surgical staffs of hospitals in London and elsewhere sent a letter to the press urging the building of 'adequate bomb-proof shelters' because 'no medical organization can cope under present conditions with the probable number of casualties in air-raids'. And they added that some authorities estimated that there would be three psychiatric cases for every physical one. A psychiatrist, Dr E.B. Strauss, had lectured the Royal United Services Institution on the need for suitable psychological precautions against the spread of panic in the five-hundred-bomber raids which could be expected. He said it was important that the Government should not become regarded as 'the people who allow us to be bombed'. He said people had had an uneasy feeling the previous September that the truth was being kept from them. Every medical psychologist knew the danger of fobbing off children when they sought information on 'the facts of life' and the same principle applied to air-raid precautions.

It was not until 17 January that it was officially announced that an order had actually been placed with the steel industry for the home shelters which Sir John Anderson had promised to protect occupants of small houses against blast, bomb splinters and falling masonry. The same day the Liberal Party executive met and passed a resolution saying it shared 'the profound and almost universal misgiving at the lack of proper provision and organization for ARP and demands bomb-proof underground shelters which, as experience in Spain has proved, can alone provide adequate protection'.

At the same time the Government was preparing the machinery for what it called 'National Service' on a voluntary basis. Eighteen million copies of a buff-coloured handbook detailing the way in which people could serve the nation if they chose were distributed to households free on 24 January. (By some local post office error fifteen hundred of them had actually appeared prematurely in Bristol a fortnight before and had had to be hurriedly recalled in embarrassment, for fear they might prejudice the atmosphere of Chamberlain's meeting with Mussolini.)

Sir Auckland Geddes, a civil servant who had been Director of National Service in the 1914–18 war and was now adviser to Sir John Anderson – himself now described as Civilian Defence Minister – revealed that a skeleton 'Ministry of National Service' was in fact already in existence with an unnamed 'young active man' already selected as Minister. 'As an island nation,' he announced, 'we have been accustomed to war which allowed us a period in which to make the necessary arrangements after the beginning of the war. This position is now past.' He went on to say that the first phase now was 'evacuation'; the second,

Anderson steel shelters being delivered free to Londoners.

Herbert Morrison, chairman of the Labour London County Council, and Conservative Home Secretary Sir John Anderson (*right*) sink political differences to recruit for ARP.

'a putting to sea of the Fleet and cutting of the aggressor's lines of communication'; and then 'only after that phase has been successful do we come to the sort of war we had before. . . . Despite what the critics say, everything is ready in the machinery of Government to bring in all the arrangements which will be required for phase three.'

It was not clear what 'the aggressor' would have been doing in the course of phases one and two.

On the same day as Sir Auckland Geddes delivered this reassurance a demonstration took place in London, but it had nothing to do with ARP. One woman and fifty men of the National Unemployed Workers' Movement held up traffic in Oxford Street for about a quarter of an hour by lying in rows across the roadway in pouring rain. Other members of the organization paraded the locality with posters saying, 'We Want Winter Relief'. The demonstrators offered no resistance when the police asked them to move.

The full campaign for national service was introduced by a BBC broadcast from Chamberlain on the night of 23 January in quiet tones:

> I want to speak to you tonight about the Government Scheme of Voluntary National Service and about the handbook which will be delivered to your homes this week. . . . It is a scheme to make us ready for war. That does not mean that I think war is coming. You know that I have done, and shall continue to do, all I can to preserve peace for ourselves and for others too . . .

The next evening the campaign was officially launched at a great meeting at the Albert Hall at which Herbert Morrison, Labour leader of the London County Council, sat together with Sir John Anderson. Sir John, having first stressed that – while they had to reckon with the possibility – 'we do not expect war either now or in the near future', went on nevertheless to elaborate a little on the new type of war of which his adviser had spoken. 'This war will differ from anything that this country has known for nearly a thousand years. It will be an invasion of our country, an invasion by air – sudden – swift – perhaps almost continuous . . .'

Herbert Morrison, while making clear his political differences from present Ministers of the Crown and saying that if only they had pursued a different foreign policy 'the peace of the world and the security of our country would have been in a better shape than they are at the present time', ended by saying that the point was that British people 'must preserve the right to decide upon the Government and the social order of its choice. It must refuse to be either bombed or cajoled into slavery.' Which was why they must all make ARP efficient and adequate to its purpose.

The meeting concluded with the singing of Blake's 'Jerusalem'.

The National Service Handbook contained a catalogue of the activities for which people could volunteer under headings such as 'Mainly for Younger Men (Auxiliary Fire Service, Territorial Army, etc.)'; 'Mainly for Older Men (Air Raid Wardens, Ambulance Drivers, Police War Reserve, etc.)'; and 'Opportunities for Women (Air Raid Wardens, Auxiliary Fire Service, Civil Air Guard, etc.)' – together with details about how to apply. Its impact was slightly diminished by the publication on the same day of an extremely detailed list of several hundred so-called reserved occupations on which restrictions for enlistment in wartime were to be placed. These ranged from 'Anchor, chain (not roller link) maker – shackle striker (aged 21)' through jewellers, laundry workers, lighthouse keepers, the medical profession and prison warders, to third hand furnacemen, tappers, helpers and refinery men – aged twenty-one – in zinc manufacture, and practitioners of many other more esoteric skills. The reality of the Government's approach was also put in question by the town council of Dover, which found to its amazement that it was scheduled as a suitable evacuation area.

Sir John Anderson had recently made a statement to the effect that Britain had been accustomed to lose every battle except the last, but that it was the last which counted. This struck even *The Times* as being 'not in these days an altogether satisfactory guarantee of national survival'. However, the latest moves seemed to have reassured the paper's leader-writer. The right steps were being taken, it seemed, to fill the undoubted gaps in the defence system 'if this is to prove adequate for a modern war'.

Two modern wars were already in progress. In China, in one which the poet Auden, even though almost on the spot at the time, reported as thudding 'like the slamming of a distant door', the Japanese had just launched their heaviest air-raid to date on Chungking. Twenty-seven Japanese planes had appeared over the city in three flights around 1 p.m. and dropped their bombs from 6,000 feet. Some Chinese fighters had gone up to intercept them but to little avail. Air-raid shelters had not been completed and between two and four hundred people were killed. Another 130 people were killed when Wahnsien, down the Yangtse from Chungking, was also bombed.

In Spain a war on the very doorstep of the western democracies had reached its climax.

9

On 17 January Herbert Matthews, the *New York Times* correspondent in Barcelona, wrote: 'The fighting in Catalonia was less important today than at any time since the rebel offensive started ... which may be symptomatic of the approaching end of the battle.' The implication was that Franco's main advance was running out of steam.

But two days later Matthews was reporting a new assault at six points on the Government line which ran between the Pyrenees and the coast – a Spanish 'Maginot line' some were calling it. The *Daily Telegraph*, describing the new unceasing artillery and air bombardment as one of the most intensive of the whole Spanish war, noted that this line was as yet unbreached. General Gambara, commander of the Italian Divisions, had been wounded and was directing operations from a camp-bed; there were hopes on the Nationalist side that there would be a revolt in Barcelona.

But from Barcelona came only reports of a strengthening of morale. 'In its long history of sieges and warfare,' wrote the *Telegraph*, 'Barcelona has probably never given so freely of its manpower as it is doing today in a supreme effort to save the capital.'

Morale had been strengthened on the morning of the 17th when people in the streets were able to cheer the shooting down by Government fighters of a two-engine German Dornier reconnaissance plane. 'For the man in the street,' wrote the *Telegraph*, 'the drama is tremendous. No one forgets General Franco's list of two million suspects. The determination to resist is remarkable and it is likely that there will be a tremendous battle, despite the difference in the strength of the two forces.'

But the *Telegraph*, like the *New York Times*, was also now commenting on the very noticeable shortage of arms on the Government side. Some Government artillery units which should have had twelve guns now only had one. There were not enough rifles to go round and only eight machine-guns to a brigade. The population were commenting bitterly on the international ban which prevented their Government from getting arms.

There was indeed now mounting agitation in Britain, France, and the United States for this ban to be lifted. In Britain the Labour Opposition leader, Clement Attlee, wrote to Chamberlain asking for an immediate recall of Parliament, not otherwise due to meet for over a fortnight. In view of the withdrawal of the International Brigades, and the continuing German and Italian intervention, Attlee said, it was obvious that non-intervention was now simply preventing the Spanish Government from getting arms with which to defend itself against the

the aggression of foreign powers. This was 'inimical to the honour and interests of this country'.

Chamberlain replied that he had given the matter careful consideration but decided that to lift the embargo 'would inevitably lead to an extension of the conflict with consequences which cannot be accurately foreseen but which would undoubtedly be grave'. He saw no reason for the recall of Parliament before its scheduled meeting.

In France there was mounting pressure on the Government to let arms and ammunition through the Pyrenees.* On 20 January a debate began in the French Chamber of Deputies on a motion to open the frontier. It became very heated and had to be suspended when the former Air Minister, Pierre Cot, accused the Right of being under the influence of Nazi propaganda. The debate was eventually adjourned until the following week but commentators reckoned that if a direct vote on opening the frontier had been taken that day, as had originally been proposed, the Daladier Government might well have been beaten, or at least would have had only a very slim majority.

From Rome the *New York Times* reported that the fighting in Spain was now turning the Franco-Italian dispute into a real threat to peace. As Mussolini had put it: France and Italy had been on opposite sides of the barricades; now these barricades were alarmingly close together. The *New York Times* correspondent wrote:

> If the French Government should yield to popular pressure and open the frontier, there is not the slightest doubt in some quarters here that the Italian Government would immediately send fresh reinforcements to General Franco. Mussolini has already made this clear. This would certainly lead to war. The present situation has all the makings of a major crisis. Yet the Italians are curiously calm. . . . The reason is not only the fact that all Europeans are becoming callous to crises. They are like passengers in a plane making a series of nose-dives, each one from a lower altitude than the last. The real reason is that no one believes France will reassess her policy on Spain at this stage. The general feeling is that Britain will be able to convince the French that the Italians will indeed withdraw from the peninsula as soon as the war ends.

Although the Italian press was happily reporting France as a decadent country with whom armed conflict was now only a matter of very little time, the French Cabinet was said in fact to have decided categorically against help for Barcelona. The announcement that the Foreign Minister, Bonnet, was not to speak until the conclusion of the debate in the Chamber on the following Tuesday made this

---

* The frontier itself had first been closed on 2 July 1938 on condition that all foreign volunteers were to be withdrawn from Spain within forty days. The Republic had complied with this, though somewhat tardily: the disbanded International Brigades being at this very moment on their way out of Spain. But the intense pressure being exerted by the Italians against the government munitions centre and fortress of Igualada on the Barcelona defensive line was once again evidence that withdrawal of 'volunteers' had been a one-sided affair, leaving the Republic very much at a disadvantage.

clear enough. Realism rather than equity was the principle on which both British and French Governments were now conducting their Spanish policy. 'Britain Firm For Inaction' was a small headline in the *New York Times* which summed things up well. And their London correspondent reported at this crucial moment for the Spanish Government that it was being widely assumed in both London and Paris that Barcelona was doomed and that the war would be over in a few months' time. Chamberlain himself was enjoying a long weekend at Chequers, 'less worried over the international situation than most of his colleagues and advisers and looking for a relaxation of tension in Europe as soon as the Spanish Civil War was over – whenever that may be'.

But Chequers was a long way from Barcelona that weekend. Franco's drive towards that city continued with such intensity that two points of the defensive line, Vendrell and Calaf, fell in spite of what even his own troops described as stubborn resistance all along the line. His tactics were to drive tanks and motorized columns ahead of the infantry, allowing them to form pockets which he knew the Republicans had insufficient resources to squeeze, while his bombers were in action continuously and virtually unopposed. The *New York Times* counted between eighty and a hundred planes operating over the front.

Igualada still held out against the Italians, who had been blocked there for ten days as they had been blocked previously for ten days at Borjas Blancas – a remarkable feat on the part of the Government troops, exhausted after fighting day and night continuously for twenty-seven days, while Franco was able to rotate his own troops in forty-eight-hour shifts.

'When these facts are considered,' wrote the *New York Times*, 'one can better understand what is happening in Catalonia ... it explains the Government's confidence ... it feels that if the army could resist at such odds ... it will not take too much to turn the tide.'

'Surrender!' cried the Franco broadcasts beamed at Barcelona, 'there is not the slightest hope for you.' But the Government General Vicente Rojo, a man said to be noted for his shyness, had made a moving reply when he broadcast back on the evening of 19 January:

> You can conquer more ground with material strength but you cannot conquer the people because liberal Spain cannot perish and even if you succeed in crushing it you could be sure that from the bones of our dead there would rise the ideal of liberty and independence which is fed by the blood of our soldiers.... The edifice you seek to raise above Spain's ruins is already cursed by good Spaniards because you have committed the great error of cementing it with hate ... life means nothing to us, absolutely nothing, if we and our sons have to live it contemptibly.

The next day it was reported that Igualada had fallen. Barcelona's first defence line was broken and Government troops withdrew to their last line running from Solsona through Cardona to Manresa and down the Llobregat river to the sea. Despite this advance of Franco's troops, however, to within twelve miles of the city and an almost continuous succession of air-raids the *New York Times* man in Barcelona continued to report morale as high. As Chamberlain rested at Chequers there were nineteen raids in thirty-one hours on Barcelona, in the course of which at least twenty-seven people were killed and sixty-eight injured. Three British freighters in the harbour, the *York Brook*, the *Dover Abbey* and the *African Mariner*, were damaged and the *York Brook* finally sunk.

The closeness of the front meant that Government fighters were now in an easier position to take on the bombers and when on the afternoon of the 21st a Messerschmitt was shot down by a Government Chato and the pilot was seen to bale out over the sea, people danced in the streets and shouted and cheered for joy.

All men were now mobilized for fighting or some sort of war work. Women took over from the waiters in the hotels, women served at petrol stations, women took over jobs in shops and factories. Otherwise there were still few outward changes to life. A new series at the opera was to begin the day after the Messerschmitt was shot down and newspapers gave as much attention to sports and foreign news as ever. Cinemas were still well attended.

Then, on Tuesday the 23rd, as bombs fell almost continuously on the port and surrounding district, reducing it to an inferno and sending the British ship *African Mariner* to join the *York Brook* at the bottom of the harbour, as thousands of citizens poured out of the city to help fortify the Llobregat line, the authorities declared Barcelona under martial law. Reports began that the Government was planning flight and it was even said that some Government departments had already quietly left. Negrín, the Spanish Prime Minister, however, insisted that the Government was staying put.

In the United States, still enjoying the coldest weather for three years with upstate New York and New England sheathed in ice, the former Secretary of State Henry L. Stimson wrote to the *New York Times* an impassioned plea on behalf of the Republic.

The embargo imposed by the United States Government on the sale of arms to the Spanish Government should now be lifted.... Intended as a protection against conditions which would endanger the peace of the United States, the embargo is now shown by events of the last two years to be a source of danger to that peace. Any danger that may come to the people of the United States from the situation in Spain would arise not from any lawful sale of munitions in our markets to the Government of Spain but from the assistance which our embargo has given to the enemies of Spain. It is the success of the lawless precedents created by those enemies which would create our real danger. There is no reason why we should facilitate and accentuate that danger ... still less reason why we should violate our own historical policy to do so. The prestige and safety of our country will not be promoted by abandoning its self-respecting traditions in order to avoid the hostility of reckless violators of international law in Europe.

In Britain, Anthony Eden, the former Foreign Secretary, speaking at Leamington said:

> Franco is . . . advancing on Barcelona by reason of air power and artillery power more formidable than this civil war has yet seen . . . everyone knows who provides this armament and who will continue to provide it in open violation of agreements and pacts signed and re-signed with Britain pledging the contrary. How can any of us deny that if Franco wins, his victory will be a foreign victory?

On Wednesday 24 January, William Carney, the *New York Times* correspondent with Franco's troops, found himself standing within a mile or so of the suburbs of Barcelona which shimmered through a haze of sunshine as flight after flight of bombers went in to the attack. The defences, he reported, seemed to have crumpled up. General Yagüe's Moroccan troops, who had been advancing at the rate of twenty miles a day and whose rope-soled shoes were now often in ribbons, had taken the airport and there seemed no serious obstacle between them and the city itself. In the air-raids leaflets were mixed with the bombs, calling on the population to surrender 'to avoid useless bloodshed', but Government officials were still saying that Barcelona could be defended as well as Madrid and that General Miaja was on his way to Barcelona by sea with reinforcements, some 12,000 of whom had already arrived.

'The taking of Barcelona', broadcast the Government radio, 'will not be an easy matter. The population of Barcelona is ready and the city will be defended inch by inch, street by street and house by house.'

While the *New York Times* man watched the bombing of the city his colleague within it reported that there was 'no less hope here now than Madrid had in the first week of November 1936 when the rebels were halted on the outskirts'.

The night before he wrote that despatch there had been a demonstration in Times Square, New York, which the police estimated at about three thousand strong, marching and shouting, 'Lift the embargo on Loyalist Spain'. There was no disorder beyond occasional arguments with spectators who shouted approval of the embargo. An American Catholic priest who had made a radio appeal to keep the embargo reported that he had had 100,000 telegrams of support, against which the Secretary of the North American Committee to Aid Spanish Democracy said a quarter of a million people had sent telegrams to Washington urging that it should be lifted. The American Institute of Public Opinion indicated from a poll that seventy-six per cent of the US population backed the Spanish Government. And under the auspices of the American Friends of Spanish Democracy a letter had been sent to Roosevelt by 250 Protestant and Jewish clergy, including seven bishops, from thirty-five States asking him to lift the arms embargo.

President Roosevelt's reply was that Government lawyers were investigating whether or not he had the legal power to do this or whether it had to be the decision of Congress. The Secretary of State, Cordell Hull, to whom in fact Stimson had written privately before publishing his letter in the *New York*

ABOVE General Franco's cavalry, still 'rebels', on the advance in Catalonia. BELOW
Republican women ready to defend Barcelona, whiie Franco's General Solchaga
(*right*) pushes on up the coast.

Times, said that the former Secretary of State's letter was receiving full consideration but that he was not in a position to say anything else at the present time.

The growing conviction of departmental lawyers that only Congress could lift the embargo was very convenient for Roosevelt since it left, as one journalist put it, this hot potato in the lap of Congress rather than that of the President. The US cruiser *Omaha* dropped anchor in Barcelona harbour to take off refugees, as did the British cruiser *Devonshire* and destroyer *Glowworm*.

In France the Foreign Minister, Bonnet, had again postponed his speech in the Chamber, this time until Thursday the 26th – a gesture of prudence since tempers were flaring so high in the debate. In Italy Mussolini called up a new class of reservists to deter France from opening the frontier, in the fear either that Daladier would give way to left-wing pressure or even be superseded by the former Socialist premier Léon Blum. In fact in France the victory of Franco was now increasingly, though on the Left reluctantly, regarded as probable. The question was now not so much should the frontier be opened, but what attitude would France take up if Mussolini tried to exploit Franco's success by strengthening his demands in a way which French opinion found unacceptable. It was on this issue that the Government determined to make its stand when the vote came rather than on the question of intervention.

But for the general public in Paris uncertainty began to create something of the same sort of atmosphere as in the critical days of the previous September, or so the *New York Times* correspondent found. What, people wondered, were Hitler's intentions? Would he back Mussolini? Would France possibly land on Minorca at the invitation of the Loyalist Government in order to hold it as a hostage against the Italian evacuation of Majorca? What, in short, was to happen if Mussolini, instead of withdrawing from Spain as promised after a Franco victory, used his troops as a means of sabre-rattling against France? That would indeed cause a major crisis. *Le Temps* wrote: 'It would be unpardonable if responsible governments did not take necessary precautions to be in a position to deal with all eventualities.'

At the frontier with Spain the French were unlimbering anti-aircraft guns which had been hooded for months, and manning searchlights.

In Barcelona itself people turned their eyes bitterly towards France, where they saw the vital decision being continually postponed. All the newspapers were still coming out in the Catalan capital and the cries of the street-vendors hawking them were part of the sound of returning normality after each nightmare air-raid. Those who read the newspapers saw the headlines in the Communist *Frente Rojo*: 'Barcelona is endangered! Fervent mobilization to defend her! Once more erect the barricades of July 19th!' (a reference to Madrid in 1936). And according to the *New York Times*, those who had seen Madrid in November 1936 said that Barcelona was showing 'today [24 January] for the first time the spirit and determination to resist that has saved Madrid'. Most of the bombing that day was done by German Dorniers, flying nine at a time in leisurely fashion over the city and then turning back to drop their bombs over the port, which was now completely shattered. Such tactics were particularly unnerving since it was found that the bombers *not* dropping their bombs provided almost the worst strain of all. The *New York Times* man counted thirty three-engined bombers flying over the city itself without actually dropping their bombs.

The weather turned colder with blustery winds but there was no sign of rain and visibility was clear. The Government finally closed all cinemas. Electricity, water and telephone services became erratic but continued to function up to a point. The beautiful, well-kept Ramblas were now bleak with their shop-fronts shuttered. Two distinct streams of traffic were now noticeable, one moving north to safety and the other southwards towards the front. It was admitted that many Government ministries were moving, in spite of what Negrín had said only a day or two earlier, but it was insisted that this did not mean that the city was about to fall. The Government was simply withdrawing to Gerona or Figueras.

Like any good newspaperman, Herbert Matthews of the *New York Times*, who had consistently reflected the mood of brave optimism in Barcelona while it lasted, immediately switched to a new realism when that mood broke sharply on the night of the 24–25 January. He found the telephones no longer working and a great exodus from the city under way. He conceded that the Government order to fortify the defences had not been a success. Many people had gone to work on the fortifications but there had also been a sort of passive sabotage at work. A mood of apathy had descended and only the Communists really retained their morale. It was said that a hundred people who had shirked their work on the fortifications had been shot in the streets. The army itself appeared exhausted. They had been fighting now continually for five weeks and were virtually at the end of their resources. The failure of the Madrid zone to relieve pressure on Catalonia had been fatal, and no one understood why such a weak effort had in fact been made there. It was thought that if that was the best that Miaja could do, there was little hope left. Up to the previous week the morale of the troops had been amazingly good but now they were mad with fatigue and bewildered at being asked to make such hopeless efforts. The units under General Enrique Lister were still fighting hard and well but the majority were 'through'. But even now Matthews could still not quite relinquish the old spirit of optimism he had breathed so long. 'All this discontent', he wrote, 'may prove temporary. The Loyalists performed the miracle of Madrid and perhaps they can perform another.'

But, realistic again, he saw little hope of this. There were brigades with only 120 men left, companies with only twenty-five rifles, no machine-guns and between fifteen and twenty cartridges per man. The once great army of the Ebro ('the ghost of an army' he called it) had thrown itself across the southern and western sides of the city, but it was broken already by its gallant stand of thrity-three days and nights against a vastly superior enemy.

At about 2.30 on the afternoon of 26 January, Franco's troops entered Barcelona almost without firing a shot.

The London *Times* reported that a few isolated machine-gun nests, in which Republicans clung grimly to their weapons long after the area behind them had been evacuated, occasionally held up a battalion for an hour or so; but the main body of the Republican army, which for the past three days had provided the only semblance of organization in the city, had gone.

There had in the end been only a very limited response from the citizens to appeals by the Republican leaders to reproduce the spirit of Madrid.

'We shall fight in the streets, at every cross-roads and corner,' Negrín had said only a few days before. And the Secretary of the Syndicalist Union, the CNT, had broadcast, only the night before Franco entered, a despairing appeal to the population to erect barricades and man them to the last. But apathy, induced as much probably by long endurance of the Byzantine quarrels of Anarcho-Syndicalists, Communists, Socialists and plain Catalan radicals on the Government side as by the long physical strain of air-raids and food shortages, had sapped the general will to resist.

The *Times* correspondent's car entering the Plaza de Cataluña with Franco's forces was surrounded by excited crowds cheering and waving the red and gold Nationalist colours and raising their right arms in the Fascist salute. Many people who had been living in the underground railway with their chairs, tables, bedding and other household goods all about them now emerged to breathe freely again in the open air. Broadcast promises from Franco's side of the past few days that he would not bomb the civilian population had failed to reach them, for wireless sets had, according to *The Times*, been requisitioned by the authorities some days before. Now for the first time for many months the street lights of Barcelona were lit again.

In Italy that morning members of the Fascist party had been told to take their uniforms to work and to change into them afterwards and report in front of the Palazzo Venezia in the middle of Rome at 6 p.m. By 7 p.m. the square and all the side streets surrounding it were packed with scores of thousands of people. All the surrounding buildings were floodlit and searchlights played over the Vittore Emanuele monument. Out onto the balcony of the Palazzo Venezia came Mussolini, smilingly contemplating for a moment the cheering and applauding human sea stretched out before him. Then he motioned them to silence. He told them that Barcelona had fallen. 'The shout of your exultation,' he cried, 'which is fully justified, blends with that rising from all the cities of Spain liberated from the Reds. Franco's magnificent troops and our fearless legionaries not only have beaten Negrín's government but many others of our enemies are now biting the dust.' At this point his voice was almost drowned by the applause. He went on: 'Their motto was "*No pasarán*", but we did pass, and I tell you we will continue to do so.' There were cries from the crowd of 'We want Corsica!', 'We want Tunisia!' and 'Down with France!', and Mussolini had to come back onto the balcony again and again as the crowds continued to demonstrate for half an hour longer. Their enthusiasm was in no way dampened by a shower of rain as they paraded the nearby streets afterwards.

Special editions of the Italian newspapers appeared with eight-column head-lines: 'The Greatest Event Since the Beginning of the Anti-Bolshevik War!' The Spanish victory was declared a major defeat for French policy and evidence of a further weakening of France's position in Europe. Mussolini had told the crowd: 'This is another chapter in the New Europe we are creating.'

Europe's anxiety had already reached something of a peak on the eve of Barcelona's fall. The *New York Times* correspondent in Britain reported that London's nervousness was more acute than anyone could remember except at the time of the previous September crisis. In some ways things were worse now because this time no one knew precisely where or how the next crisis would develop. 'The sense of unknown, invisible danger in the immediate future is what is preying on public and official minds,' he wrote, 'so that the steady old London of former years is almost unrecognizable.'

The paper's leader-writer listed the unanswered questions. What price would have to be paid by Franco for the help he had received from the Fascist nations? Would the prestige of being on the winning side satisfy Italy and compensate for Italian lives lost in Spain? Or would Mussolini now seek some compensation? And if so, what would it be? The Balearic Islands? Or a concession in Tunisia from France? And would Hitler back him? As Barcelona fell, the paper wrote of a 'lull after a storm which may be the prelude to a larger storm'. The same searching questions remained. For Italy, was the game worth the gamble of war? For Germany, was more to be gained or lost by supporting Italy? 'For the two democracies of Western Europe, France and Britain, it is the same dogged question from which there is no escape in the long run: at what point do these nations draw the line of real resistance to dictatorship on the march? At what point do constant threats of force call for a blunt answer? At what point are vital French and British interests touched?'

Of the United States' own Neutrality Act the *New York Times* wrote that it was ironic that 'a law designed in the name of peace is today a powerful bargaining-point in the hands of two aggressor nations'. But the American case against lifting the arms embargo in Spain had been stated strongly in the paper by a New York attorney and prominent Catholic, Martin Comboy who, in a letter only a few days before, had looked at the American experience of inter-vention in Europe in World War One. 'We achieved nothing for ourselves,' he wrote:

Nor did we succeed in bringing peace to Europe as was evident in 1935, and is still more evident now. Congress was surely justified in insisting that we must try to avoid the consequences of avoidable errors ... it is demanded that legislation designed to keep this nation at peace shall be replaced by legislation that would lead to our again being trapped into war. In my humble judgement the people of the United States will have none of it. Our preferences, either as to Spain or to the world at large, may be poles apart but when it comes to endangering the peace of the United States over the quarrels of other peoples, the solid good sense of the people of the United States is certain to prevail.

The reverse opinion was canvassed in an Open Letter to the Government and People of the United States prepared by a number of eminent Americans, principally in the literary field, which occupied a full page of the *New York Times*. It stated:

> While you read this message a major human tragedy is taking place. A question of the greatest importance to our country and to the entire world is being decided. A brave nation is fighting against terrible odds, not only for its own independence and freedom but for the very life of democracy everywhere.... The whole world knows now that the 'Franco Revolt' is in reality an invasion. Hitler and Mussolini are bent on destroying the Spanish Republic.... It is clear that they intend to use Spain as a means of crippling French and British democracy and as a powerful springboard to South and Central America where their agents have for years been busy spreading propaganda against democracy and for fascism.... The hard fact is that by our embargo against Spain we are giving aid to Hitler and Mussolini and all they stand for. Our embargo is helping to destroy a republic which stands as a powerful bulwark against the fascist plans. If that republic is destroyed, much of the responsibility will be ours.

After quoting the former US Secretary of State Henry Stimson's letter to the paper of a few days before and Roosevelt's own speech to the seventy-sixth Congress in which he said that the Neutrality Laws 'may actually give aid to the aggressor and deny it to the victim', the statement went on to declare: 'It is not too late, the Spanish Republic still lives. Its people who still control central Spain with Valencia and iron-willed Madrid have no intention of surrendering. A simple act of justice on the part of the United States of America can still turn the tide in favour of democracy.'

The force of the appeal, which carried a coupon to be cut out and sent to Senators or Representatives on Capitol Hill in Washington, was rather diminished by the somewhat esoteric status of the signatories who included, with Henry Morgenthau and Paul Kellogg, writers such as Robert Benchley, Louis Bromfield, Van Wyck Brooks, Dashiell Hammett, Edna St Vincent Millais, and Dorothy Parker. The names of Yehudi Menuhin, Ernest Hemingway, Theodore Dreiser, Upton Sinclair, John Steinbeck, Frank Dewey, Pearl S. Buck, and Maxwell Anderson were also added as examples of eminent Americans who urged that the Spanish embargo should be lifted.

President Roosevelt continued to be protected from any serious need for immediate decision on the issue by the constitutional problem, on which his lawyers were working, as to whether or not he did in fact have the power to lift the embargo, or whether only Congress could decide. He was already in difficulty with Congress, where the Republicans in the Senate, in alliance with recalcitrant Democrats, had knocked $150 million off the sum of $875 million he was asking for to subsidize his Works Progress Administration. The vote reflected a growing restlessness among Senators after six years of extensive government spending by the President. Indeed, they had only just completed a remarkable display of hostility towards the administration in debating Roosevelt's recent nomination to his Cabinet of Henry Hopkins as Secretary of Commerce. Hopkins's eventual nomination by fifty-eight to twenty-seven votes followed a bitter and acrimonious debate which the *New York Times* described as being 'without precedent in the Roosevelt Administration.... So deep was the feeling manifested in most of the speeches that voices were raised above the usual pitch and spectators at times found it hard to realize that all the speakers were discussing the same man.'

'I never would have approved of him,' declared Senator Glass of Hopkins. 'I do not approve of anything he has done, or anything as I recall that he has said; but I think he has done it all and said most of it in the confident belief that it would be sanctioned if it had not been directed by the administrative power.'

Senator Neally on the other hand, waving his arms, charged the Senators with crucifying a man whom he ranked with the great martyrs of history, including Socrates, Lincoln and Jesus Christ. Asked by Senator Bridges if he really put Mr Hopkins on a par with the Saviour, he replied that of course he didn't do so literally, but 'he has rendered a real service to the human race and with a holy enthusiasm, comparable to that of St Paul, Father Damien or St Francis of Assisi'.

As Senator Schwellenbach rightly commented, most of the speeches were made not against Hopkins but against the President of the United States in an effort to break down confidence in him. Schwellenbach went on to make his own partisan point: 'You are doing precisely the same thing in this country which was done so successfully in some European countries which resulted in the destruction of democratic government in those countries. This is no time for that.'

It was also clearly no time either for Roosevelt to commit himself on the Spanish embargo while he still had a respectable constitutional excuse for not doing so. Indeed among the democracies in general, the cause of the Spanish Republic was drifting into a focus for abstract idealism rather than any realistic action.

In France, the country most immediately able to do something for the beleaguered Republic, the protracted debate in the Chamber of Deputies ended on the day Barcelona fell. Daladier, the Prime Minister, seeking to obtain a unanimous vote of confidence, had tried to concentrate attention on France's determination to stand up to Italian threats rather than on the plight of the Spanish Republic itself. 'France', he declared, 'will let no one touch her territorial integrity or her colonial empire.... She will not concede a single acre or concede a single right.... I am measuring the full gravity of my words.' He did however make a gesture towards higher things, saying that, with the hour of peril approaching, 'there is an ideal to defend as well as that material Empire'.

But when Léon Blum, for the Left, tried to put his idealism to a realistic material test, by proposing an amendment 'to regulate the application of the Non-Intervention Agreement in the same way as is done by the other signatory states' (i.e. to open the Spanish frontier), a vote was enforced and the amendment defeated by 360 to 234 votes. The subsequent vote of confidence in the Government was carried by 374 to 228.

In Britain, since Parliament had not been recalled in spite of the request of the Opposition leader, Attlee, not even the formal expression of idealistic identity with the Republic which the French Left had been able to vent in Blum's amendment was possible before the scheduled reassembly of the Commons at the end of the month. Shouts of 'Arms for Spain!' were heard from time to time in the streets, and Sir Stafford Cripps, on the same day as his expulsion from the Labour Party for consistently urging a Popular Front against Chamberlain with Liberals and Communists, addressed a large meeting in that cause. Herbert Morrison, leader of the London Labour Party, sent a letter to Chamberlain pointing out once again the inequitable working of the Non-Intervention system and the need to give the Spanish Government the right to buy arms. But as day after day passed with Franco and his Italian allies advancing closer and closer to the Pyrenees, the cause became increasingly abstract and forlorn.

In Barcelona itself the *New York Times* correspondent reported that there was no doubt that many citizens welcomed Franco and were overwhelmed with joy at the end of the ghastly nightmare they had been through. The city still presented in many ways a strange appearance. There were machine-guns on the street corners but orders had been given to open all shutters after dark and admit a maximum of light onto the streets in which, littered with refuse and debris as they were, crowds wound their way in and out of the sleeping troops and mules. No bars or cafés were open so there was no drunkenness in the crowd; people were just deliriously happy to be released from the horrors of war and the constant menace of air-raids. The Plaza Cataluña was full of exhausted Moorish troops who had flung themselves down anywhere, while their hungry mules nibbled the palm trees and ate every plant and flower in the Municipal Gardens. Some soldiers lit fires with wood wrenched from doorways, and through the haze of smoke and firelight children without parents advanced timidly to ask for food. Later, groups of soldiers and children could be seen sleeping peacefully among the fires. Most of the food shops were bare. There was no bread and a mile-long queue for it stretched outside the newly-opened office of the Falange down the Paseo de Gracia. But the real tragedy now was being enacted on the road to the frontier at the Pyrenees. Herbert Matthews of the *New York Times* reported that one of the greatest mass migrations in history was there under way.

The Loyalist army in Catalonia, he said, had now to all practical purposes been destroyed, but when he interviewed the Republic's Prime Minister, Negrín, and Foreign Minister Julio Álvarez del Vayo in Figueras, they told him that the Spanish Government was determined to carry on. He did not question their sincerity but thought there seemed no possibility of that being done in Catalonia. Negrín was still making bold, optimistic assertions in public too, declaring that if the enemy hoped that the fall of Barcelona meant the end of the Republic, their hopes were destined to be frustrated. Army units, he said, were coming from Central Spain. The difficulty of obtaining new war materials was being overcome. His soldiers had ample war material and infinite courage. 'When I could not give you hope,' he declared, 'I said nothing; today I can categorically assure you that we are safe.'

Franco's spokesmen reported that it was only by courtesy that Government opposition in the region could be called genuine military resistance. His advancing troops often lost contact altogether with the retreating enemy making for the Pyrenees. The French had rushed between 4,000 and 5,000 troops to the frontier with orders to let only women and children through and send the soldiers back, but as the Prefect of the Pyrénées Orientales quickly recognized, guns would have to be used if they were really going to try to keep the Republican troops out. They were coming across the mountains in scattered groups of varying strengths and when pushed back again simply returned via other routes at different points. About 10,000 troops were across by Sunday, 29 January.

The condition of the far greater number of civilians who had fled was desperate. Most of them had not eaten for two or three days and they grabbed hungrily at the chunks of bread given them on the French side of the border by the relief organizations. Every mountain near the frontier seemed swarming with refugees and fires on the mountainside showed where they camped, with snow inches deep and bitter winds blowing. In the valleys themselves it was raining hard. As they came across, some on foot, some on carts and wagons, blocking the roads for some four miles before it, they presented a pitiable sight. A *New York Times* correspondent described them as filthy, squalid and evidencing the lack of hope of people 'for whom the world seemed to have come to an end'. Recently-born children sucked desperately at indescribably dirty rags as they lay in the cold wind on the open road. By that same Sunday in January some 40,000 had crossed the frontier and they were continuing to come across at the rate of between 15,000 and 25,000 a day.

The French had made considerable preparations for dealing with the emergency, sending motorbuses and large supplies of food and medical stores into the area as well as Senegalese infantry, two squadrons of dragoons and numerous Gardes Mobiles. A railhead for evacuation from the frontier was organized at Le Boulou, but the problem seemed for a time overwhelming. The London *Times* correspondent described some heart-rending scenes:

An old man appeared on a donkey. 'Pas d'animaux,' said a gendarme. But the old man had no legs.

A forlorn woman was carrying a bundle. 'Let me examine that,' said a

Customs Officer. It contained a dead baby. 'Don't take him from me,' pleaded the woman. 'I can't leave him behind.'

Two blind men were led in hand-in-hand. On one mountain pass a bootblack sat disconsolately behind his foot-rest and polishing-box. A knife-grinder sat beside his wheel. One haggard woman with a child in her arms and a ten-year-old clinging to her skirts had walked the forty miles from Gerona in a day and a night. More and more soldiers were coming, many of them wounded, hobbling with their arms and legs in plaster, and heads bound with soiled dressings. The *Times* correspondent saw one officer, on crossing the frontier bridge, tear off his badges of rank and throw them into the stream below. Others removed the red star from their tunics. But others still came over wearing their badges of rank, and carrying their arms, which were removed by the French police. In the frontier railway tunnel at Cerbère thousands had taken shelter from the cold and the rain, waiting for barricades at the frontier to be lifted. 'Women, childen, wounded soldiers, and deserters all slept pell-mell among each other.'

'Is it not about time,' wrote Lord Alfred Douglas, Oscar Wilde's former friend, to the London *Times* from Hove – 'is it not about time for someone to point out that these people for whose sad plight we are asked to shed tears of sympathy are simply running away from safety and security?'

It was true that far behind them Barcelona was returning to normal. Blankets and mattresses were disappearing from the underground. Wood was beginning to be available again. The first hot rations were being issued – some of the 500,000 rations distributed daily. People were exchanging their old banknotes for the new currency of Nationalist Spain. The prisoners who struggled in long lines up the road leading to the Montjuich prison fortress were now Republicans. Republican guards had abandoned it the day before Barcelona fell but not before executing numbers of the prisoners they held, including women, whose bodies were still lying on the western slopes of the hill.

As the Government itself, beset by grim reality, withdrew closer to the frontier, eventually virtually indistinguishable from the straggling tens of thousands of its own refugees, the capitals of the western democracies, for all their apparent stability, were themselves beset by much uncertainty and doubt.

Although the *Giornale d'Italia* declared that those in London and Paris who thought that Italy would strike for her claims soon after the fall of Barcelona were making an error of interpretation, it did so in a manner designed to produce minimum comfort. 'Italy's claims do not belong to the politics of *fait accompli*,' declared the paper, 'and are not linked with this or that episode. They are founded on precise facts and documented rights ... until they are satisfied they have the character of permanence.' In any case the *Relazioni Internazionali* was much more forthright. France's refusal to make concessions, it said, would lead to war unless she changed her negative policy. If France were to try to occupy Minorca 'the Italian people will rise in arms and cross the frontiers'.

Nor was the German press more accommodating. The leading article in the

Frankfurter Zeitung of 29 January said: 'Germany will defend Italy's rights with the same determination with which Mussolini supported the just and therefore obtainable aims of the Reich.'

The poet W.B. Yeats had been by the Mediterranean all week, taking short walks in the garden of a pension at Roquebrune between heart-attacks. He died at the weekend, an event principally concerning other poets*, though it was noticed on the centre page of *The Times*, a worthy tribute in view of the urgency of the international news.

'Whether a Franco victory is also a prologue to a Mediterranean Munich', wrote the *New York Times*, 'is a question overshadowing every capital this weekend ... A crisis of unpredictable dimensions draws near as General Franco pushes on.'

And the crisis cast its shadow over Washington no less than over London and Paris. The Senate's apprehension that Roosevelt was using a national defence programme to add dangerously to European uncertainty caused continued querying of the National Defence Bill and Senator Nye of North Dakota declared: 'This country is closer to war than it was in 1916.'

Nor was the Mediterranean the only source of danger.

* See W.H. Auden's poem: 'He disappeared in the dead of winter...'

10

The impression created in the Beck–Hitler talks at the beginning of the month that German–Polish relations were on a fairly even keel had been strengthened when on 25 January Ribbentrop paid an official visit to Warsaw to celebrate the fifth anniversary of the German–Polish Pact of 1934.

A Polish Guard of Honour met him at Warsaw station and a police band played *Deutschland über Alles* and the *Horst Wessel Lied* to welcome him.

The crowds, however, who lined the streets outside to watch him were silent.

At a dinner that evening Ribbentrop reaffirmed that the 1934 Pact was a sure foundation for relations between the two countries, saying that both Poland and Germany could look to the future 'with complete confidence'.

It seemed that the subjects discussed at Berchtesgaden were again gone over, and again Polish official circles stressed that there were no changes or surprises involved. Commentators said that subjects such as the Ukraine, relations with the USSR, and Danzig were all touched on and that 'on these three points at least the Foreign Ministers have harmonized their policies for the present and immediate future'. On Danzig, it seemed, the Poles had no intention of obstructing its Nazification, while the Germans were prepared to recognize Poland's rights and privileges in the port. But the correspondent of *The Times* wrote that among Poles there was 'near unanimity about what would happen if the Germans sought to include Danzig in the Third Reich. Poles, in or out of office, and the average intelligent man in the street, if asked, reply: "That would mean war." If told they would have no chance of winning in an armed clash with Germany they reply: "Poles fight for their rights even when there is no chance of winning."'

Ribbentrop and Beck met again for over two hours after lunch the next day and the official statement published at the end of the visit spoke of its showing 'once again that the collaboration between Poland and the Third Reich, tested for the last five years, has not only contributed towards the continual development of Polish–German relations but has become, in the new situation, a valuable contribution towards present appeasement in Europe'.

The Polish press were in general agreement that such consolidation of relations between the two countries was for the good of Poland, though some newspapers stressed that it was of even greater value to Germany since her hand was thus freed to tackle whatever problems she might have in the West. The *Kurjer Polski* said that the Polish–German understanding provided 'the key without which Germany would have difficulty in unlocking doors she wished to open'. It seemed that the particular doors meant were those by which she might again acquire colonies. Some papers commented that the results of the visit would confound those prophets who hoped that the coming political storm would burst in the East rather than in the West.

This feeling that a storm of some sort impended, though there was no clear indication where it would break or even whether it would break at all, permeated many minds as the first month of the year drew to its close. Nor did such minds have to be primarily interested in international affairs. The most cursory newspaper reader could not escape the signs. The storm-clouds gathering in the Western Mediterranean alone were enough to suggest that the Poles might be right in thinking that when the storm came it would burst in the West.

In such times even optimism tends to acquire a neurotic quality. Those like the editor of the London *Times*, whose belief in the efficacy of Chamberlain's visit to Rome was coupled with respect for the 'greatness and moderation' of Mussolini, treated those who warned of danger with an irritability suggesting less confidence than they professed. At the beginning of the year the *Daily Express* had sounded a note of almost hysterical calm when George Malcolm Thompson declared categorically in its columns: 'There will be no great war in Europe in 1939. There is nothing in our present situation which affords any ground to suppose that an upheaval must or will come.'

Asking what it was that 'makes the prophets of evil quake in their shoes' Thompson reassured the public by saying that dictators were a natural form of government for many countries in Europe and that as for the high-speed rearmament that was now going on, this had in the past merely been the accompaniment to 'phantom fears'. The Napoleonic invasion against which the Martello towers had been built had never come, nor had the French fleet against which we had fortified Chatham and Portsmouth in the middle of the nineteenth century.

'The pedlars of nightmare', he added, might also consider facts such as that Britain was now stronger in Europe and would be stronger in Asia when the Singapore base was ready later in the year. France, still the strongest land power in Europe, was strong also at sea and her people were in good heart. Both Germany and Italy were suffering from internal crises. There was no coal in Berlin at Christmas and people could not eat the Sudetenland. War, he concluded, was growing more and more impossible for the great powers: 'The destruction is too great.' The article was headed, 'This Is Why You Can Sleep Soundly In 1939'.

And at the end of the month, as the world waited for what Hitler had to say in his speech on the sixth anniversary of his accession to power, the British Home Secretary, Sir Samuel Hoare, at a meeting at Swansea in turn attacked 'those who go about the world with white faces and trembling lips asking each other which day of the week and of the month the world war is going to begin'. He continued:

These timid panic-mongers are doing the greatest harm. They are undermining public confidence. They are creating a feeling of the inevitability of war when there is no such inevitability at all.... I am told that in the United States of America there is a class of people who sit listening in hysterical excitement to what is called 'hot music' and waiting for the final crash. Americans in their forcible language call them 'jitter-bugs'. There are many people in Europe today who seem to be behaving in much the same way. They sit listening to all the hot music of the scares and alarms waiting helplessly for the crash that according to them will destroy us all.

A letter-writer to the London *Times* the next day, however, took Sir Samuel Hoare to task, saying that the British citizen was afraid neither of Hitler nor of Mussolini but was worried by the spectacle of inefficiency and complacency in high places. Sir Samuel Hoare deserved to be given a new version of the apocry-phal landlady's reply to her lodger: 'If there are jitterbugs here you brought them yourselves.'

This correspondent was likely to be a supporter of Winston Churchill and other recalcitrant Tories, increasingly unpopular now within the body of the Conservative Party since warnings that the dictators were unreliable and a war probable were equated with that most reprehensible of all Conservative political sins, 'party disloyalty'. Churchill himself was already under increasingly severe criticism from within his own constituency party in Epping.

But anxiety among the British general public about the international situation expressed itself on the whole in less articulate terms than it did in Churchill's mind. It was probably as well formulated by Stanley Baldwin, Chamberlain's predecessor, as by anyone when at the end of January he said: 'People are worried because they are puzzled. They do not know. They have had a great shock. [A reference to the September 1938 crisis.] They want to know the truth. They all want to do something for their country and they do not know what.' If war were to come, he added, 'the civilization that was shaken twenty years ago would be shattered and the pieces would hardly be worth picking up'.

That a certain panicky instability was indeed to be found in the air of Britain was revealed by the extreme sensitivity of the Stock Market. Beverley Baxter, writing in the *Sunday Graphic* on 23 January, had attacked the new inexplicable susceptibility of the British to rumour-mongers. In the previous week, he re-ported, the Stock Market had sagged badly for an hour after a broker friend of his had telephoned asking excitedly, 'What's this news the evening papers are afraid to publish?' And later another broker had telephoned him saying that the German army had cancelled all leave for March.

'I cannot remember', wrote Baxter, 'any time when rumour was at such a discount.... Have we gone a little mad in Britain? Is the national character deteriorating, or is it possible there are influences at work which genuinely desire war, or at least a condition of nerves and suspicion which makes real peace impossible?'

The London correspondent of the *New York Times* had already reported that he found the capital's nervousness more acute than anyone could remember except at the time of the crisis in the previous September. He did, however, find this peculiar to London and reported the atmosphere in the North and Midlands as being much calmer. There was also a certain cynicism afoot. 'A German mobilization against Rumania or Poland', he said, 'would leave British nerves unmoved; a show of force against the West would be quite a different matter.' He said that it had long been the hope of the Conservative leaders that Hitler would turn east after Munich towards an ultimate collision with Russia. According to this reasoning, nothing Hitler could do in Eastern Europe should cause the slightest concern west of the Rhine, but with the crisis in the Mediterranean and a report of two German divisions being equipped for desert operations and moved to the Italian border between Klagenfurt and Villach, where they were only a short distance by rail from the Mediterranean, things did not seem to be working out this way. Hitler's friendly exchanges with Colonel Beck of Poland, and his reception of the Foreign Ministers of Hungary and Czechoslovakia gave the impression that his own main anxiety was to secure his eastern border while he devoted his attention to the West.

There was also another significant consideration, continued the *New York Times*. If Germany went east there would be no pickings for Italy but if Germany were to demand colonies or economic concessions or naval bases at the expense of the West, Italy could demand her share, too. Germany and Italy could execute a squeeze together. This, reported the *New York Times* correspondent, was the cause of London's 'jitters'. All waited anxiously for Hitler's speech on the coming Monday, 30 January.

Chamberlain was due to speak at Birmingham two days before.

But of course even those worried in this way found many items of day-to-day interest in their newspapers to divert them from the international situation. If sport could continue to distract the inhabitants of Barcelona under bombs and shells until the very moment of Franco's arrival, it was natural that it should maintain its traditional hold over societies concerned only about theoretical disturbances of their peace. Boxing, the sport most straightforwardly simplifying conflict and sublimating human instincts of aggression and defence, captured the attention of both sides of the Atlantic in the last week in January.

In New York, where the wintry spell was cold enough for the 110th Street lake in Central Park to be open for skating and the Connecticut River was frozen over from Hartford to Long Island Sound, Joe Louis, the heavyweight champion of the world, met his fifth challenger for that title, John Henry Lewis, against whom the bookmakers were offering odds of eight to one. The only conversation the two were reported to have had at the weigh-in was appropriately laconic:

'How do you feel, John?'

'All right, Joe.'

It was a quarter of a century since two negro boxers had fought for the heavyweight title. It was to be a fifteen-round bout, but majority opinion was that the fight would be over just as soon as Joe Louis caught his opponent with a clean solid punch. Still, upsets had been known before, one of them involving Louis himself who, when clearly on his way to the top and conquering all comers, had been knocked out by Max Schmeling. He had had his revenge on Schmeling in June 1938 when he knocked him out in a few minutes, and some such treatment was now expected for his present challenger.

Lewis was indeed down for a count of three after a minute, and on getting up retreated groggily under a hail of blows to sprawl over the lower rung of the ropes. While the referee counted two he slid down the rope and managed to bounce up again from the canvas, only to be leapt after by Louis and hammered all round the ring. The *New York Times* reporter, James P. Dawson, described the hesitation of the referee as he kept one eye on the clock and the other on John Henry Lewis's reaction to 'a perfect shower of pile-driving lefts and rights to head, face and body'. Louis, having worked Lewis on to the ropes again, stepped back before leaping in once more to finish him off. Dawson continued:

> From all angles the champion struck, missing some, landing most blows in a frenzied effort to finish the work which an earlier right-hand drive to the jaw had started ... Helpless to defend himself but with that instinctive desire for self-preservation that is innate in most fighters, John Henry Lewis managed miraculously to avoid disaster for a time. He hobbled alert somehow and drew up his arms in a feeble defence while the champion, stalking panther-like, poised his right. At last the opening came.... A hail of lefts and rights and John Henry swayed drunkenly to the ropes and finally one devastating right to the jaw toppled the game Westerner.

The heavyweight champion stepped back to a neutral corner. His work was finished. After a count of five the referee stopped the fight.

'I hope John Henry isn't hurt badly,' commented the victor, 'because I sure put everything I had into my punches.'

There were complaints in *The Times* that the BBC was putting out too much news of international affairs that was depressing. Evelyn Waugh wrote to offer those 'who find themselves painfully excited by the BBC an economical and unfailing solution. We are fortunate enough to live in a country where listening-in is not yet compulsory. I have no wireless machine and find my morning newspaper a perfectly adequate source of information.'

Murder, rarer in occurrence in Britain than in the United States and more effectively focused upon and dramatized by a national rather than a regional press, had been vying as usual for the attention of the British public. There had been two particularly shocking and unpleasant cases during January, each of which was eventually to be the source of some additional interest beyond the mere sensation of their central event. In the first case the actual murder had taken place on Christmas Eve, 1938. A jeweller named Ernest Percy Key, a man of sixty-four, had been found at 11.40 a.m. on Christmas Eve lying in a pool of

"Shall I take over through town?"

1 MOVEMENT INSTEAD OF 4

OLD WAY... *For every stop you 1. brake, 2. declutch, 3. move gear lever into neutral, 4. release clutch. For every start you 1. declutch, 2. go into gear, 3. let in clutch, 4 accelerate.*

DAIMLER WAY... *To stop you BRAKE (engine idles in gear). To start you ACCELERATE (Daimler glides smoothly off).*

NO NEED—NOW WE HAVE THIS NEW DAIMLER '15'!

TRAFFIC driving is made 4 times easier in the 2½ Litre Daimler '15.' No clutch or gear lever to worry about. To stop or start needs just one movement instead of four! It's not magic—just the wonderful Daimler 'fluid flywheel,' new to *you* perhaps, but tried and proved by Daimler owners for over 7 years. And on the open road the powerful new engine sweeps you ruthlessly up to 75 if you want it. While independent front wheel springing gives superb steadiness and riding comfort. There's a thrill in driving this Daimler —and never a trace of worry.

BY APPOINTMENT TO
HIS MAJESTY THE
LATE KING GEORGE V

SPORTS SALOON (*as illustrated*) OR SIX-LIGHT SALOON
Both with the powerful new 2½-Litre engine ·· **£485**

Daimler Fluid Flywheel Transmission is licensed under Vulcan-Sinclair and Daimler patents

2½ LITRE Daimler FIFTEEN

... *ENDS YOUR DRIVING WORRIES*

blood in the back room of his shop in Victoria Road, Surbiton. He was still alive, but had thirty-one vicious stab wounds on his head, face and neck, and sixteen more on his hands, and he died before reaching hospital in Surbiton. It was on 7 January that an unemployed driver of Hampton Hill, Middlesex, a man of thirty-four, married with children, named William Thomas Butler, was charged with the murder and on 18 January committal proceedings were begun against him. The Home Office pathologist explained, with grisly detachment, how the victim appeared to have come by his wounds. A struggle had begun in the shop and transferred to the back room with the jeweller, Key, desperately trying to ward off blows from a knife and eventually being hauled up by the collar as the stabbing knife rained down on him from behind until he was brought finally to the floor. The wounds on his hands had been inflicted as he tried to defend himself against the knife.

The evidence against Butler seemed overwhelming. A gold watch and chain, missing from the jeweller's shop, had been pawned by Butler. A baby's silver rattle, also missing from Key's shop, was found at Butler's address, as were Key's bloodstained gloves which it appeared Butler had been wearing to cover thirty-six cuts which he himself had on his hands. A blood-stained bowler hat was also found in Butler's house and this too seemed a telling piece of evidence because it appeared that before noon on that day Butler had gone to a gents' outfitters and bought himself a new bowler hat, though they only had one that was too small for him. He had then gone to Kingston Station and taken a taxi to hospital. The taxi driver had noticed the blood on his gloves. Bizarrely, the hospital was the same one as that to which the corpse of the slashed jeweller had just been admitted, and Butler was even treated for the wounds on his hands by the very doctor who had just examined the remains of Key.

Butler's wounds took two hours to dress. He said that he had got them from a wood-cutting machine. He later made a different statement to the police, declaring that he had been knocked down by a motorcycle. Other sections of his statement to the police were equally inexpert. He had a garbled story about being taken to the shop that morning by a certain Detective Reeves, who, he said, had borrowed his coat, gone into Key's shop and come out wearing a different one, which he had forced him to put on after a struggle and in the pockets of which he, Butler, had found the gold watch and chain, which he admitted he had pawned. When arrested, Butler had had on him thirteen visiting-cards printed in the name 'Detective Reeves, CID', with two fictional telephone numbers. There was no such Detective Reeves in the CID.

Butler was, understandably, committed for trial.

The other murder case, a particularly horrifying one, remained until after the end of the month a tantalizing mystery. No one had yet been arrested for it though one of the biggest hunts in all British criminal history had been mounted to try and find the murderer. On the morning of Thursday 19 January the body of a nine-year-old schoolgirl had been found naked and trussed with a length of flex 'like a chicken', as one eye-witness put it, in a ditch near the RAF aerodrome at Hornchurch in Essex. She had been assaulted, sexually interfered with and strangled with a piece of white cloth torn from her undervest. Her body was found by a nightwatchman cycling home, who went to the nearest house, that of an RAF Wing-Commander, whose wife telephoned the police. The police spent the rest of that day, helped by 300 RAF men from the aerodrome, searching the neighbourhood for the dead girl's clothing or any other clues, and were still searching with torches at midnight.

The victim, Pamela Coventry, had lived on a new housing estate near by. On the previous day she had attended school in the morning and then come home for a lunch of potatoes, peas and sausages. She left home at 1.15 p.m. to return to school but never arrived there. Sir Bernard Spilsbury, the Home Office pathologist, concluded that death had taken place between 1.15 and 2.15 that afternoon. Her body had been trussed with black cable to which were attached pieces of tarred string, green cable, thick string and insulating tape, and had been tied up in such a way that the thighs were completely flexed against the stomach. Between the child's thigh and her chest, however, was found a cigarette-end which, in the opinion of Sir Bernard Spilsbury, must have got there while the tying-up was taking place.

Over the next ten days the police took statements from four thousand people living in the area. They were said to be looking for a man, or possibly a woman, with a scratched face. They were also looking for any missing radio aerial or earthing wire. In addition to interviewing householders, sometimes for as long as half an hour at a time, they were searching every hut and allotment in the area. On Monday, in a garden shed in East Romford, they found something like the flex they were looking for, but in the end decided that it did not tally. There were a number of half-leads of this nature, but they appeared to go nowhere. By 26 January it was reported that though the police had still not found Pamela Coventry's clothing, having to wait for the river Rom, swollen by the recent snowfalls, to subside, they had nevertheless considerably narrowed the area within which it was thought the murderer was being shielded.

On 31 January it was reported that laboratory tests of an undisclosed nature were being carried out and that 'should these prove favourable to a theory held by the police, swift developments may be expected'. A continuation of this report stated that a Scotland Yard detective-sergeant had been to Bristol with a photograph of a man not seen in the Hornchurch area since the girl's body was found. But the story itself now had temporarily to recede before reports from the international scene.

Although it was the speech of Hitler on Monday 30 January for which the world was waiting, the British Prime Minister, Chamberlain, actually spoke first, at a Birmingham Jewellers' Association dinner the previous Saturday, providing a sort of overture for the German Chancellor.

Chamberlain began by telling the assembled jewellers: 'If it were not for one consideration I should be disposed to take a rosy view of the prospects of business during this current year. . . . But I am bound to record that at the present time there exists a certain amount of political tension in international affairs which may or may not be well-founded, but which is undoubtedly holding back enterprise.' He went on to defend the Munich agreement against its critics (which, he thought, were mostly in Britain itself). He had no regret or any reason to suppose that any other course would have been preferable: 'War today is so terrible in its effects on those who take part in it, no matter what the outcome may be; it brings so much loss and suffering even to the bystanders that it ought never to be allowed to begin unless every practicable and honourable step has been taken to prevent it.'

He defended in the same vein his recent visit to Mussolini in Rome, complaining reasonably that he had been criticized before going, for what he was going to do and then told when he came back that it was not worthwhile having gone because nothing had come of the visit. Apart from a better understanding of each Government's point of view, the visit had yielded a demonstration of the friendliness of the Italian people, and their passionate desire for peace, which, he maintained, was shared by the peoples of Great Britain and Germany. Recognizing, however, that 'though it takes at least two to make a peace, one can make a war', Chamberlain went on to illustrate the improvements that had been made in Britain's defences on land, sea and air in the past month, drawing particular attention to the country's anti-aircraft defences which, he said, were vastly improved: 'The deficiencies which were apparent last September have now been removed.'

He summed up:

Today the air is full of rumours and suspicions which ought not to be allowed to persist. For peace can only be endangered by such a challenge as was envisaged by the President of the United States in his New Year message – namely, a demand to dominate the world by force. That would be a demand which, as the President indicated, and I myself have already declared, the democracies must inevitably resist. But I cannot believe that any such challenge is intended, for the consequences of war for the peoples on either side would be so grave that no government which has their interests at heart would like to embark on them.

Chamberlain's speech was warmly received in Rome. It was favourably contrasted in the *Voce d'Italia* with Roosevelt's 'drum-beating alarmist policy'. Roosevelt's intemperance, said the paper, was totally contrary to the spirit of Chamberlain's speech which was 'clear, honest and willing . . . nobody in Italy can think of discouraging this tendency of the British Prime Minister to seek a definite peace formula for Europe with goodwill and negotiation'. The British Prime Minister's spirit was very different from those who sought 'to pour on young nations still excluded from equality rights and world position perennial suspicion of aggressiveness and non-existent plans of world domination' – such as President Roosevelt had sought to revive with his 'customary intemperance in his unhappy New Year message'.

The German press, though, was less enthusiastic. It found Chamberlain's speech not very clear and Goering's *Essener Zeitung* found similarities between it and Roosevelt's, saying that the line had been diplomatically worked out together beforehand.

Moreover, some fairly belligerent noises were starting to come out of Germany in anticipation of Hitler's speech the following Monday. A Nazi district leader, speaking at Cologne University, had stressed that Germany still had many claims to make, and, if refused, was strong enough to get them by war. Another Nazi leader at the same meeting spoke of the 'great decisions they were to hear from the Führer in his coming speech'.

The world wondered, as it was intended to wonder, what these were likely to be.

It was the general opinion of political commentators that any possible German move in the east had been postponed and that Germany was preparing herself in the rôle of a brilliant second to Mussolini for a showdown in the Mediterranean which would involve the re-partition of Africa and with it a settlement of German colonial claims. The *New York Times* correspondent in Berlin wrote that while the world still talked of a Mediterranean crisis, Germany was already talking of an African crisis. He discounted alarming reports abroad about German troop movements but himself said: 'It is freely predicted here that events might begin moving by March.'

In Munich the governor of Bavaria had given some indication of what Hitler might be expected to say, declaring that to identify German claims for colonies with an attack on the peace of the world was to deny the necessities of life to a Germany which had reached the limit of her economic production. He also reiterated the familiar charge that in this respect as in many others the Treaty of Versailles had been a swindle. Nevertheless, semi-official quarters in Berlin played down any sensational expectations from Hitler's speech, saying that though it might disappoint the world it would also give it some comfort.

At eight o'clock in the evening of Monday 30 January, in the Kroll Opera House, Berlin, Hitler spoke. His audience, presided over by Goering, consisted of all the members of the Nazi Reichstag from the new Greater Germany, here assembled for the first time. Hitler spoke for two and a half hours.

He began by referring to the rescue of Europe from Bolshevik chaos, a rescue which Italian Fascism had initiated and which National Socialism had continued, and a further stage of which was now being witnessed in Spain: 'the same drama of a brave triumph over the Jewish international attempt to destroy European civilization'. He celebrated the new sense of greater German unity which, he said, had not been achieved without struggle, 'in spite of what the senseless bourgeois may think', and he went back twenty years to the principle of self-determination enshrined among President Wilson's Fourteen Points on which a new world peace was to have been established when Germany laid down her arms after the Great War. This principle, he said, the Allies had applied hypocritically simply as it suited them: 'Thus they refused to return Germany's colonial possessions, alleging that it would be wrong to return the native inhabitants of the colonies to Germany against their will . . . but while the Allies thus upheld the right of self-determination for primitive Negro tribes they refused in 1918 to grant to a highly-civilized nation like the Germans the rights of man which had been solemnly promised them.'

He recounted the steps by which in accordance with the principles of self-determination he had brought ten million Germans back into the Reich in 1938 and paid tribute to 'the highly-appreciated readiness of Mr Chamberlain and M. Daladier' to help him do this. But he was soon back to the theme of colonies:

> Germany has undoubtedly always been in a very difficult position economically . . . what is the cause of all our economic difficulties? It is the over-population of our territory. . . . In Germany there are 135 people to the square kilometre living entirely without their former reserve . . . there are countries in the world where instead of 135 people to the square kilometre there are only between five and eleven, where vast stretches of fertile land lie fallow, where all imaginable minerals are available. The great German colonial possessions which the Reich once acquired peacefully by treaties and by paying for them, have been stolen. . . . The theft of the German colonies was morally an injustice. . . . The objection that these colonial possessions are of no importance in any case should only lead to their being returned to us with an easy mind. . . . Germany does not require her colonial possessions at all in order to set up armies there for she has a sufficiently large German population for this purpose at home – but to relieve her economic difficulties.

He complimented National Socialism on the way it had dealt with these difficulties in spite of the lack of colonies:

> We can smile today at an age when economists were seriously of the opinion that the value of currency was determined by the reserves in gold and foreign exchange lying in the vaults of the national banks . . . instead of that we have learned to realize that the value of her currency lies in a nation's power of production, that an increasing volume of production sustains a currency, and could possibly raise its value, whereas a decreasing production must, sooner or later, lead to a compulsory devaluation.

He then turned to those who were hostile to the Reich, naming specifically

such agitators as Churchill, Cooper, Eden or Ickes [Roosevelt's Secretary of the Interior] . . . we therefore owe it to the security of the Reich to bring home to the German people in good time the truth about these men. The German nation has no feeling of hatred towards England, America or France. All it wants is peace and quiet. . . . The nations will in a short time realize that National Socialist Germany wants no enmity with other nations, that all the assertions as to our intended attacks on other nations are lies – lies born out of morbid hysteria or of a mania for self-preservation on the part of certain politicians; and that in certain States these lies are being used by unscrupulous profiteers to salvage their own finances, that, above all, international Jewry may hope in this way to satisfy its thirst for revenge and gain, that on the other hand this is the grossest defamation that can be brought to bear on a great and peace-loving nation . . .

He went on:

In connection with the Jewish question, I have this to say. It is a shameful spectacle to see how the whole democratic world is oozing sympathy for the poor tormented Jewish people, but remains hard-hearted and obdurate when it comes to helping them, which is surely, in view of its attitude, an obvious duty. The arguments that are brought up as an excuse for not helping them actually speak for us Germans and Italians. For this is what they say: 'We' – that is the democracies – 'are not in a position to take in the Jews.' Yet in these empires there are not even ten people to the square kilometre. While Germany with her 135 inhabitants to the square kilometre is supposed to have room for them!

Second, they assure us: 'We cannot take them unless Germany is prepared to allow them a certain amount of capital to bring with them as immigrants.'

For hundreds of years Germany was good enough to receive these elements although they possess nothing except infectious political and physical diseases. What they possess today, they have by far the largest extent gained at the cost of the less astute German nation by the most reprehensible manipulation. . . . If the rest of the world cries out with hypocritical mien against this barbaric expulsion from Germany of such an irreplaceable and culturally eminently valuable element we can only be astonished at this reaction. For how thankful they must be that we are releasing apostles of culture and placing them at the disposal of the rest of the world. In accordance with their own declarations they cannot find a single reason to excuse themselves for refusing to receive this most valuable race in their own countries. Nor can I see a reason why the members of this race should be imposed upon the German nation, while in the states that are so enthusiastic about these 'splendid people' their settlement should suddenly be refused with every imaginable excuse. I think the sooner this problem is solved the better, for Europe cannot settle down until the Jewish question is cleared up. It may very well be possible that sooner or later an agreement on this problem may be reached in Europe, even between those nations that otherwise do not so easily come together.

The world has sufficient space for settlement, but we must once and for all get rid of the opinion that the Jewish race was only created by God for the purpose of being in a certain percentage as a parasite living on the body and the productive work of other nations. The Jewish race will have to adapt itself to sound constructive activity as other nations do, or sooner or later it will succumb to a crisis of an inconceivable magnitude. . . . Today I will once more be a prophet. If the international Jewish financiers in and outside Europe should succeed in plunging the nation once more into a world war, then the result will not be the Bolshevization of the earth and thus the victory of Jewry, but the annihilation of the Jewish race in Europe!

After explaining how National Socialist and Fascist volunteers had gone to help General Franco as part of a crusade against Bolshevism, he extolled the cultural influence of Fascism, and in his reference to the Mediterranean crisis, he went on: 'It can only serve the cause of peace if it is clearly understood that a war of rival ideologies waged against the Italy of today will, once it is launched and regardless of its motives, call Germany to the side of her friends.'

He ended however on a pacific note:

Germany has no territorial demands against England and France apart from that for the return of our colonies. While the solution of this question would contribute greatly to the pacification of the world, it is in no sense a problem that could cause a war. ... I have stated over and over again that there is no German, and above all no National Socialist, who in his most secret thoughts has the intention of causing the British Empire any kind of difficulty. From England, too, the voices of men who think reasonably and calmly express a similar attitude with regard to Germany. It would be a blessing for the whole world if mutual confidence and cooperation could be established between the two peoples. The same is true of our relations with France ... Germany is happy today in the possession of peaceful frontiers in the west, south and north.... Our relations with the United States are suffering from a campaign of defamation carried on to serve obvious political and financial interests which, under the pretence that Germany threatens American independence, is endeavouring to mobilize the hatred of an entire continent against the European States that are nationally governed. We all believe, however, that this does not reflect the will of the millions of American citizens who, despite all that is said to the contrary, by the gigantic Jewish capitalistic propaganda through the press, the radio and the films, cannot fail to realize that there is not one word of truth in all these assertions. Germany wishes to live in peace and on friendly terms with all countries, including America.

Next day the London *Daily Telegraph* ran a headline: 'A Reinforcement of Hopes for Peace'. Hitler's speech, it said, was polemical in tone, but then allowance had to be made for his temperamental tendency to be polemical. His matter was comparatively mild and not lacking in a note of reassurance. It contained phrases which if taken at their face value were calculated to induce a certain sense of relief.

II

The day after Hitler's speech prices on the London Stock Exchange and Wall Street, which only a week before had been at their lowest since Munich, soared rapturously. 'Stock Exchange rise on Hitler vagueness' was a *Manchester Guardian* headline.

The London *Daily Express* leapt in with its own personal form of rapture: 'The jitterbugs asked in quavering voices if Hitler would attack us in 1939. The *Daily Express* said "No!" Now we know that Hitler agrees with the *Daily Express*. He says that he expects that there will be peace for a long time. We were right. We have got the confirmation straight from Hitler's mouth. There will be no war involving Britain in 1939.'

In the House of Commons, which reassembled the next day, Chamberlain was able to give his own reaction in the Debate on the Adjournment: 'I very definitely got the impression that it was not the speech of a man prepared to throw Europe into another crisis.' And he added: 'It is untrue to say that the policy of appease-ment has failed. On the contrary, I believe that it is steadily succeeding.'

To Opposition objections that the world only had Hitler's word for it that he was as pacific as he claimed, he replied: 'The worst way of ensuring that a man who has given his word will keep it is to tell him that you do not believe for one moment what he has told you, and to base your action on the assumption that he is not telling the truth.'

The German press was delighted by such reactions. 'London Free From Nightmare' was the headline in *Der Angriff*. 'Hitler's will for peace smashes warmongering campaign.' The *Berliner Börsenzeitung* wrote that it would not be necessary today for Samuel Hoare to make the jitterbug speech he had made the week before.

However, the old national leader in the Great War, David Lloyd George, struck a note of caution. Hitler's speech, he said, was 'exceedingly clever' because by prophesying a long period of peace he made people jump to the conclusion that all was well and that the policy of appeasement had at length triumphed. He warned people to read the speech again and predicted, incidentally, that Germany and Italy would not leave Spain before making demands on Britain and France in the Mediterranean which, if granted, would virtually give them control of it.

A re-reading of the speech, at least as published in the *Völkischer Beobachter*, gave some cause for misgiving in Poland. This official version left no doubt that what Hitler had said about Germany's frontiers was that she was happy in the possession of peaceful frontiers in the *west, south and north*. The absence of the word 'east' might in any case have given some cause for reflection, but what now caused the Poles concern was the translation of the speech as put out for Polish consumption; for in that version the word 'east' had been inserted, as if to allay any misgivings that might arise from the correct translation. The Polish telegraphic authorities made it clear that the alteration had come directly from Berlin. But since apprehension in the present crisis centred on the Mediterranean and tension between France and Italy, this curious episode attracted only marginal notice; and the apparently unmistakable indication in Hitler's speech that he saw nothing likely to give rise to war seemed temporarily to take the pressure out of the Mediterranean crisis itself.

It was from the other side of the Atlantic that the first sounds came momentarily to ruffle the new sense of international ease. President Roosevelt had had a meeting with his Senate Military Affairs Committee. After this some of the Senators, who in routine fashion had been sworn to secrecy, in routine fashion leaked to the press. The general drift of Roosevelt's remarks had clearly been that he was prepared to do much to help the democracies with military supplies from the United States. Some 600 aircraft, for instance, were going to be delivered to France. But one leaking Senator actually had it that what the President had said was that 'America's defence frontier is now in France'. The President subsequently hotly denied that this was what he had said, but the general sense of his remarks was clearly in line with the general tenor of his earlier speech at the beginning of the year. And this restatement of policy in private was clearly enough to re-arouse those misgivings which Roosevelt's political opponents had been voicing since the beginning of the year.

'Are we on the road to war?' asked Senator Johnson of California. 'If our present dealings with the French Air Mission now in America or any secrets now whispered about Washington indicate this, the American people are entitled to know it.'

Ex-President Hoover, speaking in Chicago, was more forthright and warned explicitly that the new foreign policies of the United States might well lead to war. The *New York Times* commented: 'Not since the World War has the Senate been in such a state of excitement.'

The German press too, naturally got itself into some state of excitement over the alleged 'frontier in France' quote, echoing Hoover with its own particular emphasis. Dr Goebbels's paper *Der Angriff* declared that Roosevelt was driving America to war as the sacrificial victim of world Jewry. Headlines in other German papers ran: 'Roosevelt Agitates America as Judah's Burnt Offering to War'; 'Roosevelt Peace Enemy Number One'. The American newspapers themselves were on the whole unfriendly to the President; those which reacted unfavourably to the purported leaks from the Senate Military Affairs Committee were easily in the majority. Roosevelt's Secretary of the Interior, Harold Ickes, had to go so far as to issue a statement in which he declared that there was 'no danger of the USA becoming involved in war under the present Administration'.

In Britain a new cause for alarm had suddenly made its appearance, distracting attention for the moment from the international scene with trouble from an old familiar quarter.

Those who had suspected that the blowing up of a Customs hut at Tullydonnell on the border of South Armagh between Eire and Northern Ireland on New Year's Day might be the prelude to a new campaign of violence by the clandestine Irish Republican Army had been proved right when on the evening of 15 January proclamations were posted in Dublin and in every city of Northern Ireland beginning: 'The hour has come for the supreme effort . . .', and calling on Britain to withdraw her institutions and representatives of all kinds from Ireland. It was signed on behalf of the Irish Republican Army by six men, including Sean Hayes and Sean Russell, a veteran of the campaign of 1920 to 1921.

The next day, 16 January, explosions had occurred at electricity, gas and water stations in London, Liverpool and Manchester. In Southwark, in south London, where copies of the IRA proclamation were found to have been pasted up, hundreds of windows were shattered by an explosion outside the control room of the Central Electricity Board. At Harlesden in north-west London an attempt was made to wreck a bridge carrying cables across the Grand Junction Canal and at Enfield in Middlesex an explosion at Brimsdown Power Station caused a temporary blackout in adjoining districts. In Liverpool there were explosions in the Crosby district while in Manchester three explosions from bombs placed in manholes caused the death of one man and injuries to two others. An electricity pylon at Alnwick in Northumberland was blown up. Other pylons were found to have bombs attached to them but the accompanying alarm clocks, set to trigger the explosive mechanism, had stopped prematurely – one in Birmingham, set for 6.15 a.m., at 3.15 a.m.

The round-up and arrest of suspected Irishmen in all these areas followed and on 2 February twenty-one people were remanded in custody in Manchester and London on charges of preparing explosive devices in the United Kingdom in the name of the IRA.

At six o'clock in the morning on the very next day there were explosions in the London Underground at Leicester Square and Tottenham Court Road from bombs which had been placed in attaché cases and left in the Left Luggage offices on a threepenny deposit ticket. Eight people were hurt, two of them seriously.

One hundred search warrants were issued and Mills bombs were found at Stoke Newington, while a package containing forty cartridges and a detonator were mysteriously found behind a roller in the front garden of a former Assistant Superintendent of Works at Hampton Court Palace. Two days later incendiary devices started fires in stores in Coventry when envelopes containing magnesium and nitric acid ignited among the stationery and books in Woolworth's, between bundles of shirts in Marks and Spencer's, between the pages of an order book in Burton's, and in the drawer of a wardrobe in Owen Owen Ltd. The devices were technically primitive but ingenious – the delaying device being provided by a toy balloon into which the nitric acid was placed and left to burn through the rubber until it ignited the magnesium. A more conventional attempt to blow up Walton Jail the same night caused little damage. But awareness that a conspiracy of unknown dimensions was at work caused sufficient alarm for the King and Queen to be given special guards and a police escort when driving that day between Windsor and Aldershot.

That the police had arrested some of the right Irishmen was confirmed when the following day twelve men were remanded at Bow Street Magistrates' Court for a week. These were mostly working-class – a porter, a butcher's roundsman, a labourer, a scaffolder, etc. – and on one of the accused 103 balloons such as those used in the envelopes at Coventry were discovered. Also discovered with them were suitcases and documents giving details of a so-called S-plan.

'In order to exercise maximum world effect,' ran this latter, 'the diversion must be carried out when no major war or world crisis is on, but if it is carried on when trouble is anticipated with jumpiness and nervous expectation of the Government as well as the nervous potential panic of the people it can be exploited to the full.'

It was revealed that on 13 January a letter had been received by Lord Halifax at the Foreign Office from the IRA, delivering an ultimatum which demanded the complete evacuation of Irish territory and territorial waters by British forces. 'The Government of the Irish Republic', this ran, 'believe that a period of fourteen days is sufficient notice for your Government to signify its intention in the matter of evacuation. If at the expiration of this period of grace these conditions are unfulfilled our Government reserve the right to take appropriate action.' It was signed 'Patrick Fleming, Secretary'.

This and further evidence produced in another hearing at Manchester in the following week, at which eight men and two girls were remanded in custody, seemed to show that the police had at least started on the right track. The Manchester arrests had been made on the day after the explosions there, 16 January, and one of the men had declared outright: 'What I did I did for Ireland.' In the overcoat of another were found 'Battalion Orders parts one and two' which began: 'The time is now opportune to attack England, the oppressor of Irish freedom.'

The arrests did much to reassure public opinion. And in Ireland itself the head of a Government freely and democratically elected by a majority of the Irish people made his own views on such events known. Mr Eamon de Valera, who was then in power, had of course at one time himself been in favour of using force through an earlier Irish Republican Army to bring about a sovereign independent and united Ireland. Now the inevitable adjustment which all skilful politicians must make to their idealism in the light of political realities inspired him to define his present attitude in his own inimitably exact style. Announcing in the Eire Senate on 7 February bills which he intended to introduce in the Dail to suppress the IRA, he said:

If things happen which we do not wish would happen when we are trying to concentrate public opinion on a certain issue we can only regret it. I am not going to refer to certain matters which are *sub judice* at the moment. But there is another matter which is a definite challenge. We have been elected by the firm vote of the people in two elections. We are the rightful lawful Government of this country. No other body has any right to talk to the Irish people but ourselves.

His main argument was compressed into a simple but telling thought: 'There is no use appealing to force if it is obvious that force is not going to be effective.'

In Britain for the rest of the month Irishmen and women continued to be arrested and remanded in custody on a charge of conspiring to cause explosions. Forty-four had been arrested by the end of it.

On the domestic scene new developments in the case of the murdered Hornchurch schoolgirl Pamela Coventry held British opinion quite as grippingly as the arcane pursuits of the IRA.

On Tuesday 1 February, after the return to Hornchurch of the Detective-Sergeant who had paid the mysterious visit to Bristol, it was announced that an arrest was expected shortly. At eleven o'clock the following night a man living in the district in which Pamela had been murdered was driven to Romford Police Station, where he was still being interviewed in the early hours of Thursday, and later that day he was charged with her murder.

He was Leonard Richardson, a twenty-eight-year-old chemical worker of Coronation Drive, Elm Park, Hornchurch, a short thin-faced man with light brown curly hair and blue eyes. He appeared in the dock at Romford Police Court looking pale and with his hands deep in the pockets of a light tweed overcoat. Crowds had been waiting outside the court to get at him but were successfully misled by the police to the wrong entrance. Richardson seemed to have some difficulty in hearing the proceedings and so was brought up to the front of the court. He was a married man with two children, one of whom had been born only three weeks before. His wife had in fact still been in hospital at the time of the murder. She now attended the court. Asked if he wanted legal aid he said: 'I'd like to get in touch with my friends first.' He was remanded in custody for a week and taken, again evading the mob, to Brixton prison. When he reappeared at Romford again a week later he was again remanded for a week, the police saying that it would be some weeks before they were ready to present their case. Richardson was granted legal aid and the public had temporarily to suspend their curiosity.

The other sensational murder case of the year, however, that of the jeweller Ernest Key for which an unemployed driver, William Butler, was being tried, was now resolved. The trial, in which he was defended by David Maxwell Fyfe, lasted only two days. Butler had changed his story to something considerably more plausible and clearly not very far from the truth. On that narrow margin which might or might not separate it from the truth his life was to depend.

His story now was that he had gone to see Key, who owed him money for some rings he had sold him. Butler, who was prepared to go into the witness-box in his own defence, said that he was married with two children and being out of work had become very depressed and had taken to house-breaking. He admitted to seven such cases and implied that Key knew perfectly well the source of the rings he had sold him. According to Butler, when he had asked him on this occasion for the money he felt he was owed, Key had . . . 'suddenly turned round and picked up a knife. Then I managed to get the knife. We were both mad. Suddenly Mr Key fell to the floor . . .' Butler had taken money from the jeweller's pockets, exchanged overcoats with him because his own was covered in blood, lost his bowler hat, snatched up some rings and a rattle, and bolted.

Asked categorically by his defence counsel: 'Did you kill Mr Key?', his reply was: 'I did not. I acted in self-defence and Mr Key was killed because he attacked me.'

A crucial piece of evidence turned out to be the knife with which the various wounds to both parties had been inflicted. It was a knife of an unusual sort with a little nail in it, used for soling shoes. The nail was exactly like others found in Butler's tool chest. The jeweller's son swore that he had never seen a knife like that in his father's shop.

The jury took fifty minutes to reach their verdict. There were three women among them and one of these came back into court weeping and buried her head in her hands. They found Butler guilty of murder, and the judge, finding this to be based on 'the clearest evidence', sentenced him to death and a date was set for his execution. Agitation for his reprieve, however, now began.

Meanwhile, on the French side of the Pyrenees a human tragedy of vast proportions was being enacted.

The disintegration of the armies of the Spanish Republic in Catalonia after the fall of Barcelona had been cataclysmic. The last meeting of the Republican Cortes took place in the dungeon-like vaults of the old citadel of Figueras on 3 February, with only 60 out of the 470 elected members able to be present. It was so cold that some of the Ministers and deputies kept on their overcoats. The Prime Minister, Negrín, appealed for resistance to the bitter end, stating the Republican war aims to be a guarantee that Spain would be the perpetual arbiter of her own destiny, and a guarantee that after the end of the war there would be no persecution of anyone. He received a unanimous vote of confidence. The next day Gerona fell and four days later, Figueras itself. Some 150 men of an Anarchist unit of the Republican army made a last suicidal stand at Puigcerdá, fighting to the last man, but by 10 February Franco's forces had reached the frontier at Le Perthus, Cerbère and Bourg-Madame, the three points at which civilian and military refugees had been pouring into France. By that date there were reckoned to be between 250,000 and 300,000 of them there.

The French had almost at once had to abandon their earliest intentions of, first, keeping all refugees out and then letting only civilians through. Such original intentions at the end of January had graphically fired the revolutionary indignation of Sir Stafford Cripps in the active campaign he was now conducting for a Popular Front after his expulsion from the Labour Party. Speaking just after the fall of Barcelona, in London, he had declared:

> Our foreign policy in the last seven years has been an attempt by the ruling classes of Britain to get protection for its interests by the utilization of other militarist or fascist powers to suppress working-class power in all other parts of the world, because working-class power was by the spread of its ideology a threat to British capitalism. ... Armed soldiers of France are keeping back the refugees from finding safety in France. What is to happen to those who are crowding the roads tonight? To such depths have sunk the democracies of Western Europe.

By the middle of February armed soldiers of France were containing, often with little sympathetic regard for the emotional trauma through which Spanish Republican soldiers had just passed, the shattered remnants of that army in concentration camps where the conditions were so bleak and miserable that just under half of the more than one hundred thousand militiamen who had crossed had already opted to return to Franco Spain, whatever the consequences. Two hundred and fifty thousand civilian refugees were being accommodated further inland. Those members of the Republican Government itself who had crossed the frontier either flew back to Government-held territory in Central Spain or moved temporarily to Paris for desperate discussions about the future of the Republic. Among the later was its now openly-pessimistic President, Azaña.

The shattered and straggling legions of the Republic's armies had been flowing over the Pyrenees for over a fortnight. Some came as deserters; some in desperate groups of beaten men determined to continue the struggle somehow, somewhere; some came merely bewildered and exhausted by defeat; some came in reasonably good order with quantities of equipment including artillery, tanks, armoured cars and machine-guns which seemed to give the lie to the many reports of shortage of arms. There were many wounded in all groups. 'Where are we going?' said a member of the Enrique Lister Brigade echoing a newspaperman's question. 'Why Valencia, of course, or Madrid!'

Together with the defeated came some 15,000 prisoners under guard, many of them civilians but between 6,000 and 7,000 of them prisoners-of-war including eighty German and Italian airmen now turned technically to victors by the tide of battle. Such prisoners were sent back under the chairmanship of the Red Cross, haggard and exhausted but, according to the London *Times*, managing to form up into columns and march off with enfeebled shouts of 'Franco! Franco! Franco!' They were more fortunate than at least one batch of the Republic's prisoners – forty-two of them, including the Bishop of Teruel, whose corpses were soon to be found in the Pyrenees riddled with bullet wounds and finished off with the *coup de grâce*. The Republic's Foreign Minister, Álvarez del Vayo, had signed an accord with the French Ambassador before leaving Barcelona, guaranteeing the bishop's safe passage to France, but clearly his guards had taken matters into their own hands.

The French began to collect the abandoned war material into dumps and prepared to sink small-arms and ammunition in the Mediterranean, sending two large lighters to Port-Vendres for that purpose. The dumped human material was collected into vast internment camps at Argelès-sur-Mer, St Cyprien, and at other points along the frontier. The only features of these camps which really distinguished them from the bleak landscape in which they were situated were the barbed wire which surrounded them and the Senegalese sentres with fixed bayonets who guarded them. On the coast great stretches of beach and sand-dunes were enclosed. At Bourg-Madame in the mountains 20,000 men lay about in the snow and mud.

The *News Chronicle* correspondent described the 100,000 men in the camp at Argelès-sur-Mer as 'a picture of human wretchedness'. There were few roofs for shelter. The defeated militiamen simply dug themselves holes in the wet sand and huddled there, covered by scraps of clothing. The dressing-station was a wooden summer pavilion. 'Here on the gritty sand of the beach or the coarse grass that fringes it, sick and wounded men, some with terrible wounds, sat or hobbled about waiting for their turn to be treated.' Once treated, the wounded lay with their splints and plaster casts in the wind-blown sandy hollows.

In such camps, wrote the *Manchester Guardian* correspondent, men were dying every day, the fields around being already strewn with the carcasses of dead mules. The mistral blew so strongly that it was difficult to stand up in it and sand and litter of all sorts were continually blown into one's face. He, too, described the little hollows the men had dug for themselves as shelters: 'as ineffective as children's sand-castles'. And when the *News Chronicle* correspondent returned to the scene a week later, on 20 February, he described it as 'a new Hell on earth'. 'The human degradation', he wrote, 'and the misery and suffering are almost beyond the power of one mind to grasp.'

Though the French made some effort to provide temporary accommodation, it was of only the scantiest sort, some second-hand circus wagons being provided, for instance, at Argelès. But the feeling was inescapable for many that the French authorities were not anxious to make the camps too bearable, lest France be burdened indefinitely with the task of somehow supporting this forlorn army. Every day loudspeakers went into the camps inviting those who wanted to be sent to a Nationalist Spain to present themselves at the gate. According to *The Times*, cries of 'Long live the Republic!' came in response, but as the morning wore on more and more men lined up for repatriation, to be sent in trains to Hendaye or in lorries to the Catalan frontier. Some 60,000 had been repatriated by the end of the first fortnight in February, many of them to find other concentration camps 'of rehabilitation' waiting for them on the Franco side of the frontier. But the bulk of them, now about 150,000, remained where the tide of war had brought them, human flotsam on the windy and litter-strewn Mediterranean beaches while the world wondered whether the government of that Republic for which they had fought could continue to survive, holding now as it did only about one quarter of the country's territory in central Spain.

A bizarre further humiliation awaited some seventy-six officers and two men of the once crack Enrique Lister brigade. On leaving Figueras castle, last seat of the Spanish Cortes, Lister had ordered them, before blowing up that edifice, to load themselves with as much of the castle's jewellery and gold treasure as they could carry. Their further orders were, on crossing the frontier, to deliver this treasure in the name of the Spanish Republic to the Spanish Consulate at Perpignan. Understandably in the circumstances some succumbed to the temptation to forget to do this. They were arrested for smuggling by the French authorities, and given prison sentences. The correspondent of the London *Daily Herald*, a former International Brigader, even found himself under arrest among them for a time.

A more successful salvage of national treasure had taken place when, as one of the last acts of government in Figueras, the Foreign Minister Álvarez del Vayo had agreed that the League of Nations should take the pictures from the Prado which had accompanied the retreating Government in a number of lorries on the hazardous road from Barcelona, and transport them to Geneva. At the moment of signing the document in Figueras there had been an air-raid and the electricity had been cut off so that it had to be signed by the light of matches. But the paintings of Velásquez, Goya, El Greco and others were successfully brought across the frontier, surviving sporadic air-raids, and safely transported to Geneva.

While the President of the Republic, Azaña, stayed in Paris, the Prime Minister, Negrín, and his colleagues returned to Madrid after flying from Toulouse to Valencia on a regular flight with Air France. They arrived in the middle of an intense artillery bombardment in which a hundred shells fell on the city, mainly damaging the Calle Alcalá where cafés and cinemas were hit and sixteen people killed in a cinema queue. Half an hour before midnight Negrín issued a declaration: 'In this decisive moment all depends on unity. I recall to you the spirit of resistance which has immortalized Madrid throughout the war. The spirit must be extended to all that remains of uninvaded Spain.'

An understandably desperate note was entering the Republican rallying-cries. Álvarez del Vayo had given an interview to the French paper *Le Populaire* the week before. 'Nothing can ban the Republic from our hearts and from the hearts of the immense majority of our heroic people. The Republic will win in the end.' In Madrid itself, General Miaja, now Supreme Commander-in-Chief, in a similar cry had however voiced what was now probably the principal serious hope of the Republicans, namely that a European crisis in which the democracies, with America's support, were ranged against the Fascist powers would rescue the Government from its dire predicament.

'As long as there is a plot of ground left in my zone,' he had said on 7 February, 'we shall fight on and I hope as we hold out that the democracies will become convinced that it is on our Republican soil that the future of millions of people outside Spain will ultimately be decided.'

Oblique confidence of this sort was not just confined to the minds of Negrín and his colleagues. From Perpignan the correspondent of the *New York Times*, Herbert Matthews, told those of his readers who might be thinking the Republic's situation hopeless and capitulation near that 'everything points to the contrary possibility'. In the first place, he said, Franco had nowhere expressed any merciful intentions towards any soldiers of the Republic except drafted ones, or to any civilians except those who had taken no part in the war on the Government's side. This did not encourage surrender. Secondly the Loyalists (as he called them) had the deepest and sincerest convictions for which they were willing to die. Finally with the possibility of a European war in the spring the Loyalists felt sure they could hold on until April and May. 'Who knows', wrote Matthews, 'what will happen in Europe before then?'

The *Manchester Guardian* correspondent in Madrid reported on the day of Negrín and Álvarez del Vayo's arrival there: 'The morale of the people remains high. Even during the critical days in Catalonia there was little sign of wavering. Newspapers are unanimous that the government is still strong.'

In parts of the international press there did begin to appear rumours that Miaja was considering negotiations with Franco in return for guarantees that there would be no reprisals against the defeated. The *New York Times* man in Paris, disregarding his colleague Matthews, had even reported on 8 February: 'All indications are that the Spanish Civil War will be over in the next two days.' And the *Manchester Guardian* itself wrote on 20 February in a leader which likewise by-passed its correspondent's report of high Republican morale: 'One thing seems certain of the Spanish Civil War – that it will quickly end.'

Yet when the *News Chronicle* correspondent, William Forrest, interviewed Miaja in Madrid on 23 February and asked him how things were going, Miaja – a man of 'few words' according to Forrest – said: 'It is the business of the Government to talk, mine to act. I can tell you in one word how things are going with us: they are going fine.' He admitted that things had been difficult after Catalonia but Valencia, he said, was a different proposition and Madrid was Madrid.

The Communists on the Government side of course spoke on a harsher, though equally confident note. Jesús Hernández, once Minister of Public Instruction and now Chief Commissar for the Republican armies in Valencia, declaimed at a public meeting: 'All that we have so far sacrificed for the independence and liberty of our land is little in comparison with what we have to give. Let no one waste time looking for a frontier by which to escape. We have lost the frontier and we have got to reconquer it.'

Barcelona, he said, was lost not because the army hadn't fought well – the army of the Ebro had fought like tigers – but because the rearguard had not mobilized itself in time with defences for the army to fall back on. The citizens of Valencia must see that the same thing did not happen there.

The *New York Times* correspondent in Paris again ventured a forecast on 25 February – even bolder than his premature assessment of the 8th. This time he wrote: 'The end of the long Spanish Civil War appeared to be only a matter of hours away tonight.'

Yet, when William Forrest reported for the *News Chronicle* from Madrid on 27 February, he was able to do so as if the Republic was in no particular distress at all. The official communiqué of that day read as it had done for some days past: 'All quiet on the various fronts.' Only a few spasmodic bursts of fire in fact came from the University City. The sun was shining and bootblacks at the Puerta del Sol plied their trade on the sunny side of the square. Workmen were repairing parts of the tram-tracks damaged in last week's shelling. The bar at the Ritz was crowded with officers arriving by car from the front only ten minutes away, from which they were able to ring and book seats for the theatre. Someone was advertising in the newspapers the loss of a dachshund 'answering to the name of Maus'. Forrest was unable to get food at the Ritz, where he had a room, but he could get soup and bread at another hotel. He met Dolores Ibarruri, 'La Pasionaria'. 'We will fight on,' she said. 'We fully realize how grave the situation is but place our confidence in the people. And we still have confidence in the democratic forces of the world. Some day we hope they will rally to our help. Meanwhile we carry on with the fight.'

But the democratic forces of the world had already given them up for lost. On the very day on which Forrest wrote his dispatch both France and Britain recognized General Franco as the legitimate Government of Spain and the United States and other countries quickly followed suit.

For people on the Left in Europe and the United States, the democratic idealism symbolized by the Spanish Republic had always tended to obscure the shortcomings of its Government's political reality. Conversely, for people on the Right, less inclined by disposition towards abstract idealism, political reality had always tended to obscure the appeal of an idealistic democratic cause. Now, the reality of the Republic's stark predicament lent desperation to the Left's idealistic aspirations and consolidated the unsentimental pragmatism of the Right.

Of course the Left and particularly the British Left did its best to give their cherished ideological symbolism a realistic appearance. Thus, in an article in the *News Chronicle* on the last day of January, a month before recognition of Franco, but when the débâcle in Catalonia was virtually complete, Philip Jordan had written:

Today the greater part of Spain is under German and Italian control ... the French now have a third front to defend – the Pyrenees. .... As for Britain, a glance at the map indicates the tremendous threat to our country a Fascist regime in Spain must mean

– both in the Mediterranean and even on the long sea route. The safety of the British people is quite literally at stake in the Spanish struggle, and the British people are being forced by their Government to stand by impotently while their safety is destroyed.

Attlee himself, the Labour Opposition leader, had made the same point in the debate on the adjournment in the House of Commons that day, deploring what he called 'the growing opinion in the country that the Government had made up its mind that it wanted General Franco to win …' Many people, he said, were beginning to realize that if Spain became more dependent on the Axis powers the strategic consequences to Britain and France were very serious indeed.

Chamberlain on the other hand emphasized the pragmatic attitude of the Right almost to the point of cynicism when he declared of the refugee influx then gaining momentum across the Pyrenees: 'No one could read accounts of the pitiless procession of wounded men, old men, women and children, some of them mutilated, struggling up the mountains which divide France from Spain in conditions of terror, without feeling what a terrible thing war is, even in its secondary effects and how much more it would mean if hostilities were extended.' Conservative cheers greeted this skilful humanitarian defence of appeasement. The Prime Minister neatly went on to state his conviction that a removal of the arms embargo in favour of the Spanish Government 'must inevitably lead to an extension of the conflict in Europe'.

A demonstration took place in the streets of London that day with thousands (including 'hundreds of women, young and old, some in fur coats', according to the *Daily Express*) chanting 'Arms for Spain' in a quarter-mile-long column. It hardly carried any serious hope of persuading Neville Chamberlain to change his mind but did successfully vent indignation at the Government's attitude. Some demonstrators stormed buses, and the unemployed even slipped a coffin into the precincts of the House of Commons. Restaurants closed the grilles of their doors, fearing invasion. The police – a hundred mounted and fifteen hundred on foot – were accused of using unnecessary force. The Bow Street magistrate with cold reason next day told those demonstrators who had been arrested for lying down in Piccadilly: 'You will only get run over if you lie down in Piccadilly and it will make no difference to the people of Spain.'

Also that day 3,000 people in Liverpool expressed the city's 'indignation at the Prime Minister's connivance in the murder of the Spanish people and the capture of Barcelona by Mussolini', demanding 'Arms for Spain', a neutral zone for refugees, and the Prime Minister's resignation. Headed by a loudspeaker van they proceeded to the Italian Consulate in Liverpool to express their detestation of the Italian invasion of Spain. However, the Italian Consul underlined the emptiness of their demands and indeed of this particular gesture, by not being there. The Spanish Republican Consul was at home, though – not to be replaced

Clement Attlee, leader of the Labour Party, deplores recognition for Franco, in Trafalgar Square, London.

Some of Britain's two million unemployed chain themselves to the railings of Stepney Labour Exchange.

by Franco's representative until official British recognition ousted him at the end of the month – and when the demonstrators arrived to see him he thanked them for their support.

This meeting had been organized by an Association of the International Brigade, of which the last remnants were then on the point of crossing the Pyrenees into France. Seven hundred of them came through on 7 February, to be reviewed by the French Communist leader André Marty and the Italian Socialist Pietro Nenni. Three hundred Italians came through singing 'Bandiera Rossa' and 170 Americans, Canadians and Britons singing the Internationale, though some British had come through the day before singing 'Tipperary'.

The British Government had felt its way towards recognition of Franco with some hope of acting as a mediator between him and the Republicans. There had been a small rehearsal of such a role when on 8 February the British cruiser *Devonshire* had gone to Minorca, the important strategic island which, unlike Majorca, had remained in Republican hands. There the Captain negotiated a settlement between representatives of the two sides on the island, which was handed over bloodlessly to Franco while several hundred Republicans and their families were allowed to withdraw on the *Devonshire* to safety. The action was carried out after full consultation with Paris. Although the smoothness of the operation was marred by an air-raid on Minorca during the course of the negotiations, this, it transpired, was evidence not of duplicity on Franco's part but of irritation on the part of the Italians whose aircraft based on Majorca next door carried out the raid on their own initiative. The Italian press openly expressed resentment of this British 'intervention'. The German press too, sneered at what it saw as an attempt by Britain to sneak into Franco's favour after all this time, hoping to benefit financially from his commercial needs, and acquire strategic advantage for France in the Mediterranean.

The one concession which the hard-pressed Spanish Republicans might hope to gain from Franco in return for an agreement to cease fighting was some guarantee of lack of reprisal for their two-and-a-half-year resistance, and some gesture of national reconciliation. It was in this respect that the British and French Governments hoped to present their good offices. There was little news to date of what was happening to Republicans in the parts of Spain newly occupied by Franco. The Republic's Senior Prosecutor in Barcelona had been captured and given what seemed like a fair trial before being convicted, sentenced to death and executed. But since he himself had been responsible for the sentencing to death and execution of many Franco supporters this did not seem to detached observers an unreasonable occurrence. Franco himself had, for all his notorious list of one or two million wanted names, always insisted that only those among the Republicans who had committed crimes themselves had anything to fear. His supporters in the democracies continued to express confidence that his attitude would be as merciful as could reasonably be expected and his procedures correct. However, a personal statement which he issued on 22 February dampened hopes that democratic governments might be able to intercede successfully on behalf of defeated Republicans. He declared that:

> The Press of neighbouring countries which has been an accomplice of all the crimes and all the robberies committed by the Reds should have the decency to be silent now. Its flattery today offends me more than its abuse in the past, and this press dares to give me counsels of 'moderation'. It is as vile as the people it has so far defended.

Thus when on Monday 27 February official recognition was finally given to Franco by both British and French governments they were in almost as weak a position *vis-à-vis* Franco as their own Opposition was *vis-à-vis* them. In the House of Commons the Labour Opposition leader, Clement Attlee, tried to make the constitutional point that the Cabinet had not sufficiently consulted the House of Commons before coming to their decision, but this point was enfeebled by the knowledge that the House of Commons had, as was shown in the Chamber that day, a solid majority for the action. Attlee had made the main emotional point effectively in a big demonstration by Labour in Trafalgar Square the day before.

'By their action', he had declared, 'the British Government have not only betrayed the Spanish people but democracy throughout the world. All must feel degraded at the way the British Government has sold the Spanish people.'

The Square had been packed and after the speeches there was a march to Downing Street with routine shouts of 'Arms for Spain!' and 'Chamberlain must go!' Attlee and Herbert Morrison personally took the demonstrators' resolution of protest to Number Ten. But the weakness of the British Left as an effective realistic force was revealed in the course of the speeches themselves when Herbert Morrison in particular, speaking for orthodox Labour, was continually interrupted by Communists and supporters of Stafford Cripps and his Popular Front.

The *News Chronicle*, the following Tuesday, said the decision to recognize Franco followed logically on Government policy which for two and a half years had connived at Franco's Fascist insurrection and placed every possible obstacle in the way of Spanish democracy's legitimate defence. Recognition was 'a shameful culmination of one of the blackest chapters in this country's history'.

For all this, as William Forrest was showing in the same paper, the Spanish Republic was itself still not dead; and a sense of international unease remained. This had been partially stilled by Hitler's generally pacific speech of 30 January, but the general cause for it remained in that sense of still-unfulfilled and as yet inexactly defined aspiration of some sort on the part of the Italian and German dictatorships. To this there was added the uneasy contradiction in British policy to which the Labour peer, Lord Strabolgi, had drawn attention at the Trafalgar Square meeting.

Referring to increased expenditure for the armaments programme which Chamberlain had just announced in the House of Commons, he pointed out that while Britain's present and future credit was pledged to piling up arms, she was at the same time destroying her natural allies: first Czechoslovakia, where she had lost the help of a million men and a thousand planes, and now Spain.

Chamberlain replied to such charges by saying that the armaments were there as a precaution, lest the dictatorships should be so unwise as not to take advantage of his own conciliatory approach. Yet this stance was weakened by a persistent refusal to accept such lack of wisdom on the part of the dictators as likely.

'Perhaps', said Chamberlain during the Commons debate on the armaments programme on 21 February, 'it would not be a bad thing if we ourselves were to show a little more confidence, and not allow ourselves to believe every tale that comes to us about the aggressive intentions of others.'

And he appeared to undermine his own belief in the necessity of stepping up the armaments programme when he went on: 'If it be true that others have no more intention of aggression than we have, then the conclusion we must come to is that we are now piling up these ruinous armaments under a misunderstanding. I am very much inclined to believe that there is a great deal of truth in that statement.'

That day the King launched the new battleship named after his father, George V, at Newcastle and the Admiralty announced the placing of orders for two new battleships of the same size. The *Manchester Guardian* commented:

> It has always been a mystery how Mr Chamberlain can on the one hand order huge armaments (£1,500,000,000 to be spent) and on the other apparently erase from his mind at will the events which explain his action. It seems sometimes as if yesterday's statement that he believes that the various 'assurances' he has received have closed an evil chapter, produced a moral revolution and brought the days of aggression to an end. But the aggression is not at an end; it is still there. Japan still wages the most barbarous of wars against China; Mussolini and Hitler still brutally crush the Republicans in Spain; Hitler still pledges his help ... to Mussolini if he makes demands on France.

Chamberlain himself saw no inconsistency in his policy, principally because he sincerely believed that the essential importance of that policy lay in having obtained those assurances which closed an evil chapter. He made this clear when he spoke on Wednesday 22 February at Blackburn. He was speaking admittedly in an area of high unemployment, when the national unemployment figure had reached a total of 2,039,026 (by 17 January) and in Blackburn the figure was, some estimated, as high as 30% of the working population. But there was a personal belief deeper than political opportunism behind his speech:

> It is a most significant fact that the easing of international tension which made itself felt after the German Chancellor's speech at the end of last month produced an instantaneous improvement in the trade reports ... that is a circumstance which coupled with the prospect of a speedy termination to the Spanish war and various other indications, encourages me to hope that the forces making for an upturn in the

Winston Churchill on the sidelines, February 1939.

trend of trade may be allowed this year to have an opportunity of developing their effect unhampered by political anxiety. If I am right we shall find the reward of our foreign policy not only in a more settled peace of mind but also in the increase of employment among our people.

A fortnight earlier, Sir Horace Wilson, the senior civil servant who had so closely advised Chamberlain at the time of Munich, had been promoted Permanent Secretary to the Treasury and head of the Civil Service. *The Times* had then commented that for all his new administrative responsibilities his special functions were likely to continue. Something of his closeness to the Prime Minister's ear could perhaps be sensed in the Blackburn speech and in Chamberlain's words in the Commons the day before.

Other democratic statesmen were less sanguine about prospects on the international scene. This was made dramatically clear when President Roosevelt, two days before Chamberlain's speech at Blackburn, announced suddenly that he might well have to cut short the fortnight's cruise on which he was embarked with the US fleet because of 'disturbing reports from Europe'. According to the *New York Times* man in London the British were perplexed by this statement. No particularly alarming news seemed to have come in in the last few days and the outlook was even slightly more hopeful than it had been. Certainly Chamberlain in his Blackburn speech had shown no signs of being perturbed by any developments. However, the *New York Times* leader-writer of 19 February may well have reflected something of the US Government's feeling when he wrote that the swift development in Spain had created a situation in which a new test of strength of rival views and theories might be expected. Italy feared that Britain and France might now gain some favour with Franco because what he wanted was money and markets. 'The belief', wrote the paper, 'that Italy may be excluded from a share in the fruits of Franco's success unless a bold step is taken now may prompt Mussolini to gamble at this time on a showdown over his long-developed claims for new power in the Mediterranean.' Next day came news that France, in reply to an increase of Italian troop strength in Libya to nearly 90,000 men, had put her own forces in Africa on the alert. She had also re-occupied an area between French Somaliland and Italian Eritrea once ceded to (though not accepted by) Italy. The *New York Times* commented:

> At least one thing is clear. The situation today is no mere parallel of that leading up to Munich. In that earlier series of events the demands of the totalitarian powers were at the expense of a third party, the small State of Czechoslovakia. This time the demands could be granted only at the direct expense of France itself. ... Moreover this time it is the weaker of the two Axis powers that is making the demands.

'Fresh war crisis near, Paris Fears', was a headline in the paper three days later, as the presence in Tripoli of several German generals was reported, together with news of French troop reinforcements and the arrival of the French Mediterranean fleet at Bizerta.

The German *Börsenzeitung* played down immediately what it called 'theatrical confusion' in Washington. The American President, it said, was grasping at any measure to save his tottering position and systematically attempting to sow unrest in the world. The *Nachtausgabe* commented: 'Europe's desire for peace will prove to be greater than all the efforts of certain American circles to find a way out of their own financial and political difficulties.'

By contrast German press reaction to Chamberlain's speech at Blackburn was sympathetic. The *Deutsche Allgemeine Zeitung* spoke of it as a warning to American 'war-inciters', approving particularly the passage in which the Prime Minister had said that Britons should not let themselves believe any tale that came to their ears about the aggressive intentions of others. And in reply to a broadcast by Senator Pitman, Chairman of the Senate Foreign Affairs Committee, in which he had charged Germany, Italy and Japan unequivocally with aggressive intentions, the paper declared: 'There is one fundamental difference between Mr Chamberlain and President Roosevelt – the Prime Minister's sense of responsibility for Europe.'

Although there were indeed clear differences of emphasis in personal style between the approaches of Chamberlain and Roosevelt to the international problem of the dictators, it seemed little more than wishful thinking for the Axis press to perceive any essential disharmony in policy. The *New York Times* leader-writer summed up the harmony that prevailed on 21 February when he wrote, with a curious look back to other days, that it was one of the signs of the present times and of changed values in the contemporary world that the present greatest of all British armament programmes should cause no concern

> on our side of the Atlantic. . . . We do not ask for parity as we once did in this or that category of naval strength. We welcome it. For we know that while there can be no question of an alliance between the British and ourselves, the facts of geography and the lessons of history have created a common interest between Britain and the United States. That common interest is an orderly and stable world.

That forces for instability continued to be active was shown by the Italian *Telegrafo*, which two days later warned France that she would be 'led to the slaughterhouse on the day the Anglo-Saxon nations decide on a war to make the world safe for democracy'.

Speculation as to what might be about to happen was compulsive in the press and elsewhere.

'What is the aim of the Axis powers?' wrote the diplomatic correspondent of the *Manchester Guardian* on 27 February. 'To secure acceptance of the German and Italian hold over Spain as well as such concessions in Tunis, for example, and perhaps in the African colonies as will make Germany in conjunction with Italy what she has never been: a Mediterranean power. Then the next step, German and Italian domination of the Mediterranean and North Africa can be attempted.' He spoke of the prospect of a 'Mediterranean Munich' and then prophesied that Germany would turn against Rumania because discontent within Germany over the economy was increasing and she needed further conquests to help her enlarge her supplies of raw material, foodstuffs and oil.

Chamberlain himself had, of course, added to the speculation by his Commons speech about armaments on 21 February particularly when, in foreshadowing the need to borrow £800 million to meet what he called 'the ruinous costs' of armament he had spoken of '. . . the folly of the course we are all pursuing, which if persisted in must bring bankruptcy to every country in Europe . . .' and then, with unusual emphasis, had added: 'In my view it would be criminal to allow this situation to go on developing as it has been developing without making some determined effort to stop it.' This left Members of the House of Commons wondering whether, as the *News Chronicle* put it, 'the Prime Minister had anything up his sleeve'. And uncertainty as much about the defensive posture of the democracies as about the aggressive aspirations of the dictatorships continued to contribute to the unease.

Attlee, the Opposition leader, said in the House of Commons that day:

> In spite of the spirit of complacency shown by the Prime Minister, there is a widespread feeling in the country that he has sacrificed moral principles of the utmost importance. . . . There are hundreds of young people who wish to bear their part in the defence of the country, who are discouraged and hesitating because they do not believe that the present Government stands for the real thing for which this country ought to stand.

A few days earlier, the Berlin correspondent of the *News Chronicle* had written that Hitler was said to be undecided at present between brusquely challenging the western democracies on a Mediterranean issue and risking US intervention – a policy said to be recommended by Ribbentrop – and a more moderate policy – said to be recommended by Goering – which would take advantage of the deadlock in the Mediterranean to consolidate Germany's position in the east. Responsible circles in Berlin, he wrote, judged that it was not yet possible for Germany to fight the western powers and survive.

The German press seemed to bear him out. Goebbels in the *Völkischer Beobachter* was running a peace campaign rather like that of the London *Daily Express*. 'The totalitarian states', he wrote, 'are peace-loving and are not playing any ideological crusade against the democracies.' And the *Frankfurter Zeitung* wrote: 'No European government is engaging on a warlike policy. Everybody wants peace in Europe.'

The *Daily Express* itself had in fact been lately rather more war-conscious in its approach, though only possibly because it found itself with an opportunity to carp at Britain's presumed allies in any war, the French. Chamberlain, in reply to a question in the House of Commons at the time of the arrival of Franco's forces at the Pyrenees, had given a pledge that any threat to the vital interests of France, from whatever quarter, would evoke immediate cooperation from Britain. On 20 February the *Express* leader commented: 'The French Government ask us to send an army to the Continent if we are required to implement our pledge of assistance to France. The country is utterly opposed to such an expedition. . . . The war of the future will be decided in the air. Britain will hold the waterways and defend the cities. France must look after her own frontiers'.

Thus all speculated, all wondered, all waited without the certainty that there was anything specific to wait for. Journalists in all countries indulged the acknowledged freedom of their trade to sound more prescient than they really were. None however seemed so concerned with urgency as to have to invoke the cliché of the Ides of March, a calendar date which was in any case over a fortnight away.

12

What even the democracies, infected verbally at least by the racialist policies of the dictatorships, had to call the 'Jewish problem' remained an awkwardly constant feature on the international scene, for all the general unpredictability of events. The problem for Britain was made doubly awkward by her involvement in the League of Nations Mandate in Palestine. Many Jews, and the official Zionist organization itself, impatient with British restrictions on immigration, saw Palestine not only as a natural refuge from German persecution but one to which they had literally a God-given right. But the British authorities there were engaged in fighting a dangerous Arab revolt for having allowed into the country as many Jewish settlers as they had done (300,000 since 1920, of whom 40,000 were recent Germans). That such a confrontation with the Arabs had come about as the result of an ambiguous policy pursued by earlier British governments, designed to please both Jew and Arab in the interests of Britain, was now only of historical relevance. The present reality was that Britain found herself trapped in an attitude which pleased neither party; and the new moral factor introduced by German persecution of the Jews was something which the Arabs saw no reason to acknowledge as their concern.

This arid prospect for Palestine was reflected in the total deadlock with which the conference opened by the British Government in London in February had ended and in which it had indeed been gripped from the very start. The British never even managed to get the Jews and Arabs to sit together and were obliged to present their own third-party views to each delegation separately, together with those of the opposing delegation. None of these proved reconcilable.* The British could do nothing but work out their own proposals which they prepared to publish in a White Paper. Meanwhile they had to continue to deal with the Arab revolt.

There had been sixty-nine British soldiers and police killed in Palestine in 1938; seven Military Crosses and fourteen Military Medals were about to be awarded for gallantry there. Some British people, feeling that their country's shouldering of responsibility in that land had already been painful enough, and aware that charity, through the Lord Baldwin Fund, was giving what it could to help refugees settle in Britain and elsewhere, saw no particular reason why they should feel further excessive individual obligation to deal with the 'problem'.

In any case, machinery for dealing with it on an international basis – the so-

---

*Weizmann had presented the Zionist case with the words: 'The fate of 6,000,000 people is in the balance ...'

called Inter-Governmental Committee for Refugees – had already been established in July 1938 when the meeting of thirty-two countries had taken place in Evian. It had however immediately become apparent then that the concern of these countries was as much to protect themselves from the difficulties created by the problem as to solve it. The London *Times* ran an article which said that the governments, faced with a migration comparable with the great migrations of history, recognized it as a serious menace to themselves. It went on:

> The fears of the governments are only too apparent; their task of economic self-protection is complicated by the risk that in opening the doors they may themselves help to create minorities and thereby stimulate anti-Jewish centres. It is this that leads them to hedge all their proposals with conditions and contribute to the general stock the absolute minimum of practical measures. They seem prepared to exchange information to any extent but not to declare a positive policy. Several countries have declared that in the matter of accepting refugees they have now reached the stage of saturation.

The Americans had made a gesture at the beginning of the 1938 conference by increasing their quota for German immigrants to 27,3000 per year. But the British representative, the Chancellor of the Duchy of Lancaster, Lord Winterton, had stressed the limited extent to which co-operation could be given by Great Britain or by the British Colonies or Dominions. The British Government, he said, were 'stretching their policies as far as they could in view of the economic situation of the country'. By mid November 1938, 11,000 German-Jewish refugees had been allowed to settle in Britain and some 4,000 to pass through it. But over half a million Jews altogether were seeking refuge from Germany.

South American countries at the Evian conference had expressed sympathy and a willingness to continue liberal policies towards the Jews but also a determination not to allow any mass migration that would dislocate their own labour markets or establish any large new individual community within their borders. The conference had ended with a summary of the situation from the League of Nations High Commissioner for Refugees in which, pointing out that since 1933 150,000 refugees had left Germany and 120,000 had found asylum, he said that there was very little chance of any large-scale settlement being carried through in any of the overseas countries and that infiltration was likely to produce better results than mass migrations.

An interesting feature of that conference had been the presence of two delegates from the Jewish community in Vienna who had come, obviously with the approval of the German Government, to which they were authorized to report back on any specific proposals for a wider opening of doors on the part of the receiving countries. This, of course, was the embarrassing aspect of the problem for the rest of the world, as Hitler pointed out in his speech of 30 January 1939 – or, as Goebbels had already put it: 'We want the rest of the world to be so friendly to Jews as to take our German Jews off our hands.'

Many British consciences were disturbed. In the House of Commons, after the Evian conference a Conservative Member, Captain Cazalet, had declared: 'History will condemn many of this generation for the appalling sins of commission against the Jews but we shall also have to answer for the sins of omission if we fail to find a solution.'

The statement had been greeted with cheers all round the House. But Lord Winterton, the Government Minister responsible, in the same debate had again revealed how circumspect it seemed necessary to be.

'Most careful and delicate treatment', he said, 'is required if the position of these most unfortunate people in their country of origin is not to be made worse. Mere denunciation of those responsible for the circumstances in which these people find themselves will not benefit them.'

The aim, he said, must be to regulate emigration rather than suffer chaotic traffic from Germany, and infiltration of other countries rather than mass emigration to them should be the governing principle. He went on:

'We live in an age of intense suspicion, acute nationalism and every sort of restriction of economic character, and to declare against mass emigration is not to show any anti-Semitism but rather to accept the facts.'

Of the five applications in the Domestic Situations Required column of *The Times* on the day he made that speech, all were from Viennese Jewesses, taking advantage of the arrangement between the Home Office and the Ministry of Labour by which entry permits could be secured for refugees seeking to maintain themselves by such or similar-type work. Otherwise every refugee had to have his or her self-sufficiency guaranteed, either by individuals or by a charitable organization.

The barbaric pogrom organized by the German authorities against Jews after the murder of a German diplomat in Paris by a Jew in November 1938 had troubled the consciences of the world anew. The British House of Commons then passed an all-party motion deploring the pogrom and declaring that in view of the growing gravity of the refugee problem it would welcome an immediate concerted effort among the nations, including the United States of America, to secure a common policy. However, no spokesman for the Government had been able to show any very fundamental change in attitude. Samuel Hoare, the Home Secretary, who at the end of his speech had been congratulated for his handling of the matter by Labour Members, had spoken of the large number of unemployed and the inevitably keen competition with foreign countries which, he said, made it 'difficult for any of our fellow-countrymen to make a livelihood' and the 'also underlying current of suspicion and anxiety about any immigration on a big scale'. It was a fact, he said, that there was the making of a definite anti-Jewish movement and that this was to be seen not only among Fascists: 'I have to be careful to avoid anything in the nature of mass immigration. That would inevitably lead to the growth of a movement which we all wish to see suppressed . . .'

The Prime Minister himself had been unable to offer any large constructive proposals, though he had made some tentative suggestions. In principle, he had said, the number which Great Britain could agree to admit either for a temporary stay or for permanent settlement was limited by the capacity of the voluntary organizations dealing with the refugee problem to undertake the responsibility of selecting, receiving and maintaining them. There was no territory in the Colonial Empire where suitable land was available for the immediate settlement of refugees in large-scale numbers, so the interests of the millions of natives there must not be prejudiced. There were, however, certain territories where there were small-scale possibilities, and he mentioned that the Governor of Tanganyika was prepared to consider the possibility of settlement on 50,000 acres in the Southern Highlands and the Western Province. Similarly there were possibilities for small-scale settlement in Northern Rhodesia and Nyasaland, while one small experiment had already been started in Kenya. The best prospects seemed to lie in an area of at least 10,000 square miles and possibly more of British Guiana, but careful surveys would have to be made there first because of the unfavourable conditions in some areas and the lack of communications. He welcomed the fact that voluntary organizations were going to send out representatives to conduct such a survey.

'Finally', he said, 'I must mention Palestine. It is generally recognized that that small country could not in any case provide a solution of the Jewish refugee problem; but Palestine has been making its contribution.'

The same evening Lord Winterton broadcast to the United States on the subject, saying that special facilities were being granted by the British government for the admission of large numbers of Jewish and non-Aryan children under seventeen for education in Britain. Britain was, he announced, with an obvious feeling of generosity, taking as many as the voluntary organizations could provide for. But he did remind his listeners that the number of people for whom emigration from Germany must somehow be made possible was 600,000 and that it was out of the question for any one government to do more than touch the fringes of the problem.

Other fringes were touched at a meeting of the Inter-Governmental (Evian) Sub-Committee in London at which it was announced that France might be prepared to take 10,000 for Madagascar and that Australia would take 15,000 over three years. There were said to be 'hopeful prospects' in Argentina and Brazil, and the United States itself had announced that it was extending the temporary visas of some 12,000 to 15,000 Jews, whose visas were due to expire, for another six months and beyond if necessary, because it was unthinkable to allow them to be sent back to Germany. Meanwhile *The Times* on 22 December 1938 looked objectively at the financial conditions which the Germans insisted on imposing on emigrating Jews.

'Without palliating in any way', it wrote, 'the cruel exactions ... it must be admitted that Germany's difficulties in procuring an adequate supply of foreign exchange have been a plausible excuse for not allowing would-be emigrants to take with them more than an insignificant fraction of their money.'

It added that many Jews in Germany with friends abroad willing to help provide them with opportunities to earn a living were being prevented from getting out of the country by the entanglements of red tape on the British side.

As for Palestine, just before the February Conference opened the *Daily Express*, a highly successful populist organ of the period, was to declare:

> The Jews must realize that the Arabs are the native people of the country. The fact that the Jews settled in Palestine thousands of years ago should not give them priority now. The Romans settled in Britain two thousand years ago. But that does not mean that the Italian restaurateurs in Soho can claim the right to control the Government in Soho. .... The immediate solution of the problem depends on the prohibition of any more Jewish immigrants into Palestine.

Thus the important question remained as always: where were the Jews to go? This and not any unwillingness in principle on the part of the Germans to let them go was the central difficulty, though the Germans much aggravated the difficulty by their insistence on extracting almost all their money from them before doing so. But on the face of it the German attitude was straightforward enough.

'The Jewish problem will be solved only when the last Jew has left Germany,' Alfred Rosenberg, Head of the Nazi Party Foreign Section, repeated in Berlin on the day the Palestine Conference opened in London.

Negotiations between George Rublee, the American lawyer President of the Inter-Governmental Committee and the German Government continued from the middle of January, seeming to reach something of an impasse over the extortionate German financial conditions. They were then interrupted by the surprise dismissal of Dr Schacht from office – though his dismissal was clearly for high political and economic reasons unconnected with the negotiations themselves. In fact Goering himself told Rublee that it did not mean negotiations were broken off, and they were resumed on 25 January in Berlin with a new German representative, Helmuth Wohltat, so-called specialist for 'Aryanization problems in the Four-Year Plan'.

The *New York Times* reported that the talks began again in an optimistic atmosphere. Nothing less than 'the evacuation of Jews from Germany' was the subject under discussion and though the meetings had to be suspended over the following weekend this was not because there was a hitch, but because Dr Wohltat had to refer everything back to his superiors. Circles close to Rublee expected negotiations to be completed in the following week.

Meanwhile signs of positive German co-operation could be interpreted from an agreement reached with the Poles over 10,000 Polish Jews. These had been due to be brusquely deported from Germany to join a similar number living unwanted after such deportation in primitive camps on the Polish side of the border. The Germans were now prepared to give the new batch time to 'liquidate their businesses', after which they would have to leave by the end of July, taking only any property they could carry with them. Their money and the value of any real estate they possessed had to be paid into blocked accounts in Germany which would be subject to negotiations later. Harsh though such terms were, the decision did amount by contemporary German standards to some recognition of humanitarian sensibilities. For those hopeful, as George Rublee was, of eventually reaching agreement over the evacuation of all Germany's Jews, further optimistic indications could be discerned from the fact that ever since mid-December groups of Jews had been released from concentration camps in Dachau and Buchenwald and had been arriving in Vienna, most of them with their emigration formalities ready to be completed. One such group had arrived in Vienna on 21 January: 110 men of all ages from nineteen to sixty-one. Eye-witnesses described them as looking tanned after work in the open, many of them weak and fatigued, but not in ill-health. All those released would say was that they had had enough to eat but that work had been very hard.

Zionists themselves emphasized that the core of the 'problem' lay not in getting the Germans to agree to let the Jews go, but in the extortionate and humiliating terms on which they were prepared to do so. Even while the Rublee negotiations were under way again an American Rabbi, Joseph Zeitlin, at a synagogue at 25 West 100th Street, New York, summarized the prospect with haughty idealism: 'That the world would not be willing to pay ransom to Germany for the release of the Jews is evident without question. The resolute refusal on the part of the remains of the civilized world to have any dealings whatsoever with a government that has recourse to the methods of the outlaw is one of the most effective ways to bring humanity back to sanity and justice.'

The World Jewish Congress had been saying the same thing in Paris the week before. Nahum Goldmann had then rejected any 'philanthropic' approach to the question of Jews in Germany, and had specifically criticized the League of Nations for accepting Jews expelled from Danzig.

The Congress's final resolution categorically refused to co-operate in the organization of Jewish emigration with governments which in their dealings with Jewish subjects did not accept the principle of equality of rights, and opposed any settlement of the problem which gave the Third Reich a bonus for the expulsion and expropriation of the Jews. It also firmly rejected any proposal for a Jewish colony in Abyssinia.

But such idealism tended to undermine a sense of urgency about the need, given the restrictions on Palestine, for the Jews to go somewhere. A letter in the London *Times* from a Fellow of Magdalen College, Oxford, made a bold and intelligent attempt to circumvent this central difficulty by proposing the Negev – south of Beersheba. This territory in ancient times, with skilful irrigation, had maintained a large and prosperous agricultural population together with a number of towns; it should be the subject of a bargain between the Arabs and the mandatory power. Only the occasional Bedouin roamed the Beersheba area today, and in return for a promise by the British to cut off all further immigration into the rest of Palestine the Negev could be handed over for settlement to the Jews.

When Chaim Weizmann wrote to *The Times* a few days later he ignored the academic's letter and merely reiterated the traditional Zionist case for Palestine. He did concede that with some half a million to be evacuated from Greater Germany and many millions to come from Eastern Europe no suggestion could be lightly rejected. But, citing failures in Latin America, he stressed that no Jewish settlement anywhere had ever been a success except in Palestine and that Palestine settlement was a success because 'every furrow ploughed there and every tree planted is sanctified into an act of national redemption'.

A lady who had just returned from a comprehensive visit to post-war Jewish settlements in Latin America maintained that, contrary to what Dr Weizmann had suggested, these could be described as in 'a state of renaissance' with the drift to towns among Jews far lower than among other immigrant settlers.

Christopher Sykes wrote to *The Times* to point out the glaring omission in Weizmann's letter. He had never once mentioned the Arabs. 'If the Arab contention that the small size of Palestine limits immigration were admitted ... the newly-settled Jews of Palestine could feel confident in a tranquil country that their future and the future of their country was assured. In a state of continued Arab-Jewish discord, what hope have they?' he asked.

In Britain a relative quickening of the pace was discernible. The Domestic Help columns of *The Times* contained daily applications from Jews in Germany for such posts. The special permission required to work was granted freely to those willing to work as servants and several hundred refugees were admitted weekly in order to do so. Winterton's promises of places for children was being fulfilled. And the *New York Times* reckoned that at the present rate of immigration more than 17,000 Jewish refugees would have been settled in Britain in the twelve months from November 1938 to November 1939. Such numbers, however, represented only a still infinitesimal proportion of the total number in distress.

Demand for access to Palestine, persistent from Zionist organizations, was explicitly articulated by the Jewish representation at the London Palestine Conference. Before sailing to it from New York, Dr Stephen Wise, President of the Zionist Organization of America, had said he hoped Britain would see that in this time of the gravest crisis for Jews in Europe the doors of Palestine must be kept open and that there would be no attempt to limit Jewish immigration there. It was a point of view which had had some interesting support in the States from Jan Masaryk, the former Czech Ambassador to London and now in exile after Munich with his former President, Dr Beneš. Masaryk had addressed the United Palestine Appeal Conference in the Mayflower Hotel, Washington, which had called for a doubling of the admission rate of 50,000 in two and a half years and urged 'as of right under the Mandate and even more of desperate need' the lifting of the temporary restrictions imposed by the British Government. One hundred thousand German refugees could be settled there in 1939. Masaryk in his speech revealed that in private conversations he had had with British colonial administrators they had told him that there was room for many more Jews in Palestine. He added:

> The British are not always given to direct answers or to complete answers, but these people in the privacy of our conversations, when they did not feel that their words might be construed as promises or obligations, assured me that Palestine has room for many more Jews. One distinguished personality mentioned the figure of millions of Jews. ... And this can be done without jeopardizing the rights of the Arabs, without minimizing their opportunity for economic success or national expansion.

It was with some hope of reconciling the latter part of this aspiration with reality that the British Government had called the London Palestine Conference.

George Rublee had left Berlin a few days before the Conference met 'with good hopes that a satisfactory arrangement for Jewish emigration from Germany would be made', and had scheduled a meeting of the Inter-Governmental Committee for 13 February, by which date he hoped a *modus operandi* would have been achieved. On the 13th he unveiled the German plan to the Committee. It was, in the words of the *New York Times*, 'the first time since 1933 that Germany had offered large-scale co-operation in solving the refugee problem forced on the outside world by the advent of the Hitler regime'.

The new plan was for the emigration over three to five years of 150,000 Jewish potential wage-earners aged between fifteen and forty-five. As soon as they were established abroad they could be followed by their wives or children or other dependants. The first aim would thus be fulfilled, of providing regular emigration instead of a panic-stricken flight, and host countries would be ensured of a refugee population that could support itself. The Germans promised that those Jews waiting to emigrate would have the right to work and that, for those wage-earners waiting to go, retraining facilities would be provided. There would be no tax on emigration and all personal belongings might be taken with the exception of jewellery and works of art. A German Commissioner for Refugees was to be appointed; passports would be issued; Jews would be released from concentration camps as soon as emigration began. An assurance was given that the elderly would not be persecuted unless another case similar to the Paris diplomat's murder were to occur. Some Jewish businesses would even be allowed to re-open. Those unable to work would be supported by a trust fund made up from impounded Jewish property consisting of one quarter of all Jewish property left in Germany. This trust fund, which was to be administered by two German trustees and one foreign, would also finance emigration and buy equipment and capital goods for Jews.

Not surprisingly all this was recognized as being a considerable improvement on the terms originally put forward by Dr Schacht. In this way the emigration of all Germany's Jews would be achieved in five years. The Inter-Governmental Committee also gave some run-down of new prospects for settlement then being examined by three Commissions: one for the Philippines which were prepared to absorb 1,000 refugees a year; another for the Dominican Republic which had declared itself ready to accept 100,000; and another in British Guiana where, as Neville Chamberlain himself had stated last November, at least 10,000 square miles were available for settlement. The *New York Times* concluded its account of the meeting optimistically with the words: 'The doors for colonization are now opening. Nothing emerged from the Committee so much as signs that other nations are really willing to take emigrants from Germany – that a few months ago stubbornly refused to open their doors.'

But optimism was tending to blanket reality. Even in Britain a German Social Democrat refugee had only recently been sentenced to a month's imprisonment for being in the country without permission, and an Austrian girl working as a maid in Queen's Gate, Kensington, was to commit suicide because a Scotland Yard Inspector had told her she must leave the country. In Germany itself only ten days after the provisional agreement reached between Rublee and the Inter-Governmental Committee Goering announced new measures against the Jews which seemed a complete contravention of its spirit.

This new German decree stated that before 7 March, i.e. in a fortnight's time, all German and stateless Jews must surrender all jewellery, gold, silver-plate, pearls and other precious stones. All these items including silver tableware were to be declared to special 'agencies', mostly local pawn-shops, where they would be exchanged for compensation to be fixed by the Ministry of Economic Affairs. Failure to comply was punishable by imprisonment with hard labour for a period of up to ten years. A cynical twist was given to the new measures by a statement that they did not contravene any provisional agreement with Dr Rublee, which had promised no new compulsory measures against the Jews; the present decree was technically not new but issued under an Ordinance already made for the registration of Jewish property on 26 April 1938.

In one way certainly this did not seem to augur well for the future. Nevertheless the fact that such cruelty was designed primarily to get the Jews out of the country seemed reinforced by a new decree reported from Berlin the next day ordering the Jewish community there to produce a hundred Jews daily, who would then have to leave the country within fourteen days. Depending on the success of this operation the same principle would be applied throughout the country. The reply of the representatives of the Berlin Jewish community was that they were only able to find places for Jews abroad at the rate of 3,000 a month over the whole country. Now they were being asked to find the same figure for one city alone and this was impossible.

An official German statement then summarized 'progress' to date. Of the 650,000 Jews in Germany when the Nazis came to power, 240,000 had left, but

Adolf Hitler, German Chancellor: '[It is] shameful how the democratic world oozes sympathy for the poor tormented Jewish people, but won't help them.' BELOW His troops enter Wenceslas Square, Prague.

almost as many had been added again by the Anschluss of Austria. Apparently 100,000 had left since the previous November. A glimpse of the precarious future which even 'successful' emigration might hold was given the same day when it was reported that sixty-eight German Jewish refugees arriving in Uruguay by the Italian liner *Conte Grande* had been refused permission to land. Their passport visas, granted in Paris, had been cancelled and they had now to return via Buenos Aires to Europe. Another 165 German Jewish refuges were refused permission to land the same day in Georgetown, British Guiana, one of the very sites on which the Inter-Governmental Committee was hoping to settle large numbers of refugees.

Either way, plainly, the prospect for the Jews of Germany was full of hazard. Advertisements appearing in the newspapers for the Lord Baldwin Fund carried a disturbingly inexplicit undertone: 'Get them out before it is too late!'

13

As the month of March 1939 opened, it was the Mediterranean crisis which still dominated the minds of those concerned with international affairs. Italian newspapers reported from Tunis that trains crowded with French troops were arriving continually from Algiers and were being sent on to the Libyan frontier. War material was being landed; leave was cancelled or cut short; guns were being placed beside railway lines; there were sentries on bridges, and instructions for civilians in the event of air-raids were being posted in the city. On 3 March the *Daily Telegraph*'s correspondent in Berlin reported that Germany's attention was at present concentrated on events in North Africa. He had information, which he believed reliable, to the effect that a number of volunteers in the German army had recently been inoculated against malaria and that khaki uniforms suitable for service in hot climates were being issued to troops in certain technical troop units.

But for all the press concentration on the Mediterranean – and it was still being assumed that Roosevelt's decision to cut short his cruise with the US fleet had been connected with that – a sense of imprecision about the direction from which any crisis might develop persisted. The sort of public utterance in which, for instance, Field Marshal Goering indulged on the 1st of March, German Air Force day, encouraged this. 'Let us not delude ourselves,' he declaimed, 'the world political situation is confused and full of problems. The poison-gas clouds of Jewish agitators and warmongers drift over the continents and confuse the good sense of their peoples.'

The next day, however, it was announced that Goering would be leaving for a holiday on the Italian Riviera on 5 March. It was reported that he would be in no great hurry to return and was likely to remain there some weeks. He was feeling the effects of overwork during the last few months, and indeed had lost over a stone in the course of them. The announcement took a subsidiary place beside the news of the election on 2 March of a new Pope, the former Cardinal Pacelli, as Pius XII. A routine column in the London *Times* that day was headed 'Prague and the Provinces – growth of Slovak separatism'.

One of the star correspondents of the *New York Times*, Anne O'Hare McCormick, then in Warsaw, was reporting an unmistakable relaxation of tension there and a distinct local optimism. 'In the most authoritative Polish quarters', she wrote, 'there is no doubt that at present Germany has definitely given up the idea of pushing eastwards.' Mussolini, it was felt, had sharply reminded Berlin that it was his turn to profit from the partnership and therefore Hitler had to turn towards the Mediterranean and concentrate on the quest for colonies.

It was of course quite easy to think, if one wanted to, that both Hitler and Mussolini were largely engaged in a game of international bluff and that Hitler in particular had problems on his hands. The diplomatic correspondent of the *Manchester Guardian* wrote on 4 March that there had been a 'perceptible deepening of public discontent in Germany during the last few weeks, though most of the symptoms seem to show that the German people are weary of the regime rather than incensed by it'. People were weary of parades, demonstrations, speeches and propaganda; housewives were weary of the difficulty of buying eggs, butter, onions, etc. There was resentment of the extravagance of building the grandiose Reich Chancellery while ordinary people had housing difficulties. Corruption was rife; it was for instance possible for Jews to pay money in order not to be sent to concentration camps. Above all there was the fear of war. There were, reported the *Manchester Guardian* correspondent, more 'jitterbugs' in what he with characteristic remoteness called the Third 'Realm' than there were in Britain.

In the second week of March a plainly inspired campaign appeared in the British press designed to communicate the Government's optimism about the future. On 10 March the *Manchester Guardian*'s political correspondent wrote from Westminter: 'The British Government's view of the foreign situation, it is authoritatively made known, is that it is less anxious and arouses less concern over possible unpleasant developments than it has done for some time.'

And the *New York Times* man in London, referring openly to his source as a 'Government spokesman', wrote:

> It became known today that such optimistic reports of the general international situation had been received in British Government quarters that the possibility of disarmament talks before the summer is out were being discussed. ... Generally it is agreed that the governments of the principal European powers are now on closer terms of friendship than readers of the German press, for example, would surmise.

Italy's Foreign Minister, Count Ciano, it appeared, had assured Great Britain that Italy had no hostile intention towards any nation in increasing her armed forces in Libya. The general improvement in the international atmosphere, it was felt, could be ascribed to a recent apparent firmness of intent manifested by the British Government. In the first place there had been the declaration that in the event of war an expeditionary force of 300,000 men would be sent to France and there was thus no question of Britain's fighting merely a self-defensive war from her own island; secondly, very considerable increases in the British naval and air rearmament programmes had been announced. Then there was what the *New York Times* man called 'a substantial recovery of morale and economic strength in France, in marked contrast to the continuing economic deterioration in Germany, and the unmistakable swing of the United States Government towards amending the Neutrality Act'.

The *Daily Telegraph* reported a similar optimistic trend: the nearing end of the Spanish Civil War would be the prelude to an important improvement in the European situation to which the next essential contribution would be the settlement of differences between Italy and France. Optimism in the Cabinet over this was 'equally prevalent where relationships with Berlin are concerned'.

Winston Churchill had written an article in the *Daily Telegraph* the day before, in which he took comfort from the new defence estimates. He wrote of 'this extraordinary rearmament which can be financed without any serious embarrassment to British credit'. He did, however, warn readers to beware of supposing that the dangers in the present European situation had been removed. He would be a foolish optimist who closed his eyes to the underlying gravity of the months immediately ahead. The definitive formulation of demands upon the French Republic by Italy had still to be made by Signor Mussolini. There had been no solution to the problem of German and Italian intervention in Spain. The military preparations not only of Italy but of France on the North African shore were intensifying and it had surely been serious information that caused President Roosevelt to curtail his cruise with the US Fleet. Nevertheless, Churchill did discern one encouraging feature in the international outlook, which led him to a not unoptimistic conclusion: 'The improvement in the east of Europe', he wrote, 'is however a most important stabilizing force. ... We may look with hope to what is happening in the east of Europe as well as to the growing strength across the Atlantic, as increasing guarantees against a breakdown of civilization in this anxious year.'

Six days later it was in the east of Europe that civilisation broke down.

Until a few days before, Czechoslovakia had not figured very prominently in the news of the year. After the loss of its natural geographical frontier and its formidable defences by the terms of the Munich agreement, the Republic's inevitable need had been to be as compliant with the economic and political demands of its dominating neighbour as was compatible with nominal independence and minimum self-respect. A vassal state against its better judgment, it had come to terms with that awkward condition with some vestiges of dignity. The *Manchester Guardian* had called the German pressure on the new Czechoslovak State in the first four months of its existence 'tremendous'. It was, said the paper, a wonder that the Czechs had withstood that pressure as well as they had but it reminded its readers that three hundred years under the Habsburgs had 'given them skill in parrying blows and pressure'. And as a *New York Times* correspondent put it, though the Czech nation was now 'constrained to the service of a race against which it has struggled for 1,000 years and of ideals which it hates', the ugliest anti-Semitism could largely be confined to the 400,000 German minority still left in the Republic (there had been nearly three million Germans in the Sudetenland) and Prague could still shelter a number of anti-Nazi Germans who had managed to escape there. Though public portraits of Thomas Masaryk and Beneš had been ordered to be banned to please the

Germans, the national outcry had been so strong that the Government had had to relent at least as far as Masaryk was concerned. And the same Government, while continuing to remind the public of the need to 'glance at the map which reveals our real predicament' and to practise benevolence and tact towards the German minority, had felt independent enough to ban Julius Streicher's virulently anti-Semitic *Der Stürmer* in Bohemia and Moravia together with a Nazi pamphlet, 'Hitler Frees the Sudetenland'.

Some question even arose in democratic minds as to whether it might not be unduly pessimistic to think of the new Republic as a vassal state at all. The matter was considered by the British House of Commons when the Government asked it to ratify the transfer of money promised to the new Czechoslovakia for reconstruction after Munich. The British Government, speaking in the person of Sir John Simon, the Chancellor of the Exchequer, only conceded that it was 'necessary to be diligent' to see that the money did not go to a third party (i.e. Germany). The Opposition, on the other hand, led by Mr Wedgwood Benn, was categorical. Czechoslovakia, he said, was 'a vassal state': and though the House would not resent the £4 million which, as a free gift, was to be spent to help refugees emigrate from Czechoslovakia, the further £8 million loan for reconstruction and relief of refugees from the Sudetenland within Czechoslovakia was a very different matter. If for example some of this were spent on the new canal now being built into the Danube it would simply mean giving German submarines a new entrance to the Black Sea. Besides helping refugees there was a danger that they were contributing towards the complete military, political and economic domination of eastern Europe by Germany.

Some Conservatives were more despondent than critical. One of these, Mr Harold Macmillan, said they might as well be frank and admit that a new Czechoslovakia settling down in peace and security as had been theoretically envisaged by the Munich Agreement had failed to materialize. Fifty per cent of her products and ninety per cent of her fuel had gone to Germany. The autonomy of Slovakia and Carpatho-Ukraine had become stronger. Political parties had been banned and Jews disfranchised. But at least the free gift of £4 million for refugees who wished to emigrate would cover some of the shame and indignity to which Czechoslovakia had been subjected.

Mr Duff Cooper said that however the reconstruction part of the money was spent, it was money to be spent at the dictation of the German government. He said you couldn't blame the government of Czechoslovakia. 'The prisoner could not be blamed for showing obedience and even subservience to the jailer especially as we had been partly responsible for getting him into jail.' Duff Cooper went on to raise an important longer-term issue concerning the whole way in which the post-Munich Czechoslovakia was to be regarded. As part of the Munich Agreement the British Government had announced its intention of guaranteeing the frontiers of the new State. But, said Duff Cooper, as the Chancellor of the Exchequer himself had conceded that the roads being built across the country by agreement with the German Government were German roads, it was stating the plain truth to say that we could not possibly guarantee the frontiers of a country which had foreign roads running across it.

Earlier in the debate when Wedgwood Benn had asked to what Czechoslovakia the money was being directed, that of the frontiers guaranteed at Munich or some smaller State, Chamberlain had sat silent, looking depressed. And when asked to say whether that Munich territorial guarantee still held he had gone on sitting there, with bowed head, not consenting to look up.

The Conservative Member, Robert Boothby, said he did not think it was a good thing for Czechoslovakia or anyone else to go on complaining that she was a small vassal State and was in complete subservience. He thought there was a considerable future for her. And an Independent member, Eleanor Rathbone, thought we should not treat the Czechoslovak authorities as if they were under tutelage.

The Czechoslovak authorities were meanwhile fighting a brave battle to maintain that there was some truth in what she said. But skirmish after skirmish in that battle now seemed to be going against them. This was made clear when a matter of what Mr Wedgwood Benn in the British House of Commons called 'stinging shame' was revealed by the government on 13 February. The Munich Agreement had provided that those who wished to leave the transferred Sudeten territory for the new Czechoslovakia because they thought they were in danger should be allowed to do so. Mr R A Butler, Under-Secretary of State at the Foreign Office, now blandly admitted that though at Munich there had been no question of restricting such right of option to any specific group, the German Government had made an agreement with the Czech Government that this provision should not include German Socialists and Communists, and these were now being herded into Nazi concentration camps.

On 19 February, as a result of German pressure for all former associates of ex-President Beneš to be removed from office, the Chief of the Czechoslovak General Staff, General Krejci, was forced to resign and it was rumoured that the Minister of Defence, General Sirovy, said to be *persona non grata* in Berlin, would soon be having to go too. However, the Czech Minister of Finance indulged at least some illusion of national independence and the Republic's ability to defend itself by allowing for an expenditure on armaments in his budget, though this was to be cut by a third of the amount of the previous year. A gesture at least in the direction of some political self-respect was also made two days later when the Prime Minister, Rudolf Beran, told a press conference that the Czech Fascists of General Gajda would have to stop wearing their black shirts, though he stressed that the remnants of all the old political parties and the old regime must be liquidated. Even the autonomous Slovak Premier, Father Tiso, developing his country in a stance increasingly independent of Prague, announced that in 'solving the Jewish problem' Slovaks would not imitate foreign examples, but would safeguard individual rights and the laws of the Catholic Church.

The Republic's Foreign Minister, Frantisek Chvalkovski, made clear just how difficult was the political tightrope which the new State was trying to walk. (In public speeches he even used the analogy of Blondin crossing the Niagara Falls.) There was, above all, always the awkward factor of the 400,000 German minority, which was particularly strong in Slovakia. This minority had their own leaders, Ernst Kundt in Bohemia and Moravia, and Franz Karmasin in Slovakia, both of whom were in close touch with Berlin, as had been their predecessor in the Sudetenland, Konrad Henlein. The State had considerately set up an Official Committee for the Settlement of German Complaints to which Germans were constantly turning. Kundt had in fact just returned from Berlin when, on 23 February, Chvalkovski warned the members of the National Union Party (now the only party in the State) that it was the delay in the previous year in settling the minority problem that had cost them a third of their territory and national wealth, and that they could not continue to quarrel with this minority. 'If they want to follow an ideology which dominates almost the whole German race, then we cannot prevent them from doing so, especially as Germany is our strongest neighbour. To admit that is not weakness but the law of self-preservation. We must be ready to come to reasonable compromises with Germany. We cannot tempt fate.'

The results of Kundt's visit to Berlin were soon apparent. The Czech Government conceded that Czechoslovak citizens of German descent would not have to serve in the Republic's army. All German newspapers and books were exempted from government censorship. The swastika flag now could be flown on all official festivals and indeed on other occasions to be decided by Kundt himself. It was thought that in spite of the Czech Government's conciliatory attitude he had indeed many more demands in store for them. Coincidentally with his return, the municipal council and Mayor of Prague were dismissed because they were held to be too representative of the old political parties. The Mayor himself, Dr Zenkl, had been a prominent supporter of the now exiled Dr Beneš.

A few days later, on the day on which it was announced that Goering would be going on holiday on the Italian Riviera, *The Times* ran its small article on the growth of Slovak separatism (as opposed to the existing autonomy), a movement which was receiving open support from the newspapers in Germany. And on 6 March *The Times* ran an almost equally modest piece of some fourteen column inches on its Imperial and Foreign page which began with the statement that relations between Prague and Bratislava (capital of Slovakia) had become extremely tense in the past few days. Hlinka (Slovak Fascist) Guards had been demolishing Jewish shops and Czech police and field gendarmerie were being sent to deal with them. Large numbers of such Czech Government security forces were, it was said, being held in reserve in Bratislava.

Awareness of these events was slow to filter through the relative everyday calm of the newspapers. On 10 March the *Daily Telegraph* ran a headline: 'Slovak Putsch Rumoured', but it was smaller than that which accompanied an account in the next-door column of the paper's Christmas Toy Fund, or of the Batley by-election won by the Socialists with an increased majority since the General Election. The *Telegraph*'s political correspondent, responding dutifully to his lobby briefing, expressed the Cabinet's optimism over relations with Berlin. And on the next day, 11 March, the *Manchester Guardian*, while itself beginning to report news from Slovakia, was still talking of the 'widely-advertised improvement . . . in the immediate outlook'.

But it was on that very day that the full story of a major crisis within Czechoslovakia began to break. It was carried with some prominence on the front page of the *New York Times*. The headline there stressed the important element in the story: 'Germany Prepares To Act On Slovak Appeal For Aid As Prague Ousts Premier'. However, in the report of their man on the spot the emphasis was on the apparent resolution of the crisis:

> It is clear that a halt has been called to the complete demoralization of Czechoslovakia that followed Munich. President Hacha and Premier Rudolf Beran have shown that autonomy will not be allowed to degenerate into treason. The central Government has reasserted its authority and – appropriately at the eleventh hour– preserved the new State's unity.

Even as his words were being read in the United States a very different story was unfolding in Czechoslovakia. Two days later he was writing: 'Whether the Czechoslovak Republic will remain in its present form on the map of Europe a few days hence, or whether Slovakia will become virtually a province of Germany, was still uncertain at midnight.' By the time those words appeared the future of any Czech State at all was in the balance.

What had happened was that the Central Government in Prague had, on the 10th, received word of an attempt to carry out a separatist coup in Slovakia which would overthrow the Constitution and replace the region's already existing autonomy with an independent Slovak State. The plot, which had been well planned, had been the work of the autonomous Premier Father Tiso, backed by the Slovak Fascist Hlinka Guard. Hacha and Beran for the Prague Central Government had indeed acted swiftly. They had sent Czech troops to occupy key positions in Bratislava, placed Tiso under house arrest in a monastery, dismissed his government and disarmed the Hlinka Guard. Martial law was declared in Slovakia.

The Government had acted with similar despatch the week before in Carpatho-Ukraine where the Prime Minister, Father Joseph Volushin, had also been displaying separatist tendencies. They had deprived Volushin of most of his powers and transferred these to the Czech General Prchala. However, there was one all-important difference between the Carpatho-Ukrainian situation and that in Slovakia, namely, the presence in Slovakia of a sizeable proportion of the

German minority. Tiso smuggled out of his monastery an appeal to Hitler and the leader of that minority, Karmasin, left for Germany reassuring his supporters that the Greater German Reich was watching developments closely. Indeed one of the dismissed Ministers from Tiso's government, who had fled to Austria, was already being allowed to broadcast inflammatory separatist slogans over the Vienna radio. The German paper, the *National Zeitung*, called the Prague Government's steps 'arbitrary acts as under Beneš' and Karmasin returned from Germany to say that Tiso had been illegally deposed and that the Cabinet with which Prague had replaced Tiso's had no constitutional validity. He could, he said, appeal to the Führer by telephone at any time.

In the *New York Times* the story was temporarily reduced to a single column beside two columns for a blizzard then glazing the streets of Manhattan and causing many traffic accidents including a collision between the Staten Island ferry and a tanker. But Slovakia was already unquestionably the centre of a new international crisis. The paper's Prague correspondent was now writing: 'Czechoslovakia will have to rescind Hacha's attempt or risk being snuffed out as an independent State.'

The first attempt by Hacha to form an autonomous Slovak Government of his own choosing failed, but he had eventually succeeded in establishing one under the nationalistic but loyal premiership of Karl Sidor, who went to Prague to swear unity to the State. Persistent German pressure, however, including the reported massing of troops on the Danube opposite Bratislava, forced the Prague Government to cancel abruptly its security measures in that city. Czech troops and gendarmes were withdrawn from key positions, which were then reoccupied by the Hlinka Guard, who claimed that eighteen people had been killed in clashes with the Central Government forces. The situation in Bratislava was in fact extremely obscure, for although the Central Government was strong enough to impose a 9 p.m. curfew on the streets it did not dare to ban a large demonstration in favour of Slovak independence held by some 35,000 of the German minority and addressed by Karmasin, who said that the Germans of Slovakia would fight shoulder to shoulder with the Slovak people and again described the new government as a provisional one with no validity for the German minority. Vienna radio broadcast: 'We call on all Slovaks to take their stand in the battle for a better future', and the voice of the renegade Slovak Minister, Durcansky, telling Slovaks to stand by for a historic announcement, said that the hour for which they were waiting would soon strike. There followed an uneasy pause of twenty-four hours.

Then, on 14 March, it was reported that Hitler had postponed his departure for a tour of Austria in celebration of last year's Anschluss and that Father Tiso, who had escaped from his house arrest in the monastery, had flown to Berlin where he was received with full military honours and talked with Hitler and Ribbentrop. An ultimatum was reported to be on its way to Prague, demanding complete independence for Slovakia and for Carpatho-Ukraine and the installation of a new Czech Government which would contain neither the present Premier, Beran, nor the present Minister of Defence, Sirovy. The Republic's gold and foreign exchange were to be transferred to Germany. The full ultimatum was in fact to be delivered in person that same evening to President Hacha and his Foreign Minister Chvalkovski who were summoned peremptorily to Berlin.

That morning's German papers had been full of stories of Czech terror against Germans in the Czechoslovak Republic. The *Börsenzeitung* wrote: 'Six months have not yet passed since Munich. Again the German people lie in their own blood as sacrifices to Czech hatred. ... German houses are fired on by Czech armed guards, German boys are mishandled with brass knuckles, the Czech police refuse to aid those mishandled while Jews applaud when Germans are terrorized.'

'Murder and arson rule again in the Czechoslovak Republic,' wrote *Der Angriff*, and the *Völkischer Beobachter*: 'No hair on an Englishman's head may be touched without the world Empire coming to his protection. Adolf Hitler has agreed to take on this responsibility for the German people. And we want this respected. Also in Prague. Particularly in Prague!'

Hacha and Chvalkovski arrived in Berlin at 10.40 on the evening of 14 March. Their train was an hour late owing to the heavy military traffic already moving towards the Czech frontier. Nevertheless, diplomatic niceties were bizarrely observed. As the special correspondent of the *Daily Telegraph* wrote: 'Seldom has victim been treated with such ceremony before sacrifice as the Czech President was on arrival in Berlin.'

The tiny President Hacha, no more than five feet tall, was met by the seven-foot Baron von Dörnberg, *chef de protocol* at the German Foreign Office, together with Dr Maissen, Hitler's *chef de cabinet*, Baron von Weizsäcker, Under-Secretary at the Foreign Office, and General Seyffert, commander of the Berlin garrison. A company of infantry with drums and colours were drawn up outside the station. A guard of honour presented arms and a march was struck up as the two Czechs walked out into the light of magnesium flares. It was noted that the Czech national anthem was omitted, but President Hacha nevertheless somehow managed a smile as the formalities were concluded and he reviewed the guard of honour before being escorted to the Adlon Hotel, outside which SS guards were stationed in their black uniforms with steel helmets and fixed bayonets.

Here within the hour Ribbentrop called to take him to the Foreign Office for a conference between Hitler, Goebbels and Goering, recalled from his holiday on the Italian Riviera. However, at this stage some attempt seems to have been made by the Czechs to alleviate the humiliating terms which it was proposed to inflict on them because Ribbentrop went away again to consult Hitler before the two Czech statesmen were finally summoned to the Chancellery at ten past one on the morning of 15 March. There again a guard of honour was waiting for them and a band played another march as Hacha went through the door for his interview with Hitler. Three hours later he was driven back again from the floodlit courtyard of the Chancellery through the wet and deserted streets of Berlin to the Adlon Hotel.

The *New York Times* gave a detailed account of all this, reporting him as looking tired and grave as he walked into the lobby between tin-hatted military sentries. Without issuing a statement he went straight up to his room, which was filled with flowers, grotesquely the gift of the German Government. He had signed a document together with Chvalkovski, Hitler and Ribbentrop to the effect that in order to assure calm, order and peace in that part of central Europe he had 'trustfully laid the fate of the Czech people and the country into the hands of the Führer of the German Reich'. The Czech Defence Ministry had already started broadcasting over the radio every five minutes the information that the German army, infantry and aircraft were beginning occupation of the

> Republic's territory at 6 a.m. Their advance must not be resisted. The slightest resistance will bring most unforeseen consequences. . . . All commands have to obey the order. The units will be disarmed. Military and civil airplanes must remain in airports. None must take to the air.

None did. There was no resistance to the German troops, though a number of Czech army officer suicides were reported. Only in the Carpatho-Ukraine, which enjoyed the curious distinction of being under three National flags in twenty-seven hours – Czech, its own and that of Hungary – were there some casualties as Carpatho-Ukrainians vainly tried to defend their shortlived independence against invading Hungarians.

In a codicil to the Munich Agreement the British and French Governments had stated that they were prepared to stand by their previous offer to the Czechoslovak Government to guarantee the frontiers resulting from any new agreement. And immediately after Munich the British Minister of Defence, Sir Thomas Inskip, had said in the House of Commons that, though a formal treaty of guarantee had still technically to be drawn up: '. . . His Majesty's Government, however, feel under a moral obligation to Czechoslovakia to treat the guarantee as now in force. In the event of unprovoked aggression they would certainly take all steps in their power to see that the integrity of Czechoslovakia is preserved.'

On 14 March, the day on which Father Tiso had returned from Berlin to Bratislava with Hitler's sanction to proclaim an independent Slovakia and break up the Czechoslovak State, Chamberlain had been asked by the Labour Opposition leader, Attlee, what action His Majesty's Government had taken in view of the guarantee. The reply was: 'The question of any action has not yet arisen.'

Attlee then asked if, given the influences brought to bear on Slovakia to separate from the Republic, the Government were not bound by the Munich guarantee to have a very close interest in anything which concerned the integrity of the Czechoslovak State. To which Chamberlain replied: 'Without full information I would not like to express an opinion on the first point raised. Assuming it to be true, that would not be a ground for bringing into force the guarantee.'

The leader of the Liberal Opposition, Sir Archibald Sinclair, asked: 'Does His Majesty's Government regard itself under a moral obligation in regard to the guarantee in question?' To this Chamberlain blandly replied that the position in that respect had not undergone any change.

The skilled evasiveness inherent in such replies was further emphasized when Attlee asked Chamberlain if the Government were merely waiting for a *fait accompli*. Chamberlain replied: 'It was a guarantee against unprovoked aggression. No such aggression has yet taken place.'

It was to take place within a matter of hours.

But as German motorized infantry poured through the streets of Prague to the brave jeering and booing and repeated singing of the national anthem from the Czech people on the pavements, and as Hitler himself, with heavy snow beginning to fall, prepared to take up residence for the night at Hradcany, in the old castle of the Bohemian kings over which the swastika now flew, Chamberlain still tried to preserve the illusion that nothing fundamentally destructive of his policy of appeasement had occurred. It no longer being possible to avoid cognizance of what had actually happened, Chamberlain skilfully cited what had actually happened as a valid reason for accepting it. Turning his attention to the question of the guarantee he said: 'After Slovak independence the state of affairs described by Sir Thomas Inskip which was always regarded by us as being only of a transitory nature has ceased to exist.'

'We are heading', said Anthony Eden, his former Foreign Secretary, 'for a universal tragedy which is going to engulf us all.'

But Chamberlain remained unconvinced that his hopes for peace had been basically affected by what Hitler had done.

'I have', he said, 'so often heard charges of breaches of faith bandied about which did not seem to be founded on sufficient premises that I do not wish to associate myself with any charges of that character.' He added, to some Ministerial cheers and Opposition laughter, that he didn't think that what had just taken place had been contemplated by any of the signatories to the Munich Agreement. For himself, he bitterly regretted what had taken place but did not wish on that account to be deflected from his course of pursuing peace.

David Grenfell, the Labour Member for Gower, expressed sorrow that Chamberlain should have shown such a scant amount of feeling for Czechoslovakia. 'This', he said, 'is a day of humiliation and shame for all of us.'

Chamberlain, asked the next day if the British Government had lodged any protest with the German Government on the invasion of the territory, replied: 'No, sir, we have not done so.'

Asked if it was proposed to lodge a protest with the German Government, he replied that he could not answer the question without notice. In reply to a further question from Philip Noel-Baker, the Labour MP for Derby, as to whether the Prime Minister would represent to the German Government that any attempt to attack the lives or liberties of the leaders of the Czech people would intensify the indignation in this country at their aggression, he said: 'I think it would be wrong to assume that the German Government have any such intention.'

The *New York Times* correspondent in London, Ferdinand Kuhn, found that the Prime Minister's air of measured indifference to the full scale of the event was widely mirrored at first in certain sections of the great British public. Describing the atmosphere in London on the evening on which Hacha and Chvalkovski went to Berlin to agree to their country's humiliation, Kuhn wrote:

> The destruction of Czechoslovakia tonight was not enough to shake Britain from her recent apathy towards events in central Europe, although it must have destroyed some of the favourite assumptions on which British policy has been based for the last twelve months. ... There was no sign that the implications of this immense event had been appreciated at 10 Downing Street or at the House of Commons, where the general attitude was a helpless shrug of the shoulders, or among the general public, which seemed to care far more about a cricket match in far-off South Africa than about the transformation of the map of Europe. Most of the newspaper placards in the streets today proclaimed in eight-inch letters 'Another Great Stand' – but by the British cricketers. By the British Government there was no suggestion of any stand whatever.*

But twenty-four hours later, realization of what Hitler had done had shocked many loyal supporters of Chamberlain into an awareness that complacency might no longer be enough, and even into criticism of their leader himself for his initially bland reactions. The *Daily Telegraph*, which described what had happened as 'the most flagrant and impudent act of unprovoked aggression that has been witnessed in Europe in modern times ... an affront to the whole civilized world', found particular fault with Chamberlain's remark about lack of evidence of bad faith. As for the passage in his speech in which he said that the manner and method of Hitler's proceedings had been 'not in accord with the spirit of Munich', it called this 'pushing understatement to the point of irony'. Hitler's proceedings reduced Munich 'to a complete and utter mockery'. The *Telegraph* went on: 'A ruthless tyranny is spreading its coils far and wide in Europe. Not a single one of Germany's neighbours is henceforth safe from the deadly embrace. ... The Spirit of Munich is dead and buried, for who can hope to appease a boa-constrictor?'

'Appeasement perhaps may have to be sought along new lines ...' wrote the *Birmingham Post*. 'We must be prepared to run the risk of war.'

The *Yorkshire Post*, wrote that

> Surely the foremost conclusion we must draw is that Nazi methods cannot be met by the bland and trustful confidence which has characterized the policy and outlook of the British Government of the past twelve months. ... Future students of the history

---

* The cricket in South Africa was the final Test Match there, an open-ended one which finally had to be abandoned as a draw in torrential rain after ten days – the longest Test Match in history. England scored a world record 4th innings of 654 for 5 (Edrich 219). The draw meant that they gained the rubber which had been lost to South Africa in 1936.

Dr Hacha (*centre above*), President of post-Munich Czechoslovakia, 'protected' by Baron von Neurath (Reichsprotektor) and General von Brauchitsch (*right*), whose men (*below left*) pass disconsolate Czechs on their way to Hradschin Square, Prague.

of our time will be astonished at the blindness shown towards the threat in Europe to those principles and hard-won liberties which the people of Britain hold precious over all.

Even one of the most loyal of Chamberlain's servitors, his Under-Secretary for the Dominions, the Duke of Devonshire, observed sorrowfully at Eastbourne: 'The Prime Minister is striving manfully, but warm supporter though I am, I am bound to confess that his policy is not bearing fruit, and is not meeting with the reception which we hoped it would.' Nevertheless he was able to continue: 'In spite of that I am of the opinion that his policy is the right one and that it is our duty to support him.'

The comments of anti-appeasers in Britain were predictable and summed up by the *Manchester Guardian*'s sentence: 'What is happening now is merely a consequence of what was done at Munich. If we would not fight then, we cannot fight now.' And the latter view was voiced by the Conservative anti-appeaser, Churchill, almost identically, when he declared in his constituency: 'It is no use our going to their aid now when we did not go to their aid in September.'

The Labour *Daily Herald* struck a realistic warning note. 'Many voices today', it wrote, 'as after every defeat of international justice, proclaim in chorus, "This does not concern us in any way. It was inevitable." This does concern us – and it is only inevitable because of our own failures and treacheries. It is the postscript to Munich.' The paper then called for a determined policy of co-operation with the United States, France and Russia against the common danger.

In the United States, where according to the *Daily Telegraph*'s Washington correspondent: 'Up to the very eve of the crisis prevailing comment was to the effect that the European situation had greatly improved', the event was felt as a dangerous shock. 'The twilight of liberty in Europe', the *New York Times* called it, writing: 'Hitler has been demanding colonies. He has the first of them now. Do not look on the map of Africa to find them. They lie in the heart of central Europe.'

There was a reproachful moral note to many of the US comments. 'The night-time of law in Europe', wrote the *New York Post*, 'finds no nation opposing the Führer, none even protesting.' And many found Britain and France, in the words of the *New York Times*, 'resolutely looking the other way'. But the *New York Daily News* uttered an isolationist caution: 'This to Americans should be merely an interesting show to watch, not a fight to mix into.'

And the *New York World Telegram* commented in prophetic tones: 'The Nazi juggernaut is rolling eastward. This juggernaut may not halt until, as in 1914, it collides with a superior force and spills blood all over Europe.'

In France *Paris-Soir* wrote that no one could now believe that Hitler wanted peace, and *Le Jour*: 'No man of good faith will be prepared to maintain any longer that the slightest credit can be given to Germany's signature.' The comment of *La Justice* was sharper: 'Everything takes place as if Britain and France had been erased from the map of Europe.'

The Russians, perhaps significantly, were more interpretative than indignant, and not particularly sensitive to the worries of the West. The object of the annexation, wrote *Izvestia*, 'is to cover Germany in the east when she strikes westward at France and Britain'. There was no mention of any threat to Russia. Another Russian paper wrote: 'The soup cooked at Munich is burning the tongue of some of the statesmen who helped to prepare it.' And the Councillor of the Soviet Embassy in London, S.B. Kagan, speaking personally to Walter Duranty, the *New York Times* correspondent, with what Duranty described as 'such profound disgust as I have rarely seen on anyone's face', said: 'If I had to sum up the Kremlin's feeling – now, confronted by the situation – I would put it somewhat as follows: "A plague on both their houses."'

The Italian newspapers necessarily approved of Hitler's move. The most gleeful was the *Lavoro Fascista* which wrote: 'It marks a further advantage for the Axis powers and a fresh fall in democratic values.' But other Italian papers struck a rather more muted note. 'The annexation', wrote *Il Giornale d'Italia*, 'will further increase Germany's strength and Italy, as her partner in the Axis, can only rejoice at this.' And *La Tribuna* merely expressed 'no grounds for regret at what has taken place but rather for self-congratulation'. There was some feeling that the event had taken Italy by surprise. The Rome correspondent of the *New York Times* wrote on 20 March: 'The Italian Government has mobilized all possible means of propaganda to prepare the people for the eventuality of war in the near future.' Newspapers were advising people to carry gas-masks, blue electric light street bulbs were replacing white ones in some cities. But the man to whom Mussolini had given so much help, General Franco, went out of his way to send personal congratulations to Hitler on 'the peaceful reincorporation of old Reich districts within the borders of Germany'.

After nearly three years in which he had received so much help from Germany, to the disapproval of the democracies, there was doubtless an ironic pleasure for Franco in thus being able gratefully to endorse Hitler's action with the stamp of that legitimacy which the democracies had so recently conferred on him.

Not that in Spain itself Franco's legitimacy was yet quite complete. On 28 February, a few hours after his Chargé d'Affaires in London, the Duke of Alba, had taken over the Spanish Embassy in Belgrave Square and the former Republican Ambassador had retired as a mere resident alien to a London hotel, the Republican Government of Prime Minister Negrín, which still controlled about a fifth of the country, held a Cabinet meeting outside Madrid. Before it started the Republican Foreign Minister, Álvarez del Vayo, who had just returned from France, declared: 'Here in Spain all I wish to say is that the reports published abroad of disorder, panic and demoralization in Loyalist territory are absolutely untrue. ... Everyone is at his post – Government, army and people.'

One of the leading officers in the defence of Madrid said to the *News Chronicle* correspondent William Forrest that day: 'So now I suppose it is we who are the rebels in the eyes of Britain and France ...' He added bitterly: 'Perhaps now that we are no longer legitimate, we can expect more help from abroad.'

But, for the beleaguered Spanish Republic, the finally destructive forces were, as many would maintain they had always been, within. As so often when climactic events are under way, it was not at first at all clear what was happening.

On the morning of 5 March while Franco's forces, said now to number a million men round Madrid, were reported to be threatening an all-out offensive unless the city surrendered, his 'fifth column' rose in Cartagena, the Mediterranean port which held the bulk of the Republican fleet. The fleet, however, remained loyal to the Republic and the rising was successfully suppressed after two hours in which the rebels had temporarily broadcast from the radio station there. That evening, a voice quivering with emotion broadcast a sensational message from Madrid radio to the effect that a National Defence Council had been formed in Madrid 'to take charge of the general situation in the zone abandoned to its fate by the Government presided over by Dr Negrín'. The Council was headed by a General Casado, commander-in-chief of the army of the Republic in central Spain, and was said to be supported by General Miaja, the commander-in-chief of all the Republic's forces. The statement continued: 'As revolutionaries, Spaniards and anti-Fascists, we could no longer continue in the present situation, in which we lacked guidance and organization, together with the absurd inactivity of the Negrín Government. The gravity of the moment compels us no longer to obey this handful of men in whom we have no confidence.' In other words, Negrín had been ousted as the Government of the Republic.

Afterwards Casado himself broadcast.

'We shall resist', he said, 'until we are able to sign an honourable peace. The people of Spain are struggling for their independence and they will continue the struggle until such a peace is offered to them. ... Long live the Republic. Long live Spain!'

What did this mean? It was just possible for a moment to think that a refurbishing of the Republic's fighting spirit might be under way. Though Franco's men were in no doubt that immediate peace overtures were intended by the new Council, this was not inevitable. But they soon turned out to be right.

Next day, Miaja himself was made President of the National Defence Council, with Casado as War Minister. Miaja broadcast as follows:

'We will bring tranquillity to Spanish homes by making peace, but peace as worthy of us as the war, since the honour of Republican arms has been saved in the struggle.'

However he spoke too of difficulties with 'a certain political party' on the Republican side and a later broadcast that same night referred to 'certain elements of the Communist party lamentably trying to disturb public order and neutralize the action of the National Defence Council'.

ABOVE Soldiers of the Spanish Republic, defeated in Catalonia, pour over the French frontier. BELOW Franco's men in Madrid at last.

Two days later the Franco forces round Madrid found themselves the spectators of an extraordinary battle in the arena before them between forces loyal to the new Defence Council and Communist elements in the Republic's army in full rebellion, who had seized a number of strong points in the city. Communist units came in to help them from other parts of Republican territory, where there was similar defiance of the new Government. Artillery, tanks and even bomber aircraft were sent into action against them. Casado in a broadcast castigated the Communists as 'insanity's own representatives', and added: 'It is as madmen that we are obliged to consider them.' But they fought with the ferocity of madmen too and were only finally dislodged with difficulty from buildings they had occupied in the centre of Madrid, like the Ministry of Marine and the seventeen-storey Central Telephone Exchange, after a week's heavy fighting.

At the end of the week the Communists, commanded by a Lieutenant-Colonel Barceló, surrendered in their last stronghold on the old racecourse. Food was brought into the city, which had been without bread for three days. Franco's men had not moved and Republican troops facing them in the front line had had the curious sensation of hearing fighting behind them and not knowing whether to turn to it or not.

On 19 March Barceló was shot by a firing-squad of the Defence Council which now broadcast that it was ready to enter into negotiations for an honourable peace. Franco's answer came through his Minister of the Interior, Serrano Súñer. He defined the requisite peace otherwise. 'We wish a victorious peace,' he said. 'After that will come the generosity of which we have so often given proof.'

About the extent of that generosity there was considerable doubt. A writer in the *News Chronicle*, Philip Jordan, reckoned that in Madrid alone between ten and twelve thousand people's lives were forfeit – moderate trade union leaders, doctors, nurses, teachers, etc. He said it was the British Government which, through its agents, had induced Casado to take power in the belief that he could get better terms than Negrín and he now urged that Government to take responsibility for such people and get them out because it was clear that terms given to Casado would in fact be no better than those which would have been given to Negrín.

Nevertheless the illusion that some sort of generosity might still be negotiated persisted. A gigantic wall poster of the Junta appeared in Valencia, depicting a soldier throwing down his rifle and looking up at the word 'Peace' in huge letters while the caption declared: 'We want a Fatherland in which all Spaniards can live honourably together, free from foreign interference.'

On the same day five Italian bombers dropped some fifty bombs on a slum district of the city. Otherwise there was a strange hiatus for a few days. Then on 26 March Franco began an offensive two hundred miles south of Madrid near Córdoba and penetrated the Republican lines at once up to a depth of twenty-five miles. Whole battalions raised the white flag and ten thousand prisoners or deserters were counted in the one day. On the 28th the white flag appeared over

MONTE CARLO

Winter Season 1939
Some Outstanding Dates

Jan. 16th.-22nd. Tennis—Club Championships. ★ Jan. 17th. Golf—Leon Garibaldi Challenge Cup. Jan. 18th. Concert with Mme Vina Bovy, soloist. ★ Jan. 21st.-25th. Eighteenth Annual Motor Rally. ★ Jan 21st.-31st. Opera—Wagner's Ring by the Bayreuth Company under Franz von Hoesslin. ★ Jan. 23rd.-29th. Tennis—International Tournament. ★ Jan. 23rd.-Feb. 4th. Bridge Tournament. ★ Jan. 25th. Concert with Kurt Baum, tenor. ★ Jan. 27th. Golf—Walter de Frece Challenge Cup. ★ Feb. 22nd. Concert of English Music conducted by Sir Adrian Boult. ★ April 1st. Ballet Season opens.

The HOTEL DE PARIS ranks amongst the famous hotels of the world, and the comfortable HOTEL HERMITAGE is under the same management. There are innumerable other hotels to suit all purses, particulars of which can be obtained from Messrs. Thos. Cook & Son, Limited, and all travel agencies

Madrid itself and it was entered at last, after thirty-three months of siege, by 200,000 Franco troops who never had to fire a shot. The Defence Council had fled to Valencia with the exception of Julián Besteiro, who broadcast an appeal to 'be calm and serene and accept the surrender of Madrid as the best means of salvation'. Some hint of the sort of salvation that might be expected was given when the Republican army central commander, Colonel Prada, followed him to the microphone. He had hardly begun his broadcast before listeners heard him brushed aside by a party of Falangists who had entered the studio and a voice was heard saying: 'Give us the radio. Madrid is ours. *Viva* Franco.' Besteiro and Prada were arrested.

Extraordinary scenes were taking place outside. As Franco's troops rose from their trenches and walked across no-man's-land, the Republicans who had faced them for so long got up too and walked towards them, embracing as they met and then walking back with them into the city in which Franco's flags had begun to fly from windows as his fifth column emerged into the open to welcome the incoming troops. That night for the first time for thirty-three months the street lights were turned on in the city. And the next day, 29 March, the Franco radio officially but technically prematurely announced from Burgos the end of the Civil War, after it had lasted for 985 days. The Republic formally capitulated on 31 March. It was soon noticed that women were wearing hats in the streets of Madrid again – hats for women and ties for men having been considered a sign of Fascist sympathies and inadvisable under the Republic. The Civil Guards too in their own traditional tricorne hats now reappeared for the first time since just after the outbreak of the war when they had been disbanded because of their authoritarian pro-Franco sympathies.

The London *News Chronicle*, which had throughout so fervently supported the Republic, wrote of the citizens of Madrid: 'Extremity has now forced them to yield. They lose none of the admiration of the world in so doing. The world's scorn will be reserved entirely for those British and French statesmen who, professing the name of democrat, would not raise a finger to help the democratic cause in Spain.'

But the democratic cause in Spain was now quickly forgotten, or relegated to minor paragraphs in the newspapers, as other democracies came under ever-increasing pressure themselves.

PART II
15 MARCH – 3 SEPTEMBER 1939

A German Infantryman at Practice: With a Weapon That Is Not Yet Obsolete

Portrait of the world in 1939. It is armed. It wears a steel helmet. It is making a jab at the vitals with a bayonet. But the vitals are still the vit.

14

With Hitler's march into Prague and his complete occupation of Czechoslovakia a mercurial and, in retrospect, almost innocent character which had hitherto marked the international scene in 1939 left it for ever.

The quality of bright morning, in which anything, even something rather hopeful, might develop, disappeared from the face of the year.* Those who believed in a policy of appeasement, to be backed almost as an afterthought by preparation for its failure, now confronted the awkward reality that the afterthought was likely to be the most important part of their policy. Those who had so confidently attacked appeasement, maintaining that it could only lead to a disastrous outmanœuvring of the democracies, now found themselves faced by the disaster of their own prediction; and suddenly in this situation it was less comforting to have been proved right than it had been to maintain that they would be.

The Ides of March 1939 marked the beginning of the end of what the poet Auden six months later called 'a low, dishonest decade'. And yet of course even turning-points as brutal as this one do not seem particularly like turning-points when lived through from day to day. The historical view is a luxury seldom to be afforded at any given moment. But the event could soon be seen as a divide. Dozens of little bridges of continuity, carried plausibly enough by the reappearance of the morning newspaper, simply disguised the fact that it had been traversed.

Relative trivialities in the news commanded the same interest as they had done before. On the day Hitler entered Prague, Leonard Richardson, the twenty-eight-year-old chemical worker of Coronation Drive, Hornchurch, Essex, who had been accused of the murder of the nine-year-old schoolgirl Pamela Coventry on the afternoon of 18 January, was finally committed for trial. Some fairly damning evidence had been accumulated against him at the preliminary proceedings.

On the late afternoon of the day of the murder Richardson had gone to see the doctor of whom he was a panel patient, and had told him that he had an accident at work and had been gassed. The doctor found that he was suffering from mild conjunctivitis of the eyes but there was nothing to show that he had been gassed. He said Richardson had seemed upset and in a more nervous condition than would have been expected in a normal person. His heart was a little fast and he seemed more excitable than was to be expected after a slight accident.

* The London *Evening Standard* had run an optimistic leader as late as 10 March headed 'Bright Morning'.

The Home Office pathologist, Sir Bernard Spilsbury, then gave evidence about the state of the little girl's corpse. She had bruises on her face and head and had bled from the nose. There were signs of sexual interference. She had been strangled not more than an hour after her last meal. The blows would have rendered the child unconscious and the sexual interference had taken place before death. Evidence was given that the self-rolled cigarette-end found pressed between her thighs and chest contained similar 'Digger' brand tobacco to that found in Richardson's tobacco pouch and that the watermark on the stub of cigarette paper was identical with cigarette papers found in Richardson's possession.

A length of green cable with tarred string attached, similar to that which had been used to truss up the body, was found in a hut in Richardson's back garden. The distance from the bottom of this garden to the place where the girl's body was found was 430 paces and took four minutes to walk.

Evidence was also given that some of the girl's clothing had been found near by, wrapped up and sealed with insulating tape in a copy of the *News Chronicle* of 11 January. The *News Chronicle* was the paper Richardson took and the 11 January issue was found to be missing among the old copies of newspapers in his house. His defence counsel did elicit the information that copies of issues of the *News Chronicle* for nineteen other days in January were also missing from his house, but on the other hand out of a run of days from 6 to 12 January only the issue for 11 January was missing. On a pair of flannel trousers and a raincoat of Richardson's worn by him on the day of the murder and shown to a Home Office analyst on 31 January, some bloodstains had been found. In a pocket of a brown jerkin he had been wearing was found a cigarette stub similar to that found on the trussed-up corpse. The prosecution argued plausibly that the latter might well have fallen out of his pocket in the course of the trussing.

Richardson had given a full account of his movements on the day in question to the police and when they arrived at his house and showed him a warrant to search it for the dead child's clothing, he had made no reply. On being told four days later that he was being taken to Romford police station in connection with the girl's death he said: 'Have you told my wife? Can I see her?'

When charged, he had said: 'I have nothing to say.'

He was committed for trial at the Old Bailey. It was a trial that was to produce a remarkable sensation.

It opened on Monday, 27 March, and Richardson, wearing the same grey suit that he had worn at the magistrate's hearing, answered 'Not guilty' to the charge of murder, in a clear, strong voice. His wife sat at the back of the court. Prosecuting counsel went through all the evidence that had been produced at the committal proceedings together with a good more detail such as that the knots in the tarred string used to tie up the body were similar to the knots on the tarred string used by Richardson to tie up his beans and that he had been seen acting oddly in the area in question in the crucial half-hour (between 1.15 and 1.45 p.m.)

on 18 January. Moreover it was revealed that the body when found was quite dry though it had rained hard up to 10.30 p.m. on the night after the murder. The body had clearly been kept somewhere and the court was reminded that Richardson's house was only a few hundred yards from the ditch where it was found. A milkman and his assistant had seen a light on in his house at 5.30 a.m. on the morning on which it was found.

It did not seem, on the face of it, unreasonable when at the end of the day prosecuting counsel submitted to the jury. 'All these things taken together lead you irresistibly to the conclusion that the prisoner is the man who murdered the child.'

The only real evidence the defence counsel was able to elicit on that day on Richardson's behalf was that his sister-in-law, who had been looking after him while his wife was in hospital recovering from the birth of her child, had noticed nothing particularly out of the ordinary about him on the day in question, though she had seen him in the afternoon only a short time after what would have been the crucial half-hour. She had known he had not been well so had not been surprised to find that having gone to work after lunch, he had returned almost at once and was at home in the afternoon. She said she had been lighting the boiler for him every day during the previous week and to do this had taken newspapers from a kitchen cupboard. She added that Mr and Mrs Richardson were a happily married couple in every way and that Richardson was a popular man in the neighbourhood with a great number of friends.

The trial lasted five days altogether. There was further evidence that seemed to go against Richardson. In spite of his own contention that the local milkman and his assistant had seen a light on in his house on a different morning, they repeated it was 5.30 in the morning of the day in which the body had been put by someone into the ditch, and were quite certain that they were not making a mistake about this. Sir Bernard Spilsbury, the pathologist, when recalled, said that the odd spots and smears of blood on Richardson's trousers and raincoat could have got there as a result of blood spurting from the child's nose while she was being strangled. But as Richardson mentioned in his statement to the police that the blood was the result of an injury to his knuckles caused by a spanner at work, and Sir Bernard agreed that this could have accounted for it, and as the spots and smears were not suitable for a conclusive blood test, the judge intervened to say that in his view it was not possible to make much of the blood spots and smears.

While the prosecution continued, evidence for the defence could only be built up circumstantially. It was confirmed by a workmate of Richardson's that there had indeed been a spilling of chemicals at work the day before to account for Richardson's state when he visited the doctor on the evening of the murder day. A neighbour, a woman, reported that he was 'a jolly good sort' and though she had been in her house throughout the time of the murder she had not heard a sound from next door. Her husband rolled his own cigarettes and kept the stubs to be smoked again, like Richardson, and she knew several men in the district who did that. A police inspector confirmed that when interviewed, Richardson had had injuries to the knuckles of his little fingers on both hands which he said he had got from a spanner at work. The inspector had found none of the dead girl's clothing in the house. He agreed that up to the time of the charge Richardson had borne a perfectly good character.

Another Home Office analyst agreed that it was very common for tarred string to be used in conjunction with wire cable for garden purposes. The manager of the Imperial Tobacco Company laboratory at Bristol admitted that his company sold over a million pounds a year of the tobacco which Richardson used. However, an expert from a cigarette-paper manufacturer emphasized that the paper on the stub taken from the body and that found in Richardson's possession were of identical manufacture.

On the strength of such success as he had been able to achieve in cross-examination of this type, Richardson's defence lawyer rather optimistically submitted that on the evidence on the case at present there was no case to go to the jury. He said that if a jury could not put the evidence against the accused beyond a probability, then it was impossible for them to say they were satisfied beyond reasonable doubt that the charge had been made out.

The prosecution then stated that nothing had happened to weaken its case, that it stood in exactly the same way as it did when opened.

'Oh, no, it does not,' said the judge, intervening. 'A great deal of change has taken place in this case since this morning in my opinion.'

He went on to say that the strength of the prosecution's case lay to a great extent in the fact that the accused was the only person who possessed certain materials. In that respect a great deal of change had occurred since the morning's evidence from expert witnesses. There was, he said, a period of possibly twenty-five minutes during which the murder might have been carried out by the accused. There was, he thought, a possibility that in that time a man might have attracted a little girl, a total stranger, into his house. Then it was also possible that something might have happened without the lady next door hearing it. Since the prosecution's main case was that the accused had a great number of materials in his possession that were in the hands of the actual murderer, the evidence about other people's having such material also was obviously particularly important, but he thought he must let the matter go before the jury.

This was the beginning of a turn in the case which, to say the least, was to come as something of a surprise to anyone who had simply followed the case against Richardson so far from the newspapers. In addressing the jury, Richardson's counsel again stressed the legal maxim that it was not enough for there to be a suspicion that Richardson might have done the murder: they had to be sure in the sense of being free from any reasonable doubt. He then stressed a point with which he had already made some play, but which, strictly scientifically, was less conclusive than the psychological effect of making it.

'Are they Raid Proof?' ask the *Sunday Pictorial* and others.

Advice for Sir John Anderson from the unemployed.

'What motive is suggested', he asked, 'other than sheer bestiality of this man of whom everybody has said, "he's a jolly good fellow"?'

He then exploited this point to the full by putting his client into the witness box, though, as he reminded the jury, there was no need for him to go there. In the box Richardson was taken step by step through his own story of the events, without faltering, strongly denying at the outset that he had killed Pamela Coventry, or even known her. He stood up equally calmly to prosecuting counsel's cross-examination for one and a half hours. Re-examining, defence asked Richardson to roll one of his own cigarettes, which he calmly did. It was handed to the judge, who looked at it through a magnifying glass and observed that the paper seemed to have been creased back in the rolling – what was known as a 'reverse fold'. After further evidence from a neighbour that Richardson was considered 'a really decent fellow', came the most dramatic evidence of all. The general manager of the Rizla cigarette-paper company was called. He began by testifying that his company made a million packets a week of the papers which Richardson used and which had been used for the stub found on the trussed-up body and that most of these were sold in London, Essex, Suffolk and Norfolk. He then described the contents of some envelopes he had been handed for analysis by a firm of solicitors who had in turn been handed them by Mrs Richardson during the period in which Richardson had been in custody. She had collected them from friends, workmates and neighbours who rolled their own cigarettes. The great majority of them were composed of the same paper as the stub found on the body, contained the same tobacco and had been rolled in a similar fashion, that is to say with a 'reverse fold'.

This evidence, backed up by that of another witness who substantiated Richardson's claim that his uncertain movements in the neighbourhood allegedly on the day on which the murder was committed had in fact taken place on the day before, proved conclusive for the jury. When they returned after the luncheon adjournment they handed the judge a note. The judge asked them:

'Am I to take it you do not feel there is enough evidence to justify you in finding this man guilty?'

The foreman: 'Yes, my Lord.' He added that they therefore found him not guilty.

In discharging Richardson, the judge said: 'That verdict does not in the least surprise me.'

As the court rose members of the jury shook Richardson by the hand and many friends of the Richardsons rushed forward to surround him and his wife and do likewise. After what his local paper described as 'one of the most dramatic fights in legal history' and two months on remand in which, to judge from the circumstantial evidence published in the newspapers, his chances of acquittal must at times have seemed slim, the accused went free.

For the accused in the other noteworthy British murder case of those weeks, William Butler, already found guilty and sentenced to death for the murder of the jeweller Ernest Key, there was to be no such happy outcome, though he had appealed against the sentence. The basis of his appeal by his counsel, David Maxwell Fyfe, was on the grounds that the charge should have been manslaughter. The killing had taken place, he contended, in the heat of passion induced by an argument over money which Butler considered Key owed him. The trial judge, it was submitted, had failed to direct the jury that to justify a verdict of murder rather than manslaughter there would have had to be a sufficient interval of time in the quarrel to enable Butler's passion to cool. But the Court of Appeal found no grounds to reverse the verdicts. One of the reasons given was that the evidence showed clearly that a number of blows had been delivered from behind the victim, suggesting presumably that there must have been some element of premeditation in these. Butler's wife then started a movement for his reprieve, going round from door to door in Teddington, where the family lived, collecting signatures. She even wrote to the King. But on 27 March it was announced that the Home Secretary had been unable to find any grounds to justify interference with the sentence of death. The same day the condemned man wrote three letters, two to his daughters Pat and June, aged five and ten, and one to his wife. The *News of the World* published extracts from them:

Dear little Pat,
    Be a good girl to Mummy. Daddy will be going away for a long time, as he is going abroad. Learn all your lessons at school so that you will get on well. Never forget your Daddy who will always love you.

    Your dear loving,
    Daddy

To his elder daughter he wrote:

I don't know when I shall be writing again, for I shall be a long way away and it will be difficult for me but remember Daddy loves you. I shall be thinking of you always and I hope you will not forget me.

He also wrote a letter to his wife, which she received on the morning he was hanged:

It is very hard for me to write this letter as my heart is broken and my eyes keep filling with water. . . . I have kept my chin up as well as I could but I am afraid, my love, that now I am completely done. . . . I am not afraid to meet my end but it is what is being taken from me . . .

He was hanged inside Wandsworth Prison on 29 March. In addition to the letter she received from him that morning, there was one from the King conveying a negative reply to her request.

She herself married again two months later a man who had helped her collect signatures to the petition for a reprieve.

They ordered capital punishment differently in France – also in the United

States. A few weeks after Butler's execution a mass murderer, Eugen Weidmann, was guillotined in public in front of the prison at Versailles. In America great care had been taken to give insulin to a murderer who might otherwise have died before he could be electrocuted.

A trial of a very different sort and far more dramatic in its implications had recently ended in the Soviet Union. It was a sequel to the trial in early January in which five Moldavian officials of the NKVD had been found guilty and shot in Kiev for extorting false confessions of treasonable activities from innocent persons.

The new trial took place in the city of Leninsk-Kuznetskiy in the Urals, and was of three officials of the NKVD for similar abuse of their authority. The chief of the Leninsk-Kuznetskiy NKVD himself, one Lunkov, was up before the court. He admitted that he and his subordinates had fabricated cases against a large number of children (several score it seemed) in order to heighten his reputation for vigilance against enemies of the State. His former Chief Investigator, Belousov, testified that Lunkov had told him that if they secured convictions their authority would rise very high.

To conceal the nature of the operation the children's ages had been suppressed in order to give the impression that they had been arrested for 'fascist terroristic activities'. The arrested children had been crowded into cells with common criminals as well as political offenders, had had to sleep without bedding, had not been allowed to make contact with their parents or teachers and had been questioned singly and at night. A boy of ten, Volodya, gave the court details of such questioning. He said it had been after midnight in winter when he was very sleepy that he had been called up for questioning by the four men now before the court. They had pointed their pens at him and asked him strange questions again and again over several days, such as 'were you a member of a counter-revolutionary fascist terrorist organization?', to which he had given what seemed the desired answers. He had admitted that he had begun recruiting for the members of his fascist terrorist group in 1935, when he was in fact 7 years old. The local Soviet newspaper, *Soviet Siberia*, commented on this: 'If he were recruiting members of a terrorist band at the age of 7, at what age before that was he himself recruited? Before he was born?'

All four NKVD officials were found guilty and shot and *Soviet Siberia* concluded indignantly: 'It is a provocative, criminal, foul, shameful slander on Soviet children. The investigation now has conclusively proved that the documents had been forged and that the case is artificial.'

It was presumably for perpetrating such travesties of justice that heads of the NKVD in the Ukraine, Byelo-Russia, Moscow, Leningrad, Stalingrad and other districts had, as was now announced officially, themselves been liquidated.

Trials of such people, with their consequences, seemed intended to prove two things: first, official acceptance that there had been serious abuses of justice

Have you Keen Eyes — quick to spot news?

HOW TO READ CHARACTER

EYE FOR NEWS. Full and well-rounded, with a wide-open expression of piercing penetration and steadiness, despite the slight contraction of the lids. Horizontal wrinkles at outer edges of the eyes.

VIGILANT EARS. Large, and set low down upon the head and not particularly close to the crown. The extreme top of the ear distinguished by the so-called "elfin point" associated with vital alertness and observation.

Look at your face! Have you keen eyes and vigilant ears that recognise news? Then try K4's! You will appreciate their **real Virginia tobaccos**—mild, yet satisfying. You will recognise, too, **the greatest cigarette value in all the country.** With each packet of twenty K4's you get four extra for your friends. K4's — the friendly cigarette. Yes, 4 and 20 finest quality Virginia cigarettes — one shilling the packet.

THEY'RE REAL VIRGINIA, SIR,
WHY ACCEPT LESS?

4 and 20
One Shilling
The Packet

K4's

during the recent purges; and second, that charges formulated in future by officials of the new Head of the NKVD, Lavrenti Beria, would be genuine. The *New York Times*, reporting the Siberian trial, added a rather more contentious conclusion, namely that 'the purge is definitely over, at least as far as indiscriminate arrests are concerned'.

As always, news to emerge from the Soviet Union was patchy, though such trials, supplemented by a campaign to penalize slackers in industry and reprimand managers whose corrupt or otherwise inadequate natures hindered progress in the Five-Year Plan, suggested that some sort of new phase had opened there. The suggestion was encouraged by Stalin's five-and-a-half-hour-long speech to the Eighteenth Congress of the Communist Party, which referred to the purge as having run its useful course, and incidentally also hinted (the speech was just before Hitler's invasion of Prague) that the western democracies were for their own purposes making more fuss about Hitler's threat to eastern Europe than was justified by objective assessment of the facts.

Stalin maintained that the western democracies had at Munich ceded parts of Czechoslovakia to Germany with the design of bribing Hitler to launch a war against the Soviet Union. They were, he said, working up fears that Hitler was driving eastwards with a Greater Ukraine as his ambition.

'It looks', he said, 'as if the object of this suspicious fuss is to raise the ire of the Soviet Union against Germany, to poison the atmosphere and provoke a conflict with Germany without any visible grounds for it.'

As the *New York Times* commented, Stalin was less severe in his handling of the aggressive states themselves than he was of the western democracies whose weakness of policy had permitted the aggressions to succeed. Although the notion of Hitler and Stalin sitting down at the same table had, the paper said, been hitherto one of the great unthinkables of European politics, it could not help asking what these words of Stalin might mean. Did they forecast better relations with Germany? It found the effect of the words even more confusing because very recently there had seemed to be some sign of closer relations between Britain and the Soviet Union. Mr Chamberlain had just attended a reception at the Soviet Embassy in London for the first time.

On the whole preoccupation with Hitler's present actions and future intentions overshadowed thoughts about what Stalin might have in mind. Apart from the cathartic shock in Britain to supporters of 'appeasement', it was on the Poles that the transformation of Czechoslovakia into a German protectorate had its most quickening effect. President Moscicki of Poland made an unprovocatively plain statement on 19 March, the anniversary of the birthday of Marshal Pilsudski: 'Poland was weak, now she is strong. We shall not surrender her territory to alien protection.'

Marginally more provocative and certainly gladly accepted as such by the German press were anti-German demonstrations which took place in Bydgoszcz (formerly the German town of Bromberg). Allegations of maltreatment of Ger-

mans in Poland immediately appeared in the German newspapers and the official *Diplomatisch-Politische Korrespondenz* gave a warning that such events were contrary to the spirit of the Non-Aggression Pact between Poland and Germany which Ribbentrop and Beck had so recently reaffirmed. The Polish press remained unequivocal. *Polska Zbrojna* wrote: 'Poles understand the tragic example of Czechoslovakia. Therefore Poland is ready for war even against the strongest adversary.'

But as if to flaunt his indifference to all world opinion Hitler now presented it with another *fait accompli*.

The Baltic city and seaport Memel, and its hinterland, with a population of 150,000 consisting mostly of Germans, had been ceded by Germany under the Treaty of Versailles to four guarantor Powers (Britain, France, Italy and Japan) under the League of Nations to ensure that the newly-created independent country of Lithuania had access to the sea. Memel had been under French administration until January 1923, when it was occupied by the Lithuanians, who thereupon asserted their own sovereignty over the territory. Their action obtained international acceptance. But the German population there had early become enthusiastically National Socialist and in the light of Hitler's successes elsewhere had since become even more so. On 20 March Ribbentrop peremptorily presented an ultimatum to the Lithuanian Foreign Minister in Berlin demanding that Memel should be handed over in exchange for a guarantee of Lithuania's territorial integrity and for special port facilities in the city itself. The demand was accompanied by the threat that if the matter were not resolved on a diplomatic level it would be dealt with on a military one, with unforeseen consequences. Two days later the Lithuanian Government and Parliament agreed to a treaty which ironically contained a non-agression clause binding the two contracting parties never to resort to force against one another. Most of the Lithuanian population of Memel and all the Jews moved out immediately and

163

Hitler himself arrived there on 23 March in the new battleship, the *Deutschland*, to address his delirious supporters.

'You have returned', he declaimed, 'to a new Germany which is determined to master and shape its own destiny even if this does not suit the outside world. . . . We have no intention of imposing suffering on that other world. Only the suffering which it has imposed on us has come to an end.'

Less than two weeks before, democratic governments had been expressing confident optimism about the international situation. Now there was one more reason to adjust themselves to a state of bleak resignation. Lord Halifax, the British Foreign Secretary, had already articulated the mood in the House of Lords on the day the ultimatum was delivered to Lithuania. But in doing so he had added a significant rider.

He had begun by saying that every country which was Germany's neighbour was now 'uncertain of the morrow'. He was glad to note that Rumania, which was now signing a trade treaty with Germany, denied receiving any ultimatum as reports had been suggesting, but he nevertheless viewed with the gravest misgivings the happenings of the past few days. There had, he admitted, been two schools of thought since the war about the best way of preserving international peace: the first embodied a belief in collective security; the second was primarily worried that collective security might involve dangerously indefinite commitments. However, he went on, after the sort of event they had just experienced in Czechoslovakia

> there is likely immediately to be found very much greater readiness to consider whether the acceptance of wider mutual obligations in the case of mutual support is not dictated by the necessities of self-defence. His Majesty's Government have not failed to draw the moral from these events and have lost no time in placing themselves in close and direct consultation, not only with the Dominions but with other Governments concerned.

Such bland wording clothed a suggestion of radical change in policy.

The principal Government concerned was now Poland, whose common frontier with Germany had been extended by some two hundred miles by the destruction of Czechoslovakia. On the day on which Halifax spoke, not only did the Germans apply their lightning pressure on Lithuania, but the Swiss League of Nations Commissioner for the Free City of Danzig, Karl Burckhardt, went to Geneva to discuss with the Secretary-General of the League the political situation in Danzig and the possibilities of an early crisis there. Apprehension over that possibility was not much eased when the German Nazi spokesman in Danzig stated: 'We are not looking for any immediate change in our status. . . . The time has not come for such a step. We must rely on Berlin to make the decision for us.'

In London a general apprehension for Poland was expressed by King George VI in his welcome for the French President, Albert Lebrun, on a state visit to the

'Standing together in our hour of danger': King George VI and Queen Elizabeth with French President Albert Lebrun, Mme Lebrun (*right*) and Queen Mary (*left*) at the Royal Opera House, Covent Garden, March 1939. BELOW Farewell to the Lebruns and French Foreign Secretary George Bonnet, with Princess Elizabeth, Chamberlain and Halifax in attendance.

capital. The King pledged that Britain and France would stand together 'above all in our hour of danger'. The *New York Times* correspondent in London noted that although there were still some Conservatives in the House of Commons clinging to a more than ever fragile optimism ('Things look a little better to-day, don't they?' 'Maybe it will quieten down now', etc.), such illusions were not widely held by the Government itself. Yet on 23 March Chamberlain made a statement in the House of Commons to amplify Lord Halifax's remarks of three days before which showed sadness if not positive reluctance at the prospect of having to abandon earlier illusions:

> I am not yet in a position to make a statement on the consultations which have been held as a result of recent developments. I wish to make it clear, however, that there is no desire on the part of His Majesty's Government to stand in the way of any reasonable efforts on the part of Germany to expand her export trade. On the contrary, we were on the point of discussing in the friendliest way the possibility of trade arrangements which would have benefited both countries when events took place which for the time being at any rate put a stop to those discussions. Nor is this Government anxious to set up in Europe opposing blocs of countries with differing ideas about the forms of their internal administration. We are solely concerned that we cannot submit to a procedure under which independent States are subjected to such pressure under a threat of force as to be obliged to yield up their independence, and we are resolved by all the means in our power to oppose such attempts, if they should be made, to put such procedure into operation.

As the *New York Times* noted, a certain shift of emphasis in high quarters was undoubtedly being made. But it was not yet clearly the abandonment of one policy for another. The extent to which 'appeasement' had in fact been abandoned, or was merely being given the appearance of having been abandoned, by men like Chamberlain and Halifax, to whose natural instincts it remained more congenial than a policy of confrontation, was a question that was to persist awkwardly for the next few months.

15

A mood in Britain demanding some explicit change of policy had been increasing strongly in the days after Hitler's entry into Prague, and was evidently present even among the Prime Minister's closest supporters in the Conservative Party. For when Chamberlain had spoken two days afterwards in Birmingham on 17 March his condemnation of Hitler's action had been much more forthright than it had been in the House of Commons. A number of official statements in the course of that week also served to add detail to a new sense of realism in Britain's foreign policy. Gas-masks or gas-helmets for children under two were, it was announced, now available – hoods fitted with a window which enclosed the head, shoulders and arms of the child. There were 1,400,000 of these, while another 1,300,000 special respirators had been made for children under four. A Civil Defence Bill introduced in the House of Commons on 24 March carried seventy-five clauses directed towards the improvement and acceleration of the country's preparations against air attack. The Austin Motor Company of Birmingham had completed deep shelters for five thousand of its workers and similar shelters for another ten thousand were planned. Conscription was being urged by some Conservatives including the former Foreign Secretary, Anthony Eden, who declared that it was, 'No time for half-way measures. As conditions are today every hour counts.'

Hourly too, according to the *New York Times* correspondent in Warsaw, suspicion of Germany and the determination to fight if menaced by the Nazis were growing in Poland. Danzig, he said, was uppermost in the minds of the people there. The Polish Government too was making plain its feelings. On 28 March the Polish General Skwarcynski declared: 'For our frontiers, our independence, our homes, we will fight till our last breath, till the last drop of our blood.' Next day Poland launched a National Defence Loan to strengthen her air force and measures of air-raid protection. Polish reservists were called to the colours as German troop concentrations on the frontier were reported, though these were denied in Berlin. Polish troops were reported to be taking up positions at Gdynia, the wholly Polish port beside Danzig. A German official in Danzig was quoted as saying: 'Almost every German expects confidently that Danzig and the Corridor [the Polish province of Pomorze] will become part of Germany one day. The separation is unnatural.' In its newspaper the Polish army continued to assert its readiness: 'We are ready and we will fight hard. We are ready for any kind of war with even the strongest opponent. Poles do not allow themselves to be frightened by the number of their enemy's divisions nor his technical equipment nor his political aggressiveness.'

This developing tension in Poland was now reflected in London by an apparently explicit affirmation from the Government of that change of attitude for which so many had been hoping. On 31 March, Chamberlain, in response to a request from the Opposition Front Bench spokesman Arthur Greenwood, made a statement on the European situation. He began by saying that the Government had no official confirmation of the rumours of any projected attack on Poland and that they must not therefore be taken as accepting them as true. But consultations were, he said, taking place with other Governments. He went on:

> In order to make perfectly clear the position of His Majesty's Government in the meantime, before these consultations are concluded, I now have to inform the House that, during that period, in the event of any action which clearly threatened Polish independence, and which the Polish Government accordingly considered it right to resist with their national forces, His Majesty's Government would feel themselves bound at once to lend the Polish Government all the support in their power.

He added that an assurance to this effect had been given to the Poles and that the French Government had authorized him to say that they were in the same position.

Greenwood said with some reason that this was the most momentous statement made in the House of Commons for a quarter of a century – i.e. since August 1914 and the outbreak of the Great War.

What Chamberlain had said had been delivered in his usual quiet and precise manner. It was almost as if he had caught his own dedication to appeasement unawares. After this, however much he might wish otherwise, that policy could never be quite the same again. The Polish Foreign Minister, Colonel Beck, was due to arrive in London on a visit three days later.

For many long-standing critics of appeasement the change of emphasis was still not convincing. Sir Stafford Cripps, who had been joined in expulsion from the Labour Party by Aneurin Bevan on the day Chamberlain spoke, said in a speech at Taunton: 'I do not believe in the sincerity of the National Government even in the proposals now put forward. I do not believe that this leopard, the National Government, has changed its spots.' And certainly those long committed to appeasement immediately began to show themselves restless in the restricted range of movement to which they now felt confined. Among these was the editor of *The Times*, often assumed to have, discreetly, special access to the Government's thinking. On the day after Chamberlain's statement, 1 April, he produced a remarkable leading article.

The Prime Minister's statement, it began, was one which needed to be 'read and re-read if its exact implications are to be appreciated correctly'. The exact implication to which the editor of *The Times* wished to draw attention was spelt out in the first paragraph: 'The historic importance of the British Government's declaration is that it commits them to stand for fair and free negotiation.' (This in itself was odd. The British Government had been committed to stand for 'fair and free negotiation' for many months. What was new was its specific commitment to go to the defence of a country in Europe if that country were attacked by Germany.) 'The new obligation', it went on, 'which this country yesterday assumed does not bind Great Britain to defend every inch of the present frontiers of Poland. The key word in the declaration is not "integrity" but "independence".'

The leader made no specific mention of Danzig or the Polish Corridor. But later it added: 'Mr Chamberlain's statement involves no blind acceptance of the *status quo*. On the contrary, his repeated references to free negotiation imply that he thinks that there are problems in which adjustments are still necessary.'

Some of the readers' letters that day were preoccupied with the issue of whether or not conscription was now necessary. But, possibly as if to emphasize the need for an everyday sense of proportion at such a moment, with Britain entering 'upon a course which diverges widely from her traditional aloofness from the affairs of Central Europe', the editor published as his first letter one dealing with a more appetising prospect. It came from the head chef of the Dorchester Hotel, much concerned to provide a suitable dinner for the Oxford and Cambridge boat crews after the six weeks of strict training which would end that day with the rowing of the traditional annual University Boat Race. Six weeks of grapefruit, he judged, required a choice of oysters or smoked salmon as a suitable starter, followed by clear soup, grilled sole, and chicken with new peas, 'many small potatoes', and asparagus 'with a brimming sauce-boat of melted butter'. But the course to which he paid most attention of all after their six-week deprivation of any sweets was the last. For this, he wrote, 'I conjure up in my mind the richest, most creamy, *bombe glacé* that ever *glacier* prepared.' The prospect seems to have been too much for Oxford. Certainly the race itself saw an upset of form. Oxford started as favourites but led only for the first ten strokes, after which Cambridge drew steadily ahead to win by four lengths in nineteen minutes and three seconds, a time that had only been bettered five times in the ninety-one years of the race's history.

The following Monday a letter appeared in the paper which carried two uncompromising headlines ('The Pledge to Poland' and 'Unanimous Support') but which reflected the same reasoned ambivalence behind an apparent firmness as the editor had displayed in his own leading article of the previous Saturday. The writer this time was the historian Arthur Bryant, and his letter occupied the greater part of a column.

It endorsed the pledge to Poland principally as a means of uniting British opinion behind Chamberlain in a manner which it maintained had not hitherto proved possible. (An opinion poll just conducted by the *New Chronicle* had in fact shown that popular approval for Chamberlain's policy of appeasement was consistently averaging just over fifty per cent.) But Bryant's letter went on to suggest that the policy which was to thus unite the nation by making clear its abhorrence of Hitler's methods would principally ensure peace by making it possible to negotiate with him wherever it might be politic and equitable to do so. The fatal weakness of the League of Nations had been that it provided no machinery for reviewing 'the dictated and anything but impartial settlement of Versailles'. What Chamberlain was trying to initiate was 'a new European policy of peaceful consultation and revision leading to the ultimate and gradual creation of a higher European order'. This was the only method of avoiding a war which 'with the destructive resources of modern science, would end in the destruction of European civilization for all time'. And Bryant complimented his editor on 'wisely' pointing out the previous Saturday that the British unilateral guarantee of Poland's independence did not necessarily mean a guarantee of the integrity of her present Versailles frontiers in perpetuity.

Alongside his letter civilization received homage from another correspondent under the headline 'The Progress of Television'. No one, the writer declared, who had seen for instance the great boxing-match between Boon and Danahar in February (relayed to large screens in London cinemas with varying visual success but to the amazed general approval of onlookers) could fail to understand that a new form of entertainment had arrived. The letter went on:

> I do not believe, however that any but a few people have yet realized what television is capable of giving this country. Not often does there emerge a new British industry with the clear opportunity of a lead over all other countries in the world market. Yet that is what television, resolutely, promptly and imaginatively developed, will give us. ... No other country in the world yet approaches this performance. But there are the beginnings of a public service in France and Germany; and when, this month, television makes a start in the United States a formidable rival will have entered the field. No one who has watched closely the coming of television can doubt that, sooner or later, it is going to sweep the world.

Even in such exciting new dimensions, however, everyday life was being increasingly overshadowed by international crisis.

When the commitment to Poland was debated in Parliament on 3 April Lord Halifax, in the House of Lords, nostalgically recalled the international mood that had followed Hitler's speech of 30 January. Then, as he said, 'it seemed possible to hope that nothing would occur to shake confidence in Europe and that we might have embarked on a period during which a sense of security might gradually have been established'. Now the only dissenting voice in the Lords on the Government's decision came from Lord Arnold who, in looking at what he described as 'this revolution in British foreign policy', expressed the belief that history would record that this commitment to Poland was one of the most unwise and dangerous decisions ever made by a British Government.

In the Commons, the very ambivalence of interpretation given to the pledge to Poland by *The Times* and indeed elsewhere contributed to a surprisingly une-quivocal and positive mood. Even before the appearance of *The Times* leader, on the very evening of Chamberlain's announcement of his pledge, Reuter had put out for international consumption a report that the Prime Minister's declaration was made with mental reservations, and that the Poles would be told that we expected them to get into negotiations with Germany, in the course of which they must be prepared to make substantial concessions to Hitler as the condition for our protection.

Hugh Dalton, speaking for the Labour Opposition in the debate, drew attention to this and maintained that it had very nearly been responsible for making Colonel Beck, the Polish Foreign Minister, put off his visit to London. The Foreign Office had indeed found it necessary to issue a statement the same evening, denying that such an interpretation was correct. The demand for a precise definition of the pledge had come up immediately at Question Time when R.A. Butler, the Under-Secretary for Foreign Affairs, was asked by Robert Boothby, the Conservative Member for Aberdeen, if he could assure the House that there was no truth in the suggestion contained in the leading article in *The Times* that the undertaking of His Majesty's Government to Poland did not cover existing frontiers. Butler assured him that it was the Foreign Office's statement of the previous Friday evening that was the correct interpretation.

Arthur Greenwood, for Labour, analysing what had happened as the closing of a chapter entitled 'Appeasement' and its replacement by one entitled 'Mutual Aid', also brought up the interpretation of Chamberlain's pledge given by *The Times*. He said he had understood the Prime Minister's statement to mean that should Poland become the next victim of aggression, 'immediately and without further parley Britain and France would come to her aid with all the means at their disposal'. This interpretation of Greenwood's was greeted by cheers from all sides of the House. It was important, he went on, that the extent of our commitment should be known.

Chamberlain, who was himself loudly cheered on rising, affirmed that the pledge 'does really constitute a new point – I would say a new epoch – in the course of our foreign policy', and said that he himself had been surprised that there should have been any misunderstanding. He would have thought it was 'plain and clear to all who could run or read'.

While not being concerned of course with 'some minor little frontier incident ... if the independence of the State of Poland should be threatened then the declaration which I made means that France and ourselves would immediately go to her assistance'. Again there were cheers from all over the House of Commons. Assurances previously given by Hitler, he went on, had been 'thrown to the winds' and had 'forced the British Government to make this great departure.... This country has been united from end to end by the conviction that we must now make our position clear and unmistakable whatever may be the result.' The cheers were particularly loud.

Sir Archibald Sinclair for the Liberal Opposition expressed forcibly the need for there to be 'no hedging in the policy of His Majesty's Government and no whittling-down of their pronouncements'. He had noted that newspapers which supported the Government had been swift to declare that Chamberlain's statement was intended to exclude Danzig and the Polish Corridor from the scope of the new guarantees. He insisted that Danzig and the Corridor were vital issues to Poland. He stressed that the task of constructing an alliance convincing enough to deter Hitler in the future was going to be extremely difficult 'because both in Central Europe and in Spain the weakness of the Government's policy in the past year had enabled Germany to acquire strategic positions of dominating power'. It was no longer possible to count on General Franco's neutrality, and he asked what assurances the governments of Italy and Germany may have given as to the departure of Italian and German troops from Spain. It was supremely important, he said, to bring Russia into co-operation with Britain in resistance to aggression.

Churchill, however, who had for so long criticized Chamberlain on such matters, was content now to express his 'most complete agreement with the Prime Minister' on this 'transformation' of his policy in the last few weeks and specifically thanked the Government for repudiating the sinister passages in *The Times* leading article and other attempts to whittle away the guarantees. He painted a graphic portrait of the phase through which they had been living and to which the Government's pledge to Poland was mercifully putting an end: 'Life', he said, 'is intolerable under present conditions. We wait from fortnight to fortnight for various dictatorial speeches. No one can plan ahead. Business is stifled, employment is deranged, insecurity and anxiety overcloud our happy land and lie still more darkly over Europe. A united stand must be made and be made now.'

It was left to the national leader in the Great War twenty years before, David Lloyd George, himself long in political decline, to introduce a note of uncomfortable realism. While hoping that the Government would not try and evade their commitment by inspired articles in *The Times* ('Ribbentrop is behind all that', interjected a Labour Member at this point), Lloyd George asked the House to examine calmly the position into which they had now got themselves. They could not go back again on the pledge they had given. 'The whole world would mock at us if we did.' (Here there were Government cries of: 'We are not going to do that.') Lloyd George went on to say that Britain had been admired, respected, hated, and feared, but she had never been laughed at. It was essential that, having given this solemn pledge with the assent practically of the whole people of this country and of France, we should carry it out. That meant that if Hitler marched his armies into Polish territory, with a view of annexing it to his own dominions, as he had in Czechoslovakia, France would march and we should march with her. But, he went on, was it in fact clear that we could help Poland?

If war occurred tomorrow we could not send a single battalion to Poland. . . . France could not. She would be confronted with fortifications which were infinitely more formidable than the Hindenburg line, which took us four years to break through with casualties running into millions.... What was going to happen to Poland while we were blockading Germany?

He stated awkwardly that we should also have the Italian army to face – at which point a Conservative Member interrupted him to say that he was harming the country by this sort of talk and Conservative supporters cheered the interrupter. But Lloyd George persisted in pointing out other disadvantages from which Britain was likely to suffer, including the hostility of Franco's Spain and a closed Mediterranean. Finally: 'without the help of Russia we should be walking into a trap.... I cannot think why, before we committed ourselves to this tremendous enterprise, we did not secure beforehand the adhesion of Russia. I ask the Government to take immediate steps to secure it.'

Sir Stafford Cripps was alone in wholly distrusting the Government's pledge, saying it would be foolish of anyone to place faith in the Government in the light of their actions over the last six years: they had shown a complete disregard for the principles of democracy, liberty, and freedom, which are the basis of civilization. He went on:

Fundamentally, the Government and their supporters have sympathy with the totalitarian view that it is necessary to suppress the common people and take away their freedom in order to preserve capitalism and imperialism.... I believe that the kite-flying articles in *The Times* were more truly representative of the views of the Government than the statements put out to contradict them by the Foreign Office.

But in winding up the debate, Sir John Simon, the Chancellor of the Exchequer, went out of his way once again to emphasize the unequivocal nature of the Government's pledge to Poland. He spoke of 'the unreasonable comment and quite unfounded gloss' placed by both Reuter and *The Times* on the Prime Minister's declaration, which he declared was 'perfectly straightforward. I do not think it was capable of being given some refined or unnatural meaning. It is to be understood in the fullest sense it bears.'

The leader in *The Times* the next day blandly ignored the references to itself with which the debate had been punctuated. It could not do less than applaud the Prime Minister, whose parliamentary performance, it said, had been one of his greatest, but in doing so the editor still managed to convey to those who wished to find it some of the ambivalence which had caused the trouble. Chamberlain, he wrote, was 'not concerned with details but with this essential principle of security and civilization'. A loophole was thus left as to whether or not Danzig and the Polish Corridor – otherwise unmentioned in the article – might prove to be details. *The Times*'s severest criticism of the debate was reserved for what it called the 'outburst' of inconsolable pessimism' from Lloyd George, who, it said, 'now seems to inhabit an odd and remote world of his own'.

That same day Colonel Beck, the Polish Minister, arrived in London. When he left two days later, it was announced that an agreement had been reached with the British Government on a formal and permanent expression of the pledge. The news aroused the considerable resentment of the German press, which nevertheless managed to suggest that, because nothing had yet been officially signed, it was still not too late for Poland to meet Germany's terms for a settlement of the Danzig and Corridor problems, namely the return of Danzig to the Reich and the construction of an extra-territorial autobahn under German sovereignty to East Prussia – a corridor across the Corridor. The trouble was, said the *Völkischer Beobachter*, that Warsaw had caught 'war influenza' from London. All the Polish papers, however, pointed out the purely defensive aspect of the projected alliance.

It was Holy Week, and an eventful one. The revelation that the Head Chef at the Dorchester had conned *The Times* into giving him free publicity with his letter about the Boat Race dinner would have passed deservedly unnoticed had *The Times* not published a correction on their leader page. The two university crews, it seemed, had dined separately and not at the Dorchester at all – Oxford at the United University Club and Cambridge at the Junior Carlton.

The day of this revelation also brought first reports from the Mediterranean of a concentration of Italian troops and transports at Bari and Brindisi, an indication, according to *The Times*, that Italy intended to make some move in regard to Albania. Then, at midday on Good Friday, Italians learned from their newspapers that their troops had indeed invaded Albania, 'called there by Albanian patriots who could no longer tolerate the misgovernment of the King [Zog] and to defend the lives and property of Italian citizens who were threatened and attacked by armed bands'. The *Popolo di Roma* offered a frank explanation: 'In the case of war against anybody the sure military possession of the Albanian coast is for Italy a matter of life and death.'

Signor Gayda, Mussolini's mouthpiece in *Il Giornale d'Italia*, said Italy was not entering Albania in the spirit of a harsh conquest but with a deep respect for the spirit, habits and real needs of the Albanians. Her collaboration on the largest possible scale would be devoted to directing the Albanians along the path of labour and progress in accordance with her historic mission, which in past decades had already been recognized by all foreign observers.

It had, indeed, long been accepted by international opinion that Albania reasonably belonged within the Italian sphere of influence. But it was the unilateral assertion of this influence in a new, stark form, without any further regard for international opinion or for the Anglo-Italian agreement guaranteeing the status quo in the Mediterranean, confirmed only in January, which added one more twist to an increasingly implacable sense of international crisis.

The first news from the Albanian Legation in London was that 'stiff resistance' was being offered to the invaders, but the same communiqué conceded that by

1.30 on Good Friday afternoon the main ports of the country - San Giovanni di Medua, Durazzo, Valona and Santa Quaranta - had been taken.

Resistance was not, in fact, appreciable, though the landing at Durazzo was held up for an hour or so and twelve Italians were killed and fifty-three wounded there. Enthusiasm for King Zog, however, was little more than perfunctory and he seems to have anticipated this, for he and his family fled immediately from his capital, Tirana, on Good Friday in a motor convoy, which by Sunday had safely crossed the frontier into Greece. The Italians sent a regiment of Grenadiers to Tirana by air to join up with the troops moving up the road from the coast.

In the course of a lightning campaign Italian troops often made a point of displaying tactful chivalry, by complimenting the Albanians, for instance, on their marksmanship, which had delayed the drive up to Scutari from the coast for a whole day, and at Scutari itself by replacing the white flag (which had been run up in token of surrender) with the Albanian flag to fly alongside the Italian. Officers who had fought on to the last round in the castle were treated with the full honours of war and the Albanian army itself was painlessly transformed into an Albanian gendarmerie. None of this lessened the detrimental effect of the enterprise on international confidence. It was the Italian version of Hitler's occupation of Prague – evidence, as some saw it, of Mussolini's need to show that he was not just a sleeping partner in the Axis.

The Rome-Berlin-Tokyo Axis had just acquired an honorary partner in the form of General Franco, who had brought Spain into the Anti-Comintern Pact. And the question of when the Italian troops were to be withdrawn from Spain was now sharply accentuated by the invasion of Albania. The only reply vouch-safed to the British Government so far was that the withdrawal would take place after Franco's victory parade in Madrid, originally planned for 20 April, but now, it was announced, postponed until 2 May.

On Easter Sunday, Chamberlain flew down to London, cutting short the holiday he had been taking in Aberdeenshire, for a Cabinet meeting on Easter Monday. It was the first time the Cabinet had met on a Bank Holiday since the Great War. Downing Street was packed with sightseers to watch the Ministers arrive on what in London was a warmer-than-average day for April with attendance at the Zoo nearing a record. After the Cabinet meeting, which lasted two and a quarter hours, it was announced that Parliament was to be recalled from the Easter recess to meet in two days' time. Constant exchanges were taking place, it was said, with the Greek, Rumanian and Turkish governments.

The Italian press continued to play down the invasion of Albania. Signor Gayda in *Il Giornale d'Italia* maintained bluntly that 'what Italy is doing there is no more than Britain and France have done in Egypt, Algeria and many other parts of the world'. But it was estimated that Italy must now have at least 1,250,000 men under arms. Again, as if to play down the possible implications of this, the Italian Government issued a statement saying there would be no more call-ups unless 'unforeseeen circumstances' arose.

It was not, of course, merely due to events in the Mediterranean that alarm bells were ringing all round Europe. A reminder of the simultaneous tension in Poland came from the Warsaw military newspaper *Polska Zbrojna*, which declared:

> The whole people will fight with determination for Polish liberty and independence. Nothing will be given up without a fight. Every Polish house will be a fortress which the enemy will have to take by storm. The danger from the air will not daunt Poland, which is chiefly an agricultural country.... Whoever seeks a quarrel with Poland will have more to lose than to gain.

The Dutch Government, while making clear that they did not feel directly menaced, felt sufficiently apprehensive of the general European tension to issue an Order in Council which specifically declared that there was a danger of war. It was expressed in curiously fatalistic, even poetic, tones for a government statement. 'The more calmly all of us continue to go about our work,' it ran, 'the better it will be for ourselves and the better will be the impression abroad. Our fate is not in our hands: God Almighty rules the world. This faith gives force and firmness, and prevents man from swaying to and fro like a reed.'

In the United States, the day before, President Roosevelt had taken leave of a group at Warm Springs, Georgia, with the words: 'I'll be back in the Fall if we don't have war.' The *Washington Post* commented:

> Most Americans realize today that the sweep of events has now brought Europe to the very edge of war. What is insufficiently realized is the tremendous implications of the impending catastrophe for every citizen of this country. There is speculation as to what the President meant by 'we' ... by 'we' he undoubtedly meant Western civilization. A war affecting its foundation would immediately affect us vitally, whether or not the United States was at the outset involved.... He told the Axis powers that the Administration is far from indifferent to their plotting. He made it plain that a war forced by them would from the outset involve the destinies of a nation which, as they fully realize, is far stronger than Germany and Italy united.

From this week onwards the events of the year 1939 acquired for those who lived through them a sense of inescapable momentum towards a historic conclusion such as is rare for people preoccupied with the day-to-day business of ordinary life. On the day after the *Washington Post*'s article, Harold Nicolson, the anti-Chamberlain National Labour MP, sitting in his new boat on the Hamble River and listening to the sound of people scrubbing the deck mingling with the sound of aircraft overhead, wrote: 'How happy I should be if there were no fear of war, and if I could really believe that in a few weeks I should be cresting the waves.' Chips Channon, a pro-Chamberlain Member of Parliament, had written in his diary on the Good Friday of Italy's invasion of Albania: 'The terrible inevitability of war has descended upon us.'

On 13 April, Chamberlain told the House of Commons that the Government was giving a pledge of full support to Greece and Rumania, if action were taken against their independence which they considered it vital to resist. Consultations with the Turkish Government along similar lines were also under way. The French Prime Minister, Daladier, in a special broadcast put out at 4 p.m. that afternoon, associated himself with the British Government's action. The Italian paper *Corriere della Sera* commented that, as Great Britain seemed to have a mania for guaranteeing countries which no one was likely to attack, she might like to guarantee the moon. The German paper, the *Völkischer Beobachter*, said that Britain was 'creating superfluous tensions in Europe, sabotaging natural development and bringing harmless nations into positions from which they – and not the British – must suffer. What British policy has achieved in Poland, and would like to achieve in Greece and Rumania, is simply a European crime.' And the paper referred to 'the unscrupulous war agitators of the Thames'.

Anthony Eden, speaking in the debate in the House of Commons on the pledges to Greece and Rumania, expressed the mood of Britain more recognizably when he said that there could not have been anyone at Easter who did not have feelings of horror that the world was possibly approaching a state of affairs similar to that endured not so long ago.

In Greece, however, under the immediate impact of relief, things momentarily looked more hopeful. The Athens newspaper *Hestia* wrote the next day: 'Once again the imminent danger of war has been averted and mankind can confidently expect world peace to be pursued.' From the other side of the Atlantic, on the same day, came words from President Roosevelt further investing the pursuit of peace with a high authoritative tone which could also act as a salutary warning to the European dictators. He peremptorily dismissed Mussolini's claim that he was a prisoner in the Mediterranean and Hitler's claim that he was being encircled by agreements between nations to defend each other's independence. Speaking to the Union of Pan-American States on the forty-ninth anniversary of its foundation, he held up the Declaration made by the twenty-one American States at Lima the previous December as an example of the way in which affairs between nations should be handled. He continued:

> The American family of nations may also rightfully claim now to speak to the rest of the world. We have an interest wider than that of the mere defences of our sea-ringed continent. We now know that the development of the next generation will so narrow the oceans separating us from the Old World that our customs and our actions are necessarily involved in theirs, whether we like it or not. Beyond any question, within a few scant years, air fleets will cross the ocean as easily as today they cross the closed European seas.... Our will to peace can be as powerful as our will to mutual defence.... It will have its voice in determining the order of world affairs in days to come.

That same night Roosevelt addressed a personal message directly to Hitler and Mussolini, a move immediately applauded in a broadcast by Senator Pitman, Chairman of the Senate Foreign Affairs Committee, who declared that never in history had there been 'so imminent and dangerous a threat' to the peace of the 'whole world and of civilization'. The next morning Roosevelt held a press conference at which Senator Pitman, Cordell Hull (Secretary of State) and Sumner Welles (Under-Secretary of State) were all present. Having said that he and Cordell Hull had felt no effort should be spared in trying to avert war and that they had slept with clearer consciences after they had sent the message to Hitler and Mussolini, he read out its content to the assembled journalists.

It began impressively and sombrely, though also with a faintly patronizing touch, possibly inappropriate to the politically sensitive natures of the two dictators to whom it was personally addressed:

> You realize, I am sure, that throughout the world hundreds of millions of human beings are living today in constant fear of a new war or even a series of wars. The existence of this fear – and the possibility of such a conflict – is of definite concern to the people of the United States, for whom I speak, as it must also be to the peoples of other nations of the entire Western Hemisphere. All of them know that any major war, even if it were to be confined to other continents, must bear heavily on them during its continuation, and also for generations to come.
>
> Because of the fact that after the acute tension in which the world has been living during the past few weeks there would seem to be at least a momentary relaxation – because no troops are at this moment on the march – this may be an opportune moment for me to send you this message.

After regretting in somewhat schoolmasterly fashion that the standards of international conduct which he had previously enjoined them to follow had been disregarded and that three nations in Europe (Czechoslovakia, Austria and Albania) and one in Africa (Abyssinia) had lost their independence, while vast areas of China had been occupied by their ally Japan, he continued: 'Reports which we trust are not true insist that further acts of aggression are contemplated against still other independent nations.'

He reminded them that they had repeatedly asserted that neither the Italian nor German peoples wanted war and said that in speaking thus for Americans he spoke not from selfishness or fear or weakness but 'with the voice of strength and friendship for mankind'. He advocated in general terms the solution of international problems at the council table. But first, 'as head of a nation far removed from Europe . . . acting only with the responsibility and obligation of a friendly intermediary', he sought from them an immediate statement of intent.

> Are you willing [he asked] to give assurance that your armed forces will not attack or invade the territory or possessions of the following independent nations: - Finland, Estonia, Latvia, Lithuania, Sweden, Norway, Denmark, the Netherlands, Belgium, Great Britain and Ireland, France, Portugal, Spain, Switzerland, Liechtenstein, Luxemburg, Poland, Hungary, Roumania, Yugoslavia, Russia, Bulgaria, Greece, Turkey, Iraq, the Arabias, Syria, Palestine, Egypt, and Iran?

He undertook to transmit their assurances to this effect, which he hoped could

ABOVE LEFT President Roosevelt: 'The possibility of conflict is of definite concern to the people of the United States.'

RIGHT Former British Foreign Secretary Anthony Eden and Polish Foreign Secretary Colonel Beck toast the British pledge to Poland: 'at once . . . all the support in our power'.

In the Kroll Opera House, Berlin, Hitler answers Roosevelt's 'curious telegram'.

be construed as applying to a period of ten years at the least – 'a quarter of a century if we dare look that far ahead' – to the governments concerned. He ended:

> I think you will not misunderstand the spirit of frankness in which I send you this message. Heads of great governments in this hour are literally responsible for the fate of humanity in the coming years. They cannot fail to hear the prayers of their peoples to be protected from the foreseeable chaos of war. History will hold them accountable for the lives and happiness of all – even unto the least. I hope that your answer will make it possible for humanity to lose fear and regain security for many years to come.

The reality behind President Roosevelt's forebodings was illustrated by a small incident in Poland on the same day as that on which the world read of Roosevelt's message in its newspapers. A delegation of Polish journalists visited the Polish Prime Minister, General Slawoj-Skladowski, and told him that all Polish journalists had resolved to sink their differences in order to give the Government full support in the interests of national unity and defence. *The Times* reported a universally patriotic mood in the country. 'There is no excitement, but a calm determination to defend the independence regained twenty years ago. Nobody wants war, but the country's mind is made up. It has no doubts: it will fight.'

In the British House of Commons the Government was asked specifically by Geoffrey Mander, the Liberal Member for Wolverhampton, if existing Polish rights in Danzig were covered by the British guarantee. R.A.Butler, Under-Secretary at the Foreign Office, replied that Chamberlain's recent statement had put beyond doubt the nature of the undertakings given to the Polish Government and there were ministerial cheers to support this. But when Mander asked further: 'Is it not important that the whole world should know whether existing rights are affected or not?' there was no further reply, the inference being presumably that there was no need for one.

A reminder that the international situation continued to be sensitive in the region which had given most cause for concern in the earlier months of the year came from unconfirmed reports of large amounts of German equipment arriving in naval ports and aerodromes on the north-west coast of Spain. These were accompanied by the disquieting announcement that General Franco's triumphal march through Madrid, before which Mussolini was not prepared to withdraw Italian troops from Spain, had been postponed once again, this time until 15 May.

Roosevelt's message was enthusiastically received by the democracies. The British Government said they entirely endorsed the President's estimate of the international situation and believed that the statesmanlike initiative which he had been inspired to take offered a real opportunity of averting the catastrophe which hung over Europe. In France, the London *Times* reported, newspaper-sellers on the Champs Elysées reaped a rich harvest from the many thousands of

Parisians strolling in the afternoon sun, relieved for once to have news at a weekend that did not tell of some totalitarian *fait accompli* and finding it difficult to see how the dictatorship, could openly reject the President's appeal. Surprisingly perhaps after Stalin's recent castigation of the European democracies, the Soviet Union's welcome to President Roosevelt's message was as enthusiastic as anyone's. It was described in an official cable from President Kalinin of the USSR to the American President as a noble appeal and one which would 'find the warmest reception in the hearts of the peoples of the Soviet Socialist Union, who are sincerely desirous of the preservation of universal peace'. The cable could be interpreted as lending an optimistic tinge to the two long talks which the British Ambassador in Moscow, Sir William Seeds, had been having over the weekend with Litvinov, the Soviet Foreign Minister.

Details of these conversations were not revealed, but Seeds explained to the Press that the Soviet reaction was natural, since one of the results of the British Government's efforts to steady the situation in eastern and south-eastern Europe during the past fortnight had been to fortify for Soviet Russia most of her western frontier states.

That the German and Italian press would treat President Roosevelt's message with little but scorn was only to be expected, and they duly obliged. The Hamburger *Fremdenblatt*, for instance, described it as only a tactical manœuvre to present Germany and Italy as the hindrances to a general settlement, and in this way to give moral support to the policy of encirclement. The *Völkischer Beobachter* referred to it as an infamous trick and said it was astounded that the President of the United States should lower himself to send a shabby propaganda pamphlet as a message to two Heads of State. It attacked him personally as 'the man who, more than any other statesman, has contributed to the present war atmosphere and now wants to appear, like President Wilson, in the guise of an angel of peace. If he is successful, he will be elected President a third time; if not, then he has a moral alibi, and will be able to wash his hands in innocence with the well-known pose of Pontius Pilate.'

The reply to Roosevelt's message of the two Heads of State themselves, though likely to be negative, was also likely to be presented in a more considered fashion than in the conventional apparatus of their Governments' press. But the Italian press in particular had been denouncing Roosevelt so violently as a troublemaker and even as a lunatic, that *The Times* thought it was indeed going to be difficult for 'Signor Mussolini to accept him suddenly as the artisan of world peace'. Hitler, however, whose birthday was due in a few days' time, soon made it clear that whatever the exact nature of his reply to Roosevelt, it would be an elaborate one, and one which would engage the attention of the world. He announced that he had summoned the Reichstag to meet on Friday 28 April, when he would deliver his answer to Roosevelt 'in the name of the German people'.

In the meantime Mussolini rather skilfully chose his own opportunity to deliver a public reply to Roosevelt. The occasion was the opening by himself of a new phase in the preparations for the World Exhibition to be held outside Rome in 1942. Fifteen thousand workmen were already employed on the site, and Italy's contribution was to include buildings of the proportions of the Colosseum and St Peter's, which, according to Mussolini, were to remain as permanent memorials of the Fascist era throughout the ages. Casting his eyes over the physical evidence of this elaborate and expensive commitment to the future, the Duce declared:

> If we had any intention of setting the world ablaze, we should not be harnessing ourselves to a task so enormous. If, in spite of the storm-clouds which weigh on the horizon, we have dared to start and go on with this work cheerfully it ought to be considered a hopeful sign and as proof that we do not want to attack anyone but only get on with our job.

It was, he said, unjust to put the two Axis countries into the dock. He dismissed the scheme for mutual guarantees as absurd. Equally absurd were the colossal geographical errors made by persons (and here, according to *The Times*, Mussolini's eyebrows rose in the manner of the comedian George Robey's) who had the most rudimentary notions of European affairs.

As the world waited for Hitler's reply, his admirers acknowledged his birthday in appropriate fashion. Goering saluted him as 'the greatest German of all time' and continued: 'Let the politicians and statesmen of the world forge their plans and intrigues; let journalists spout forth poison against us; for us, undisturbed by their shrieks, only the world of Adolf Hitler is valid.... Lord God, protect the Führer and bless his work.'

General Franco's press congratulated him in more measured but equally laudatory tones: 'Herr Hitler's great merit', wrote the *Diario Vasco*, 'is his sincerity, his heroic and transparent conduct contrasted with the hidden desires and false purposes of his adversaries. Neither Germany, Italy nor Spain has ever betrayed Western interests or sinned against civilization.'

There was still a week to go before Hitler was due to reply to Roosevelt and in the meantime a certain anxiety was caused in some circles, particularly among the left wing in France but also in Poland, by the news that the British Ambassador, Sir Nevile Henderson, who had been withdrawn at the time of the invasion of Czechoslovakia, was returning to Berlin. There was an uneasy sensation that this could possibly herald a return to the policy of appeasement, or at least indicate that it was still somehow waiting in the wings. Such uneasy thoughts could, in the minds of the uncharitable, receive substantiation from the welcome given to Henderson's return by the Italian press who regarded it as a sign that Britain was now turning over a new leaf and abandoning her base designs for encircling the Axis Powers. On the other hand, those who wished to emphasize the integrity of Chamberlain's new stance could point to the Government announcement on 27 April that a new Compulsory Military Training Bill for all men between the ages of twenty and twenty-one would be introduced into the

House of Commons the following week, involving, it was estimated, about 200,000 men in six months' training. Next day Hitler spoke to the Reichstag, whose members received him with great enthusiasm.

His speech, which lasted about two and a half hours, was closely reasoned and, while hardly conciliatory, could not in fairness be thought dramatically provocative. Indeed in the course of it he went out of his way to stress the sincerity of his feelings of friendship towards England. His tone was primarily one of expiatory self-justification, spiced from time to time with a certain sharp irony and even wit at the expense of the President of the United States.

'Members of the German Reichstag!' he began. 'The President of the United States of America has addressed a telegram to me, with the curious contents of which you are already familiar . . .'

Before making any direct reply, he embarked on humble thanks to a Providence which had enabled him 'to find the way to free our people from its deepest misery without any shedding of blood, and to lead it upwards once more . . . to raise my German people out of the depths of defeat and to liberate it from the bonds of the most infamous dictate of all times. For this alone has been the aim of my actions . . .'

But he said that he had never left any doubt that there was a limit to the extent to which the Treaty of Versailles should be revised and that wherever what he called 'the higher interests of the European comity' were at stake, German national interests had to be put in second place. He cited for example the two 'former Imperial Provinces' of Alsace and Lorraine, on which Germany no longer had any claim. After justifying the Anschluss of Austria, and the absorption of Bohemia and Moravia into a renewal of earlier historic, economic and cultural links between those provinces and the German Reich, and indeed between the German and Czech peoples, he denied that he had broken the Munich Agreement by occupying Prague. That agreement, he said, had specifically stated that other problems remained to be solved in the area. If the concomitant parts of Czechoslovakia had decided to turn to Germany and Italy rather than to the Four Powers as a whole for the solution of such problems and had finally split the State so that no such Czechoslovakia any longer existed, it was hardly a matter of reproach to Germany. Bohemia and Moravia were now no longer the concern of the signatories of the Munich Agreement. 'Just as English measures in, say, Northern Ireland, whether they be right or wrong, are not subject to German supervision or criticism, this is also the case with these old German electorates.'

He went on to stress in the most positive terms his wish for a close friendship and collaboration between Germany and England:

This desire for Anglo-German friendship and co-operation conforms not merely to sentiments which result from the racial origins of our two peoples, but also to my realization of the importance for the whole of mankind of the existence of the British

Empire. . . . The existence of this Empire is an inestimable factor of value for the whole of human cultural and economic life.

He said the wish and conviction that there should never again be a war between England and Germany was alive in him today, but since a war against Germany was now taken for granted in Great Britain and the press and official-dom there upheld the view that Germany should be opposed under all circum-stances and confirmed this with their policy of encirclement, he had decided to put an end to the Anglo-German Naval Agreement. No one would be happier than he at the prospect of still being able to come to some clear and straight-forward understanding with the British Government, but whoever believed that he could attack Germany would find himself confronted with a measure of power and resistance compared with which that of 1914 was negligible.

He soon turned to what he called the problem that was 'perhaps the most painful of all problems for Germany': that of relations with Poland, and specif-ically the problem of Danzig and the Polish Corridor. And he stated the essence of that problem most reasonably:

I have never ceased to uphold the view that the necessity of a free access to the sea for the Polish State cannot be ignored. . . . I considered it, however, necessary to make it clear to the Government in Warsaw that just as they desire access to the sea, so Germany needs access to her province in the East. Now, these are all difficult problems . . .

What he now proposed was that Danzig should return into the framework of the German Reich and that Germany should receive a route through the Corridor and a railway line at her own disposal possessing the same extra-territorial status for Germany as the Corridor itself had for Poland. In return Germany would recognize all Polish economic rights in Danzig, would grant her a free harbour with completely free access to the sea, and at the same time regard the present boundaries between Germany and Poland as ultimate, and would conclude a twenty-five-year non-aggression treaty with Poland – a treaty, therefore, which would extend 'far beyond the duration of my own life'.

The Polish Government, he said, had rejected his offer and merely proposed to negotiate over the question of a substitute for the League of Nations Com-missioner in Danzig and to consider facilities for transit traffic through the Corridor. This was regrettable enough, but even worse was the fact that now Poland, like Czechoslovakia a year ago, was calling up troops, though Germany had not called up a single man and had not thought of proceeding in any way against Poland. 'As I have said, this is in itself very regrettable, and posterity will one day decide whether it was right to refuse this suggestion.' In view of Poland's entry into a pact of mutual assistance with Great Britain he had decided to consider the German–Polish Non-Aggression Pact as no longer in existence. But he repeated that this decision did not constitute any modification of his attitude

Author H.G. Wells – back from trouble in Australia – lunching with friends at the Gargoyle Club in London's Soho.

Conductor Arturo Toscanini in London: 'music in the teeth of the wind'.

in principle to the problems of Danzig and the Corridor and he would welcome some fresh contractual arrangement with the Polish Government.

In these circumstances the responsibility for fresh unrest in Europe lay solely in the propaganda services of the international warmongers conducted by numerous organs of the democratic States which by constantly increasing nervousness and by the invention of continual rumours strove to make Europe ripe for catastrophe – namely the Bolshevik destruction of European civilization.

He concluded his survey of the international scene by saying that the mischief-makers had been deprived of one of the greatest of danger-spots of the European crisis – Spain – 'thanks to the heroism of one man, his nation and – I may say – also thanks to the Italian and German volunteers'.

But international warmongers in the past few weeks had been fabricating further lying assertions and publishing in numerous newspapers childish and malicious reports. Referring to a U.S. radio broadcast at the end of 1938 by Orson Welles of H.G. Wells' *The War of the Worlds* which had momentarily panicked the city of New York, Hitler noted with pleasure that nervous hysteria was now such that even 'the landing of inhabitants from Mars in the land of unlimited possibilities' was considered likely. The real purpose of the campaign was to prepare the people to accept the English policy of encirclement and support it, should the worst come to the worst. He stressed, however, that the German people could face all this in perfect tranquility, for their frontiers were guarded by the best army in Germany's history, the air above them was protected by the most powerful air fleet and their coasts rendered unassailable by an enemy power, while in the West the strongest defensive work of all times had been built. And after acknowledging and approving the Italian invasion of Albania as a legitimate spread of the civilizing work of Fascism, he stressed the hope that Germany, Italy and Japan would forge still closer relations than at present, these three great powers being 'the strongest factor in the future, making for the preservation of a true human culture, a practical civilization and a just order in the world'.

He then turned at last to Roosevelt.

He first stated that of the fourteen small wars and twenty-six violent interventions which had taken place between 1919 and 1938, Germany had participated in none. Of course in order to accept this (and it was a reservation he did not make) it was necessary to accept that the German 'volunteers' in Spain had genuinely gone of their own free will, and that the annexations of Austria and Czechoslovakia had not been violent interventions. Nevertheless, the assertion enabled him playfully to continue:

It would therefore be a mistake in my eyes to assume that the fear of war inspiring European and non-European nations can at this present time be directly traced back to actual wars at all. The reason for this fear lies simply and solely in an unbridled agitation on the part of the press, ... and an artificial spreading of panic, which in the end goes so far that interventions from another planet are believed possible and cause scenes of desperate alarm.

He then proceeded to tackle with a similar irony tinged with indignation, a number of high-minded expressions of concern to which Roosevelt had given voice. Roosevelt had said that every major war must have serious consequences for generations to come. 'Answer: no one knows this better than the German people. For the Peace Treaty of Versailles placed burdens on the German people which could not have been paid off even in a hundred years ...' Roosevelt had appealed for a peaceful settlement of political, economic and social problems without resort to arms. 'Answer: I myself have always been an exponent of this view ...' Roosevelt had said that the peoples of the earth could not be persuaded that any governing power had the right or need to inflict the consequences of war on its own or any other people, save in the cause of self-evident home defence. 'Answer: I should think that every reasonable human being is of this opinion ...' Roosevelt had asked for specific assurances that the German armed forces would not attack a specific list of twenty-nine States which he named.

Answer: I have first taken the trouble to ascertain from the States mentioned, firstly whether they feel themselves threatened, and secondly and above all, whether this enquiry by the American President was addressed to us at their suggestion or at any rate with their consent. The reply was in all cases negative, in some cases positively so. It is true that I could not cause enquiries to be made of certain of the States and Nations mentioned because they themselves – for example, Syria – are at present not in possession of their freedom, but are occupied and consequently deprived of their rights by the military agents of democratic states. Apart from this fact, however, all states bordering on Germany have received much more binding assurances and above all suggestions than Mr Roosevelt asked from me in his curious telegram ...

I must also draw Mr Roosevelt's attention to one or two historical errors. He mentions Ireland, for instance, and asks for a statement to the effect that Germany will not attack Ireland. Now I have just read a speech delivered by Mr de Valera, the Irish Taoiseach, in which, strangely enough, and contrary to Mr Roosevelt's opinion, he does not charge Germany with oppressing Ireland, but reproaches England with subjecting Ireland to continuous aggression at her hands. With all due respect to Mr Roosevelt's insight into the needs and cares of other countries it may nevertheless be assumed that the Irish Taoiseach will be more familiar with the dangers which threaten his country than the President of the United States.

In the same way the fact has obviously escaped Mr Roosevelt's notice that Palestine is at present occupied not by German troops but by the English ... and is suffering the cruellest maltreatment for the benefit of Jewish interlopers ...

After observing that it was doubtless the size of the United States that enabled President Roosevelt 'to find time and leisure to give your attention to universal problems – consequently the world is undoubtedly so small for you that you perhaps believe that your intervention and action can be effective everywhere' – Hitler said that he was content to work on a much smaller scale for his own people, believing, however, that 'this is the way in which I can be of most service to that for which we are all concerned – namely the justice, well-being, progress, and peace of the whole human community'.

It was not on the face of it the speech of a man preparing to plunge the world into a major war. One American correspondent described it aptly as a vaudeville act and Goering, sitting above Hitler's rostrum and beneath the giant Nazi eagle which dominated the audience had been observed jumping up and down in his seat with joy at his leader's sarcasm. The 862 members of the Reichstag who constituted the audience had also greeted the Führer's words with appreciative uncontrollable laughter at times and had wiped tears from their eyes when he read out the list of nations for which President Roosevelt was so deeply concerned. He was quite prepared, however, to give the assurances required and added the United States to the list for good measure.

'Hitler opens the door to negotiations', was how the *Daily Express* summed up the speech. 'If Hitler means peace, then the questions of Danzig and the Polish Corridor should not stand in the way of securing peace.'

But *Le Petit Journal* of Paris commented: 'Only imbeciles or traitors will tell us we should be entirely reassured by the Führer's speech.'

The London Stock Exchange received it well, but the New York Stock Exchange couldn't decide: stocks first rose buoyantly, then hovered and began to fall.

The *Washington Star* saw in the speech 'anything but pacific significance'.

'Hitler has spoken,' wrote the London *News Chronicle*, 'and the world breathes again.' But it summed up what he had said as 'an attempt to fan the dying embers of appeasement'.

It was indeed a speech well-calculated to appeal to appeasers. For the puzzling question of whether or not appeasement was really dead was itself still very much alive.

The puzzle was all the more impenetrable because of the extent to which those who still hankered after the old policy seemed themselves confused as to whether they really favoured it or not. There was also the difficulty of defining where exactly appeasement began and a reasonable willingness to respond, say, to Hitler's speech, ended.

Up to the Ides of March and Hitler's occupation of Prague it had seemed that British public opinion was very marginally in favour of 'appeasement' as Chamberlain had then been pursuing it. Not only did the opinion polls show him consistently commanding about fifty per cent of the British public's support as Prime Minister, but a British Institute of Public Opinion poll published on the very day Hitler occupied Prague showed those who were actively opposed to appeasement as a distinct minority. Only twenty-four per cent thought that it was 'bringing war near by whetting the appetites of the dictators'. But the poll also revealed some blurring of concept as to what appeasement actually was. It was positively approved of by twenty-eight per cent as 'a policy which would ultimately lead to enduring peace'; but forty-six per cent thought it would 'keep us out of war until we had time to rearm'.

The partial detachment from the European scene felt by intelligent American observers enabled them to gauge the European mood more coherently than those directly affected by it.

P.J.Philip, the *New York Times* correspondent in Paris, writing on the day after Hitler's speech had been digested, said it was quite clear that the day had not yet come when Britain and France were prepared to oppose Germany's forceful revision of the Peace Treaty terms on the eastern front with a definite 'No'. As Warsaw had stiffened her attitude, he wrote, so Paris and London had seemed to incline towards compromise, and having excited Poland's expectations and aroused public sentiments in Warsaw to a heroic pitch, the French and British Governments were now advising the utmost prudence on Colonel Beck, the Foreign Minister, when he was scheduled to make his reply to Hitler in less than a week's time. Both countries, wrote Philip, were apprehensive that the sudden seizure of Danzig by Hitler might cause a new outburst of patriotism in Warsaw and a summons for the implementation of the guarantee.

As informed attention increasingly focused on Danzig and the Polish Corridor, another *New York Times* correspondent, Anne O'Hare McCormick, writing from Rome, placed European concern vividly within the context of everyday living:

> One impression outstanding after a survey of more than a dozen countries is that tomorrow has come to have a very limited meaning to most Europeans. It is not next year or next month; it is just the day after today. They go to bed every night wondering what will happen in the morning. . . . Europe in the strange upheaval of recent months has lost not only the sense of future but the sense of sequence. No one plans because no one can count on one event following another in any sort of logical order. . . . The fundamental fact of the European situation is that millions of men are under arms and ready to go. This mobilization puts practically every country of this Continent on a war footing.

In the United States themselves it was still possible to take a loftier view of 'tomorrow'. On 30 April, the anniversary of the inauguration of the first President, George Washington, President Roosevelt, not particularly smarting under the reply he had received from Hitler to his telegram, opened the New York World Fair, dedicated indeed to the theme of the 'World of Tomorrow'. It was the biggest international exhibition in history, at which some sixty nations were represented and in which 1,216 acres were covered with pavilions and fair grounds. The *New York Times* described it as a spectacle of surprising beauty and magnificence, especially at night, when the lighting effects and fireworks were reflected in the various pools and lagoons. The Fair was dominated by a 700-foot three-sided beacon and broadcasting tower, the Trylon, and a 200-foot Perisphere, the supporting columns of which were screened by cluster of fountains so that the ball appeared to be poised in the air on jets of water. Inside this spectators could view, from revolving platforms suspended in mid-air, what the 'World of Tomorrow' was to be like. There displayed was a conception of the city of the future, 'Democracity': 'a conception of more and more progress in democracy and in the advance of science, industry, commerce, transportation, commercialism, the arts and the professions to bring peace and happiness to mankind'. Over half a million people attended the Fair on its first day. However, as the *New York Times* felt compelled to add: 'The world of tomorrow has a great deal of unfinished business in it.'

16

The principal piece of unfinished business immediately engaging the mind of the world was Danzig. On 1 May the *New York Times* again reported that Paris and London seemed hopeful of a compromise on the Polish Corridor and Danzig, and that there seemed to be in both capitals a 'disinclination to fight on the issue'. Indeed that Delphic source, the editor of the London *Times*, while criticizing Hitler's speech had insisted reasonably that 'the improvement of arrangements in the Corridor is not incapable of determination between a peacefully-minded German and a strong Poland'.

The *New York Times* correspondent in London, Ferdinand Kuhn Jr, discussed the hesitation felt in British Government circles about the negotiations which had been opened a fortnight before for some alliance with the Soviet Union. He judged that the traditional Tory prejudices against Bolshevism had been effectively swallowed, or the approach could not have been made at all, and Sir John Simon, the Chancellor of the Exchequer, had stated publicly that there were no ideological objections to such an alliance. At the same time there was a certain reluctance in the air about the venture, partly due to the fact that Spain, Portugal, even Japan, but above all the Pope, might themselves have outright objections to an alliance with 'the Communist Colossus'. The newly appointed Franco Ambassador in London, the Duke of Alba, chose this moment to reiterate his dislike of any dealings with 'communistic countries' and to look forward to 'a renewal of the old tradition of maritime intercourse between Britain and Spain'. Some British willingness to meet him half-way was signalled by the British acceptance of an invitation to attend Franco's Victory Parade, now finally scheduled for 19 May. But there was a further Tory objection to any pact with Russia, namely a doubt as to the effectiveness of her military prowess. The Government had been troubled by pessimistic reports which R.S. Hudson, Parliamentary Secretary of the Department of Overseas Trade, had brought back from a recent visit to Moscow. The *New York Times* man concluded:

Appeasement may re-emerge some day among British Ministers and newspaper editors, for it is not entirely dead in some influential quarters. Nevertheless the mood of the country has been revolutionized in the past few weeks; public opinion continues to run far ahead of the Government, and any Cabinet that attempted to put any pressure on the Poles as it did on the Czechs last summer would meet with instant criticism and perhaps disaster in Parliament and the country.

In Moscow itself, May Day had seen no doubts whatever about Russia's military prowess. Marshal Voroshilov, Commissar for War, had cantered into the Red

Square on a bright chestnut thoroughbred to inspect troops drawn up in front of Stalin, present on Lenin's tomb. After an NKVD band, conducted by an elderly bandmaster in white gloves and khaki uniform, who had somehow managed to outlast the three successively-purged Commissars who had been his superiors, had played part of Beethoven's Ninth Symphony, Voroshilov spoke from the rostrum below Stalin. He compared the peace and prosperity of the USSR with capitalist Europe, which he said was 'racked by aggression, intrigue, fear and cowardice'. The USSR wanted peace but would not engage lightly in small adventures; however, it was prepared to resist aggression with all its might. His Order of the Day proclaimed: 'The unbridled Fascist military aggressors intoxicated with easy victory, do not hesitate to threaten weak and frightened countries. Only the Soviet Union is watching calmly what goes on beyond its borders.'

Any misgivings about some inscrutability in this last sentence could be at least partly dispelled by the arrival on the same day of two Russian airmen at the New York World's Fair, who had just, for the first time, flown the Great Circle route from Moscow to the United States. They brought with them a letter date-stamped 28 April, containing greetings from the Russian people to the people of the United States. They were welcomed at the Fair with the words: 'You have cut off nine days from the usual time of travel from Moscow to New York. You are the outriders of the world of tomorrow as annihilators of time.'

The next day in the House of Commons, Clement Attlee, Leader of the Labour Opposition, asked Chamberlain about the fortnight-long negotiations with Russia. 'Is the Prime Minister aware that many people are disturbed at the slow progress which is being made in these conversations, and that they have not felt that the British Government are pressing on as rapidly as they might?'

Chamberlain replied: 'I cannot help it if people get that sort of idea, and I hope Mr Attlee will not do anything to encourage it.'

Inscrutability was not to be altogether a one-sided affair.

However, some in Britain spoke openly enough. Sir Oswald Mosley, the British Fascist leader, left no doubt on May Day as to his own and his party's view of the situation. All democratic parties, he declared, were now in the service of international finance. By suggesting that Britain was threatened they hoped to bring on war and reap huge profits out of armaments. But what country was threatening us? It had been said that Germany had threatened us, but Hitler in his speech recently had said no such thing . . .

The traditional British Left, in its traditional demonstration in London's Hyde Park, displayed equally predictable attitudes. The sun shone bright on Herbert Morrison as he denounced to a crowd in which Anti-Fascist chocolate was on sale at tuppence per packet, both Fascism and the compulsory military service now being introduced to combat it. To judge from the banners it was compulsory military service that was the most prominent issue at stake. 'Conscript Wealth, Not Life' was the most popular slogan, followed by 'Chamberlain Must Go'.

Spain, which for the past two years had dominated banners on this occasion, was now sadly relegated. Only the occasional slogan recalled the great ideological cause which had so swiftly disappeared from the public eye, to be replaced in the newspapers by news of the blue denunciation forms issued by Franco or by the statistics of trials and executions to which these inexorably led.

'Who Gave Spain To The Axis?' asked a banner from Uxbridge. It had the answer it required from Morrison himself, as he linked the democratic tragedy in Spain to the possibility of similar tragedy for the whole of European democracy in the near future. British capitalist governments since the war, he said, had made their own horrible contribution to the tragic state of affairs, including some contribution to the establishment of the Nazi dictatorship in Germany: 'The mischievous Cliveden Set and others associated with the Conservative Party for years maintained an attitude of sympathetic encouragement towards Hitler and those same evil influences cordially approved the shameful non-intervention policy in Spain which ultimately gave Spain to the Axis.'

Some such influences associated with the Conservative Party were now beginning to write to *The Times* in the context of Danzig. Their letters were published with prominence. Lord Rushcliffe, a former Conservative Minister, wrote that it would be a profound mistake to dismiss Hitler's recent speech with the superficial comment that it left matters exactly as they were and that it was unnecessary to pay any particular attention to it. It was, he said, the deliberate and carefully-prepared utterance of the man who 'has it in his power to plunge Europe into war – or on the other hand to make the greatest contribution to peace'. None of the matters in dispute at the moment were so intractable that accommodation was impossible, and he cited Danzig and the Polish Corridor, the Italian claims in the Mediterranean, and the German claims for colonies. He concluded: 'There is too much evidence at the moment of a policy of fatalism and inevitability which, if allowed to develop, may largely contribute to a result that all are anxious to avoid.'

Lord Ponsonby of Shulbrede, also a former Conservative Minister, wrote immediately to take exception to his fellow Peer's letter but only in one respect: namely, that where Rushcliffe had stated that 'one more' effort at settlement was needed, he would substitute the words 'another and yet another'. And yet another ex-Ministerial Peer, Lord Elton, wrote the next day to praise Rushcliffe's letter as 'wise and timely'. He regretted that the prolonged tension was producing inevitable psychological effects. People were persuading themselves that 'a world war might not be so very unpleasant after all. A few months ago they would still have seen clearly that world war must mean general anarchy, pestilence and famine for a generation.'

Unexceptionable as these sentiments appeared at one level, their airing at this moment by such people in such a place was liable to cause uneasiness to Britain's friends on the Continent, or so at least Duff Cooper thought, who wrote a letter of his own to *The Times* to this effect.

Liberal opinion in Britain too was shocked. The *News Chronicle* in particular took *The Times* to task for opening its columns to appeasement views. 'For *The Times* of all papers to take such a step is particularly deplorable, following the miserable pattern of Czechoslovakia.' And the *Manchester Guardian* under a heading 'Appeasement Reappearing' had this comment from its Diplomatic Correspondent:

> Appeasement has begun to show itself again. The visible symptoms are far from revealing the extent and the seriousness of the growth. So far there is no evidence that the Government is infected, but influential persons outside the Government, some of them very near to the Government and in constant touch with it ... are engaged in a concerted attempt to deflect British policy from its present course and to compound with Germany by concessions made at the expense of friendly Powers. Whether these persons will succeed in influencing policy is quite uncertain.

A sudden and surprising piece of news from Radio Moscow just before midnight on 3 May made this whole area of speculation particularly sensitive. It was announced out of the blue that the Commissar for Foreign Affairs, Litvinov, had been removed from his post for reasons of health. It was indeed known that he had had some heart trouble but he had been seen in apparently good health only two days before with Stalin on Lenin's tomb at the May Day Parade. His orientation in foreign affairs had always been pro-British and anti-German and, as the *New York Times* wrote: 'The possibility must not be overlooked that his removal means a turn in Russian policy towards isolation.' The paper headlined its story next day: 'Russia Switches Her Policy; Drops Collective Security; Foreign Capitals Puzzled'. It added a supplementary headline 'Reich Tie Unlikely' at the top of a story suggesting that Litvinov's dismissal might simply be shock technique on the part of the USSR to bring Britain and France quickly into a firm alliance. But its correspondent in Moscow, Walter Duranty, seemed to subscribe more to the view that Russia was isolating herself. He wrote:

> Either they got news from London that the British would not march, after all, or the Kremlin suddenly decided it was fed up with all this shilly-shallying with two Western Governments it neither liked nor trusted and said: 'Shucks, let's end this nonsense in quick time. It's not our way anyway, and if at any time now or later anyone tackles us we are ready and able to meet them.'

Duranty added honestly, in view of the fact that Moscow had just abolished censorship for foreign correspondents, that though they were now free to tell what they liked, the trouble was that they did not know what to tell. The only advantage was that there was now greater opportunity for guesswork.

The German press seemed hardly more sure of what Litvinov's dismissal meant, though knowledgeable certainty was its stock-in-trade. It saw his fall as the price of failure, but of the man who was to replace him, one Molotov, the *Lokal-Anzeiger* could only say: 'Little is known save that he is a Russian and 49 years old and that he is a willing tool of the Usurper of the Kremlin.' Such

THE NEW SPRING HATS

PANAMAS AND SMOOTH STRAWS—FLOWERS AND VEILS—NEAT SAILORS AND DEMURE BONNETS

From Our Fashion Correspondent

PARIS, JAN. 28

Well ahead of the dressmakers the Paris milliners show their spring models, and long before spring dresses are of practical interest Parisiennes are wearing straw hats trimmed with flowers and frivolous bows of ribbon.

Straw hats are first worn in Paris at the end of January and in the beginning of February. The latest models so far do not suggest any drastic changes in line. They are becoming rather than exaggerated and a free use of colour adds much to their charm. Very dark navy-blue takes the place of black as a basic by Blanche et Simone, and they may be made of net, chiffon, or jersey-tulle, the latter fabrics being gathered on to elastic bands and really forming little bags in which a chignon can be concealed.

Muffin and tambourine shaped toques look well with coloured ribbon trimmings. Some have rolled edges bound with silk. Picot-edged taffetas and satin ribbons are much liked by the milliners, who find that their decorative borders add a rococo air to hats of the romantic kind. Rose Valois chooses her ribbons in two colours, one dark, the other light, and knots them round the crowns of black picot straws, 1860 fashions or those of 1900. One pale pink gauze-straw from Suzy is made in a tiny tambourine shape with no centre to its crown. It is circled by a wreath of pastel-coloured flowers in which honeysuckle dominates and a frill of fine pink organza adds a finishing touch. Another tiny hat sweeps up in front and is banked with clusters of mauve and white lilac forming two " ears," while knots of cornflowers, smothered under a deep blue veil trim a corn-coloured felt toque for the first days of spring.

Certain designers show hats with brims which sweep up at the back or sides of the

These hats, sketched by our artist, show the trend of design for spring in Paris, where the milliners show their models ahead of the dressmakers.

terminology seemed to support the *New York Times*'s view that a 'Reich tie' was unlikely.

A leading article in the American paper made an attempt to sum up what it called 'The Russian Enigma': 'There are competent judges who think the change may mean a swing by Russia to a policy of isolation, which would be a pro-Hitler policy. There are competent judges who have held that the Stalin regime has all along been courting Hitler, or perhaps there is an aim to drive the British into a pact on Moscow's terms.'

The immediate effect in Britain was to concentrate attention again on the question of delay in the Russian negotiations. Chamberlain, when again asked by the Labour leader Attlee in the House of Commons if he was aware of the uncertainty in the country as to whether the Government was really carrying out its declared policy, and if he was aware that the delays and the dilatory action were the cause of this uncertainty, replied with considerable testiness.

'I do realize', said Chamberlain, 'that uncertainty has been created by a number of people who are all the time suggesting that if there is any fault it must be the fault of the British Government.' (Here he received a cheer from his supporters.) 'I cannot be held responsible for that.'

'Does not the Prime Minister realize', continued Attlee, 'that the uncertainty is caused by his own past record?'

Chamberlain now got really angry. 'That is a partisan observation which is characteristic of Mr Attlee.'

Again there were cheers from his supporters and protests from the Labour benches, while George Griffiths, Member for the ultra-safe Labour seat of Hemsworth, called out: 'Don't get your rag out!'

When asked by Philip Noel-Baker, one of the Labour experts on foreign affairs, whether, in view of the grave urgency of the situation in Europe, it were not time for the Government to make up their minds to accept co-operation with Soviet Russia, Chamberlain replied resolutely: 'No, Sir! We cannot accept the view that we should altogether give up our own opinions and accept without question the views of other governments.' And again there were Ministerial cheers. By the time the only Communist Member of Parliament, Willie Gallacher, came to ask him whether, to facilitate the negotiations, the Prime Minister might not consider personal contact with Moscow, Chamberlain managed to inject a certain black humour into the haughtiness of his reply. Perhaps, he said, Mr Gallacher would suggest how to make personal contact with Moscow because personalities changed rather rapidly there. And the sally was greeted with laughter.

This note of open anxiety about the delay in concluding an alliance with Russia, struck so urgently in May, was to persist, in spasmodic alternation of gloom and optimism, for almost the whole of the rest of the summer.

During that time Britain, in a characteristically routine mood of orderliness rather than thoroughness, steadily adjusted itself to the thought of war as a normal background to everyday life. The Conscription Bill passed its third reading in the House of Commons by 283 votes against a doctrinaire libertarian opposition of 133. The steel shelters for protection against blast and debris, for which the Government had officially opted in preference to a national system of deep shelters, continued to be distributed free to the population; plans for the evacuation of city children to the countryside and their billeting there with local householders were systematized; and a Civil Defence Bill, making blackout facilities in all buildings compulsory, together with the provision by industrial firms employing more than fifty people of adequate shelters for their protection (aided by Government grants), was debated in Parliament through April and May and amicably attained its third reading on 14 June. By 1 August the required enrolment of two million men and women for civil defence was short only by 100,000, and though less than half of the 2,500,000 steel shelters ordered had been delivered, protection of this sort was now available for six million city dwellers. The twelve 'Regional Commissioners' appointed in February carried out, in co-operation with local authorities, a number of ARP and blackout drills in different parts of the country – half England was blacked out on the night of 8 August – and under an adjustment to the schedule of reserved occupations some 1,500,000 men of the 7,500,000 originally protected from wartime service were made available for it. An incidental benefit from increased armament expenditure was shown in the unemployment figures, which dropped substantially every month between February and June to settle at around 1,350,000 for the rest of the year, compared with 2,000,000 in January. Recruiting figures for the regular Army, Navy and Air Force and the Territorial Army showed appreciable increases on the previous year, and since it had been discovered by the Prime Minister in April that the procedure for mobilization in wartime was 'antiquated and out of character for modern times', a Bill was introduced enabling the Services to call up reserves by an Order in Council.

In July the first of the 200,000 militiamen between twenty and twenty-one available for six months' training under the Conscription Act were called up. The principle that all were to be treated equally by the Army units to which they were attached, regardless of their social background, was stressed, as was the humane consideration with which they were to be treated. Spectacles were to be provided for those who needed them; men were given advice as to what to bring with them, though only one suitcase was recommended; and each was to have a locker in which to keep his own belongings. It was regretfully conveyed that married men could not bring their wives.

Theoretical analysis of what was likely to happen on the Home Front gave even this new dimension in modern war a certain reassuring British familiarity. 'Some things you should know if war should come' was the title of one Government leaflet distributed at the end of June. And the *Manchester Guardian* had published a measured fourth leader in the middle of May on the need for early evacuation from towns in the event of war, saying that 'the fiercest bombing attacks on the great towns of this country – the lightning stroke intended to break us – would be made in the first days of war; afterwards, for many reasons, they would probably slacken'.

Lord Chatfield, the Minister of Defence, speaking in the House of Lords, caught the sense of limbo in which the British public passed the summer with greater perspicacity than he possibly realized when he said: 'We are well on our way to achieve our aim of being more ready for war in peace than we have ever been.'

All through these months newspaper readers in Britain, familiarizing themselves with the idea of life in a wartime of which all that was really known was that no one knew what it would be like, received a series of fluctuating and often bafflingly contradictory reports on the progress of negotiations for that alliance with Russia which nearly all military experts said was vital if the war were to be fought successfully. The salient point about the negotiations seemed to be that although they continued desultorily, punctuated by occasional flurries of activity or disappointment, no actual progress was ever positively made. As early as the 8th of May, Lloyd George, expressing in the House of Commons the continuing anxiety after what was then only three weeks of negotiations, declared: 'Without Russia our guarantees to Poland, Rumania and Greece are the most reckless commitments any country has ever entered into. I say more – they are demented.'

And though his concern was widely shared, not only by the official Opposition itself but also by the Churchill-Eden-Duff Cooper faction within the Conservative Party, the relative complacency of Chamberlain's supporters was revealed by the war hero Sir Roger Keyes who, while conceding that Lloyd George would be remembered in history for his determination and will to win in the Great War, said he would also be remembered in history for what would be regarded as the very dangerous speech he had just delivered.

Ten days later, however, Lloyd George was again pressing Chamberlain to say exactly what was standing in the way of progress in the negotiations and asking what help we could possibly give Poland without a Russian alliance. 'It is very vital that we should know,' he said.

Chamberlain replied testily: 'I am not going to answer. It might be vital to Mr Lloyd George but I think it might be damaging to our policy.'

A less opaque indication of the difficulties involved was however given by Chamberlain when he said: 'We are also aware that the direct vast participation of the Soviet Union in this matter might not be altogether in accordance with the wishes of the countries for whose benefit and on whose behalf these arrangements were made.'

The difficulty, it could be deduced, was the reluctance of perhaps Poland but certainly the Baltic States (Latvia, Lithuania and Estonia) to give Russian troops free entry to their territory. However as Churchill said, Chamberlain's was 'not a very clear account'. The Prime Minister, he continued, had not reassured those who felt a deep misgiving about the present situation. Churchill concluded:

Margot Fonteyn and Robert Helpmann in *The Sleeping Princess*.

Chelsea and Manchester United at Stamford Bridge football ground.

Without Russia there can be no effective eastern front. If the Government, having neglected our defences for a long time, having thrown away Czechoslovakia with all that means in military power, having committed us without examination of the technical aspects to the defence of Poland and Rumania, now reject and cast away the indispensable aid of Russia and so lead us into the worst of worlds, into the worst of wars, they will ill have deserved the confidence – and I will add the generosity – with which they have been treated by their fellow-countrymen.

A Gallup Poll that week showed that ninety-two per cent of the British people were in favour of a Russian alliance (only sixty-one per cent favoured conscription). Even the London *Daily Express*, which had been opposed to the pledge to Poland, was in favour. 'We shall get the alliance,' it wrote in its leader column on 22 May. 'The marriage will take place. Wedding-bells will ring. For an alliance with Russia follows logically on the commitments in Eastern Europe. These should never have been made. Now we have got these liabilities there is no reason we should not extend them further.'

A few days later even Chamberlain himself was suddenly optimistic in the House of Commons: 'I have every reason to hope', he said, 'that it will be found possible to reach full agreement at an early date.'

And the *Manchester Guardian* Diplomatic Correspondent reassured its readers: 'Mr Chamberlain's statement will have removed whatever doubts there may still have been with regard to the alliance between the Western Powers and Russia.'

Two days after that, on 27 May, the *Manchester Guardian* reported that Marshal Voroshilov, the Commander-in-Chief of the Soviet Army, was coming to London to attend British Army manœuvres. 'It is confidently expected in London', the paper wrote, 'that final agreement with the Soviet Union will have been reached by the end of the week.'

Readers of the American press, informed of this particular bout of optimism, were in a better position to approach such news warily. Indeed throughout the whole summer they were more realistically in touch with this situation than were readers of British newspapers.

Immediately after Litvinov's dismissal the *New York Times* correspondent in London had written:

The British have wanted Russian support as a window-dressing to convince Herr Hitler that an attack on Poland or any other country would not be worthwhile. If such a window-dressing should not prove possible it would make Britain's new commitments in Eastern Europe seem less attractive or more dangerous than before. It might make Mr Chamberlain more anxious than ever for a 'compromise' on the Danzig question. 'Appeasement' tendencies here might be revived in full force.

He did, however, add that British obligations to Poland were so definite that it would be hard for any British Government to wriggle out of them even if it wanted to do so.

As early as 7 May a headline in the *New York Times* had run: 'Reich Held Seeking A Pact With Russia', though it surmised that this would be a non-aggression pact rather than a straight alliance. A companion headline ran: 'Soviet Said To Plan Baltic Occupation', beneath which it was explained that the Russians wished to have Estonia, Latvia, Lithuania and even Eastern Finland as a buffer for their self-protection. On 9 May the *New York Times* correspondent in Berlin reported specifically that Hitler was seeking a deal with Stalin. 'It is no secret here', he wrote, 'that the Soviet Government itself has been in favour of such a development; it took active steps to bring it about ... as late as last February.' (A reference to abortive preliminary trade negotiations which had taken place between Russia and Germany at that time.) Again it was emphasized that if indeed some move of this sort were planned by Stalin it would be in the direction of 'neutralization' or 'normalization' of relations between the two countries rather than an alliance. The story appeared adjacent to a report of cautious optimism in Britain and the belief there that the displacement of Litvinov did not necessarily mean any major change in Soviet foreign policy. Grounds for such optimism could be found in the news that it was the British Ambassador in Moscow, Sir William Seeds, who was the first diplomat to see Molotov after his appointment as Commissar for Foreign Affairs, while Litvinov took himself off to the theatre.

On 20 May, Halifax, on his way to Geneva, headquarters of the League of Nations, for talks with the Russians and the French about the prospective alliance, stopped off in Paris for preliminary talks with Daladier and the French Foreign Minister, Georges Bonnet. French officials let it be known that they expected an agreement to be reached within the next three days. The *New York Times* again injected a note of detached realism. The British, it seemed, wanted to limit any such alliance's application to a tripartite guarantee to Poland and Rumania against aggression, supplemented by agreement for concerted action should any of the three be attacked in implementing such guarantees. The question of the Baltic States and, reciprocally, Holland and Belgium, was to be studied in consultation. The *New York Times* correspondent in Geneva commented that, quite apart from difficulties over the Baltic States, such an alliance was 'obviously a pretty hard dose for a British Government representing Big Business as well as all the tradition inherent in the old school tie to swallow'. It pointed out that the Russians could have sent Molotov himself to Geneva but instead had merely sent their Ambassador in London, Ivan Maisky, whom Halifax could have seen in London at any time by simply asking him to take a taxi around to the Foreign Office. The two had even travelled together to Geneva in the same sleeping-car.

The Geneva correspondent further commented that if Russian opinion as privately expressed was a true reflection of the mind of Joseph Stalin, then all such manœuvrings were quite useless. The Russians were letting it be known that they disliked all the talk about consultation, seeing in it too many chances for 'other partners to wriggle out of an awkward situation on another Munich formula'. What they wanted was a clear-cut definite alliance. Moreover, wounded Russian *amour propre* made the whole thing difficult. The Russians thought they were being 'invited to enter this new mansion of Democracy by the service entrance instead of the front door and they did not like it. Both France and Britain on the other hand – Britain especially – are somewhat appalled when they contemplate the propaganda to home Bolsheviks of front-door honours to Russian Bolshevism.'

It was soon announced, from the British side, that the Geneva talks had run into an impasse and that no more conversations were contemplated at present. However, even this correspondent concluded that the impasse would have to be circumvented sooner or later and that the probability was that it would be the British rather than the Soviets who gave way.

Chamberlain's optimism as expressed in the House of Commons successfully infected Britain itself for the rest of the month.

'Agreement With Russia Is In Sight' was the headline of the liberal *News Chronicle* on 25 May, and on the 31st: 'Last Obstacle To Pact With Soviet'. The *Daily Express* had even had a headline on the 25th: 'Soviet Pact Agreed'.

Study of the German press suggested that things were unlikely to be so simple. On 19 May in the *Völkischer Beobachter* Goebbels signalled what looked very much like a switch in propaganda tactics. All mention of the previously denounced Bolshevism was avoided in his article and venom concentrated on the war-and-panic-mongers in London, Paris and Washington. Germany and Italy, he said, were 'the great proletarians among European nations, robbed of their natural living rights by plutocratic States that have amassed vast riches by plundering and oppressing whole continents but they now hate the have-nots with all their capitalistic hatred disguised by hypocritical church morality'. And an article in the *Westdeutscher Beobachter* a week later reminded readers that Stalin in his speech on 10 March had said he refused to be enrolled in a crusade against Nazi Germany. The article went on:

> National Socialism does not want war against a State because that State has a different content from our own. ... The Anti-Comintern Pact does not strike primarily at the Soviet Union but ... at Bolshevism when it reaches out beyond Russia's borders ... it is therefore possible for the German Reich and the Soviet Union to maintain diplomatic relations with each other.

Such straws in the wind – if that was what they were – seemed to attract less attention in Britain than in the United States. In any case, both in Britain and the United States there were many distractions from such matters altogether.

At about 7.30 on the morning of 23 May one of the newest of the US Navy's submarines, *Squalus*, which had been launched only eight months before, sailed from the Portsmouth Navy Yard, New Hampshire, for trials in the area of the

New Hampshire lobster grounds. Its crew of five officers and fifty-one enlisted men, supplemented by two Navy Yard observers and a representative of the contractors, came from homes covering twenty-eight States of the Union. At 8.40 a.m. the *Squalus* signalled that it was preparing to dive for two hours. By 11 o'clock it had not returned to the surface. At 11.20 an attempt was made to get in touch with it by radio. This was unsuccessful. At 11.30 the *Squalus*'s sister-ship, *Sculpin*, went out from Portsmouth in search of her. An hour later at a point about five miles south-east of the Isle of Shoals off Hampton Beach she saw a red smudge on the sea.

This was from a smoke-bomb which the *Squalus* had released from her position on the sea bed some 240 feet below. On the same spot the *Sculpin* picked up a yellow marker buoy with a brass plate on it on which was written 'Submarine *Squalus* sunk here. Telephone inside'; 350 feet of telephone wire connected it with the *Squalus* which was settled at an angle on the bottom. Up this telephone the captain of the *Squalus*, Lieutenant Oliver Naquin, reported that it appeared that a high-speed induction valve had been left open during the dive. He suggested that an attempt should be made to raise the vessel rather than try to attach the Navy's dome-shaped diving-bell escape chamber to it at that depth. But at that point the telephone cable broke and there was no further communication with those trapped inside until 9.45 p.m. when divers, who had in the meanwhile been brought out from Portsmouth, received a message tapped out on the hull: 'Conditions satisfactory but cold. Forward engine-room, after engine-room and after torpedo-room are flooded.'

Navy officials said that the men had emergency rations, water and plenty of oxygen and would be able to maintain themselves there for several days. Admiral Cole, Commandant of Portsmouth Navy Yard, said he thought he had 'a pretty good chance of getting the men out'. This would be the first priority rather than saving the ship, which apparently had been Lieutenant Naquin's concern. It was assumed that the men in the submarine would be lying as still as possible to conserve their precious store of oxygen.

By first light next morning the salvage vessel *Falcon*, from which the rescue operations were to be conducted, was in position. With it was the ten-ton dome-shaped metal chamber which was to be attached by divers to the forward escape-hatch of the submarine, and into which it was hoped eight to ten men could enter at a time. It took a long time for divers to fix it to the submarine at such a depth. The spot on the open sea which the day before had been marked by a single red smudge was now, as one reporter put it, 'as busy as a traffic intersection at Times Square'.

At 1.18 p.m. on 24 May the dome-shaped chamber broke the surface beside the *Falcon* and the first dungaree-clad figure stepped from the hatch to a burst of cheering from the onlookers.

The escape bell made four trips altogether. On the last of these the lines became jammed some ninety feet from the bottom. It took three hours to free them, but the rescue was then resumed and by the end of that day thirty-three men had been safely brought to the surface. From them it was learned that the twenty-six others were trapped in flooded compartments and that there was only the slenderest possible hope for them, though their relatives naturally clung to this throughout the night.

The entombment of the twenty-six had followed an agonizingly quick but necessary decision on the part of those who survived. An electrician's mate had only just managed to get the watertight door between compartments which were flooding and the rest of the submarine shut in time, after allowing through five men who had called to him desperately, 'Keep it open! Keep it open!' as he was already trying to shut it. Among those whom he had had to shut in was a friend at whose marriage to a girl from Denver he was to have been best man on the following Sunday.

When the divers took the escape chamber down again the next day they found, on opening the escape hatch on the deck of the submarine, that there was only water to be seen inside. Still, the rescue as far as it went was something of a triumph over disaster, a cause for rejoicing as well as mourning – a small American drama partly, at any rate, successfully concluded, quite detached from the affairs of Europe.

On the other hand the extent to which the United States in fact daily concerned itself with the European crisis was striking, and indeed struck forcibly the *New York Times* correspondent Anne O'Hare McCormick who returned to the States from a long working spell in Europe in the second half of May. She wrote:

> The homecoming American is startled by our intense preoccupation with European affairs. .... It is an exaggeration to say, as many returning travellers do, that we are more excited than Europe over Europe's troubles. We are merely noisier and more articulate. We fume and stutter because we still believe we can do something to maintain rights and remedy wrongs. We have never yet struck the dead centre of hopeless fatalism. In Europe, fear and anxiety shake the depths of being; here the same disturbance frets and foams on the surface.

She went on to say that European peoples were increasingly interested in the States only as a possible ally or enemy in war, and commented that English people themselves were constantly surprised at the extent to which Americans were interested in their affairs. One Englishman had said to her, only the day before her return: 'I assure you that you listen to Mr Chamberlain and read our White Papers more than we do.'

Of course there was one perfectly good sense in which Americans' concern for Europe was also a personal concern for themselves. Their major underlying political consideration was whether Roosevelt's linking of his New Deal to support for the cause of the democracies might not drag the United States unnecessarily into another war, and the political sensitiveness of this question was made more acute because the President faced a difficult Congress. Attention focused on the attempt Roosevelt was about to make to amend the Neutrality Act as Congress prepared to adjourn for the summer in the middle of July.

When the proposal for the adjournment came up in the Senate it was immediately opposed by Senators Johnson of California and Connelly of Texas on the grounds that some step involving the United States in a European war might be taken if Congress were not in session during the crisis. Senator Johnson made plain his own sense of extreme urgency, saying:

> The consequences of war to this country are such that I tremble when I think of them. The consequences of war are that this Government of ours will be gone. And there will be no remedy by which we can resurrect it in our lifetime. . . . I regard the dictators with every feeling of horror that can activate anybody. If we go to war in an endeavour to destroy those two dictators we shall have a dictatorship in the United States and it will be with us for ever. . . . Let us go on and prevent any provocative utterances, prevent if we can various things which may be construed as warlike on the part of this Government. Let us be ourselves and for the people of the United States; let us keep out of war!

On these last words applause of 'extraordinary proportions' broke out in the public gallery and had to be silenced by the attendants.

The next day Alfred Landon, the Republican leader who had been presidential candidate in 1936, 'crossed the floor', as he put it, to back Roosevelt in his appeal for peace, but in the process he managed to get in a pretty strong isolationist diatribe. Hitler's speech at the end of April had, he said, still left the door slightly open. And he went on:

> The United States of America is the one great Power that has not yet been fully drawn into the balance of power game and the ancient boundary-line disputes which have prevailed in Europe since before the Roman Republic. And, please God, may we never be! . . . We cannot be sure what nation we can rely on in Europe. For centuries they have been engaged in the art of double-crossing each other. Never has there been a more urgent call to be Americans, first, last and all the time.

He warned Americans against what he called 'weasel words'. Aggression, he said, was simply the 'weasel' word to fool the American people into sending their sons to Europe to fight in boundary-line disputes which had been going on in Europe and Asia since before the dawn of civilization.

'Let's face the fact frankly that economic assistance means in the end doughboy assistance. Let's stop fooling the American people that economic guarantees and economic assistance mean anything less than sending American boys into the cockpit of Europe to fight.'

A Gallup Poll taken about the same time and asking the question, 'Do you approve or disapprove today of Roosevelt as President?' received an answer of 56.1 per cent in approval, a drop of two per cent since January but still a figure slightly higher than in December of the previous year.

For supporters of Roosevelt, surveying the ground for the coming battle over the Neutrality Act, the classical answer to Landon's argument was that the Act might give aid to an aggressor and deny it to the victim, and that to lift the embargo against selling arms in war-time was a measure of preserving peace and not bringing war nearer. Potential war-makers must be made to believe that the odds were too great if the United States supported Britain and France against them.

In Britain, as Anne O'Hare McCormick had noticed, the European crisis was instinctively assessed at a quieter level. There the national temperament was more at ease, treating crisis as though it were routine. In France a sense of crisis was reported to be pervading even the cultural scene: all but the most important concerts were being cancelled, and theatres were poorly attended. In Britain cultural business was as usual. Toscanini was conducting a series of concerts to crowded audiences. Of one of them the *Manchester Guardian* music critic wrote: 'The great wheel of his right arm never ceased; on and on we were driven; the rhythm beat into the brain. It was as though we were listening to music in the teeth of a wind.' And, being a man of individual discernment, he added:

> And at times I, for one, craved for a momentary place of shelter, for a softer and more yielding touch. . . . It was when Toscanini came to the Fourth Symphony [Beethoven's] that some of us, for all our admiration, began to chafe and privately rebel [against] an unsmiling purposefulness and a sense of the inexorable. The introductory *adagio* is one of the most romantic in music . . . but Toscanini's first granite-like chord of B-flat sent fancy running for cover like a startled deer. . . . Throughout the entire Symphony, Toscanini's basic and dominating rhythms beat out the unbreakable girders of his formalism.

This same *Manchester Guardian* music critic, Neville Cardus, was also the paper's cricket correspondent. The seriousness of the British attitude to sport traditionally provided an alternative to the seriousness of other matters, as that American correspondent had testified who had been confused by Test Match posters on the day Hitler seized Prague. And on the morning of 27 May, with the Anglo-Russian pact 'in sight' and its 'last obstacle removed', Cardus sat down at the Manchester cricket ground of Old Trafford to report the traditional Battle of the Roses between Yorkshire and Lancashire:

> a cool morning with low drifting clouds hiding the sun, which broke through from time to time making shadows so that the cricketers were followed about by bright light like characters in the ballet. Bill Bowes [Yorkshire] at mid-off indeed performed at least one *pas de seul* as he stopped a hit by Paynter [Lancashire]. Bowes found the breeze and the atmosphere helpful to his own deadly skill with the new ball and caused much concern to Washbrook . . .

When Yorkshire's innings started, Cardus described the veteran opener Sutcliffe's batting as wearing 'an ominous appearance'. He said a good ball would be needed on the coming Monday to prevent his making a hundred.

His prediction was fulfilled. Sutcliffe made 165. But Monday also produced a

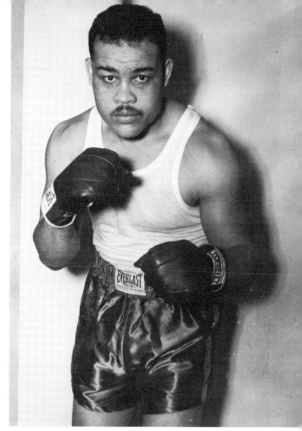

Sporting life: Oxford undergraduates at Henley regatta; Joe Louis, world heavyweight boxing champion, in New York; and English cricketers near Horsham, Sussex.

remarkable athletic event at the White City stadium: what was described as 'an almost unbelievable mile' by S.C. Wooderson who ran the distance in 4 minutes 7.4 seconds. Apart from the time, what was remarkable was that he led from start to finish. The *Manchester Guardian* wrote: 'A more remarkable individual effort without the slightest help from pace-makers there has never been seen. ... Watching him to-day one no longer thought of a mile in four minutes as out of the question.'

That most traditional of all British sporting events, the Derby, had been won the week before by Lord Rosebery's colt Blue Peter, also in very good time, but the Royal Ascot race meeting in the middle of June was, at least from the point of view of *The Times*, disappointing in its traditional rôle of fashion parade. This was partly because the King and Queen were not present, having left the country the previous month for that transatlantic visit to Canada and the United States which H.G. Wells had deemed of so little relevance when writing at the beginning of the year – a judgement in which he was to be proved spectacularly wrong.

Their absence from Ascot, however, troubled *The Times*, as did the weather which, it complained, provided an afternoon more like one in April than in June. There was little sunshine and there were a number of cold showers and the paper almost seemed to detect a hint of the old social order changing in some slightly ominous way:

> Yesterday it was a case of furs, some no doubt borrowed at the last moment from the hostess with whom visitors might be staying, of overcoats, of few silk hats and many grey ones, and still more soft hats or bowlers. It was indeed a sad Ascot from the point of view of fashion, whether of men's clothes or women's. It is many years since so few new clothes have been seen. And yet there is evidence that many new clothes were ordered.

In London that afternoon arrangements were being made for the holding of a judicial tribunal into a serious naval accident to a submarine which had recently taken place off the coast of North Wales.

By an odd coincidence it had occurred only a few days after the loss of the American submarine *Squalus*. The event, for many, eclipsed an important speech by the new Russian Commissar for Foreign Affairs, Molotov, made the day before in which he cast sudden strange doubts on the prospects for an Anglo-Russian alliance after all, adding at one point: 'We do not refuse to improve our trade relations with Germany.' But this was all rather obscure. The naval news was plain enough.

At ten o'clock on the morning of 1 June the British submarine *Thetis* sailed from Birkenhead for trials in Liverpool Bay. After the required surface trials had been completed she dived at 1.30 p.m. for a three-hour underwater test. Four hours later she had not resurfaced and nothing had been heard from her. Just before dusk one of her emergency marker buoys was spotted in the sea off Great Ormes Head near Llandudno and by first light on 2 June holiday-makers on the

A salvage vessel alongside the sunken British submarine *Thetis* on the seabed of Liverpool bay with ninety-nine men trapped inside and less than twenty-four hours of oxygen.

Relatives waiting for news.

promenades of the popular holiday resorts between Llandudno and Blackpool could see destroyers out at sea searching for further signs of her while flying-boats joined in a patrol overhead. There were thought to be fifty-nine naval personnel on board the submarine, together with nineteen representatives of the makers, Cammell Laird Ltd, and a Mersey river pilot.

It was known that the *Thetis* carried thirty-six hours' air supply, of which 16½ hours would have been exhausted by 6 a.m. on 2 June. There was therefore some cause for hope, particularly since, by contrast with the waters in which the *Squalus* had foundered the week before, Liverpool Bay was relatively shallow.

It was not long after dawn that the destroyer *Brazen*, which had been searching all night, sighted an object protruding from the water sixteen miles north of Great Ormes Head. Racing up, she found that it was the stern of the submarine sticking up almost vertically on her nose which was buried on the bottom some 130 feet below. As the tide fell, more of the submarine became exposed until eventually eighteen feet of the stern was sticking up out of the water. The Admiralty announced: 'There is nothing to indicate that the men are other than safe.'

The crew of the *Brazen* coming alongside the wreck in open boats had tapped out messages in morse code on the hull and had received a reply that all the men in the *Thetis* were alive. This news was flashed to Cammell Laird offices at Birkenhead, where wives and relatives of those missing were waiting. They burst into tears of relief on hearing it. When first news of the accident had been brought to the wife of the commander of *Thetis* the day before she had been in a Liverpool cinema watching a newsreel of the rescue of the *Squalus* survivors.

Other vessels now closed in on the submarine and at about half-past nine two heads bobbed up from below to the surface, encased in Davis escape apparatus: two naval officers, to be followed a few moments later by a stoker and one of the Cammell Laird representatives. They were immediately taken aboard and, though suffering badly from carbon dioxide poisoning, reported that, except for two men who had drowned while trying to get through the escape hatch and another who had gone mad there and died, all in the submarine were still alive though some of the older men were suffering from lack of air. The waiting ships gazed anxiously into the water for more escapees but ten o'clock came and went and nothing happened. No more heads appeared. It could only be assumed that something had gone wrong with the escape mechanism. No diving-bell such as that which had been successfully used on the US submarine *Squalus* was available.

It was known that at about 4 p.m. the high tide would be likely to cover the submarine and frantic efforts were made first of all to pull her off the bottom by a cable attaching the *Thetis*'s rudder to a tug. The grey fin did indeed rise higher out of the water for a moment but then the cable snapped and the hull slipped back again. Attempts were then made to cut a hole in the hull through that part which was sticking up, with an oxy-acetelyne cylinder. But this was beaten by the tide which, with one surging swell, as a journalist reported, caught the *Thetis* and forced the men working on the hull to jump for safety. The submarine itself then rolled like a great fish below the surface.

Theoretically there should still have been enough air inside to last until after midnight. But those who had escaped had revealed that there had in fact been 103 men on board, which meant that there were still 94 within it trying to breathe. The time the air supply could be expected to last was thus considerably reduced. Cables were now passed under the hull and attached to pontoons in the hope of floating the submarine off, or at least keeping the stern up until the tide fell again. However, when the tide did start to fall two hours later the stern did not reappear as expected.

The Admiralty sent another message: the hope of saving any further lives was dimming. And soon after midnight a Cammell Laird spokesman told a crowd of about a thousand people waiting at the shipyard gates: 'I am sorry, but there is no hope. The best thing you can do is to go home.'

In the stunned silence, broken only by weeping women, someone suddenly yelled: 'Where are your experts?' But he received no reply. It was a question of the sort which the newspapers were to be asking within a few hours.

'For the ordinary man, ignorant of the technical problems involved,' wrote the *Daily Express*, 'it seems an almost intolerable thing that the vessel should be visible for hours and yet the crew remain unsaved.'

And the *Daily Mirror* echoed this: 'Why,' it asked, 'five hours after the stern had been above water, had not a hole been made?'

Ninety-nine men altogether had died. It was to answer such questions that a tribunal was being set up.

From Spain there was news of tribunals of a different sort. It was announced there that there had been 688 executions of Republicans by firing squad in the two months since the end of March – in Madrid, Toledo, Ciudad Real and Albacete alone. Spanish official circles pointed out that there had in fact been a thousand death sentences promulgated altogether but 312 people had been reprieved by Franco. Daily trials, it was said, were 'contributing to the total normalization of the life of the nation ... indispensable for initiation of the second era of empire'.

It was reckoned that 1,200,000 informations had been received of assassinations by Republicans, robberies, burnings of churches, treason, and imprisonment of Nationalist sympathizers. Some 46,000 people were already scheduled for trial and accusations were coming in at the rate of 380 a day. Such news – in itself only the beginning of something – put a sort of finishing touch to the ceremonial with which the end of the Civil War had at last been officially celebrated in Madrid on 19 May.

It took 150,000 troops, including 10,000 Italians and 5,000 Germans, nearly five hours to march past General Franco in his dark blue Falange shirt and red *Requeté* beret. The Italians were given the honour of heading the review and they came past in a fine drizzle with the band playing *Duce A Noi*. It was an hour before the first entirely Spanish detachment passed the stand, by which time the gold and red ribbon which crossed Franco's chest from shoulder to waist had become thoroughly sodden. Umbrellas were provided for the Cardinals and for some of the diplomats but the top-hats of the US Chargé d'Affaires and others were seen to suffer 'woefully' by one correspondent.

It cleared up for the Germans, though. At about one o'clock the German Kondor Legion marched past, led by Baron General Richthofen, and as they passed the stand the announcer recited their Civil War achievements. Their equipment included artillery, anti-aircraft guns and machine-guns. To their own shouts of '*Viva España*', the crowd replied, '*Viva Alemania*'.

A week later the full remaining complement of this Kondor Legion (some 6,000 altogether) finally left Spain for Hamburg aboard five German 'Strength-Through-Joy' liners. When they arrived in the mouth of the Elbe they were escorted up it by the pocket battleship *Graf Spee* while shore batteries fired a salute. On shore, women pelted them with flowers and they goose-stepped triumphantly past Field Marshal Goering, General von Brauchitsch (the German Commander-in-Chief), Admiral Raeder and General Keitel.

The much larger number of Italians still in Spain, some 20,000, came home in patriotic triumph at the end of that week, to be reviewed by Mussolini in Naples and praised as 'the nightmare of the pluto-democracies'. It was officially announced that the maximum Italian force in Spain had been 40,000, and that the final casualty list had been 3,132 Italians killed (including 174 airmen) and 2,000 permanently disabled. Eighty-five planes had been lost in the two years and nine months of the Civil War.

In the official eulogies which were now lavished both in Germany and in Italy on the 'volunteers' who had been sent to Spain, there was no longer any pretence that their intervention had been only in response to intervention on behalf of the Republicans. It was proudly confirmed that both Germany and Italy had responded to General Franco's call for help from the very first days of the Civil War, when they had helped transport large numbers of his troops from North Africa to Spain itself. Hitler, reviewing in Berlin some 15,000 goose-stepping men who had served in the Kondor Legion at different periods of the Civil War and 2,500 sailors who had served during it in Mediterranean waters, publicly proclaimed what he had been denying for nearly three years, namely that he personally had given the orders for them to go. A contingent of 330 Hitler Youths carried silver placards framed in gold, each bearing the individual name of a man who had been killed in Spain. It was the first official intimation of German casualties there. Including wounded these were now said to be about a thousand altogether.

One other feature of Hitler's speech caused interest. It was noted that in contrast with references to the Civil War in earlier days it was no longer called 'a war against Bolshevism'. It was now simply a war against 'the Christian democracies and international warmongers'.

17

On 25 May Colonel Josiah Wedgwood, the Labour Member of Parliament for Newcastle-under-Lyme, had addressed a letter to the Home Secretary, Sir Samuel Hoare, from the House of Commons. It ran:

> Dear Home Secretary
>
> It is not creditable to our country to play so poor a part in helping the persecuted Jews of Germany. ... Washing our hands like Pilate is bad for our consciences and our traditions ...

Having stated that there was now little practical difference between slavery and their present existence in Germany, he drew attention to the fact that at present the only Jews permitted to come to Britain and stay there were: (1) unmarried women between eighteen and forty-five who were suitable for domestic service; (2) those over sixty whose support was guaranteed for life; (3) those still with some capital to start a business.

No more doctors, dentists, professors, nurses were now being allowed in and even those over sixty had practically ceased to arrive since the rules for immigration had been tightened earlier in the year. All other Jews allowed into England had to be trans-migrants and none of these, except for trainees, were allowed to work. Charitable organizations such as the Lord Baldwin Fund alone made it possible for such Jews to survive.

In the reply Colonel Wedgwood was to receive from the Home Secretary it was stated that since the beginning of the Nazi regime in 1933 just over 29,000 refugees from Germany had been admitted into Britain, of whom 3,873 had re-emigrated. Since 1 January permits had been given for 7,170 to be taken into domestic service; 2,184 over 60; 5,000 children; 10,000 who were scheduled for re-emigration and a few hundred nurses, doctors and midwives.

It was now some seven months since Chamberlain, speaking just after the pogroms of November 1938, had said that he was greatly impressed by the urgency of the problem. But since then very little had been done by the world at large for the persecuted Jews of whom Germany was anxious to be rid. The talks with Germany through the Evian Inter-Governmental Committee for Refugees had got nowhere in the past few months since their apparently reasonably hopeful opening earlier in the year. The crux of the question was still money. The Germans wanted all Jews to emigrate but wanted to take almost all their assets from them before they could leave. The nations making up the Evian Committee had so far refused to commit themselves to the considerable amount of financial aid necessary both to sustain refugees in any initial phase of their emigration and also to help them finally settle somewhere.

Even the London *Times* had made an attempt to stir consciences in a leader in April and now, after Colonel Wedgwood's letter, the *Manchester Guardian* spoke out with an equally high moral tone. It said that the British Government, the representatives of a quarter of the world's surface, had a special responsibility. The Government was attempting to make a peace front against aggression and gather together the moral forces of the world, but as a moral leader its record was poor and its somewhat enforced conversion to the principle of collective security did not redress the balance of the picture. If, said the paper, the British and Allied Governments wanted to figure as the defenders of world civilization, they should act now in the tradition of the West. Christianity with its roots deep in Jewry urged them to find homes for the refugees.

Apart from money, of course, the problem remained: where were the refugees to go? The United States had a strict quota list for immigrants. A Commission was sitting, to examine the possibility of Northern Rhodesia and British Nyasaland for settlement. There was still talk of homes in British Honduras and in the Dominican Republic. Further enquiries were being made into possibilities in the Philippines. A report had just been published by His Majesty's Stationery Office on British Guiana saying that it did not, after all, seem suitable for large-scale settlement but that some 5,000 could be tried for a start at the cost of some £600,000. Chamberlain said that the Government hoped 'that large-scale settlement might prove possible', yet he also said that the experimental settlement would have to be financed from private sources. The *Manchester Guardian* wrote:

> Everyone knows that until the Evian Governments assume full responsibility and act, nothing will happen at all. But each of them hangs back, talking of their problems of unemployment and the sensitiveness of their own public opinion. . . . The Jews look to their home in Palestine which they have been promised. Here the British Government, though it knows from the refugee question itself that Europe's Jews must go somewhere, has almost shut the door on immigration.

The British Government had, in fact, just published on 17 May its proposals for the future of Palestine, in the form of a White Paper. The opening paragraphs admitted that these proposals were unlikely to meet with much acceptance since they were virtually those which had already been rejected by both the Arab and Jewish delegations to the London Conference.

The four fundamental obligations of the Mandate conferred on Britain by the League of Nations in 1922 were listed: (1) to protect and provide access to the Holy Places; (2) to establish in Palestine a national home for the Jewish people, and to facilitate Jewish immigration and a close settlement by Jews on the land; (3) to ensure that, in doing this, the rights of other sections of the population were not prejudiced; (4) to lead the country to self-governing institutions.

The inherent problem in trying to reconcile the second and third of these obligations was immediately faced by the White Paper when it said that the 1917 Balfour Declaration, while providing for a Jewish national home in Palestine, did not mean that the whole of Palestine was to be converted into a Jewish National State. 'His Majesty's Government therefore now declare unequivocally that it is not part of their policy that Palestine should become a Jewish State. They would indeed regard it as contrary to their obligations to the Arabs under the Mandate ... that the Arab population of Palestine should be made subjects of a Jewish State against their will.'

But whatever exactly the new Jewish national home was to be, His Majesty's Government reaffirmed that there was to be one and that it was to be in Palestine 'as of right and not on sufferance'. Attention was drawn to the fact that since 1922 some 300,000 Jews had come to Palestine and that the population of the national home had risen to some 450,000, or a third of the entire population of the country.

As to the difficulties created by the exchange of letters between Sir Henry McMahon for the British Government and the Sherif of Mecca in October 1915 in which McMahon undertook to recognize and support Arab independence, it was the British Government's view that the whole of Palestine west of the Jordan was excluded from that pledge.

What, then, were Palestine's self-governing institutions to be? The answer in theory was an easy one: 'It should be a state in which the two peoples in Palestine, Arabs and Jews, share authority in government in such a way that the essential interests of each are secured.'

The Government therefore declared its intention of creating such a State within ten years, preceded by a transitional period in which the people of Palestine were to acquire an increasing share in government. Steps to implement this would be taken as soon as peace and order were sufficiently restored. In referring in this context to the citizens of the new State, only the term 'Palestinian' was conveniently used.

The more controversial matter of Jewish immigration was then examined. The limitations imposed by the Mandate had been that it should not be so great as to exceed whatever might be the economic capacity of the country nor, at the same time, be a burden upon the people of Palestine as a whole nor deprive any section of them of their employment. Hitherto it had been the first of these considerations that had seemed paramount; and it could not be denied that a large number of the Jewish immigrants who had been admitted so far had been successfully absorbed economically. However, His Majesty's Government now made clear that they did not regard the country's economic absorptive capacity as the only test for further Jewish immigration. It was clear that the Arabs were afraid that a continued indefinite influx would lead to their domination by the Jewish population and to 'consequences which are extremely grave for Jews and Arabs alike and for the peace and prosperity of Palestine'.

The 'lamentable disturbances of the past three years' and the Arab terrorism to which the White Paper gave 'unqualified condemnation' had made Arab apprehension plain enough. If immigration, determined only by the economic absorptive capacity of the country regardless of other considerations, were to continue, 'a fatal enmity between the two peoples will be perpetuated and the situation in Palestine may become a permanent source of friction between all the peoples in the Near and Middle East'. Neither the obligations of the Mandate nor considerations of common sense and justice required this situation to be ignored.

There were only two alternatives: to expand the Jewish national home indefinitely by immigration against the strongly expressed will of the Arab peoples of Palestine or to allow further Jewish immigration only if the Arabs were prepared to acquiesce in it. His Majesty's Government had now decided that the time had come to adopt in principle the second of these alternatives. They were rejecting one proposal which had been made, to the effect that all Jewish immigration into Palestine should be stopped forthwith, but they had now decided that for each of the next five years a quota of 10,000 Jewish immigrants a year would be allowed into Palestine and, as a contribution towards solution of the Jewish refugee problem, a further 25,000 for the whole period would be admitted as soon as it was clear that adequate provision for them could be made. After the end of that five years no more Jewish immigration would be allowed into Palestine unless agreed by the Arabs. Any illegal immigrants who might come into Palestine in the meantime and could not be deported would be deducted from the yearly quotas.

The White Paper concluded with one sentence at least which was likely to meet with general agreement: 'His Majesty's Government cannot hope to satisfy partisans of one party or the other in such a controversy as the Mandate has aroused.'

Enough of this had been anticipated for world Jewish indignation to be ready to express itself immediately. After all, except for recognizing that an additional 25,000 Jewish refugees might in the exceptional circumstances of the present have to be admitted over five years, the White Paper argued as if the only premises to consider were those of the McMahon Letter, the Balfour Declaration and the Mandate of 1922. But as David Ben-Gurion, Chairman of the Executive of the Jewish Agency for Palestine, had said in Jerusalem just before the White Paper appeared:

> Anyone aware of the position of Jews in Eastern Europe today will not for one moment believe that they will cease coming to their homeland because some law terms it illegal. They will never recognize the moral validity of this term. Jews who must choose between utter extinction and immigration to Palestine under conditions called illegal will not waver for a moment in their choice.

As the *New York Times* wrote: 'A return to barbarism in Europe unimaginable when the contract [i.e. the earlier Balfour Declaration] was made has transformed the Holy Land from a symbol into a real place of refuge, changed it from a spiritual home into the expanding nucleus of a national State.'

It found the White Paper a shattering disappointment. 'Intolerable and unacceptable,' Dr Nahum Goldmann, President of the Zionist Organization of America, called it. He urged President Roosevelt to act on behalf of the Jews. And an American Rabbi, speaking to Jewish women's organizations at the 'Temple of Religion' in the New York World's Fair, confronted Britain with unequivocal moral blame: 'The doors of their ancestral homeland have been shut in the faces of the most pitiable refugees in the world today because of the failure of a great nation to maintain the sanctity of its pledged word to a weak, small people.'

In Palestine itself the confrontation was physical.

The day after the White Paper was published there were riots in Jerusalem and Tel Aviv. 'The Bible Is Our Mandate; England Cannot Annul It' was one of the banners carried in the demonstration in Tel Aviv. In Jerusalem the police were stoned by Jewish demonstrators when trying to prevent them from going to the District Commissioner's office and the affray lasted some three hours. Over a hundred Jews were hurt, as were five British constables; one British constable was killed by a bullet fired from a Mauser at close range. At least one sergeant and two constables appeared with swastikas on their helmets, shouting 'Heil Hitler!' It so happened that the issue of the *New York Times* which reported the riot also had a report with a Munich dateline, stating that one thousand stateless former Polish Jews had been ordered to leave Germany by 31 July or be sent to Dachau.

The next day was quiet but tense. The three British policemen who had appeared with swastikas on their helmets were suspended pending disciplinary action. The commander of the British forces said that while appreciating the three years of restraint shown by the Jews during the Arab revolt, he would suppress all violence unflinchingly.

The protest of the Jewish population was massive but, on the part of the majority, non-violent in its approach. The Landlords' Association, for instance, announced that it was starting a campaign of non-cooperation, refusing to pay rates and taxes. Demonstrations themselves were intended to be peaceful. On 22 May a procession of 2,000 Jewish women carrying banners saying 'We Won't Give In' took a document of protest to the Chief Secretary of the High Commissioner for Palestine. It described itself as 'a cry from the broken hearts of thousands of Jewish mothers who showed marvellous restraint for three years of terror when so many of our young sons were killed, who turned the desert into a paradise. On behalf of the Jewish mothers of the world we pray that this terrible mistake may be rectified, preventing the greatest catastrophe to the Jewish people.'

The procession was watched by a large detachment of steel-helmeted police carrying batons and backed up by two armoured cars. But it dispersed peacefully enough.

Jewish ex-servicemen from the British forces called a meeting in Palestine to approve the return of their war medals to the War Office.

It was clear from the start, however, that reaction would not always continue to be moderate. It was thought that extremist Jewish youth might well get out of hand and resort to violence in the belief, apparently substantiated by the effect of the Arab revolt, that violence was the only way of making Britain take notice. A few days even before the White Paper was published a clandestine Proclamation had been posted throughout Palestine. 'As soon as the White Paper is published,' it said, 'Israel's sword will be drawn from its sheath.' It was signed 'By command of the Covenant of Warriors for Motherland and Liberty.'

Israel's sword was now indeed drawn by such extremists in the form of bombs and bullets directed principally at the Arab population. By the end of May six Arabs had been killed and twenty wounded. Zionists of the Revisionist school were held responsible. There were wholesale arrests of Revisionists, of whom two hundred were in Acre prison by the end of the month. Both British and moderate-minded Jews found themselves amazed that Jews could sink to the level of Arab terror tactics. It was even reported by one Hebrew evening paper that Vladimir Jabotinski, the Head of the Revisionist Movement, who was still in Poland, was himself deploring the use of violence.

However deplorable, the British were now clearly caught up in a vicious circle of terrorism which made itself painfully felt on 2 June when four British soldiers, together with three Jewish police, were killed in an ambush near Tulkarm while patrolling the railway line there. Bomb explosions at the Jaffa Gate in Jerusalem killed five Arabs, injured nineteen others and destroyed a number of telephone lines in the city.

The British punished this latter act by suspending bus services in the city for a time. Similarly, when an Arab was shot dead a few days later in Tel Aviv, they stopped all motor traffic in and out for twenty-four hours. Their punishment of the Arabs who had ambushed them at Tulkarm was more direct. They surprised the gang in the same area and killed fourteen of them. Three days later the young Jewess who had planted the time bombs at the Jaffa Gate was arrested and sentenced to life imprisonment.

There were more bombs in Tel Aviv on 13 June and on 19 June an explosion in a bus station in Haifa killed nine Arabs and wounded twenty-four. In six attacks by Jews on Arabs on the roads on 29 June eleven Arabs were killed. The British started introducing collective fines on neighbourhoods. The Zionist General Council issued a statement which condemned 'the shedding of innocent blood which is likely only to stain the purity of the Jewish people's struggle for liberation'. The grave consequences for Jews and Arabs in Palestine which the White Paper had specifically hoped to forestall were upon them already.

But one moderate Jewish voice still saw time for a further warning note. Albert Einstein, speaking to the Jewish National Workers' Alliance in New York, said: 'There could be no greater calamity than a permanent discord between us and the Arab people. ... We must strive for a just and lasting compromise with the Arab people.'

Meanwhile terrible things were happening to Jews elsewhere – not only those still in Germany but those who, provided they could reconcile themselves to the loss of their possessions, were leaving it as fast as they could.

The relatively small number of Jewish refugees welcomed in the outside world by contrast with the number available to leave Germany could be gauged from the official figures given this summer by the two countries most willing to receive them, the United States and Britain. Between July 1932 and the beginning of 1939 the United States had received 65,404 refugees from Germany – more than a quarter of those in the last six months of 1938. There had been no significant increase in the rate of arrival in 1939 and indeed some opposition to a plan to bring one about. A Senate Resolution which provided for the admission to the United States of 20,000 Jewish refugee children from Germany under fourteen over the following two years was opposed by the American Legion on the grounds that the Legion did not believe in the break-up of families; and that there were thousands of underprivileged children in the United States, 'many of them in need, and housed in tar paper shacks without adequate food or clothing'. Congress eventually passed the Resolution.

The figure for Britain since 1933 as given by the Home Office in response to Colonel Wedgwood's letter had been 29,000. Yet there were still some half a million Jews in Germany and many millions living in other European countries where anti-semitism was widespread and, as in Italy and Hungary, actually becoming enshrined in law. And if there was a tragic disproportion between those of whom Germany wanted to be rid, and those for whom there was a welcome elsewhere, the experiences of those who did manage to get on their way was often heart-rending.

Distressing scenes multiplied as Jews who had left a country in which life for them had been made humiliating and fearful, tried to find one in which they could live without humiliation or fear. Both rich and poor, as Jews, were equally liable to rebuff, though some less liable than others, and these inevitably the rich. Baron Louis de Rothschild, arrested by the Gestapo at the time of the occupation of Austria in March 1938, and held for over a year on an upper floor of the Hotel Metropole in Vienna, which became their headquarters, was released on 12 May in apparent good health and flew to Zürich, where he had no difficulty in being accepted. From there he moved to Paris, where it was said he intended to stay for some days before going to the provinces for a much needed rest. But wealth had not always ensured so smooth a transition to freedom.

A party of twelve Jewish refugees from Czechoslovakia including a wealthy iron dealer and his daughter had arrived in a specially chartered plane at Croydon airport, London, on the night of 29 March via Copenhagen and Amsterdam. They were told that they would have to be held pending enquiries and were taken for the night to Wallington police station. The Home Office found that there was apparently no refugee organization sponsoring them and the refugees were told that they would therefore have to be sent back to where they came from. They were returned the next morning to Croydon aerodrome in a police van. But on their arrival, when an official called out that the plane was waiting, a hysterical scene took place. The refugees screamed, shouted and refused to move – except for two who somehow got away and were later recaptured trying to hitch a lift in Purley Way. The others eventually had to be carried to the aircraft, screaming and shouting, by aerodrome police and porters. Once inside it, their distraught state became so acute, with several threatening to throw themselves out in flight, that the pilot refused to take off, and they were sent back for a second night to Wallington police station. Finally the British Committee for Refugees from Czechoslovakia agreed to act as guarantors together with some private individuals and the Home Office allowed them to stay for three months.

Three other refugees from Czechoslovakia, who had spent the night in police cells in the aerodrome itself, were not so lucky and were sent back to Poland – one in such a state of desperation that he had to be 'assisted' out to the aircraft. Croydon was in fact the scene of more than one such incident. One Czech who arrived from Holland on Monday 27 March and was sent back the next day returned on Wednesday, was sent back again on Thursday, and returned again on Friday. This time the immigration authorities detained him.

A week later *The Times* in a leader, the main purpose of which had been to welcome Colonel Beck to London, had made clear that an indiscriminate welcome for Jews as refugees from Europe was far from being one of the Establishment's top priorities. The passage ran as follows:

> The Polish Government are known to be very anxious to come to some arrangement by which room can be found within the British Empire for some of those who are described as the 'surplus Jews' of Poland. Readier sympathy will be given to the wish of the Warsaw Government to obtain special facilities for access to raw materials.

And in Parliament Colonel Wedgwood had had no hesitation in accusing the Government of callousness. He said:

> The appalling delay on the part of Government departments in granting visas to refugees is responsible for a large number of the suicides in Prague during the past month. ... All the time there is this desperate attitude of permanent hostility on the part of the Government reflected in the attitude of the voluntary organizations because they take their orders from the Government. How long is it to continue? How long is our good name to be smirched by the Government's attitude of deliberate hostility, instead of their behaving like a Christian Government and giving help where it is needed?

The Times itself was sometimes critical of progress. 'It must be admitted that the fulfilment of the task of rescue leaves much to be desired,' it had written in its leader of 20 April.

The voluntary organizations ... are battling bravely but in some respects vainly against the disorganization of overwork and the complete inadequacy of their funds. And it must be said that the Government might at least lend them the nucleus of a trained staff, without recanting that refusal of official responsibility which, it appears, all receiving countries consider essential.

It was by no means only the British Government that was dragging its feet. In other territories scenes such as those at Croydon were being enacted on a far harsher scale.

During May and June on the borders of Poland and Germany in Silesia several thousand Jews were being cruelly shuttled backwards and forwards between two sets of contemptuous authorities as they were deported by the Germans only to be rejected by the Poles. Those who subsequently avoided a return to the concentration camps, from which they had originally been released on promising to leave Germany lived, unwanted by anyone, in makeshift encampments in a temporary no-man's-land between the two countries.

Boatloads of Jewish refugees from Germany were also arriving haphazardly at different ports around the world from Shanghai to Buenos Aires by regular commercial shipping lines, or cruising desperately off the shores of Palestine in flimsy craft, hoping for illegal disembarkation. Even those who arrived abroad as fare-paying passengers on the regular liners often found a cruel welcome awaiting them.

At the beginning of May, 937 German Jews sailed for Cuba from Hamburg on the Hamburg-Amerika liner *St Louis*. Most of them were already on the quota list for immigrants into the United States, though their individual numbers had not yet come up and they were going to Cuba to wait for them to do so. All had Cuban immigration visas obtained from Cuban Consuls in Europe and signed by the Director-General of the Cuban Immigration Department, granting them permission to enter the country though not to work there. They had had to pay for these permits, as of course also for the tickets, being required by the German line to buy return fares lest difficulties should arise over their landing and reception. Many of them had spent all their remaining money on the voyage. Friends and relatives who were already in Cuba awaited them.

The *St Louis* anchored in the long narrow harbour of Havana on 27 May. While it had been at sea a new decree had been issued by President Federico Laredo Bru of Cuba, requiring further documentation, of which very few of the passengers were in possession, together with a $500 bond posted ahead of their arrival and sufficient funds with them to prevent their becoming a public charge. There were now 9,000 Jewish refugees in Cuba already, most of whom had arrived in recent months to await their turn on the US quota list. Feeling had been growing against them, fanned by campaigns on the press and radio, and these stricter regulations were the result.

Of the 937 passengers only very few were regarded by the Cuban authorities as having their papers in order and the rest had to stay on board in the harbour, hoping that somehow the next day the President would cut through the red tape on their behalf. Otherwise the *St Louis* would have to sail back again for Hamburg on 30 May. When the day came and nothing had happened, last-minute efforts were made by American Jewish relief organizations and the vessel's sailing was postponed. But despair was beginning to set in. One of the passengers, Max Loewe, a forty-eight-year-old lawyer from Hamburg who had sailed with his wife and two children, slashed his wrists and jumped overboard into the bay. He was picked up by a launch and taken to hospital. The next day the ship's Captain, Gustav Schroeder, said he was afraid of 'a collective suicide pact' among the passengers if he had to sail for Hamburg, and there was indeed a second suicide attempt when a young Jewish lawyer on board took poison in his cabin. Ship's officers had to break down the cabin door and he was saved by a doctor. A representative of the Cuban President spent several hours on board that day but it was announced that the President was sticking to his decision. Attempts were being made, it was said, to get President Roosevelt to intervene.

On 1 June President Laredo Bru signed a decree ordering his navy to conduct the *St Louis* outside Cuban waters, having first seized anyone who had managed to disembark and returned them to the ship. The Captain posted up a ship's bulletin:

> The Cuban Government requires us to leave the harbour but has allowed us to remain until tomorrow morning so we shall sail definitely at 10 a.m. The shipping company is going to remain in touch with various organizations and official bodies in an endeavour to effect a landing outside Germany. We shall try to stay in the vicinity of South American countries.

Late that afternoon the *St Louis* was surrounded by small boats filled with relatives and friends of those on board, though police boats prevented anyone other than officials from coming too close. But people in the boats were able to talk to the passengers lining the rail of the *St Louis*, many of whom were sobbing desperately. Letters too could be exchanged. As each small boat turned back again to the shore it was followed by anxious cries of 'Auf Wiedersehen!' At nightfall huge spotlights from the *St Louis* shone out onto the surrounding waters. A thirty-six-man vigilance committee was appointed on board to watch for attempted suicides.

Max Loewe, the lawyer who had slashed his wrists, was said to be in a grave condition in hospital and unable to leave with the ship, but it was hoped that his wife and two children would be allowed to stay behind with him. However, when in fact the ship did set sail the next morning, cleared for Hamburg, and escorted by twenty police boats watching for people jumping overboard, the authorities would not relent. Frau Loewe and her children had to leave with it.

Captain Schroeder was still worried about mass suicide attempts. He let it be known that he would probably anchor outside the twelve-mile limit while negotiations with the Government continued. A report was spread to the effect that the United States Government had authorized the landing of the passengers in New York, should the Cuban negotiations fail. Officials in Washington, however, denied this. The American Trade Union leader, John Lewis, cabled the military leader of the Cuban Government, Colonel Fulgencio Batista, asking him to reconsider the decision and reminding him that if returned to Germany the Jews would immediately be sent to concentration camps. The only action taken by the Inter-Governmental Committee for Refugees had been to request the German authorities in Berlin not to let refugees leave the country unless sure that they would be allowed to land in the country of their destination.

Certainly the prospects for those on board the *St Louis* did not look good, though Captain Schroeder seemed in no particular hurry to return to Germany. On 4 June it was reported cruising leisurely in Caribbean waters off the coast of Florida, with a United States coastguard patrol boat out of Fort Lauderdale standing by to prevent any attempt to jump overboard and swim ashore. The passengers were said to be quite cheerful, which may have been reaction to the news that a New York attorney from the American Joint Distribution Committee was in Havana still pleading with President Laredo Bru to change his mind. But multiplying reports of the fate of other boatloads in the region contained little comfort and suggested only that the attitude of Latin-American governments in general was becoming increasingly implacable towards Jewish refugees. In Costa Rica, twenty who had actually been given permission to land were now ordered to leave with the exception of one woman who had just had a baby. Further south, 200 Jews on the liners *Caporte*, *Monte Olivia* and *Mendoza* who had first tried to get into Paraguay and then Argentina had been refused by both and ordered to return to Germany. And 104 Jews who had arrived at Havana on the French liner *Flandre* the day after the *St Louis* and had been sent on to Vera Cruz in Mexico, were reported on 3 June to have been sent back again to Havana. Perhaps they too had some hope for a moment that President Laredo Bru would change his mind. Indeed some tentative agreement seems to have been arrived at, though not satisfactorily implemented, by which, in return for a bond deposited in a New York bank to cover all refugees at a rate of $500 a head, some consideration would be given by the Cuban Government to the idea of temporary refuge in a camp on the Isle of Pines. However, on 5 June President Laredo Bru issued a sombre statement to the effect that 'the post that I occupy has painful duties which oblige me to disregard the impulses of my heart and follow the stern dictates of duty'. And the next day the New York attorney who had been negotiating in Havana was told, to his consternation, that the offer had now expired and that all doors were now closed. The *St Louis* set course for Hamburg. 'No plague ship', wrote the *New York Times*, 'ever received a sorrier welcome. ... The *St Louis* will soon be home with her cargo of despair.'

Such cargoes of despair were now to be found scattered across the seas of the world. Five hundred Jews from Austria and Czechoslovakia who had escaped

down the Danube in river boats to Constanza on the Black Sea had been trying
for a month to find ships to take them to Palestine. Unsuccessful, they had been
expelled from Constanza and were now in a state of desperation at Balchik near
the Rumanian-Bulgarian border. Another party who had left Hamburg as early
as 22 April for Alexandria had, on being refused permission to land in Egypt,
tried to get to Palestine, failed, landed in Turkey but were expelled from there
and had returned to Alexandria where they were again barred and told they
must return to Germany. Eight of them, six men and two women, tried to
commit suicide in Alexandria harbour. The 626-ton steamer *Colorado*, flying
the Panama flag, was ashore at Fethiye opposite the island of Rhodes with 226
refugees who had no prospect of being accepted anywhere.

On 1 June the 573-ton Greek cattle boat, the *Liesel*, carrying 906 Jews
including 300 women and sixty children from Poland, Rumania, Germany and
Czechoslovakia was apprehended off the coast of Palestine. The Captain had
already taken passengers off two other similar boats. All were now taken to
Haifa, where to their relief and joy they were given permission to stay in
Palestine. However, their number was deducted from the total number of 10,000
allowed in for the year under the new rules of the White Paper. Their good
fortune meant that 906 Jews in other cattle boats would one day be turned away.

From Central and Eastern Europe many such cargo and cattle boats, often
unseaworthy and always overcrowded, were taking on Jewish refugees with the
promise to take them to Palestine. Their captains were often extortionate and
had even been reported as extracting gold teeth in payment when a refugee had
no other money or possessions left. They were also sometimes unscrupulous,
dumping, so it was said, small groups of helpless refugees on small islands and
even barren rocks in the Eastern Mediterranean, rather than risking confrontation with immigration patrols off the Palestinian coast. One party of 500 Danzig
refugees was in June stranded in Crete, reportedly destitute and starving, though
a similar group had successfully reached Palestine. Meanwhile a scattering of
flimsy vessels cruised endlessly up and down the Palestine coast looking for a
chance to land their suffering cargo undetected by British patrols, interception
by which led to confiscation of the boat and heavy fines. Lately captains had
taken to cruising just outside territorial limits and sending refugees off towards
the shore in lifeboats. If caught, their numbers too were deducted from the
regular quota.

To most ordinary newspaper readers in the democracies these events seemed
of course remote and were difficult to grasp realistically, even if read about. To
the ordinary German newspaper reader they were even more remote, though
there was some suggestion that the fate of the *St Louis* passengers, or possibly
just the publicity which accompanied it, had caused concern to informed public
opinion in the Reich. It was thought that this might have had something to do
with the apparent willingness the Hamburg-Amerika line was now showing to
consider diversion of the ship to some other port outside Germany. But if the

democratic world had too much on its mind to be able to give more than fragmentary sympathy to the Jewish predicament, it is perhaps not surprising that the Germans, indoctrinated in any case to view the Jews less sympathetically, found little here to reflect on the essential quality of their culture. It was clear after all from their newspapers that their Führer was a cultured man. In the middle of June, while all these things were happening, he gave a luncheon for Richard Strauss on the occasion of the composer's seventy-fifth birthday in the Imperial Hotel, Vienna.

On 4 June it was reported that the Hamburg-Amerika liner *Orinoko*, which had just sailed from Cuxhaven for Cuba, on learning of the experience of those on board the *St Louis* had turned back to unload 200 Jewish passengers. These were said to be dejected and uncertain of what would happen to them.

Many such Jews now wandering the high seas in alternate fits of optimism and despair knew all too well what would happen to them if they were returned to Germany. People in the democratic countries knew too, up to a point. At the time of Chamberlain's appeasement visit to Rome at the beginning of the year there had been the newspaper photograph of Jewish inmates of Sachsenhausen concentration camp in their striped prison pyjamas being inspected by the visiting Italian Minister of Culture. Now in the middle of the year, with the final destination of the *St Louis* still uncertain, readers of the *News Chronicle* could learn of the sort of thing that went on in such places from an article by a Jew recently a prisoner there who had been lucky enough to be accepted as a refugee in Britain.

They read how, on arrival at Sachsenhausen with its grim landscape of camp barracks, high electrified wire fence and watchtowers manned by guards with machine-guns, he and his fellow-prisoners were greeted by SS men armed with whips and sticks who beat them mercilessly as soon as they had descended from the lorries. He himself only had a little finger broken though some were beaten so severely that they had to be carried into the camp unconscious. Once there, they were made to stand motionless for nearly five hours to await the striped clothing marked with a yellow and red triangle. Their heads were shaved.

Work, which lasted from 6 a.m. to 6 p.m. each day with a half-hour break for dry bread, consisted of carrying heavy loads of cement, sometimes at the double. Working in the winter mud prisoners often fell under the load and were beaten with rifle butts until they rose again. Eight men out of the sixty in the transport in which the writer had arrived died in the first week in the camp.

Being stopped one day by the camp commandant, Baranowski, and his entourage, this prisoner had been asked why he was there, and had replied that it was because he was a Jew. Baranowski had immediately struck him viciously in the face.

Soon after arrival the writer's attention had been caught one day by the sinister banging of a distant drum. He discovered that it was being carried by a prisoner who, while banging it, was made to march three times round a vaulting-horse, across which he was then strapped to be given twenty-five strokes with a steel cord whip. After fifteen strokes the man had collapsed. He was then carried to a water hydrant where, as he screamed in agony, the nozzle was pushed up his anus and water forced through it. His body swelled up and dirty water gushed out of his mouth. He was carried away screaming and died later.

The first part of this punishment was one which the writer of the article had seen repeated frequently, though the camp commandant had forbidden further use of the hydrant. Other punishments in the camp consisted of – the mildest – standing for four hours outside with hands above the head; or 'hanging' or 'crucifixion' which consisted of being hung from a beam by the arms for one to two hours and which frequently caused dislocation of the joints. The standard punishment was whipping. There was no day on which he had not seen one or other of these punishments inflicted. The death-rate in the three months he was in the camp was around ten per cent of those imprisoned there. He himself had contracted pneumonia and had eventually been released on condition that he left Germany within a certain period. He was warned that if he did not do so he would return to the concentration camp for life.

As the St Louis still proceeded with its 900 despairing passengers back towards Hamburg – though at slackened speed so that the negotiations for some alternative destination could continue – it was reported from Berlin that thousands of Jews had received new orders to leave the country or be sent to concentration camps. They were appealing to their community leaders to find them homes outside but had to be told that this was possible for only very few. It was also reported that what were called 'transports' of Polish Jews in Germany, of whom more than 10,000 had received written notices to leave or be sent to a concentration camp with time limits varying from a few hours to four weeks, were being 'today organized by the police'. Among these were several who had been arrested the previous autumn and released on giving a promise to emigrate. The fate of these Polish Jews living in Germany was particularly precarious because Poland was refusing to have them back on the grounds that they had lived too long abroad. The estimated 11,000 Jews living in East Prussia had all been ordered to get out by 20 June. In Leipzig 4,000 Jews had been told to leave within one month, and similar moves had been made against Jews in Dresden, Breslau, Kassel, Hannover, Kiel, Bremen, Nuremberg, Karlsruhe, Bamberg, Würtzburg, Darmstadt and Cologne.

In the end those on board the St Louis were among the lucky ones. After a meeting in Paris of the Liaison Committee of the League of Nations High Commissioner for Refugees from Germany it was reported on 14 June that Britain, France, Belgium and Holland would accept the 900 passengers between them. But Captain Osbert Peake, Under-Secretary at the Home Office, replying to a question in the House of Commons, made one thing clear. 'It is essential', he said, 'to emphasize that the special arrangements made in this case cannot be regarded as a precedent for the reception in future of refugees who may leave

Germany before definite arrangements have been made for their reception else-where.'

Britain's share of the *St Louis* refugees, 287, eventually arrived at Waterloo Station in London on 21 June. Some shed tears of relief. Every sort and condition of refugee was revealed by the seventy tons of luggage: expensive leather dressing-cases sitting side by side with cheap fibre cases and cardboard boxes. Some of the refugees were in working clothes, others wore immaculate tweeds and suits and costumes from the finest tailors in Berlin and Vienna. There were forty small children, including babes-in-arms, a sixty-seven-year-old Rabbi, and a woman who had only been able to wave from the deck of the *St Louis* to her husband, who had come out into Havana harbour in one of the small boats. Some of the refugees were now going to stay with relations in Britain; others were going to the camp at Richborough in Kent; others had been found temporary homes by various Jewish Aid Committees.

It was a very English sort of day on which they arrived. P.G. Wodehouse was made an Honorary Doctor of Letters at Oxford. And a married man of thirty-one with two children was ordered twenty strokes of the birch and six months' imprisonment for taking a handbag from a woman walking her dog, after hitting her several times with a stick. He was told by the judge: 'We rather pride ourselves in this country on not having this class of crime.'

As the *St Louis* refugees came into Waterloo Station they found it decorated with flags and bunting. Some of the children thought this was for them. In fact it had been for the King and Queen, who had returned from their tour on the other side of the Atlantic the day before.

18

After a highly-successful 7,000-mile tour through Canada, King George and Queen Elizabeth had, on the evening of 7 June, crossed the border by train at Niagara Falls on to – as the *New York Times* put it – soil wrested from the British Empire 160 years before. It was the first visit in history by a British Sovereign to the United States, and the royal pair were welcomed by Cordell Hull, the Secretary of State, bowing deeply and wearing morning clothes (though the King was still wearing only a dark blue chalk-stripe suit) and by Mrs Hull, who did not curtsey.

On the left-hand side of the front page of the issue of the *New York Times* that reported this event there was a headline: 'Britain Is Sending Expert To Moscow To Hasten Accord'. This was a reference to the despatch of a Mr William Stràng, Head of the Central European Department of the Foreign Office, to help and advise the British Ambassador to Moscow in the negotiations there. The paper suggested that Lord Halifax, the Foreign Secretary, might have been more acceptable to the Russians but it quoted the Prime Minister in the House of Commons as saying reassuringly that in London, Paris and Moscow there was now general agreement as to the main objects to be attained.

Washington that day was chiefly concerned with preparations for the arrival of the King and Queen. Vast crowds were expected and did indeed turn out to welcome them on their drive from the Union Station up Delaware Avenue to the Capitol and along Pennsylvania Avenue to the White House. It was estimated to be one of the largest crowds ever seen in the streets of Washington, some 600,000, exceeded perhaps only by that which had welcomed Colonel Lindburgh after the first transatlantic flight in 1927.

There were those who had been worried about the success of this visit of the King and Queen of England to the United States. The *New York Times* wrote afterwards that it had been 'a chancy business'. There was, as the paper put it, not far below the surface of American political opinion 'a suspicious nerve where the British are concerned'. It was nothing like so sensitive as in the days when the Irish question was acute, or as in the early days of the Great War when British orders-in-council were held to be infringing US rights as a neutral, yet there were still those in politics who maintained that Britain's policy was to use the United States as a catspaw and asserted that 'the British are never polite to us except when they want something'. 'Strong also in the American consciousness', added the paper, 'is the memory that our independence was won by military resistance to a British King.'

It was this latter historical fact and its traditional emotional importance for

Americans which had to be acknowledged, albeit good-humouredly and dismissively, from time to time throughout the four-day tour. Even the friendly *New York Times* in its welcoming leader, found it necessary to argue that for all the memory of his predecessor, George III, there need be no hesitation in welcoming George VI. 'A true-born American will not be disloyal to his country's best traditions if ... he says today quite sincerely: "God Save The King".'

That anthem was of course played formally, together with the 'Stars and Stripes', following the twenty-one-gun salute when President Roosevelt met the Royal couple at the Union Station – the first time any President had thus come to meet a Head of State. But it was the occasional snatches of the tune from crowds on the pavements which signified the unmistakable sound of success of the visit almost from the start. Its significance too on the level of international affairs was also discernible from the start.

It was just this aspect that had worried a paper like the *Chicago Daily Tribune*, so proud of its isolationism. The visit indeed presented the paper with something of a dilemma, for while it did not want to ignore the royal couple's popularity – it boasted that never before in newspaper history had a 'true-colour picture of a faraway spot news event' been brought to its readers' breakfast-tables so fast as its own of their arrival in Washington on the back page of its issue of 9 June – but it also had serious political reservations to express.

Its fear was that the visit was being exploited politically by Britain and France with the aid of President Roosevelt, as a means of entangling the United States in dangerous commitments to the democracies. While the King and Queen were still in Canada the paper had run a leader (on 3 June) in which it said categorically that it was the intention of the royal tour to swing America into the orbit of British and French imperialism. If, it said, it worked out as intended, the United States might be led into the diplomatic vassalage desired by promoters of the alliance which put America's frontier in France or somewhere in Africa. Such a visit, it suggested, might be acceptable to France which, although a Republic, did have a monarchical historical tradition, but here in the United States things were very different. And it pulled out every stop in the States' own aggressively republican historical tradition to confront the courtly but sinister intrigue to which it now felt the country was being subjected. It wrote:

> The incongruities of two opposed systems of society defy the efforts to demonstrate that they have everything in common. ... American national usage, customs and habits of thought are to be eclipsed by the image of a feudal mediaevalism moving across its face. ... Nor can a larger acquaintance with the institutions preserved by the British caste system for its own protection be very stimulating to the American belief that a man's worth is wholly in his own qualities. ... The United States receives them [the King and Queen] cordially if with mental reservations.

But with the popular success of the visit displayed on its front pages it expressed those reservations modestly enough in its headlines, simply providing

The King says goodbye to his ministers before leaving for Canada: (*right to left*) Sir Thomas Inskip (Defence), Lord Halifax (Foreign Secretary), Samuel Hoare (Home Secretary) Neville Chamberlain (Prime Minister) and Lord Crewe (Liberal Opposition leader).

HANG ON TO YOUR POCKETBOOK, UNCLE

WELCOME

HEP! HEP!

HOORAY FOR THE KING AND QUEEN!

FOREIGN INTRIGUE

AMERICAN ISOLATION FROM EUROPE'S QUARRELS

Chicago Daily Tribune cartoon by Orr.

formulae into which isolationists could read their own disapproval if they so wished – 'F.D.R. Drinks Toast To King'; 'Their Majesties Dine In Splendour With Roosevelt'; 'British Rulers Shake Hands Of US Law-Makers'. The strength of its feelings was confined to its cartoons. On 9 June it showed Uncle Sam waving a flag of welcome above crowds crying, 'Hooray for the King and Queen' as their motorcade approached the Capitol. But his hand was over his wallet in his back pocket, which was wrapped round with the slogan 'American Isolation From Europe's Quarrels', while a pair of hands marked 'Foreign Intrigue' moved surreptitiously towards it. The cartoon was entitled 'Hang On To Your Pocket-Book, Uncle'. The next day a bewildered Uncle Sam was seen standing in the middle of the American continent on which the Capitol was tied to a steaming tug moving towards Europe flying a Union Jack and piloted by a smiling John Bull. 'Europe's Quarrels' was marked on a buoy pointing in the same direction while Uncle Sam himself, feeling nervously for his hat, cried, 'I Seem To Be Drifting Again'. The picture was headed: 'In Tow?'.

On that first day in Washington the President and the King in his Admiral's uniform in the first open car were followed by Mrs Roosevelt and the Queen, in a whitish long dress of crêpe material, similar loose boxy jacket and high-crowned small hat with a feather, in the second. They were escorted by the traditional motorcycle police and baby tanks (one of which was to catch fire and burn out) while naval bluejackets manned the route and ten of the new Flying Fortresses flew overhead in formation with forty fighter aircraft – 'a flight of goodwill and friendship', as the *New York Times* wrote, adding 'but the roar of their engines was an awesome sound'.

The Queen particularly captured everyone's hearts, as she was to do throughout the whole of the tour. 'The King's tour, the Queen's triumph,' wrote one correspondent. 'Give her a crowd and she mows them down,' remarked another as the motorcade moved up Pennsylvania Avenue. Her hair, they said, was blacker, her eyes bluer, her figure slimmer, her complexion more gardenia-like with a flush of healthy colour than people had expected. But it was her charm and magnetic personal appeal which held the crowds as she peered eagerly among them and even stood up for a moment in the car with Mrs Roosevelt so that she could see them better.

Rapturous crowds turned out again for the royal couple when the President took them on a personally-conducted tour of the city. Next day they travelled in the President's yacht down the Potomac to George Washington's house at Mount Vernon, laid a wreath on the tomb of the Unknown Warrior at Arlington Cemetery and went to the Capitol to meet members of Congress. About four-fifths of these came to applaud them loudly in the Rotunda where, as few failed to point out, the King and Queen faced a painting of Cornwallis's surrender at Yorktown and another of Burgoyne's surrender at Saratoga alongside it. A life-size statue of Thomas Jefferson holding the Declaration of Independence stood on the Queen's left. Some of the remarks made by Congressmen, not accustomed

King George VI and Queen Elizabeth sail down the Potomac from Washington with President Roosevelt on the presidential yacht. BELOW 'The King's tour, the Queen's triumph' – Queen Elizabeth talking to a US girl scout outside the White House.

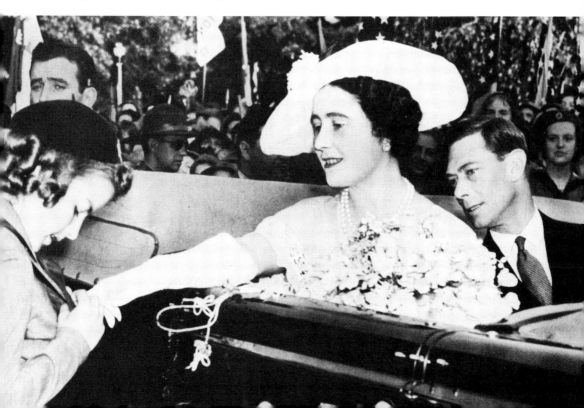

to keeping their voices down, were so clear that it was felt she could hardly have helped hearing them'. 'She's lovely!'; 'She's just as sweet as she can be!' – and certainly one Representative told her to her face that she was 'a good sport'.

The British press were delighted by the welcome. 'The news of it touches the hearts of the British people,' wrote the *Daily Herald*, describing the visit as a spontaneous expression of friendliness between two great English-speaking nations. The *News Chronicle* thought that the good relations between the two countries, than which there was no surer guarantee of peace, had been wholly enhanced.

The visit to New York was an even greater success than that to Washington, at least in terms of numbers. It was reckoned that 3,500,000 people turned out to see, cheer, sing and wave at the King and Queen as, after travelling up New York Bay on a United States destroyer flying the Royal Standard for the first time in history, they were welcomed at the Battery by Mayor La Guardia and made a 51-mile tour of the city to visit the World's Fair on Flushing Meadows – where, as Americans could be reminded without the occasion becoming soured in any way, 'the redcoats of George III had fought George Washington's ragged Continentals'. Mayor La Guardia afterwards revealed that in the car he had told the King and Queen that their visit 'had negotiated a treaty of friendship that would take many years to revoke' and that it was a visit which had done 'more good than the sending of twelve Ambassadors or the interchange of fifty diplomatic notes'.

'It is very kind of you to say so,' replied the King.

La Guardia also gathered that, rather than the roundabout route which had been laid down for them, the King and Queen would have preferred the traditional ticker-tape route through the city via Broadway and Fifth Avenue. But this, it was said, had been vetoed by Scotland Yard, anxious for the royal couple's security, lest a whole telephone book, or worse, should be dropped down the steel-and-concrete canyons of New York onto their heads. Nevertheless, whether on the Express Highway to 72nd Street, along 96th Street, or between the Queens end of the Triborough Bridge and the Fairgrounds, there was an almost unbroken line of cheering people. Again it was the Queen who captivated everyone. La Guardia's secretary had said to her before the drive began at the Battery: 'You've been here about four minutes and all New York is in love with you.'

His prediction proved true. One journalist described New York as 'melting before the cordial friendliness and personal magnetism of the beaming little consort of King George', singling out her 'faculty for rapt attention to persons presented to her' and her 'quick intelligent grasp'.

But the volume of goodwill for the royal couple meant that the King too received praise in his fashion. Going round the World's Fair, where 'the British monarchs captured the hearts of the world of tomorrow', the King was seen to look tired, showing his fatigue in the rather mechanical way in which he wearily

King and President, goodwill and friendship, though not far below the surface of American political life lies 'a suspicious nerve where the British are concerned'.

The King and Queen at the New York World's Fair.

waved his right hand to the crowds, but this was interpreted wholly to his advantage: 'His serious, gravely-smiling countenance, and the faraway look in his eyes as if he were gazing far over the heads of the people in front of him and seeking to penetrate the mysteries of the world of tomorrow in earnest, gave him an appealing aspect that made people feel sympathy for the cares that rest upon a crowned head.'

The royal visit to the Fair was seen clearly not only by the crowds present at the time but on television by 200 'sight-sound receivers', as the term went, in the metropolitan area of New York. General Electric also laid on a special demonstration of the new medium in the Hildeberg Hills some 130 miles away. Officials of the company were reported as being pleased thereby to have disproved the current theory that television could not be received beyond the normal horizon.

The King and Queen were given a rest on the last day of their visit to New York, which was the last day of their visit to the States, spending it quietly with the President in his Hyde Park home. He drove them about himself that day and went swimming with them. The King was able to wear an open-necked shirt in which he had the pleasure of eating his first hot dog. Soon afterwards the hot dog sellers on Coney Island were reported to be selling their wares under the slogan 'By Special Appointment to His Majesty the King'. That night the royal couple returned to Canada to begin their journey home.

'Thanks, America!' wrote J.L. Garvin in that Sunday's *Observer*. He struck a note which suggested almost that a historically new phase had developed in Anglo-American relations:

> Among the victories of peace none is greater than the assuagement of ancient bitterness. In the things that chiefly matter to the world, the American people and ourselves hold the same standard of right and wrong, look with the same eye upon claims of tolerance and mercy and resent with the same intensity whatever violates the precepts of the Christian tradition. When two great peoples have that bequest in common from their searching past, it can be no mere featherweight in the scale of fate.

The reactions of the German press too seemed to suggest that something quite important had happened. On the one hand there was an attempt to mock the whole visit, curiously by sympathizing with the traditionally courtly-mannered royal couple faced by the crudeness of American behaviour. *Der Angriff* raised an eyebrow on their behalf at the cowboy hat which had been seen at the British Embassy reception and at Vice-President Garner who had flexed his muscles, pretending to be a boxer, against the restraining ropes and had patted the King on the shoulder. A supplementary attempt to disparage American standards by contrast with more stately British ones was made by the paper in criticism of the security arrangements for the visit, which had indeed been massive (it was estimated by the American press that 20,000 policemen had been mobilized for the two-day New York visit alone). 'By its all-too-public organization of its safety measures the United States gave itself the aspect of a gangster Eldorado,'

Cartoon by Low in London's *Evening Standard*: 'And three cheers for you, too, brother.'

Chicago Daily Tribune cartoon by Orr: 'In tow?'

wrote *Der Angriff*. It was possibly on more relevant ground when it noted that the King's and Queen's reception at the Capitol had been boycotted by nearly one-fifth of all Congressmen. On the very Sunday on which Roosevelt had been driving the King around Hyde Park, Representative Hamilton Fish, Chairman of the National Committee to Keep America Out of Foreign Wars, addressed a rally at which he said that if Roosevelt had his way over the Neutrality Bill he would make the United States 'the potential slaughterhouse and arsenal for Britain and France' and would eventually drag the country into the next world war. 'It is none of our business', he added, 'what form of Government exists in any foreign lands.'

However, there was no doubt that the visit had been far more than a mere ceremonial success. The *New York Times* probably summed up the effect as well as anyone: 'Like all Britons, George and Elizabeth hope of course for something nearer an alliance between the United States and Britain than ever will be made.' But, said the paper, they were well coached in fact. They knew that the President's foreign policy powers were limited; they knew the importance of Congress; they knew the popular resolution in the States never again to send troops to a European war; they knew the consequences of the British default on war debts; and the criticism in the States of appeasement. Nevertheless, 'they left an even better impression than most optimistic counsellors had ventured to expect'.

While the *Völkischer Beobachter* joined in mockery of the vulgar reception in the 'Jewish metropolis' and of the predicament of ladies of the American press, who at the press conference in Washington 'in their excitement almost invariably stumbled over their own legs trying to curtsey', the editor of the *Münchener Neueste Nachrichten* wrote that it was not right to underestimate the effect of the visit in tying Britain and the United States closer together. He stressed the particular importance of the personal rapport between the President and the Crown. Roosevelt was the key to future United States policy. If Roosevelt were not to go for a third term, he said, neither Vice-President Garner nor the Democrats nor any Republican candidate 'would dream of entering similarly adventurous paths such as Roosevelt has sought in the past few months'.

In Germany itself the prevailing mood was by the middle of June difficult to assess. Hitler had made two bitter speeches the week before the King and Queen returned to Britain, protesting against 'encirclement' and suggesting that the crisis was deepening or even approaching an impasse. Yet the *New York Times* man in Berlin found many people there wondering why. Even leading Nazis agreed that neither Danzig nor the Polish Corridor was in any sense a vital or urgent problem though it would have to be resolved one day. Ninety per cent of the population – ninety-nine per cent one German told him – would have liked simply to rest on the laurels Hitler had won so far and, thinking wishfully perhaps from this premise, felt confident that the peace would be kept. They argued that Hitler did not want a war and that Britain and France did not want one either. 'Thus', went on the correspondent, 'Hitler will draw back at the right

The King and Queen with the President, his wife and mother at Roosevelt's house, Hyde Park, on the Hudson River.

The last day of their visit: Roosevelt at the wheel and hot dogs by Royal Appointment on Coney Island.

moment and so will his opponents – this seems to be the predominant German view. Yet the whole game is to see which can go furthest without drawing back. It seems a somewhat unsatisfactory basis of peace and the welfare of 500,000,000 people.'

19

While what had been happening to the Jews seemed, understandably, to Jews themselves – and particularly to Zionists – of agonizing and overriding importance, to the rest of the world it remained something to be balanced realistically against other demanding considerations. Some of these were of local concern such as, in Britain, the IRA bombing campaign which had persisted irritatingly since the beginning of the year, in spite of many arrests and convictions, these usually followed by long terms of imprisonment – up to twenty years. The young Irishmen at these trials often declared themselves proudly to be soldiers of the Irish Republican Army and, as at the trial in March of those accused of the Manchester explosions which had killed a man, had to be declared by the Court 'mute of malice'. When five men were each sentenced to twenty years on this occasion (two women being given seven) they ceased abruptly to be mute and cried, 'God save Ireland!' and 'Up the Republic!' in the traditional fashion before warders clapped their hands over their mouths and took them below. After this trial the police issued a warning that such terrorist acts were likely to take place for some considerable time to come. And indeed they continued regularly throughout the spring and summer. There were explosions in Coventry at the end of March, and in May, on the day that Litvinov was dropped as Soviet Foreign Minister. Shortly after two Irishmen had been sentenced at the Old Bailey for a bomb that had gone off harmlessly at Hammersmith, there was an outbreak of 'bomb outrages' in London, designed it seemed to cause damage and inconvenience rather than loss of life. Tear-gas bombs went off that day in two London cinemas and fifteen people had to be taken to hospital. A musical instrument maker's shop in Charing Cross Road had a bomb through its letter-box, and windows were broken in the showroom of Commercial Motors in Euston and of Crittall's Manufacturing Company in Holborn. The balloon and acid bombs used earlier in the year were again the principal weapon.

The man behind the IRA campaign in Britain, Sean Russell, was in the United States at the time, and at the end of May Britain applied for his extradition. As if in reply to this move, a few days later balloon acid bombs exploded in twenty-seven letter-boxes and two post offices in different parts of Britain. Most of these were in London, where the Metropolitan Police immediately put every letter-box in the City under guard. At Wimpole Street post office a worker was injured when a parcel exploded as he was stamping it. And six men were injured and a number of letters destroyed in the main post office in Manchester. The same day, in Scotland, an Irishman was sentenced to ten years' imprisonment for stealing explosives with the intention of making bombs. He had told the jury that it was the British Government which was responsible for the wave of bombings because of its refusal to withdraw British troops from Northern Ireland. This latest wave of letter-bombs, which was reported on the same day as that on which the King and Queen arrived in New York, enabled the *Chicago Daily Tribune* to place a congenial headline above the royal news, 'Mails In England Bombed'.

In Ireland a fortnight later Eamon de Valera, the Irish Taoiseach or Prime Minister, made his own move against his comrade of former days, Sean Russell, and declared the IRA an illegal organization there. This coincided with the news that the new Lord Mayor of Dublin was Mrs Tom Clarke, widow of the first signatory of the Proclamation of the Rising against the British of 1916. She declined to be invested with the Mayoral chain of office because from it hung a medallion portrait of William III. 'Don't put on King Billy's chain', a voice from the council chamber had called to her, and she had complied.

A few days later the illegal organization struck again against the British, injuring nineteen people in various bomb explosions in London. A few late visitors were leaving the Waxworks Exhibition in Madame Tussaud's, and the manager was making a routine search of the Hall of Kings when he saw a flash under the figure of King Henry VII, who was blown up and burnt to nothing with all his clothes. On the next floor the manager was just in time to spot a bomb hidden under the pillow of the wolf's bed in the Red Riding Hood set; he just succeeded in getting it into a bucket as it went off.

A Prevention of Violence Bill was rushed through the House of Commons enabling the police to fingerprint and register, and if necessary deport, Irish people they had reason to suspect. Full figures were then given of outrages since the introduction of the IRA's 'S' plan at the beginning of January. There had been 127 of these, fifty-seven in London and seventy in the provinces; one man had been killed and fifty-five people injured; sixty-six Irishmen had been convicted. While the Bill was being rushed through there were two further IRA explosions in King's Cross and Victoria stations in London.

At the beginning of July an Irish labourer who gave his name as Gerard Lyons, but whose real name was said to be Gerard Anthony Dunlop, had been found guilty with four other Irishmen of causing explosions in High Holborn on the night of 3 May and given a sentence of twenty years' imprisonment. Asked if he had anything to say from the dock, he squared his shoulders and said: 'I believe it a just and Christian thing to try and overthrow tyranny. It is a Christian thing to strike at it and the British Government have tyrannized Ireland. While it exists it is the duty of every Irishman to try and overthrow this tyranny, and I believe I have done my duty to my country.'

He was not to be the last to think like this. Less than a fortnight later another Irishman, also sentenced to twenty years' imprisonment for his part in IRA bombings, said that when he came out, 'If there are only half a dozen men with walking-sticks fighting for Ireland, I shall join them'.

*   *   *

At the other end of the world, in China, fighting of a sort which, though it had only started two years before, also seemed to have settled into a pattern with no foreseeable outcome, continued on a massive scale. But this military campaign, conducted by Japan since 7 July 1937 in pursuit of a new political and economic order which would reduce China's sovereignty to mere nominal status, only surfaced periodically for attention in western newspapers. When it did so it was often because of the heavy casualties caused by Japanese bombers on Chinese cities in air-raids which, like those in Spain, seemed harbingers of what the whole world might soon find in store for it.

The first really heavy air-raid of the war had taken place in the first month of 1939, when twenty-seven Japanese bombers had flown over the new Chinese capital of Chungking, to which General Chiang Kai-shek had withdrawn his Government. Bombs had been dropped from 6,000 feet in the early afternoon, killing some 200 people. Air-raid shelters in the town had not yet been completed. A further 130 people were killed when Wahnsien, down the Yangtze from Chungking, was also bombed. But far worse raids were to come. The town of Ichang was bombed in March, leaving 1,800 Chinese civilians dead and 4,000 injured. On 3 May there was another heavy air-raid on Chungking when, on a bright sunny day at noon, forty-five Japanese planes dropped bombs on a mile-long zone along the populous Yangtze waterfront. Some Chinese fighters went up to intercept them but only one Japanese bomber was shot down. Some 1,500 people were killed. Madame Chiang Kai-shek herself personally directed rescue operations. A total eclipse of the moon that night seemed a sinister omen to the citizens, who pounded drums and pans for hours hoping to prevent Heavenly Dog from eating the Queen of Heaven. To no avail. The next day there was another equally devastating attack by twenty-seven Japanese planes.

On land, however, the Chinese, by the second anniversary of what had originally been known as the China 'incident', could be said to have more or less stabilized the situation created by the Japanese invasion and to be successfully holding what was left of their own. On that date just under half of all Chinese territory, mainly in the North, was occupied by the Japanese armies, but the strength of Chinese guerrilla activity behind the lines was such that the Japanese really only had a firm hold on the towns, the railways and the ports. And though they had captured more towns in March and April, a big Chinese offensive in April along a 1,500-mile front, supported by extensive guerrilla activity, had, it was claimed, recaptured some 70,000 square miles of national territory. The scale of the operations in the China 'incident' was revealed by the casualty figures released by both sides on its second anniversary, each incidentally implausibly detailed though the general picture was clear enough. The Japanese claimed that 896,496 Chinese had been killed and gave their own dead as 59,999. The Chinese figure for their own dead was not far short of that given by the Japanese: 835,618, but their claim for Japanese dead was 870,215, together with 20,000 prisoners.

It was the stranglehold which the Japanese were in danger of establishing over the Chinese supply system which was perhaps the most serious threat to the Chungking Government, for the Japanese held all the main seaports and had virtually cut off access to French Indo-China in the South. A new road, however, from Burma into Chungking-held territory, spectacularly accomplished in the previous year, was now proving its worth. British financial support to the Chinese dollar was of considerable importance in maintaining Chungking's economic strength.

Indeed resentment of the British Government's support for Chiang Kai-shek and its refusal to countenance in any way the puppet Chinese regimes set up by Japan in the north and in the Kwangtung province round Canton in the south, played a significant part in what was truly at first only an 'incident' but which now, in this summer of 1939, brought the aggression of Japan in China to the notice of a larger British public. This was the blockade inaugurated by the Japanese on 14 June against the British Concession in the port of Tsientsin in the Japanese-occupied north.

By previous treaties with Chinese governments a large number of ports in China provided special facilities to foreign governments and their nationals. Under such treaties twenty-five ports were open for British residents and trade, but in two of them, Tientsin and Canton, there were special British 'Concessions' - areas leased in perpetuity to a foreign government for occupation by its nationals. On 9 April a Chinese customs superintendent of the Chinese puppet government had been assassinated inside the British Concession in Tientsin - part of a pattern of patriotic terrorism recurring throughout Japanese-occupied territory. But the British refused to hand over to the Japanese or to their Chinese puppets the four men alleged to have carried out the assassination. The initial demand that these 'terrorists' should be surrendered, which Britain refused on the grounds that a proper case must first be made out against them, was soon supplemented by a more serious one from the Japanese authorities in Tientsin to the effect that the British should reverse their pro-Chiang Kai-shek policy in China and recognize the Japanese New Order in Northern China and co-operate with it.

Six hundred British subjects lived inside the Tientsin Concession, protected by a battalion of the Durham Light Infantry. The Japanese had originally said that food would be allowed in but Chinese traders were in fact being kept out. British subjects were not allowed to leave or enter the Concession without searches which often included slappings, proddings with bayonets, studied insults and general humiliation. A Mr and Mrs Finlay, employed at the International Country Club outside the Concession, were typical victims of this procedure. Mrs Finlay complained that she had been stripped and allowed only to retain her 'hip-girdle' while being searched by a Chinese policewoman in full view of a Japanese sentry who had only momentarily turned his back. When she was released from the searching hut she found her husband outside wearing only

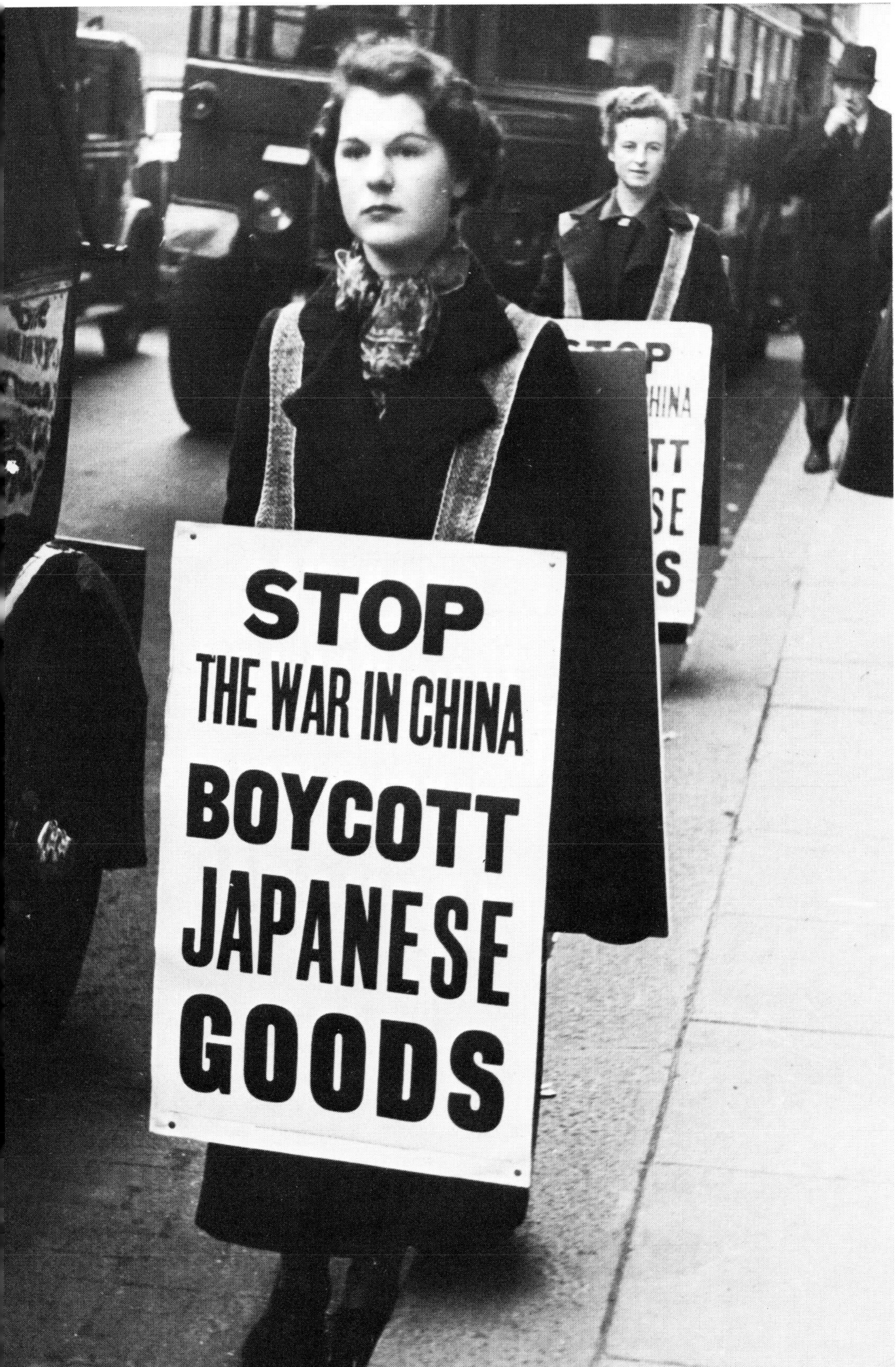
STOP
THE WAR IN CHINA
BOYCOTT
JAPANESE
GOODS

his vest, with his clothes thrown after him into the street, where he had to dress in public. Fifteen British subjects had been humiliated in similar circumstances by the end of the month, though Mrs Finlay was the only woman.

Such treatment of the nationals of a once proud British Government was of course a source of great joy to Dr Goebbels in the *Völkischer Beobachter*, but also a source of consternation to British newspaper readers, accustomed to thinking, particularly in hot foreign parts, of the British Lion. British verbal protests were severe. Chamberlain himself made clear at once that something much more far-reaching than the question of handing over the four men was at issue and the Foreign Office issued a statement taking 'the most serious view' of the fuller demands which had been raised and which they said 'would mean the abandonment under threats of force of the policy which His Majesty's Government have followed in the past'. Two escort vessels of the Royal Navy, HMS *Sandwich* and HMS *Lowestoft*, were sent to Tientsin. They were to affect the practical situation little.

However much Chamberlain might say, as he did in Cardiff on 24 June, that 'no British Government can tolerate that its nationals be subjected to such treatment and no British Government can submit to the dictates from another Power as to its foreign policy', gunboat diplomacy was irrelevant in the presence of the armed might of the Japanese. But protests by His Majesty's Ambassador in Tokyo, Sir Robert Craigie, seem to have had some effect because on 27 June, General Homma, in charge of the occupation forces in Tientsin, ordered that no more people going in and out of the Concession should be stripped. The blockade itself continued while negotiations were to proceed between the British Ambassador and the Japanese Government in Tokyo. Different degrees of militancy between the Japanese Government and the occupation authorities on the spot seemed part of the difficulty.

What happened next needs to be seen in the context not only of the inevitable British military weakness at Tientsin but also in terms of the closer European tension which preoccupied His Majesty's Government. Churchill himself, long acknowledged as the most powerful critic of appeasing attitudes, said of the events at Tientsin in a speech to a City Carlton Club lunch on 28 June: 'I am glad the Government were not provoked into taking their eye off the target. These studied insults and affronts from the Japanese – a nation hitherto renowned for their good manners – may well have been a trap to lure us away from the seas, where any major trouble which may arise will be decided.'

At such a moment Chamberlain in particular was no man to be imprudently belligerent.

While Britain still refused to hand over the four men accused by the Japanese of the murder, it became clear from a speech he made in the House of Commons on 17 July that his mind was moving in the direction of some accommodation with the Japanese. He referred to reports that the Japanese regime had been insisting on a fundamental reversal of British Far Eastern policy as a condition of the negotiations, and reiterated that 'this country will not and cannot so act in regard to its foreign policy at the demand of another Power'. But here he sought comfort in the apparent differences of emphasis between what was said by the Government in Tokyo and by its military authorities in Tientsin. Although only the month before he had seemed to accept that the demand for a change of policy was what the Japanese had been making, he now went on to draw attention to the fact that His Majesty's Government had received no such demand from the Japanese Government. In the opinion of the British Ambassador in Tokyo, he said, the Japanese attitude 'would be more accurately described as a desire that Great Britain should endeavour to regard the Sino-Japanese hostilities with more understanding of Japanese difficulties and of Japan's side of the case. His Majesty's Government share the Ambassador's view that to attribute to the Japanese Government intentions which might be found to have no basis in fact would only be calculated to prejudice the success of the forthcoming negotiations'.

Japanese army leaders continued to stress the need for what they called 'radical changes' in Britain's attitude to China and threatened strong measures if these were not made. The British Government continued to insist that it would not change its foreign policy at the behest of another government. But it was now clear enough which way things were going. A preliminary agreement with the Tokyo Government was reached on 21 July and its terms were announced by Chamberlain in the House of Commons on the 24th:

> His Majesty's Government fully recognize the actual situation in China where hostilities on a large scale are in progress and note that, as long as that state of affairs continues to exist, the Japanese forces in China have special requirements for the purpose of safeguarding their own security and maintaining public order, and that they have to suppress or remove any such cases or acts as will obstruct them or benefit the enemy [sic]. His Majesty's Government have no intention of countenancing any act or measures prejudicial to the attainment of the above-mentioned object by Japanese forces.

Asked in the House if this would not mean *de facto* recognition of the Japanese occupation in China, he denied it. The man with whom the agreement had been made, however, Baron Hiranuma, had different views. The day after it was reached he stated that its basic principle was to apply to the whole of China and not just Tientsin. He said that British rights and interests would only be recognized if Britain would recognize the relations of interdependence between Japan and China. He did not think that Britain would assist Chiang Kai-shek by granting credits or otherwise. If they were to do so the action would be regarded as hostile to Japan.

After this it was virtually a foregone conclusion that the four suspect terrorists would be handed over. An attempt by British Liberals headed by Professor Norman Bentwich and Miss Margery Fry to obtain a writ of habeas corpus on their behalf failed since it was maintained that habeas corpus did not apply outside the United Kingdom. The four Chinese were handed over on 5 September, by which time the British Government and public had other matters on their minds.

To the Chinese Government what had happened at Tientsin was deeply troubling. On the day after Chamberlain's statement a spokesman of the Chinese Foreign Office had said that his Government could not 'conceal their disappointment'. And General Chiang Kai-shek himself declared that 'any understanding affecting China which might be arrived at between Great Britain and Japan without the cognizance and consent of the Chinese Government would be regarded as without validity'.

In the British House of Commons it was the Labour Member, Philip Noel-Baker, who most effectively expressed the Chinese sense of concern. He asked that China be made part of the 'peace front' against aggressions.

In doing so he provoked from Chamberlain a classic exposition of those tortuous tactical skills with which, in these difficult times, both in the Far East and Europe he now found himself impelled to operate. Chamberlain said of Noel-Baker:

> I have always found a difficulty in answering him, because he always appears to try to push the Government to go a little further in their statements, pledges and assurances than I think they ought to go – and it puts me in this position that, in refusing to put my foot upon what seems to be unsound ground, I may seem to be less willing, to go less far than I really am going.

On a more straightforward course the Chinese managed to hold the Japanese more or less where they were to the end of the year.

The great convulsion taking place in Asia was, for the ordinary Western newspaper reader, always something of a background event – Auden's off-stage war still 'the slamming of a distant door'. But at least the remote news attaching to it could be attributed to physical distance. The similar sense of remoteness attaching to what was happening to the Jews was harder to explain, for that was a great convulsion much nearer home. The phenomenon, of course, was partly due to Western newspaper readers' ever-growing preoccupation with the personal danger which Hitler now posed to themselves. But the fact that in the United States, Britain and even in France anti-Semitism was an insignificant enough force to seem politically irrelevant may also have made it more difficult to apprehend the volume of its horror elsewhere.

Both in Britain and the United States evidence of anti-semitism seemed little more than one of the many freak details that made up the normal background of everyday life. A newspaper run by Mosley's supporters, the *Blackshirt*, spoke facetiously of 'the Refujew' and disparagingly of an appeal for the Baldwin Fund as a 'levy imposed on the people to keep the garbage of Germany in ease on the money of the people'. But the *Blackshirt* and its readers counted for almost

Japanese air-raid on China's new capital, Chungking.

The Japanese blockade of the British Concession of Tientsin, China: humiliation and stripping.

nothing in British political life. Other people in Britain who, somewhere in their minds, might have felt something of the doubt which the *Blackshirt* so crudely expressed, would usually have taken care to couch it in more acceptable terms. Similarly Mosley's ranting cry at a meeting at Earl's Court in July: 'A million Britons shall not die in your Jews' quarrel!' would not have been the way most of those who were beginning to warn of an unnecessary war over Danzig would have liked it put. Mosley's significance now, as a political figure on the extreme Right, had shrunk to mere nuisance factor by contrast with the days when he had been a darling of the Left, ten years before.

By a curious coincidence a would-be Fascist leader of exactly the same name, although slightly differently spelt, acquired a sudden notoriety in the United States this summer: a recently-retired Major-General, George Van Horn Moseley, also a man with a distinguished past.

Borne in Evanston, Illinois, sixty-four years before, he graduated from West Point in 1899 and served in the Philippines, the Mexican border campaign of 1916-17, and was on the staff of the American Expeditionary Force, 1917-19, when he became Commander of the Fourth Corps and won the Distinguished Service Medal twice. While still in the army he had stirred controversy by advocating sterilization for refugees coming to the United States, and just before he retired in September 1938 had criticized Roosevelt's national policy for 'lack of outstanding leadership' and 'untried theories and ideas upon which we have lavished the greatest peacetime appropriations in our nation's history'. The administration's Secretary for War had then felt stung to reply that these remarks had been made out of pique because Moseley had not been made Chief of the General Staff as he had expected to be. The Secretary criticized him for being 'flagrantly disloyal'. Now Moseley was to achieve momentary prominence again as a result of some peculiar revelations that had been made to the House of Representatives Dies Committee on un-American activities.

After a session of extraordinary secrecy in which a number of witnesses had been heard, the Committee announced that it had evidence of a well-organized anti-semitic campaign which had been developed in the United States and which had attracted the attention of Major-General Van Horn Moseley. Some of the evidence which they released included a letter written by Moseley to a New York National Guard officer in which he said: 'The most serious problem confronting America today is just this problem of the Jew and how to get rid of his influence definitely – locally, nationally and internationally.' It appeared that material had been circulated containing 'highly-inflammatory racial statements calculated to arouse racial hatred among those to whom they were disseminated'. But perhaps the most sinister document of all was a letter which spoke of some sort of GHQ in Atlanta 'to build an army and secure leadership', and spoke of the need for a General who would skilfully get at the Reserve Army Officers' Association – 'they would resign their commissions and enlist with us for this American-Jewish war, for that is all it is, a war fought with money and propaganda instead of rifles'. Moseley was subpoenaed to appear before the Dies Committee on the following Monday, 22 May.

The General was not one to let the interval slip by without making his views known. He gave a statement to the press to the effect that he was on his way to Washington from his home in El Centro, California, where he now lived but was going to stop off in Atlanta to collect some files. He said the fact that he was being called a Fascist was simply proof of what a previous un-American Affairs Committee had discovered, namely that the constant misuse of the term 'Fascist' as synonymous with anti-Communism was significant of Communistic misrepresentation and deceit. In fact, he said, he was merely following those patriotic Christian American principles which had governed him for a lifetime in the service of the Republic – 'particularly during this period of emergency in assisting as far as I am able ... in saving America from herself. ... Do the American people not realize that we are in the midst of the greatest battle in our history, first: the battle to keep America out of war, and second, to save us from those enemies prospering within our gates?'

He said it was strange that it should be possible to discuss openly Irish, Italian, and German problems but if one but mentioned any internationalism or Zionism and their increasing control of America, one got summoned before a committee in Washington.

His own appearance before it was impressive. A tall, slender, erect figure scarcely showing his 64 years, he was followed into the room by a retinue of attorneys and the right-wing Representative Thorkelson of Montana, who had recently been described by a far-Right journal called *Silver Shirts* as 'a new statesman rearing high above this miasma of skulduggery'. Moseley immediately said that he wished to make a speech, having brought a prepared document. Permission was refused him. He expostulated:

'The American people want to hear this. Aren't you interested in un-American activities?'

Whereupon the acting chairman of the committee, Representative Healey of Massachusetts, assured him: 'Yes'.

'Bull!' replied the General.

He spent a turbulent five hours before the committee, shouting and pounding the table and issuing constant exhortations to American patriotism. He defended organizations of the extreme Right such as Fritz Kuhn's German-American Bund as 'an antitoxin for the disease of Communism'. He had nothing but praise for the Bund, having, he said, attended a meeting in Madison Square Garden on George Washington's birthday which he had found 'impressively patriotic'. Its only purpose was to see that Communists did not take over the country. He denied any sinister conspiracy and said that the Communist threat could be handled in five minutes from the White House. He would simply issue an order immediately discharging every Communist in the Government and everyone giving aid and comfort to Communism in the Government. He would also release the army from its present position of constriction whereby it could make plans for attacking Germany, Italy and Japan but 'it can't do a damned thing to defend itself against the enemies within our gates'. Asked point-blank if he were an anti-semite, he replied that he had nothing against individual Jews. He was eventually allowed to read a shortened version of his statement which contained details of the alleged Jewish conspiracy, but it was afterwards accounted irrelevant and struck from the record.

A certain amount of indignant resentment of the General's views was voiced in the days following this outburst. It was said that the War Office was considering whether or not he should be court-martialled and the Council of US War Veterans Incorporated urged that he should be.

They maintained that Moseley's court-martial was to be the first step in a vigorous campaign against Fascism in the United States. However, the Dies Committee took him less seriously and the General withdrew again into the patriotic shadows of retirement. The Committee went on to concern itself with the German-American Bund.

This had been known until 1936 as the Friends of the New Germany and had been founded by two veterans of Hitler's Munich *putsch* of 1923 who had since become American citizens, Heinz Spanknoebel and Fritz Gissobl. Under a new leader, Fritz Kuhn from Detroit, it had in March 1937 changed its name and its original uniform of black breeches and riding-boots, similar to that of the SS, to one modelled on that of the American Legion. The Bund cooperated with 125 other organizations, also concerned to oppose Communism and international Jewry. For tactful diplomatic reasons the German Embassy had nothing to do with it, and in 1938 the Bund had changed the flag it carried from the national one of Germany to a United States flag, flown alongside a special Bund flag which carried a swastika as 'a sign of Aryan supremacy'. It claimed a membership of 8,299, two thirds of whom were in the metropolitan district of New York. The previous February it had held a meeting in Madison Square Garden of some 19,000 people. But it seemed that its membership list showed its numbers as only 6,617 and there was an allegation that Fritz Kuhn had been embezzling the funds.

What the Dies Committee at least seemed to have made clear was that there was significantly little positive political Fascist anti-semitic feeling in the United States. Far more representative than General Moseley of the mood of distinguished citizens was, for example, Gene Tunney, the former world heavyweight boxing champion, who in the middle of June joined the Committee of Catholics to fight Anti-Semitism.

The reigning holder of the world heavyweight championship, incidentally, Joe Louis, had other things on his mind that month. He took on his third challenger of the year on 28 June in the shape of Two-Ton Tony Galento who had sworn to knock Louis out. Galento did in fact give Louis a nasty shock in the first round, actually knocking him down for the count of one. But, as the *New York Times* man put it, 'he missed the title because in his awkward, heavy-footed way

he could not muster the accuracy to uncork another left hook to the jaw, such as that which had floored Louis'. Louis finished him off in the fourth.

When the *Chicago Daily Tribune* bade farewell in a leader to the King and Queen after the end of their visit to the States, having reluctantly had to admit that their democratic and unaffected demeanour, together with the agreeable qualities of their personalities, had made a tremendous hit wherever they appeared, it summed the whole matter up with the words: 'So far no great harm has been done. . . . The possible damage would be found in legislation prejudicial to the welfare of this country. . . . Probably the first test will be in action on the Neutrality Bill.'

Roosevelt had said at the outset of the year that the Neutrality Act, which could actually favour the dictator countries in time of war, ought to be revised. Under its current provisions it was illegal in time of war to export any arms or war material to the war zone, to give loans to belligerent governments, or for United States citizens to travel on belligerent vessels. Two other provisions of the Neutrality Act had lapsed on 1 May. These laid down: one, that no United States ships could carry certain other articles or materials to belligerent states, and two, that no foreign ship could carry them unless it had paid for them first and the ownership had been thus transferred. This latter clause was known as the 'Cash and Carry' clause, and it was held that in operation it naturally favoured those maritime countries like Britain and France with greater control of the seas. In view of the expiry of these clauses, the Senate Foreign Affairs Committee had for some weeks been working on proposals for an amendment to the Neutrality Act, but no lead came from the President or the Secretary of State, Cordell Hull, for so long that even a supporter like the *New York Times* was driven to chide them for the delay. It was essential, the paper said, to lift the embargo on arms in order to deter war-makers; it would be a peace policy, not a war policy. When Cordell Hull eventually made the administration's proposals known, they were much as expected and met the expected opposition from those determined at all costs to keep America out of any war. The embargo was indeed to be lifted and the 'Cash and Carry' clause was to be restored. These amendments were plainly favourable to the democracies and were treated as such by the isolationist opposition in Congress.

There was a sense of urgency behind the administration's efforts. A clear declaration of American policy in the event of war might – would, was how they put it – prevent war. Thus, though the embargo could of course be lifted after war had been started, it would have failed in its preventive rôle which was what the administration was stressing. It would also then appear actively as a way of taking sides rather than, as now, preserving neutrality. Thus Representative Bloom of New York who sponsored the administration's Bill in the House of Representatives presented it as a measure for keeping the United States at peace. It would, he said, 'cushion the United States from the impact of any general conflict'. He denied any ulterior motive such as that the new Bill was intended to support a democratic alliance, to which argument Representative Hamilton Fish replied: 'In this Bill you are taking the road to war'.

The second reason for urgency was that Congress was due to adjourn for the summer in July and Roosevelt wished to have the power to sell arms to the democracies should war break out before its reassembly, which in the normal course of events would not be until January 1940. Indeed it was thought that the administration had actually hoped to get a favourable report on the Bill from the House Foreign Affairs Committee in time for the visit of the King and Queen at the beginning of June, and it was chided for this in committee by Representative Tinkham of Massachusetts, who said the object of reporting the Bill was to get it through – 'not a Neutrality Bill and drawn wholly in favour of England' – in order to give it as a present to the King on his arrival. There had at that time been a question on the floor of the House, as to 'whether the unprecedented visit of the King does in fact signify an *entente* between the administration for the preservation of the British Empire at the expense of American blood and American treasure?'

Such isolationist opinion was on the whole very anxious to make clear that its point of view was in no way identifiable with support for the dictatorships. Senator Borah, Dean of the Senate and of the Senate Foreign Relations Committee, summarized the case against Roosevelt when he wrote to a correspondent that the administration was

> constantly talking about neutrality and proposing at the same time legislation that is unneutral – not a neutral plan and not intended as such. We are seeking to enact legislation which will enable this Government, under the guise of law, to take sides and become associated in the Imperialistic war now being waged, openly or covertly, between two great Powers of Europe, Germany and Great Britain. ... Of course we do not believe in the ideology of Germany and Italy – it is contrary to everything in which we believe. But as Chamberlain has said, ideology does not come into it. What really is happening is this: a great controversy is going on about territory and raw materials – purely imperialistic matters – and that is the issue. To talk about any others is to mislead the American people.

There was enough strength of feeling behind this view to prevent successful progress before the date of the adjournment. And Roosevelt had to enter the summer recess without the power to help the democracies with arms and raw material, should an emergency arise.

20

Towards the end of June 1939 the British Institute of Public Opinion carried out a poll with the question: 'Do you think the risk of war has increased or decreased since last Autumn?' Fifty-seven per cent replied that it had decreased; thirty per cent that it had increased; thirteen per cent had no opinion. A similar poll conducted in the United States put the question: 'Do you believe there will be a war between any of the big European countries this year?' Only thirty-two per cent replied 'Yes', whereas in April the number had been fifty-one per cent.

These results were in some respects a reflection of the extent to which it was the Berlin–Rome Axis which not only set the pace of public events in Europe but also dictated the mood in which they were received, holding the world partially hypnotized to its will. In such moments of relative calm there was always a tendency in Britain for the ghost of appeasement once more to reappear, or at least for a tentative note to be struck which could make people wonder if it were about to reappear. Thus, early in June when, rightly or wrongly, the pressure was sensed as being temporarily off Danzig and the Polish Corridor, Lord Halifax, the British Foreign Secretary, delivered a speech which again caused some to doubt whether they really were represented by a positive will in that fatalistic limbo to which Hitler seemed to have consigned them. As his fellow-Peer and Opposition leader in the Lords, Lord Snell, put it, the foreign policy of the Government sometimes seemed to resemble the winds of heaven – 'whence it came and whither it goeth no man knows'.

Halifax began with a reassuring account to their Lordships of a number of contemporary aspects of foreign affairs, not least the fact that he was in no way worried about the amount of war material the Germans and Italians had left behind in Spain. 'There is nothing on earth', he said, 'to prevent the Germans and Italians selling or giving war material to General Franco. ... There is no ground for complaint against the Anglo-Italian Agreement.'

He said that with the exception of one or two difficulties such as the problem of the Baltic States the Anglo-Soviet proposals to the Soviet Union met in all essentials the points on which there had been difficulty and that Molotov had confirmed this in his recent speech. (That seemed on the whole a strange interpretation of what Molotov had said. The *New York Times* had described Molotov's speech as a 'bombshell' and said that it evoked 'the lurking spectre of a Nazi-Soviet *rapprochement*'.)

Halifax said that it was important, for the negotiations which were being conducted by the British Ambassador in Moscow, that he should be as fully informed as possible of what was in the Government's mind. A day or two ago they had asked him to come home, but it was because he had influenza, that 'in order to accelerate the negotiations', they were sending the senior Foreign Office man, William Strang, to Moscow 'to convey to His Majesty's Ambassador there all information as to the Government's attitude to all outstanding points'. In case this might seem to some of his hearers a less than urgent approach to the matter, he reminded them of an alliance 'somewhat similar in character and purpose, concluded in the fourteenth century, which had withstood the changes and chances of five hundred years of European politics – our alliance with Portugal'.

He then warned the House against the danger these days of using exaggerated language or jumping too hastily to insecure conclusions:

> Above all, we must be sensible of the extreme importance of doing our utmost to understand the point of view of other nations, and of getting them to understand our own. While there must be many people in Germany who, like ourselves, disapprove of the treatment of the Jews and the final destruction of Czech independence, such people may feel, too, that Germany would never have secured consideration for claims that seemed to her people eminently reasonable and just, unless she had been prepared to back them by threat of force. It is no long step from this for the patriotic German to accept the view that British policy consists in the blocking of any and all of Germany's aspirations, whether racial, political or economic. What is really dangerous is that the German people as a whole should drift to the conclusion that Great Britain has abandoned all desire to reach an understanding with Germany. ... The British people have sought, and still earnestly desire, if they think it possible, to reach such an understanding. ... They have been very ready to admit many mistakes, made both at and after the conclusion of the war, and there is a widespread desire to rectify what might be legitimately rectified. That desire found practical expression in the successful negotiations for the evacuation of the Rhineland before the time laid down in the peace treaty.

There were a number of people in Britain a good deal less happy to reflect that it had been Hitler's occupation of the Rhineland that had laid the foundation for his later forceful successes.

Halifax emphasized how it had been the destruction of Czech independence that had brought about an instinctive drawing together of countries determined to contest any threat to dominate the rest of Europe by force. He stressed that the same spirit animated the French as well as the British people. Having said this, he returned to the hope of new opportunities for peaceful settlement, saying how encouraged he had been by a speech of Mussolini's last month to the effect that he saw nothing ahead which could logically justify a universal war. He even extracted a certain macabre political comfort from the fact that both Hitler and Mussolini had sent messages of condolence to the King on behalf of their peoples on the occasion of the *Thetis* disaster. And the rest of the speech was dotted with phrases which could inevitably cause some disquiet to those concerned that the determination to appease might be stronger than the determination to resist aggression:

> provided that the independence of nations is recognized, His Majesty's Government are not only willing but anxious to explore the whole problem of economic *lebensraum* not only for Germany but all European nations. ... Any of Germany's claims are open to consideration round the table. Great Britain is only anxious to see the rival claims adjusted on a basis that might secure lasting peace. ... It is the duty of statesmanship to work for such a *détente* in feeling as might make a real change in the atmosphere through which an approach to the problem has to be made. ... No settlement by negotiation could be worse than or as bad as a settlement achieved by war ...

to which there were cries of 'Hear, hear!'

As often hitherto, such language in its own right was quite unexceptionable but viewed in the context of what it had led to before, particularly its consequences for Czechoslovakia, it could have for many people a sinister ring. *The Times* found the speech 'valuable' and 'of exceptional importance' and a 'solid contribution ... to the understanding of the foreign problems of the hour'. Others were less happy. 'MPs Wonder If Appeasement Is Coming Back' was a headline in the *News Chronicle* which told of considerable speculation in Parliament about the marked conciliatory character of statements such as Halifax's and one that Neville Chamberlain had made in Birmingham on the same day, in which incidentally he talked of the forthcoming General Election, though he said he had not yet made up his mind about the date. The *News Chronicle*, printing some letters which protested against Halifax's speech, added that it had received a very large number of such letters from readers. The paper itself was amazed that a mere Foreign Office expert, William Strang, was being sent to help the negotiations in Moscow. 'It is hardly possible to conceive a step more maladroit', it wrote, adding that Halifax himself should have gone.

A few days later in the House of Lords, Halifax went out of his way to say that his speech should not be read as appeasement. This did not prevent one of his fellow-peers, Lord Davies, from saying that it once more demonstrated the cleavage in the Cabinet between those who were in favour of appeasement and those in favour of collective security. Certainly to some it seemed to have the effect on German policy which those who opposed appeasement always predicted.

In Danzig the situation suddenly became much more tense and it began to look as if some sort of coup were being prepared. At the beginning of the month it had seemed to some in both neutral and German circles in both Danzig and Berlin that Hitler was not going to press for its return to the Reich immediately, though it was equally assumed that the pressure would be put on later, probably in September – 'a date mentioned with foreboding in Danzig', wrote the *New York Times*. However, by the middle of the month – whether or not stimulated

The Free City of Danzig waits to 'return to the Reich'. Most of the population were German and the local administration was Nazi, but the port was, for the Poles (*below right*), 'the sun of our national life'.

by Halifax's 'conciliatory' speech – pressure was already building up unmistakably.

The administration of the Free City and its 400,000 citizens, ninety per cent of whom were of German blood, was in any case virtually in German hands; the Danzig Nazi Party under its leader Albert Forster held complete control of the Senate, and German laws, including the Nuremberg laws under which the entire Jewish population had been expelled, were largely duplicated there; even the car licence plates were replicas of those in Germany. The inhabitants, who perhaps had not been particularly in favour of annexation before pressure for this started from the Reich, now looked forward to it as a release from the tension, which was in itself bad for the trade on which Danzig's merchants had always thrived, and as a release from the threat of destruction by the Polish army should war break out, which would be even worse for trade. The relatively trivial sacrifice of certain everyday commodities less easily obtainable in the Reich, such as butter, eggs and coffee, seemed a small price to pay for that long-term security on which all real prosperity must depend. Throughout June arms and ammunition were pouring into Danzig by sea and over the East Prussian border, while several thousand so-called 'tourists' who were said to be partly soldiers and partly SS and SA men in civilian clothes were pouring in with them. A Freikorps similar to that which had been formed in the Sudetenland of Czechoslovakia before the Munich crisis had come into being. On 18 June Goebbels visited Danzig and indicated something of Germany's response to the ambivalence of the British Cabinet: 'Great Britain has given Poland a blank cheque and is attempting the encirclement of Germany and Italy as in 1914. But she is mistaken if she thinks she has before her a powerless bourgeois Germany. We regard the speech-making of London and Warsaw as noisy shadow-boxing to conceal with words a deficiency of determination.' He said that Hitler had called Danzig a German city and said that it would return to Germany, and everyone knew that he kept his word.

Winston Churchill, whose addition to the Cabinet was beginning to be strongly urged in many quarters, addressed himself in the speech he made to the Carlton Club lunch on 28 June at one point specifically to Hitler: 'Pause,' he said. 'Consider well before you take a plunge into the terrible unknown. Consider whether your life's work – which may even now be famous in the eyes of history – in raising Germany from frustration and defeat to a point where all the world is waiting for her actions, consider whether all this may not be irretrievably cast away.' He went on to convey his own sense of the grim urgency of the hour: 'Considering the German preparations, the tone of the government-controlled press and Party leaders, there can be no conclusion but that the worst could happen and happen quite soon. I must consider – I think we must all consider – July, August and September as months in which the tension in Europe will become most severe.'

Perhaps Churchill's words had some effect on the Foreign Secretary himself.

On 29 June, the day after Churchill had spoken, Halifax made another speech, this time at a dinner of the Royal Institute of International Affairs. And this time his tone was very much stronger than in the speech he had delivered earlier in the month. This time there was no talk of negotiation and when he said things like 'in the event of further aggression we are resolved to use at once the whole of our strength in fulfilment of our pledges to resist it', it sounded as if he meant it. He stressed the new military strength Britain had acquired in recent months. 'Our Air Force, still undergoing expansion which has outstripped all the expectations of a few months ago, has now nothing to fear from any other. I have little doubt that its personnel, in spirit and in skill, is superior to all others.' And he concluded with further clear reaffirmation of Britain's new position: 'Our immediate task is to resist aggression. I would emphasize that tonight with all the strength at my command so that nobody may misunderstand. And if we are ever to succeed in removing misunderstanding and in reaching a settlement that the world can trust, it must be upon some basis more substantial than verbal undertakings.'

The new resolution behind Halifax's words was immediately acknowledged and commended by those political opponents hitherto most sensitive to the apparent lack of such a quality in the Government's foreign policy. The Labour spokesman, A.V. Alexander, at the same dinner, said at once with disarming candour: 'I believe I shall be speaking the thoughts of at least a large number present tonight when I say that I was most surprised at the power and strength and firmness of the great utterance to which we have just listened.'

'Britain Set For War', cried the United States tabloids, while the *New York Times* more coolly but equally sombrely declared in a leader that statesmen did not utter words as ominous and clear as those of Lord Halifax unless they felt themselves in the presence of a danger they believed real and imminent. The Left in Britain seemed convinced at last that the Government meant business. Will Lawther, the acting President of the Mineworkers' Federation of Great Britain stated: 'No member of either the Trade Unions or political movements would disagree with what Lord Halifax's speech implied.' And the *Manchester Guardian* called the speech the finest on foreign policy made by a Minister of the National Government since it came to power.

In France, papers as far apart politically as *Le Temps* and *Le Populaire* acknowledged the speech's firmness with applause. The reaction of the German and Italian press also revealed recognition of a new firmness. The *Populo di Roma* found Halifax's speech 'bitter and threatening' and the *Deutscher Dienst* wrote: 'What London is hastening to undertake bears all the marks of a preventive war game.' Goebbels in the *Völkischer Beobachter* exchanged his mocking tone of a few days before for one of peevish outrage: 'The British are very angry with us', he wrote.

They regret our brusque way of speaking. With many 'oh, how shocking's' they play the rôle of the governess of civilized humanity. The British Prime Minister said recently he longed for the moment when one could talk reasonably to reasonable people. We are in the not-too-enviable position of the harmless pedestrian in the midst of a dark wood who has been robbed of all his belongings and who is being invited to a friendly conversation by the one who took his watch and dangles it provocatively in front of his nose. When in such a situation one does not attach too much value to good manners.

It was the Poles of course who nominally held the key to the question of whether or not there would be war. For if they were at the last moment to decide that Danzig would not be worth a war for themselves, then there would be no cause for Britain to go to war with Germany, for Poland's independence would not be threatened. However, President Mosicki of Poland put a final stop to any speculative doubt on this score by stating clearly on the same day as Halifax's speech: 'Any attempt to change the status quo in Danzig, either by a move within or from without would be a cause of war.' He described the Corridor and Danzig as 'the air and sun of our national life and the basis of our economic and political independence'.

The British National Council of Labour, representing the TUC and the Labour Party, addressed an appeal to German workers, urging them, as if such matters were really within their power, to settle disputes by reason and not by war, but the address itself expressed the sense of urgency of the moment. 'The nations arm and arm ... the feverish preparations for war proceed. Everyone is asking, "Will it be war?" and now people are asking, "Are we on the edge?"'

The real answer to this question, for all Halifax's speech and a would-be equally firm statement by Chamberlain the next day, lay in an area where no man could be certain of what was to be found: namely the true resolution of the British Cabinet when something more than words would be finally required. This indeed was one of the reasons why such a strong public campaign was being waged by the beginning of July for the inclusion of Winston Churchill within that Cabinet. No one, least of all the Germans – and this was the real peace point in the campaign – doubted that Churchill meant, and would do, what he said. No one could ever be equally certain that whatever Chamberlain and Halifax might say, they would actually do it – perhaps not even they themselves. Certainly not the Germans.

'Reports reaching Whitehall', wrote the London evening paper *The Star*,

show that even the recent speeches of Lord Halifax and the Opposition spokesmen have failed to dispel the illusion of the Nazis that Britain would remain passive before an attempt to change the status of Danzig by force. Those who know the Nazi psychology best say that the return of Mr Churchill and Mr Eden to the Cabinet would do more than a hundred speeches to convert the Nazis to a belief in the sincerity of our intentions.

Eden himself, though with an instinctive oblique courtesy, hinted in the same direction in a weekend speech in which he struck a guardedly optimistic note saying that though the immediate future was grave, even dangerous, it was not yet desperate and that war was not inevitable. He meant that there would be no war if the true firmness of will and purpose of Britain could be understood abroad.

The *Manchester Guardian* put the matter more pointedly in its leader of the 3rd July in which it said that the Prime Minister's inexperience in foreign affairs was such that he fell an easy victim to illusions that would never have deceived a less simple mind: '... As it is, there is genuine uneasiness at home, and every speech made by Ministers, however harmless in intention, is anxiously scrutinized by our friends abroad, dreading to find in it some hint of another Munich.'

Thus even a recent 'firm' statement by Chamberlain in which he had categorically said that while recent occurrences in Danzig suggested that some internal surreptitious action was afoot, this could not be regarded as a purely local issue and would raise issues affecting Polish national existence and independence – even this statement contained a short passage to worry nervous ears. Of Danzig itself Chamberlain said: 'While the present settlement is neither basically unjust nor illogical it may be capable of improvement. It may be that in a clearer atmosphere possible improvements could be discussed.' (The point to stress, an anxious critic might surely feel, was not that in a clearer atmosphere there was a possibility of a solution, but that the atmosphere was being intentionally clouded.)

'It would be of interest to historians', wrote the *Manchester Guardian* in a leader on 11 July, 'that this was an epoch in which a British Government had continually to be restating its intentions on the same subject.' The paper reiterated that if the Government had, as it did have, a somewhat sceptical audience both at home and abroad even after its apparent change of policy, this was a scepticism inevitably attaching itself to those who had previously pursued appeasement with such dedication. Not that *Manchester Guardian* readers were themselves altogether free from some ambivalence, even at this point in the summer.

On 4 July the Marquess of Tavistock wrote to the paper to say that as things appeared to be boiling up for another crisis, '... it is earnestly to be hoped that we may not see another demonstration of the fact that the better-prepared nations are for war, the more likely they are to go to war for quite inadequate reasons – and the withholding from Germany of the mainly German town of Danzig is a quite inadequate reason for a world war'. He suggested that one reason the Government might find themselves forced into such a war for Danzig would be that they were afraid to face the charges of cowardice and bad faith which might be levelled at them by their bellicose critics. But he added: 'The one thing which is worse than making a foolish promise is keeping a foolish promise. ... No considerations of honour justify the slaughter of millions for a cause not perfectly adequate, especially when the lives to be sacrificed are not those of the men responsible for the imprudent and unjustifiable undertaking.'

Two days later Mr Thomas Campion of Goldbourne near Warrington wrote to support him. Lord Tavistock, he said, had stated what many others felt. War over Danzig was morally indefensible. If there was to be a war against aggression the case needed to be much clearer than it was likely to be over Danzig and Poland should not be the sole arbiter.

Such feelings were also to be found in France, and Marcel Déat, writing in the radical paper L'Œuvre on 10 July, said he was only giving his own views but felt that negotiations were in the air. 'After certain exaggerated alarms there is an impression that the desire for useful conversation is in the air and that it will come about.'

Whatever else might or might not be in the air, if German action over Danzig were going to be called off only in response to the absolutely certain conviction that Britain and France would thereupon honour their pledge to Poland, there was enough doubt of their firmness around to make such German action possible so long as there was no change in the Cabinet. There was still too much room in Britain's attitude for people to hear whatever they wanted to hear. The official Polish Gazette, for instance, was delighted by Chamberlain's recent speech, which it said left Germany in no doubt. Italian papers, on the other hand, seized on the same speech to say it 'hinted at the possibility of another Munich'. 'Considering his words came after a fighting speech by Lord Halifax,' wrote the Popolo di Roma,

> we may safely say that the Prime Minister's intervention contained a certain return to common sense. Those who expected a severe tone in yesterday's speech were somewhat perplexed to hear that Danzig, in spite of the alleged advantages of her present status, is susceptible of an even better arrangement. . . . It is to be noted that Chamberlain avoided pronouncing the phrase expected and demanded of him in some British journalistic quarters: 'We British will fight for Danzig.' Undoubtedly British diplomacy is in the midst of a psychological crisis.

This crisis was to prove to be of an enduring nature, susceptible to those fluctuations of mood so often associated with disturbed psychological conditions in human beings. *The Times* itself manifested the symptoms, applauding Lord Halifax's speech of 29 June and saying that if there were any further attempts to alter the boundaries of Europe by force the British people would not only approve but demand action, but on 1 August it went out of its way to stress that there was *nothing* (author's italics) in the Danzig question that 'sane statesmanship could consider worth a war'. Within three weeks of that leader the situation had so changed that, as the paper wrote on 21 August, Danzig itself had become a side issue. Germany was now demanding not only Danzig but the whole of the Polish Corridor and Polish Silesia as well.

The fact that Chamberlain's reality was still very different from Hitler's had been shown on 2 August, when the Prime Minister had proposed the regular adjournment of Parliament until 3 October – again raising the possibility of a General Election in November – and apparently seeking to draw credit from the fact that the House would thus reassemble some three weeks earlier than normal, to be prepared to deal with any eventuality. There was marked criticism of this decision from the Labour Opposition, who wanted Parliament to be recalled on 21 August. Arthur Greenwood, speaking in place of the official Labour leader, Attlee, who was recovering from an operation, said that there was 'a suspicion that once the House rose the Government would take the wrong turning'. A considerable number of Members of the House, he said, did not trust the Government.

Winston Churchill, while regretting that Chamberlain did not agree to a much shorter adjournment, said he accepted in good faith the Prime Minister's assurance that there would be no departure from the Government's declared policy without a recall of Parliament. But he stressed that bad faith was not the only point at issue: there was also the possibility of bad judgement.

> It would be a very hard thing to say to the House: 'Begone! Run away and play. Take your gas masks with you. Don't worry about public affairs, leave them to the experienced Ministers' – who so far as defence is concerned landed the country where it was landed last September, and who in foreign policy have guaranteed Poland and Rumania, after having lost Czechoslovakia and without having gained Russia.

But Chamberlain was adamant, meticulously resisting further appeals from his own back benches as well as from the Opposition and saying that while he was grateful to Churchill for trusting in his good faith though not his judgement he was rather inclined to say, where judgement was concerned, 'tu quoque!'.

In general, Chamberlain said, there was no doubt that what was being expressed in the House was mistrust of the Government's good faith, so that the vote on the amendment for a recall on 21 August was a vote of no confidence. He expected his friends to support him, which they comfortably did – the amendment was defeated by 118 votes and the original motion carried by 116.

Curiously, one of the reasons Chamberlain had given for the desirability of such a long period as two months before Parliament's recall was that there were signs that things were not going too well in the negotiations in Moscow and that 'it would not be wise to be too optimistic about reaching a very speedy conclusion'.

21

At the very beginning of Halifax's speech of 29 June he mentioned with a sort of confident casualness that he hoped there would very shortly be a successful issue to the negotiations with the Soviet Union for an association in defence of the states in Europe whose independence and neutrality might be threatened. The same day there appeared in *Pravda* an article by Andrei Zhdanov, Secretary of the Central Committee of the Communist Party, giving a very different impression of these negotiations.

Zhdanov was often thought of as being the second most important man in Russia after Stalin. Although he stated in the article that his view was only a personal opinion and that his friends did not share it, it was thought unlikely by shrewd observers that such a view would have been expressed in such a prominent place as *Pravda* without the approval of Stalin. Zhdanov began with the question that had already been put a number of times in one form or another to Chamberlain in the House of Commons and was to be put a number of times again there: 'What is the reason for the delay in the negotiations whose favourable termination is impatiently and hopefully awaited by all peace-loving nations and all friends of peace?' He pointed out that the negotiations had been going on for 75 days, in the course of which 16 days had been taken up by the Soviet Union in preparing answers to the various British proposals, while the remaining 59 had been 'consumed by delays and procrastination on the part of the British and French'. It had taken them only a very short space of time to agree to pacts with Poland and Turkey (an agreement with Turkey had been reached on 12 May). He said the British and French objections to a pact which included a guarantee of the Baltic States, whether these States wanted it or not, were obviously insincere and could only be inspired by the wish to hinder the negotiations in order to disrupt them. What was the difference in this respect between Rumania, Greece and Turkey, for whom the British and French sought guarantees from the Soviet Union, and indeed further ones for Holland and Switzerland – the latter of which did not even have normal diplomatic relations with the USSR – none of whom had asked for such Soviet guarantees, and the unasked-for guarantee from Britain and France of the Baltic States which the Soviet Union required? He could only come to one conclusion. The British and French were not sincere in their wish to negotiate a treaty on terms of equality and reciprocity. All they wanted – and here Zhdanov repeated a phrase which Stalin had himself used earlier in the year to describe what Soviet foreign policy should be on its guard against – all Britain and France wanted was to get others 'to pull chestnuts out of the fire for them'. All, in fact, they wanted was to find an excuse for blaming the Soviet Union for the failure to get an alliance and thus to 'make easier for themselves the road to deal with the aggressors'. Curiously, the article caused no very great stir in British Government circles. The Associated Press reported from London that it was 'discounted' there; new instructions which would come very close to Russia's original demand were being sent to the British Ambassador and an agreement was 'expected next week or the week after that at the latest'.

For all the note of urgency which Zhdanov's article had seemed to inject into the situation, week after week was again to go by as hopes and anxieties alternated in London and Paris while the negotiations in Moscow continued. The headlines in Britain's papers over these weeks documented the course of those negotiations. 'Moscow Talks Again Going Badly', wrote the *Manchester Guardian* on 5 July and *The Times* in a leader agreed that they had been 'checked' and that the position was 'unhappy'. 'Making Another Attempt In Moscow', proclaimed the *Guardian* on 8 July. But there were anxious questions in the House of Commons on the 12th about the way this attempt was going and on the 14th the *Guardian* again had to report 'No Progress In The Russian Negotiations'. It added that it was coming to be realized in London that Russian procrastination was methodical and that there must be a limit to future delays. 'Moscow Talks Resume', reported *The Times* on 18 July - 'the fifth round, as it were'. Presumably for a time it was thought to be going well. On the 24th Hugh Dalton asked in the House of Commons whether in view of grave concern in many quarters over the delay the Prime Minister would give an undertaking not to adjourn Parliament until agreement was reached. He received the plain answer, 'No'. The *Observer* that Sunday declared in bold black type: 'In spite of the delays on either side there is no doubt about the eventual success of the negotiations.' On 27 July there was a confident 'Agreement Near In Moscow' from *The Times*. And the accompanying article stated: 'A defensive agreement can now be virtually assured.' The *Guardian* was only marginally less sanguine. 'Nearer A Pact With Russia' was its headline, followed by 'A Statement Soon?' The article began: 'Progress is at last being made ...'. 'Important Stage In Moscow' said *The Times* the next day and on 1 August, in a leader, went further, seeing 'unmistakable implications that the substance of an agreement between the three Powers is secure ...'.

During all this time the situation in Danzig had become, it seemed, irreversible, with men nominally masquerading as tourists and war material openly pouring into the city. But the confidence with which Germans both inside and outside the Free City proclaimed that a change in its status was imminent did little to clarify the minds of opponents of aggression. Confusion as to whether that change in status would be brought about by violence from without or within, and whether the reaction should be the same in either case, was a puzzling factor, nicely calculated to stir that slight haze of imprecision that still hung over the declared policy of Britain and France. The *Manchester Guardian*'s diplomatic correspondent had already said that the firmer type of official statement which Halifax and Chamberlain had been issuing recently seemed to carry less weight among the German leaders than certain reports made to Berlin by unofficial but busy 'appeasers' claiming to report the real opinion of Britain and France. Even that paper's own correspondence columns had shown that a British opinion which considered war over Danzig indefensible could be found if looked for hard enough; and the German leaders were doubtless looking quite hard for material with which to substantiate their optimistic suspicions about Chamberlain's ambivalence. They might even have looked as far as the Skipton Congregational Church, whose clergyman wrote to the *Manchester Guardian* on 18 July: 'Is it seriously contemplated that ten millions of the young men of Europe shall be put to the cruel death which modern warfare involves over the question whether Danzig shall be governed by Germans or Poles? Nothing more completely fatuous or lunatic could possibly be imagined.'

Obviously in Danzig itself the issues at stake seemed anything but fatuous for the Germans and Poles involved, though a certain vein of lunacy pervaded the practical situation there. For on this territory, inseparable from the interests of Polish independence, into which in any case vast quantities of arms and ammunition were being brought by sea into special wharves to which the Polish authorities were physically denied access by Danzig Nazi storm troopers, the Free City German Senate now declared that all Polish customs officials were to be removed from their posts, though it later relented and said it would only suspend seventy-three on the grounds that these were spies, the other twenty-seven being bona fide customs officials. In a way these Poles were lucky because the week before a Polish customs official had been shot dead by a Danzig Nazi. In fact the suspension of the seventy-three was not even carried out, apparently after the receipt of instructions direct from Berlin. The Warsaw Government, who after all could claim to be the final authority, sent a protest to which, it announced in a communiqué, it received an oral assurance that no such measures would be taken and that it was to get a written reply the following week.

Meanwhile reports multiplied of German troop concentrations on the Polish border and of a special force the Poles were keeping ready, standing by in case the frontier with East Prussia should be forced open by Danzig Nazis. Certainly it hardly looked probable that the Germans were still seeking a diplomatic solution, but then this might have been the way they wanted it to look, and in any case it was still not clear what sort of active solution they might select.

By the beginning of August there was again a feeling around that somehow the situation was easier. Hitler had resumed his holiday at Berchtesgaden which he had broken off for a quick one-day visit to Berlin, and the *Observer*'s Berlin correspondent reckoned that though August had at one time been thought of as the crisis month, that crisis was now likely to develop in the first ten days or so of September, or after the Nuremberg Rally of 2 September. In the interval Danzig would be kept merely slightly simmering in the German press, 'ready to

A new pope is crowned: Pius XII (formerly Cardinal Pacelli) and retinue in St Peter's, Rome, 12 March.

The Royal Family relaxes: Princess Elizabeth and Princess Margaret with their mother and father at a scout camp near Balmoral.

be brought to the boil at the right moment'. The important Italian review *Relazione Internazionale* had been running a mildly conciliatory line which, while saying that it was up to Britain, France and Poland whether there was a war or not, also said that Danzig was not worth one.

To await the moment at which the affair was to be brought to whatever 'boil' the Germans had in mind, the democracies went off on their traditional holidays. The Prime Minister, looking astonishingly well and vigorous and as if he had withstood the unbroken strain of the past few months 'amazingly', was off to Chequers and then to Scotland for two to three weeks 'to cast a line over a remote stream'. But it was stressed that he would be remaining in daily touch with London by telephone. The *Observer* summed up the mood of Britain as it prepared for the August Bank Holiday and what the paper called 'the greatest escapist month of the year', saying that many millions intended to enjoy it to the full. 'We realize that the problems, like the Dictators, are still with us. We are unperturbed. . . . The curious thing about this "war of nerves" we hear so much about is that it has precisely no effect at all. We have realized the danger and taken the precautions. It will take more than a "jitterbug" or a Goebbels to shake a serenity founded on conscious strength – if "it" comes, it comes.'

A record rush of holiday-makers was expected, with one thousand special trains laid on by the London, Midland and Scottish Railway Company alone. And the day before the Bank Holiday itself, the *Observer* added: 'Nowhere is there a shade of panic or nervous agitation. All have a pretty good idea of what the worst would be like if it came. Not for nothing has the study of ARP been popularized. But we look it squarely in the face.'

Even though there had already been so many weeks' delay and failure to make progress in the negotiations with Russia a note of urgency did not seem upper-most in Chamberlain's announcement, just before Parliament adjourned, that a military mission was being sent to Moscow to work out the practical side of the alliance. It was, he said, 'to go very shortly to Moscow – possibly this week'. The names of its members certainly gave it a ring of purposeful stability. There was one from each of the three Services: Admiral Sir Reginald Plunkett-Ernle-Erle-Drax, Air Marshall Sir Charles Stuart Burnett and the be-monocled Major-General T.G.G. Haywood. The editor of *The Times* measured out his enthusiasm at much the same pace as Chamberlain, saying 'the sending of the mission could not be other than a hopeful sign'. Another hopeful sign was that on the day his leader appeared, *Pravda* contained an article which seemed to leave no doubt as to where Russian sympathy, or at least Russian hostility, lay. 'The Soviet people', it wrote, were tranquilly watching 'the criminal activities of the Fascist warmongers'.

The Opposition in Parliament that day had been uneasy about Chamberlain's apparent satisfaction with the pace of things. Hugh Dalton for the Labour Party had described the negotiations with the Soviet Union as 'diplomatic dawdling without precedent'. He said of Chamberlain that last year three times in a month he had flown into 'the embracing arms of Hitler' and shortly afterwards he had taken Lord Halifax with him to Rome to see Mussolini. Had the Prime Minister then lost all faith in the desirability of opposite numbers meeting? Dalton was worried, too, about the fact that the Treasury had refused to give Poland a £5,000,000 loan in gold which it had asked for (Britain's own reserves being as high as £500,000,000 in gold). Was it, he asked, perhaps feared that if the Poles got too many arms too quickly they would get a bit above themselves? Had Ministers some sinister and unrevealed purpose in keeping Poland weak? If not, why ever did they not let her have the money to buy arms?

Chamberlain in reply had said that Dalton was playing Hitler's game by talking like this. Dealing with the matter of delay, the Prime Minister pointed out that the Anglo-French *entente* of 1904 had taken nine months to achieve, the Anglo-Russian Convention of 1907 fifteen months and the Anglo-Japanese Alliance had taken six months. He was in any case clearly in no mood to be panicked. Referring to the situation in Danzig he said that some reports of what had been happening there, particularly in relation to the extent of German militarization of the place, had been 'undoubtedly greatly exaggerated'. He said they would of course continue to watch the situation but 'I think my Honourable Friend [Lord Halifax] was justified in saying recently that he did not feel undue concern about it'.

In fact the official *Gazeta Polska* had just published some details of this militarization. The police force had been increased from 1,000 men to 4,500 and had been organized in regiments as in the German army. It was supported by an auxiliary force of SS men and had its own field artillery, anti-tank and anti-aircraft guns.

The military mission to Moscow did in fact sail at the end of that week and after taking another week to get there started work at once, together with a similar French mission, in talks with Voroshilov. The political talks, *The Times* had reported in the interval, were continuing 'not at all unhopefully'. It was just as well, because by that time the situation in Europe had deteriorated much as those who had opposed such a long adjournment of Parliament had forecast, possibly causing Lord Halifax and the Prime Minister to revise their opinion that there was no reason for undue concern.

Forster, Hitler's Gauleiter in Danzig, had been to Berchtesgaden to see his Führer on the weekend of the British Bank Holiday and his return had coincided with an increase in the virulence of attacks on Poland, both in the Reich and the Danzig press. A statement in the Polish newspaper *Czas* had said that Polish troops would fire on Danzig if attempts were made to incorporate it within the Reich. And it was the increasing evidence of Polish defensive firmness in view of the German threat that the Germans now seized on as evidence of Polish chauvinism and aggressive intent. Another Polish paper had pointed out, perhaps with a touch of facetiousness, that of course if Germany forced Poland into a war and Poland won it, as she would, then Poland would naturally look for some frontier rectification later – perhaps in East Prussia and Silesia. 'Poland, Look Out!' ran the headlines in the German press. The *Danziger Vorposten* accused Poland of 'laying the match to a powder-barrel which may explode any moment'. Warsaw was playing a 'mad war game'. The Berlin paper *B Z am Mittag* spoke of England's blank cheque to Polish megalomania and chauvinism. 'On the basis of the English guarantee,' it wrote, 'Poland now shows herself to be an irresponsible firebrand playing with fire.' It was the first time for some weeks that the German press had worked up this pitch of excitement. Nor was it just the press which gave grounds for anxiety. German army manœuvres had started: between 1,700,000 and 2,000,000 men were thought to be under arms, and eye-witness reports from Slovakia told of great military activity there directed towards the Polish frontier.

Britain too was making preparations in her own fashion, though these hardly looked directly towards Poland. The Reserve Fleet had, it is true, been virtually mobilized; no dramatic order had been given but reserves had been recalled in stages over the past few weeks. The King reviewed it on 9 August. But the emphasis on Britain's preparation was introspective. On the night before the Fleet review the largest ever RAF exercises involved mock raids on the Eastern counties of Southern England, and half the country was to undergo a practice blackout on the night of the 9th itself. This had to be postponed twenty-four hours because of the weather but on the night of the 10th it was revealed that the blackout, particularly in London, was far from effective. London, it was said, stood out from the air like a fire at sea in the surrounding darkness. In no sense could the capital be said to have been blacked-out. But this, after all, was what such trials were for. There was time in which to improve such matters.

A.P. Herbert, the literary humorist, then an Independent Member of Parliament, formulated an important part of the contemporary British mood in a letter to *The Times* protesting at the barbarities committed against the English language by practitioners of officialese. He said that if Nelson had had to repeat his famous signal today it would probably have run: 'England anticipates that as regards the current emergency, personnel will face up to the issues and exercise appropriately the functions allocated to their respective occupation groups.' And that, both in form and content, represented something of the spirit of Britain in this August of 1939.

Gauleiter Forster's signal to his men in Danzig on the day Herbert wrote his letter was more succinct: 'We know what is coming. We know we will return to the Reich, but we do not know when. The important thing is that we should prepare ourselves.'

From Berlin *The Times* correspondent wrote that 'according to all indications Germany is now rapidly reaching her maximum of military preparedness'. In Britain listeners to both the national and regional programmes of the BBC could hear Wagner's *Flying Dutchman* from Bayreuth. After all the really important preparations as regards Poland were going on in Moscow. The start of talks there at the weekend of 12 August and their continuation all day, even though it was Sunday, was regarded as impressive. The toasts which Voroshilov had proposed to the 'invincible' and 'glorious' British and French fighting services at the dinner after their arrival seemed to have been a good omen.

The same day, Burckhardt, the Swiss League of Nations High Commissioner in Danzig, was invited to Berchtesgaden for a talk with Hitler. The German press was still full of complaints of Polish provocation, both verbal and, in the case of German citizens living in Poland, physical, and the *Times* correspondent in Berlin spotted a curious article in the German economic paper, *Die Deutsche Wirtschaft*. Germany, said the article, was short of coal and this shortage had been made more acute by the acquisition of further territory in Bohemia and Moravia excluding, ironically, the particular territory which, until September 1938, had supplied the Czechoslovaks with much of their coal. For this territory had been ceded to Poland after the Munich Agreement. Poland, however, had an excess of coal anyway. 'Even though we have no ambition to become the coal merchants of Europe,' wrote the paper, 'we feel entitled to assert that the nation which actually needs coal most is entitled to it.' And another economic paper, *Der Wirtschaftspolitische Dienst*, stated bluntly that Poland couldn't possibly need all the coal that she had and that her coalfields should be placed at the disposal of the Reich.

Meanwhile, President Roosevelt, having failed to get his Neutrality Bill through and having suffered additional defeats on housing and lending proposals before Congress adjourned for several months, had gone cruising off the New England coast for about ten days. It was made clear that he had no intention of calling a special session of Congress unless there should be a war crisis. In that case he let it be known that he would call one in order to ensure American neutrality – by which everyone knew that what he meant was: to try to get the arms embargo repealed.

Roosevelt's recent defeats were to be seen more in the context of internal American politics than as a conclusive pointer to the likely effectiveness of American influence on the European scene. Internal American politics at this juncture, still some eighteen months away from the 1940 presidential election, meant concern for the coming Party Conventions and particularly the Democratic Convention. Anti-New Deal Democrats were manoeuvring to undermine Roosevelt's authority in the choice of a Democratic candidate for that election and above all to prevent him from presenting himself for a third term. The President had just struck a blow for himself in this preliminary skirmishing with a letter to the Young Democrats' National Convention at Pittsburg in which he had stated that were a Conservative Democrat to be chosen as Democratic candidate on an unequivocally conservative programme, he would need to make clear his own 'inability to participate in the suicide of the old Democratic Party'.

In this he was echoing what his supporter, Senator Berkeley, the Democratic Party leader in the Senate, had said when he declared that anyone who could select a candidate to repudiate Roosevelt's eight years in office 'should consult an expert on mental disorders'. The Young Democrats at Pittsburg in fact loudly applauded every reference in the Conference to a third term for Roosevelt.

The nuances of the American political situation were on the whole well understood in Britain and failure to get the Neutrality Act altered and the arms embargo lifted, while disappointing, had not been considered any long-term devastating blow to the democracies. The middle of the month came and *The Times*'s earlier advice to look to two dates, 27 August, when Hitler would speak at the commemoration of the battle of Tannenberg in East Prussia, and 2 September, when the Nazi Party rally opened at Nuremberg, for pointers as to what was likely to happen next, seemed still sound. No communiqué had yet been issued as a result of the staff talks in Moscow, but *Pravda*'s tone could be taken as encouraging. It had been running a series of articles on just and unjust wars to commemorate the anniversary of August 1914 and had written in one passage: 'The war of the Soviet Union against Fascism would be the most lawful of all the wars of humanity – a war for the liberation of humanity from Fascism and of oppressed nationalities from bondage.'

On the same weekend as that on which the military mission's talks started in Moscow – that of 12 and 13 August – Count Ciano, Mussolini's son-in-law, had visited Berchtesgaden for talks with Ribbentrop and Hitler. Conversations had lasted two days, with an evening of relaxation at the White Horse Inn on the Wolfgangsee in between. Ciano had telephoned Mussolini at least once in the course of the weekend and it was assumed that Danzig would have been discussed. No communiqué was, however, issued and correspondents in Berlin found it difficult to glean anything of what might have gone on there. Two days later, however, there was a growing impression in Berlin that there was, as the *Times* man put it, 'something in the air'.

The *Times* leader that day admitted to a certain sense of mystery about the weekend conversations but maintained that, unlike the days of the Czechoslovak crisis the previous year, the world remained calm and confident. In particular, said the editor, the French and British military missions to Moscow 'seem to be making good progress and their work invites the assurance that there will be no big delay in completion of the "peace front" by the inclusion of Russia'. There was indeed about the *Times* leader of that day almost an air of firmly resigned finality to its account of the spiritual journey which the world – and perhaps particularly itself – had completed in the past twelve months. 'It is of less importance to travel consistently than to arrive,' wrote the editor. 'In the end nations must agree or fight. The intermediate "war without guns" cannot last indefinitely nor can the temporary advantages conferred upon governments which have exploited for their own purposes the healthy detestation of war that is common to all civilized men.'

The next day there were persistent rumours from Berlin of some sort of peace plan but at the same time there seemed a sense of conviction there that haggling over Danzig was no longer possible. The only question to be discussed on the Danzig issue was how specific arrangements for the handover by the Poles were to be managed. Incidents on the German–Polish frontiers were increasing and both sides were issuing orders to their frontier guards to shoot on sight. A Polish policeman was murdered by Germans in Polish Silesia and a number of arrests of Germans followed, including that of the leader of the German minority political party there, the *Jungdeutsche Partei*, who was held for questioning for a day but then released. Indeed, of the eighty Germans arrested by the Poles, forty-four were released the next day.

All this was enough to bring the German press campaign against Poland to a new peak of hysterical violence. Many observers were reminded of the similar campaign against the Czechs in the Sudetenland the previous year. It was reported that thousands of Germans had been arrested and that refugees were fleeing in terror across the frontiers into Germany with stories of torture and of prisoners in Polish jails being beaten with iron rods and rubber truncheons. To the average trusting German newspaper-reader there could be little doubt that a reign of terror against Germans in Poland was in progress. The press talked of 76,000 refugees, though foreign correspondents suggested that this number referred to Germans who had moved across from Poland over some period, for most of them were already at work. There were 4,400 refugees in camps in the area, said the *Völkischer Beobachter*, and there were pictures of them as there had been of Sudeten refugees in the days of the Czech crisis. A 'merciless campaign against all Germans' was under way, according to the paper, which also stated: 'The problem of Danzig and the Corridor is overripe for solution, for instant solution. Every day lost increases the danger of war.'

It was clear that the Germans had widened the issue. Danzig itself was now a side issue, replaced by extreme general tension in German–Polish relations. The Germans were demanding the whole of the Corridor as a matter of course and, it seemed at times also, Polish Silesia. On the evening of Sunday, 20 August, Chamberlain came down from Scotland by sleeper to preside over a meeting of his Ministers on Tuesday the 22nd.

Nothing had been heard for some days of the talks going on in Moscow. This made it all the more amazing for readers of *The Times* on that 20 August to take in the headlines of the lead story in the first left-hand column of its centre page. These ran:

Full Cabinet To-day
Growing Tension
German Troops Massing
Nazi Pact with Russia

This last astounding piece of information had come in very late during the night and even missed some of the late London editions. The leader that day was on a different subject altogether. There was no explanation of the news in the paper and only a few brief comments on it from abroad. From Berlin it was reported that the news removed all danger of war from Europe. Great Britain, it was being said there, had suffered a grave diplomatic defeat and could now hardly carry out her obligations to Poland. High officials in Washington also described it as 'a stunning blow to Britain's peace front'. Parliament was recalled for Thursday 24 August.

There was indeed some confusion at first as to what this pact would actually mean. That the news was true was undeniable. A pact had been agreed and Ribbentrop was on his way to Moscow to ratify it with Stalin. An official statement was immediately issued from Downing Street, which said that a Russian–German non-aggression pact would in no way affect the obligations of the British and French Governments to Poland 'which they have repeatedly stated in public and which they are determined to fulfil'.

In Moscow, Soviet officials seemed to be trying to say that the pact meant no more than an attempt by the German and Russian Governments to preserve peace, but with the pact not yet officially signed it would have been natural for them to stall by thus playing down its importance. Nevertheless, the *Times* diplomatic correspondent grasped at the accommodating straw. 'That Russia would definitely throw in her lot with Germany is not believed,' he wrote. 'It is hard to imagine that Russia would allow smaller nations to be engulfed by Germany until the German frontier, for example, was brought up against the Russian.'

The editor of the paper seemed inclined to agree with him. In his first leader comment he wrote that a first general impression that the danger to Poland and the West had been greatly increased soon gave way to less grave interpretations because other talks were expected to continue. Doubts had even begun to be entertained 'whether in fact the Nazi-Soviet deal would make any material difference in peacetime or in war'.

From Berlin, however, there was reported now to be a firm belief that England would not fight.

On 23 August the pact was formally signed in Moscow, while in Berlin the British Ambassador, Sir Nevile Henderson, formally told Hitler that the guarantee to Poland stood. A 'crisis of the utmost gravity' was said to exist. French citizens were advised to leave the capital and, though no official advice was yet being given to the British there, some of them and many neutrals were already leaving. Britain's reaffirmation of the pledge to Poland was not reported in the German papers.

The next day Parliament duly reassembled – three days after the date for which the Opposition, at the beginning of the month, had asked for a recall only to be blandly rebuffed by Chamberlain. Even at this moment there was a touch of blandness about the Government's treatment of the news, at least in the House

A first visit by Prime Minister Neville Chamberlain to the Soviet Embassy in London, 18 March—'every reason to hope for full agreement at an early date'.

Molotov, watched by Ribbentrop (*left*) and Stalin (*centre*), signs the Nazi-Soviet Pact on 23 August.

of Lords where Lord Halifax, the Foreign Secretary, said he admitted that there had earlier been rumours of some change of attitude between the German and Russian governments but 'I do not conceal the fact that the announcement of the Nazi–Soviet Pact came as a surprise'.

Lord Snell, for the Labour Opposition, said he could not help asking 'how it came about that His Majesty's Government knew nothing of what was impending'. He wondered 'what our intelligence service had been doing, on which we spent so much money'. Halifax replied that he had already said he had heard rumours of a change, but that no cause for reproach attached to our ambassadors or our intelligence service. 'If there is any case for blame – and I do not admit that there is – it is to me that it should be attached.'

Chamberlain in the House of Commons also said that rumours of an impending change had been around for some time, but added of them strangely: 'No inkling of that change was conveyed . . . to us . . . by the Soviet Government.' He admitted that the pact came as 'a surprise and a surprise of a very unpleasant character', and said that it came on top of news received by the Government at the beginning of the week that German troops were moving towards the Polish frontier and that a crisis of the first magnitude was approaching.

On the solemnity of the hour all were agreed. 'The situation with which we are faced', said Anthony Eden, 'is in my judgment as grave and as perilous as any this country has faced at any time in her history.'

Little was actually said about the grave and perilous danger which faced the Poles, to whose aid, in the event of aggression against them, Britain and France were publicly pledged to go 'at once' and with 'all the support in their power'. Even when Leo Amery, long an opponent of appeasement, also spoke of the gravity of the situation, it was the British danger that he stressed. Would it not be madness, he asked, on our part not to take at once every measure that would be required if war were to come? He meant measures for the safety of Britain, such as rushing stores into the country, setting evacuation in train, and preparing a system of rationing. Harold Macmillan, also an anti-appeaser, said that we would find ourselves in a worse strategic position than in 1914 but the advantage was that there was a greater degree of unity in our hearts.

The only Member who slightly disturbed the solemn air of unity with which the Commons faced the crisis that day was Aneurin Bevan, the Labour Member for Ebbw Vale. People would want to know, he said, why the negotiations with Russia which had gone on so long had broken down. Why could Ribbentrop go to Moscow but no one of equal standing be sent by the British? The Prime Minister, he said, was the man who was responsible. He was the man on whom Hitler relied.

'Be British!' interrupted an Honourable Member.

Bevan turned on him. 'You talk to us, you Franco-ites . . .'

The *Times* leader commented the next day that the impressive unity of the House had not been broken by criticism from any 'serious' speaker.

There was a legislative purpose to the session, which was to vote the Government emergency powers with which to take measures for the Defence of the Realm directly by Orders in Council. These powers were granted without dissension in both Houses of Parliament and received the Royal Assent on the same day. 'Catastrophe has not yet come upon us', were the only comforting words Chamberlain could give the House for the future. It adjourned, but this time on his own proposal, to reassemble a week later, on 31 August.

22

Once again it had been Hitler who had called the tune and the democracies who were left to dance to it. This time, though, they seemed less ready to oblige. That the Nazi–Soviet Pact was a shock – a 'bombshell', Chamberlain had called it – to which they had to adapt themselves was obvious. But although it was in a way the most sensational of all the twists Hitler had applied to the course of world events, executed at a juncture which seemed to leave the democracies almost no room for manœuvre at all, there was now apparently little sign of that confusion which might have been expected or of that constantly ambivalent nerve in British policy of which friends were apprehensive and by which enemies set such store. The Government's statement of its own unaltered attitude had been very firm; 'impeccable', *The Times* called it. The Opposition in the House of Commons, with an ear permanently cocked for any sign of wavering, had not been worried. The extraordinarily routine mood in which the British people had been accustoming themselves to the prospect of war as one more familiar aspect of the everyday seemed to have permeated the very highest reaches of government. The apparent steadiness in policy was reflected in practical announcements to the British public. 'Get in touch at once with your Air Raid Warden if you do not already know him or his address,' advised the Lord Privy Seal's office. And it enjoined people to remember that 'Lights Out' was an injunction which did not only apply after the air-raid warning had been sounded; once a 'no lighting' order had come into effect there should be no lights shown after darkness at all, and houses that had made no provisions for blackout would not be allowed to turn their lights on. There was a run on dark curtain material and blinds at the London stores, but people were reminded that beige material of suitable weight could not only be very effective but also gave rooms a cheerful appearance. Sharp blasts on police whistles might be heard as supplements to the warbling signal of air-raid warnings. A continuous signal at steady pitch would denote that raiders had passed, while poison gas would be signalled by hand-rattles, and the ringing of bells would denote that gas had cleared. A final injunction from the Lord Privy Seal's Office ran, 'If you are going away for any length of time remember to take your gas mask with you. Those who ignore this advice may be running grave risks.'

An advertisement appeared in the papers from an insurance society, 'the oldest organization to have, in time of peace, a substantial fund for the event of war' – the Property Owners' War Risks Mutual Society – which offered low-rate premiums on private and commercial buildings and personal effects provided they were subscribed for at once. The Fund, it was stated, was non profitmaking and, should there be no war by October 1947, would provide subscribers with a remarkable sum in interest.

The raising of bank rate to four per cent from the two per cent at which it had stood since March 1932 seemed by comparison with all this a dramatic gesture. 'Half a mo, Hitler,' ran a slogan carried on the back of one small car. 'Let's have our holidays first.' And yet for the Cabinet with its own holidays cut short, and waiting as so often before to see what Hitler would do next, the reality was alarming. Article 2 of the Russo-German Pact stared them in the face: 'If one of the contracting powers should become the object of warlike action on the part of a third power, the other contracting power will in no way support the third power.' In other words, in any war between Great Britain and Germany over Poland, no help at all could be expected from the Soviet Union. Article 3 even spoke of the two contracting powers consulting over 'questions which touch their common interests', so that it looked very much as if the Soviet Union might actually be helping Germany.

In Berlin it was confidently felt, at least among the general public, that the logic of all this for 'the encirclers' would be insurmountable and that the danger of a major war was now past. Certainly the European crisis was approaching its climax. The technically illegal and unconstitutional proclamation of Gauleiter Forster as Head of the Danzig State was evidence enough of that – the clear prelude to a take-over. But though British residents were now at last being advised to leave, correspondents reported a sense of conviction that, while Poland would have to be taught a sharp lesson, Britain and France would not intervene. On the evening of Friday 25 August, Hitler, Ribbentrop and Goering, together with the Commanders of the German Army and Navy (General von Brauchitsch and Admiral Raeder), went into a conference at seven o'clock which did not end until the early morning of the 26th.

In France new classes of reservists were being called up. Horses, cars and even some premises were being requisitioned. Gas masks were being issued and civilians without urgent business were advised to leave Paris. Faces were reported as unsmiling and pessimistic. Newspapers were scanned eagerly. Much the most agitated reaction to the Nazi–Soviet Pact in France came from the Left and particularly the large French Communist Party, some of whose members were described as dazed and anchorless, while others were disgusted and disillusioned. One Socialist Deputy had even proposed that Communist Deputies should be expelled from the Chamber's Foreign Affairs Committee, but had been overruled on constitutional grounds. The Confédération Général du Travail issued an official statement condemning the Pact as 'prejudicing the peace front at the very moment when European tension was approaching its culminating point'. In the Renault factory 2,000 workers resigned from membership of the Communist Party in the course of a week. *L'Humanité* and *Ce Soir* both tried to produce an apologia for the pact and were banned by the police for their pains. Communist Deputies of the Foreign Affairs Committee evolved a statement saying that the

Russians had checked another Munich but they added that if Hitler were to start a war he would find the French people united against him. They also said that a Franco–British–Russian alliance was still perfectly possible.

The Japanese had no such reason to prevaricate in their interpretation of the pact. It was, understandably, bitterly resented by them. Their press described the Anti-Comintern Pact with irony as another 'scrap of paper'. Quite apart from the ideological revulsion the new Russo-German treaty caused them, that article which prevented either contracting party from giving support to any power with whom the other was at war boded ill for any German support for Japan in the bloody clashes taking place between Russian and Japanese troops on the borders of Manchukuo.

The Italians showed themselves quite unconcerned by any ideological embarrassment and, as always, approved a German success both in its own right and as a possible precursor of further adjustment to the world order in their own interests, as a worthy partner in the Axis. Their press contented itself with criticizing the speech Chamberlain had made in the House of Commons, particularly for his talk of 'world law' and 'the will of humanity in the world'. What he was really talking about, they said, was the British Empire and the British Empire's will. Nevertheless more attention was given to an appeal for peace made by the Pope in the Italian press than in the German press and there was a suggestion of much diplomatic activity.

As had been the case throughout the year, intense interest in the European crisis came from the United States. In New York, it was said, wirelesses were on in thousands of offices and homes with news bulletins, commentaries, interviews and descriptions of scenes in Europe virtually excluding all normal programmes. All the press, even the isolationist papers, revealed a sense of involvement, though in their case as something to beware of. Other papers stressed the need for Britain and France to be firm. 'Absolute firmness on the part of Britain and France', wrote the *New York Herald Tribune*, 'may yet pull the world through to safety.' With the Neutrality Act unamended, the *New York World Telegram* of the Scripps-Howard chain made clear the United States's own sense of responsibility. 'Whatever we do or do not do', it wrote, 'will have tremendous power; it cannot fail to swing the world balance perceptibly one way or the other. We will be unneutral if we act, we will be unneutral if we do nothing whatever.'

At a Washington press conference held on the same day as Hitler held his conference with his Commanders-in-Chief, Roosevelt let it be known that he still had a 'lovely hope' of peace, though he said he had nothing to base this on that was not also known to his hearers. Asked if he would recall Congress, he said he would do so if he thought war was 'imminent'. By 'imminent' he meant 'certain' and it was not yet certain. He had addressed appeals for peace both to Hitler and to King Vittorio Emanuele of Italy, with a copy of the latter to be shown to Mussolini. In these he had proposed that the Polish–German dispute should be settled either by direct negotiation or by arbitration, and had suggested that if the latter, one of the American Republics should be the arbitrator but not the United States. He received a polite acknowledgement from the Italian King but, as usual, only abuse in the press from Germany.

In many ways the country on which the pact made the least impression was Poland, herself beginning to experience the first effects of an approaching storm. A number of frontier incidents were taking place both around Danzig and on the Silesian border. German patrols had invaded a railway station and a court house at Makeszowa, near Katowice. The Germans had opened fire and three Poles had been wounded and one kidnapped. In revenge, Poles broke into the offices of the German newspaper in Katowice and smashed it up. The Poles, reporting this last event and fully aware of the chances it provided for exploitation by German propaganda, announced that the 'roughs' responsible for the break-in had been arrested by the police. Partial mobilization was already under way and three more classes, totalling about half a million men, had just been called to the colours. Horses and motorcars were being requisitioned and columns of reservists were to be seen marching in plain clothes through Warsaw singing patriotic songs and crying 'Long live Poland!'. William Forrest, the *News Chronicle* correspondent who had reported the last days of the Spanish Republic, arrived in Warsaw at this time and found that Germany's 'war of nerves' had quite failed to disturb the calm and courage of the people. Music and dancing continued and he found no tense faces and no tears even from those saying farewell to their loved ones going to war.

On the day on which Forrest's report appeared, his paper's leader quoted Carlyle: ' "From the purpose of crime to the act of crime there is an abyss: wonderful to think of. The finger lies on the pistol; but the man is not yet a murderer." ... The whole world waits with bated breath for enlightenment on proceedings which for millions may literally be a matter of life and death.'

In the English Midlands town of Coventry at about half past two on the afternoon of Friday 25 August the wide thoroughfare of Broadgate in the middle of the city was crowded with shoppers while in restaurants and cafés near by people were just finishing their lunch. A bomber aircraft was flying overhead. Suddenly there was a flash and a violent explosion opposite the premises of a paint and colour merchant named John Astley & Sons, and Broadgate was filled with smoke which, when it had cleared, revealed a scene described by an eyewitness as being like that of a bombed town. Glass and wreckage from premises on both sides of the street were lying all over it and on the pavements, with five people killed and a number injured, some seriously, among the debris. The dead included a man of 65, a boy of 16 and a girl of 21 who had been out buying the trousseau for her wedding in a fortnight's time. Twelve of those injured were detained in hospital.

The bomb had not come from the aircraft, though many people thought at first that an air-raid had begun: it was the work of the IRA, one of whose ammunition dumps had only twelve days before blown up in a hut on an allotment ground in Coventry. The Broadgate bomb was found to have been placed in the basket of an errand boy's bicycle. Three men who immediately after the explosion had been heard to say, 'Come on! We'll get out of this quick,' had nearly been lynched by the crowd before being taken to the police station, where they succeeded in satisfying the police that they had nothing to do with it. Two days later the police made it known that they wanted to interview a man named Adams, who also went under the name of Norman.* The same day there were more IRA incendiary bombs in Blackpool and Liverpool, and five Irishmen appeared on an explosives charge at Bow Street in London. The world's main attention, however, was on other things.

The weekend of 25 to 28 August was one of intense diplomatic activity. The 25th, the day of the Coventry explosion, saw the formal signing at last of the Treaty of Mutual Assistance between the United Kingdom and Poland. The pledge of immediate assistance already given some months before and frequently restated since was now officially formalized. Lest anyone should have forgotten of what the pledge consisted it was clarified explicitly in the Treaty's first article. If one of the parties became engaged in hostilities with a European power in consequence of aggression by the latter against that party, the other party would 'at once' give it 'all the support and assistance in its power'.

The British Ambassador in Berlin, Sir Nevile Henderson, had an interview with Hitler that afternoon in which, it was speculated, the terms of the Anglo-Polish Treaty were communicated to the Führer officially and the Führer had communicated some sort of terms for a solution to the Polish crisis to the British Ambassador. According to what journalists called 'well-informed quarters' in Berlin, these terms were more demanding than the proposals for a return of Danzig to the Reich and for a sovereign corridor through the Corridor which Hitler had offered earlier in the year, since it was now too late for these to be offered again. But they did not – still according to well-informed quarters – go so far as the maximum demand that might have been made. They offered a medium solution which would involve the return of Danzig and the Corridor itself to the Reich, together with certain border territories in the Posen area which had been German before the Treaty of Versailles. Poland would, however, still be guaranteed a Free Port on the Baltic, presumably Gdynia.

It was announced from Berlin that night that Hitler would not after all be going to the Tannenberg Commemoration on the following Monday because of the tense situation and that the Nuremberg Rally on 2 September had also been cancelled. The general air of tension in Berlin that evening was considerably increased for a time by the temporary suspension at 6 p.m. of all communications with the outside world. Reservists were being called to the colours all day and

---

*Two Irishmen named Barnes and Richards were condemned to death for the Coventry murders on 14 December 1939.

truckloads of soldiers in steel helmets and full field kit could be seen travelling through the Brandenburg Gate and down the Unter den Linden.

The French Prime Minister, Daladier, broadcast to his nation this same evening of the 25th. He said the issue was no longer just that of Danzig but far more wide-reaching matters that threatened the liberty of the Polish State. He was sure that there was not a single Frenchman who did not understand that if France were to go back on her word and allow one people after another to fall, then very soon the process would be turned against France herself. 'French men!' he declaimed, 'We wish to remain free. We cannot agree to bow down under the threat of violence and to a reign of injustice.... Frenchmen and French women, I do not need to point out your duty to you. I know that you are resolved to ensure by every sacrifice the safety of the future.'

In London, Chamberlain went to see the King and also saw his Foreign Secretary, Lord Halifax, twice. The latter was working at the Foreign Office till after midnight and the United States Ambassador, Joseph Kennedy, called there about 11 p.m. Sir Nevile Henderson, who had telegraphed an account of his meeting with Hitler in code, was coming to London in person on the morning of Saturday the 26th.

None of this particularly seemed to accord with the Moscow view of things which, as expressed in the paper *Izvestia*, held that the Russo–German Pact could only pacify the extremely tense situation and contribute to the consolidation of peace. *Pravda* was sufficiently unconcerned to be able to devote its leading article to 'vegetables'. But there was an interesting footnote for those still able to take a detached historical interest in events in an article by Voroshilov in *Izvestia*. Explaining the failure of the British and French military mission he said that effective assistance for Poland would plainly require Soviet troops on Polish territory but the British and French had been unable to agree to this. Moreover, the Polish Government had openly declared that they did not require and would not accept such assistance from Russia. That made collaboration between the USSR and these powers impossible. Assistance to Poland of materials alone did not require anything so elaborate as a treaty. But then of course any sort of assistance to a Poland attacked by Germany had just been made impossible by the new treaty which the USSR had concluded with Germany.

A party of 140 British tourists in the Hotel Metropole in Moscow were worried. They had their bookings on the next Soviet steamer out of Leningrad, but it was due to go through the Kiel Canal.

While, in London, the Cabinet considered the message which Sir Nevile Henderson had brought from Hitler – sitting for two and a half hours on the Saturday evening and another hour and three quarters on Sunday afternoon with a final polishing of their reply on Monday – further air-raid precautions proceeded steadily alongside other more normal features of British life. The football season had opened on Saturday and matches were watched by 600,000 people. Individual conical steel shelters arrived for the sentries at Buckingham Palace.

The line of the kerb in London and other major cities was painted with alternate white square dashes for guidance in any coming blackout. The twelfth-century stained glass was removed from Canterbury Cathedral to safety, as was the Seven Sisters window from York Minster; the National Gallery was closed for the storing of pictures. The personal columns on the front pages of *The Times* had the initials ARP scattered across them like a rash as people offered for sale or rent, as protection against air-raids, houses as far from London as Scotland and Somerset but also as close as Cobham in Surrey and Balcombe in Sussex. A barge at Twickenham was also offered as some sort of getaway.

It had been a long weekend of diplomatic flurry in this strange atmosphere of normality and tension: Mussolini was reported to have been involved in a number of telephone conversations; the Pope's earnest appeal for peace was in the papers; there were rumours that a five-power conference was being planned. But incidents multiplied on the German–Polish frontiers: the Poles reported thirteen instances of temporary armed German penetration of their territory; there were 200,000 German troops on the Polish frontier in Slovakia.

The Times on the Monday morning of 28 August spoke of 'this eleventh hour of the gathering storm'. The *Daily Telegraph*'s leader struck a similar half-apocalyptic vein: 'It is something gained that there has been no actual break.... The sands of time are not yet out and there is still time for reason to return.' The paper thought there was a double strand in German policy: if possible, to get Britain to save Germany the necessity of war by bullying Poland into an acceptance of Hitler's terms or, if that failed, to get the Western Powers to dishonour their obligations to Poland and abandon her to her fate.

From Warsaw itself the *Telegraph*'s correspondent reported that indeed all eyes were on London and that it was being suggested in some circles that the French were wavering and trying to drive a wedge between Britain and Poland. But there was no evidence of such wavering in the public exchange of letters between Daladier and Hitler that weekend, except inasmuch as they addressed each other as old front-line fighters who knew the horrors of war. Daladier said that destruction and barbarity would be the only victors if French and German blood should flow again in a war still longer and more murderous than the one that had started twenty-five years ago. But he went on: 'Unless you concede less honour to the French people than I to the German, you cannot doubt that France will loyally fulfil her obligations to other powers such as Poland.' At the same time he saw no differences over Danzig which could not be solved peacefully.

Hitler's 'old front-line fighter' reply sounded more as if it were trying to drive a wedge between Britain and France than between Britain and Poland. Polish intransigence, he said, was due to British encouragement, 'without which we would have peace for the next twenty-five years'. How would he, Daladier, feel if a foreign corridor separated him from one of his provinces? 'You are French, I am German; if you attempted to regain it, it is inconceivable that Germany would fight you!' Thus he made an unequivocal demand for a return of Danzig and the Polish Corridor to the Reich.

In the London *Times* on Monday 28 August there was a letter from George Bernard Shaw about the 'joyful news that Hitler is now under the thumb of Stalin whose interest in peace is overwhelming. And everyone except myself', he went on, 'is frightened out of his or her wits. Why? Am I mad? If not, why? Why? Why?' He was to be answered a couple of days later by another correspondent writing a short letter who asked: 'Who is frightened out of his wits? Who? Who? Who?'

It was a time when rumours and speculation were almost indistinguishable. One of the oddest rumours concerned a mysterious figure who arrived by Lufthansa plane at Croydon at 1 p.m. on Sunday 27 August: a man in a black homburg hat wearing a dark suit, of medium build, clean-shaven, and carrying only a small brown case. A similar man was seen to arrive at the German Embassy at 3 p.m. When he left at a quarter past six he was asked by a *News Chronicle* reporter:

'Can you tell me who you are, please?'

The strange reply came: 'I do not know who I am.'

At 7.20 p.m. the *News Chronicle* man reported: 'The mystery stranger's plane left Croydon for Heston, where it picked up three more passengers believed to be Embassy officials.'

Britain's own envoy, Sir Nevile Henderson, who had come over from Berlin, took off from Croydon for Berlin again the next afternoon. As he stepped into the plane a reporter wished him good luck. 'Thank you,' he said. 'I shall need all the good luck I can get.' He saw Hitler for an hour that evening and gave him the reply over which the British Cabinet had worked so long.

All day in London on 28 August people of importance had been coming and going. Chamberlain had again been to Buckingham Palace to see the King. Arthur Greenwood for the Labour Opposition had been to Downing Street to see Chamberlain four times. The price of gold rose sharply to just over £8.

On Tuesday 29 August Parliament met again, two days earlier than planned, recalled to hear what the Government felt it could reveal of these various comings and goings since its last report before the weekend on the 24th.

This wasn't much. The Foreign Secretary told the House of Lords that the situation had not changed substantially since 24 August and was still one of great anxiety and danger. Hitler's last note had contained a wish for some Anglo-German understanding of a complete and lasting character, but showed no change in his attitude to the Polish problem on which everything depended. His Majesty's Government were sticking by their pledge to Poland, while seeing no reason why the problem should not be solved by negotiation. 'While determined to maintain any undertakings that we have given,' he said, 'we have thrown our whole influence upon the side of resolving these dangerous issues by negotiation rather than by force.'

British holiday snaps.

There was an absolutely even placing of emphasis on both aspects of this policy so that Parliament was able to feel wholly united behind it. In the House of Commons Chamberlain made a similar statement, stressing too that the first prerequisite for any calm atmosphere for a discussion was that the present frontier clashes must cease. He repeated that the catastrophe was not yet come but 'the danger of it has in no way receded'.

Greenwood, it was true, went a little out of his way to lay special emphasis on one aspect of the policy. But then, as the Government's own emphasis had been so carefully evenly distributed, there was no disturbance of the House's unity in his doing that. 'Poland', said Greenwood, 'will not be allowed to follow to the grave those nations that were martyred by the aggressors. He who today, whether over there or outside, in this country or abroad, who would dishonour the pledges they have been given, and endorsed, re-endorsed and endorsed again, would be a traitor to the peace and freedom of the world.'

Incidentally no-one in the House of Commons had commented on the fact that the Prime Minister in his speech the week before had used a phrase curiously echoing one he had used about the Czechoslovak crisis before Munich. In September 1938 he had spoken of 'a quarrel in a faraway country of which we know nothing'. On 24 August 1939 he summed up the situation as it then stood by saying that if in spite of all efforts for peace, 'and God knows I have tried my best', if in spite of all it should come to war, 'we shall not be fighting for the political future of a faraway city in a foreign land', but for principles, the destruction of which would mean the destruction of all peace and security for the peoples of the world.

Perhaps just because of the very suspicions which some Members had had of his policy at other times, the firmness which Chamberlain was now evincing seemed particularly uncompromising. Certainly his speech had been well received in Warsaw and in Paris, where *Le Petit Parisien* described it as 'calm and full of noble firmness'. *Le Figaro*, praising it, wrote: 'With regard to the present drama there is only a Franco-British point of view just as if, if necessary, tomorrow there would be only one Franco-British military, naval and air power to defend it.' Henri de Kerillis, a strong French anti-appeaser, wrote in *L'Epoque* that Chamberlain's speech had been excellent, both in form and content.

In France too, there was the same evenness of emphasis in the approach to the problem. A former Minister, M. Pitri, echoed Chamberlain in *Le Jour-Écho de Paris* saying that the British and French line of action remained changeless. 'It is armed intervention if Poland is forced to defend herself by military means, but at the same time no chance of peace is rejected, no unblemished hand refused.' And the former Prime Minister, Léon Blum, wrote in *Le Populaire*: 'If Germany renounces the application and threat of force, a general settlement still remains possible. I am glad Chamberlain has accepted the idea in such noble terms.'

But, a week later, the time during which the even balance of the policy could be maintained was running out, for the balance was becoming more precarious every hour, and the skills required to maintain it ever more delicate and subtle. Sir Nevile Henderson saw Hitler again on the evening of Tuesday the 29th and there was a further exchange of notes.

The next day, Wednesday the 30th, there were reports from Berlin that the door remained open though the situation was still serious, but it was taken as a sign of some hope there that Hitler was said to have studied Chamberlain's latest speech in the House of Commons with care. In London there was a broad advance in the Stock Market. The *News Chronicle* described 'a wave of hopefulness' as sweeping through the City and there was similar optimism on the Paris Bourse. However, as the *Telegraph* told its readers: 'The British people face the crisis of these hours ready for any sacrifice they may be called on to make rather than the sacrifice of honour,' and added: 'Proud as we may justly be of British firmness throughout the present crisis, we recognize in the fortitude of France something even more striking.'

There were military guards at railway stations now in Britain, some of them being ordinary railmen in civilian clothes with rifles. People were covering their windows with strips of brown paper against blast. 'A waiting period is often very trying', Chamberlain had said in his House of Commons speech.

For all the wave of hopefulness in the City, the *Telegraph* correspondent in Berlin noticed an ominous change in the tone of the German radio on the evening of Wednesday the 30th. Whereas the previous evening the first news bulletin had begun with the latest information on Anglo-German 'peace exchanges' and with a full summary of Chamberlain's speech in the House of Commons, on this evening nine out of fourteen items in the first news bulletin covered bloodcurdling reports of what was being done to Germans in Poland. German women were being beaten up; German shops were being set alight, while the Polish police watched and did nothing. It was stated that more than sixty Germans had been killed in Poland since May. The Polish Government, which had increased its call-up, was accused of aggressive military preparations. The radio transmitted an outside broadcast from a German air-force station somewhere in East Prussia with a description of squadron after squadron of heavy bombers drawn up for immediate use with 500 lb and 100 lb bombs. 'Where these bombs fell,' said the commentator, 'not one stone would be left on another.' There was a description of how, after the bombers had delivered their first load, they would return to be loaded again and keep up a series of uninterrupted raids. It was announced from Berlin that evening that a German Council of Defence had been set up with Goering as Chairman and Hess as Deputy. Hitler was in conference with it at 11 p.m.

An item not quoted by the Berlin radio, but noted by the British press, was the arrival at Croydon Airport that night of the 30th of another mysterious stranger from Berlin, or possibly the same one, carrying a briefcase as his only luggage. A hired car was waiting for him, in which the driver had orders to take him to the Foreign Office. The man's name was not on the passenger list.

Such matters, together with further references to notes being exchanged between the British and German governments and further reports of the deteriorating situation on the Polish–German border (what were described as 'German diversionary bands' had opened fire near a town in Polish Silesia), were available to the general public in the newspapers of Thursday 31 August. From Warsaw it was reported that Poland would be 'absolutely ready' by midnight to meet any onslaught, while there were pink posters up in the streets there calling up all men up to the age of forty to the colours. Other posters declared: 'In case of war every man, regardless of his age, and every woman will be soldiers.' There was a ban on the sale of alcohol in Warsaw to ensure that reservists arrived at the depots sober.

In London a *Times* correspondent described how people in the East End were cheerfully filling sandbags on waste land there, while the street markets functioned as usual. Herbert Morrison issued a call to all Londoners engaged in the evacuation of schoolchildren, which was just beginning: 'Keep calm. Keep a cheerful British smile on your face.... Good luck, and a safe return to dear old London.'

The latter message could be read in the papers of Friday 1 September. Also there were the conditions at last on which Germany said she was prepared to accept a settlement of the Polish problem. There were sixteen points in it altogether, the principal ones being: (1) that Danzig should become part of the Reich forthwith in view of the unanimous wish of its population; (2) that a plebiscite should be conducted to decide the future of the Polish Corridor, to be held in one year's time under the supervision of Britain, France, Russia and Italy; (3) that pending the plebiscite, the Polish authority should evacuate the Corridor, which would be run by a similar international commission; (4) that Gdynia should remain Polish whatever the result of the plebiscite, providing an outlet for Poland to the sea; and (5) that both the German and Polish armies should be demobilized.

Too late for inclusion in the newspapers that morning was the news which became known to the Foreign Office only at about 10 a.m.: that shortly before 6 a.m., without declaring war, the German armies had invaded Poland on a massive scale and were bombing Polish towns and villages.

If Article 1 of the Anglo-Polish Treaty were now to be implemented, as it had been continually repeated that it would be in such circumstances, the balance of emphasis in British and French policy towards the Danzig and Polish problem could no longer be maintained.

The House of Commons met that evening at six o'clock with all the recently fitted blackout blinds drawn. Both Chamber and Galleries were crowded. Loud and enthusiastic cheers greeted the Prime Minister.

Chamberlain said that it appeared that an aggressive act of force had been committed against Poland in her independence and that accordingly, unless His Majesty's Government received assurances that operations had been suspended and that Germany was preparing promptly to withdraw, His Majesty's Government 'will without hesitation fulfil their obligations to Poland'.

Surprisingly, perhaps, there was no direct demur at this stage from Members to the effect that such language in itself represented some hesitation, though one Honourable Member did call out: 'Time limit?', to which Chamberlain gave a still not altogether categorical response:

'If a reply to this last warning is unfavourable,' he said, 'and I do not suggest it is likely to be otherwise, His Majesty's Ambassador is instructed to ask for his passports. In that case we are ready.' There were loud cheers for this.

The Anglo-Polish Treaty had not said anything about His Majesty's Ambassador in Berlin being instructed to ask for his passports in this eventuality. The wording was clear: 'The other contracting party will at once give the contracting party engaged in hostilities all the support and assistance in its power.'

'So much for the immediate present,' said Chamberlain. 'Now we must look to the future.' He said it was essential to organize our manpower 'this time' more methodically than in the last war. The Military Training Act would now be extended to include all men between the ages of eighteen and forty-one, or rather it would make them liable for military service 'if and when called upon. It is not intended at the outset that any considerable number of men other than those already liable shall be called up.' He concluded by stating the Government's satisfaction that throughout these last days of crisis Signor Mussolini had been doing his best to reach a solution.

When a similar statement had been made by Lord Halifax in the House of Lords the Leader of the Labour Opposition there, Lord Snell, had said that, 'as far as I can understand the noble Viscount, it would appear that an ultimatum has been sent'. But Lord Crewe, the Liberal Leader there, said that it would not be quite correct to describe this as an ultimatum, though it could be described as a frank statement of our moral and political duty. In the House of Commons, Arthur Greenwood, speaking for the Opposition, was a little more direct though not over-critical. 'The Right Honourable Gentleman appears to have left another loophole. His communication gives the German Government the opportunity of withdrawal. There can be no withdrawal. I would read Article 1 of the Anglo-Polish Treaty, which bears only one meaning.' And he did so, thus reminding the House again of those words 'at once' and 'all the support and assistance in its power'.

Chamberlain in his speech told MPs that copies of a Government White Paper were being rushed out for them, so that they could study for themselves the course of the interchange that had been taking place between the British and German governments for the past ten days. This in general bore out such surmises as responsible commentators had been making, briefed as they doubtless had been by responsible officials from time to time. One or two details, however, could now be detected that gave an additional interest as well as clarity to the flurry of diplomatic news that had been available.

The exchange of notes had begun the previous week on 22 August. The general tenor of each side's position had been clear from the start: His Majesty's Government proffered a theoretically conciliatory line once the unswerving dedication to honour and the pledge to Poland had been necessarily stated; the Germans insisted that the problem could have been solved by now on the basis of their unparalleled magnanimity in their proposals earlier in the year but that the Poles had rejected these because Britain had encouraged their intransigence.

The most conciliatory approach seemed to have come from Hitler on Friday the 25th. This was the communication to which the British Cabinet spent the whole weekend replying. Hitler said that he had been turning things over in his mind and wanted to make a move towards England as decisive as the recent move he had made towards Russia. He said that the previous day's sitting of the House of Commons and Chamberlain's speech there had moved him to think again. Here however he could not resist one of those bitterly ironical sallies which had so pleased the members of the Reichstag. He said he found Chamberlain's assertion that Germany wanted to conquer the world ridiculous. The British Empire had 40,000,000 square kilometres; Russia had 19,000,000 square kilometres; the United States had 9,500,000 square kilometres and Germany 600,000 square kilometres. 'It is quite clear who it is who desires to conquer the world.' Then he moved on to the real point of his note.

Having stated twice but without further elaboration that the Polish problem must be solved, he said he was prepared 'to approach' Britain once more 'with a large comprehensive offer'. This would require some limited deal over colonies but would guarantee the future existence of the British Empire and finally lead to general disarmament. He would make this offer as soon as he had dealt with the Polish problem. He added that he desired to stress the irrevocable determination of Germany never again to enter into conflict with Russia.

The British reply to this, which had taken so long to perfect, tried to bring Hitler back to the main point at issue, and indulged in some irony of its own. Having cited the Führer's insistence that there must first be a settlement of differences between Poland and Germany, the British note said: 'As to that, His Majesty's Government entirely agree. Everything, however, turns upon the nature of the settlement and the method by which it is to be reached. On these points, the importance of which cannot be absent from the Chancellor's mind, his message is silent.' And once again there was a restatement of His Majesty's Government's 'obligations to Poland by which they are bound and which they intend to honour'. The note then recommended direct discussion between Poland and Germany with the proviso that it should be understood beforehand that any settlement arrived at must be guaranteed by other powers – a guarantee to which His Majesty's Government would be glad to contribute. And the obligations to Poland reappeared, although this time with a slightly different emphasis. His Majesty's Government trusted 'that the German Chancellor will not think that, because His Majesty's Government are scrupulous concerning their obligations to Poland, they are not anxious to use all their influence to assist the achievement of a solution which may commend itself both to Germany and to Poland.' It hoped that such a solution could indeed lead to a limitation of armaments, the Chancellor's reference to which it had noted with interest. And it reiterated that failure to reach a just settlement of the questions between Germany and Poland would ruin the chances of any better understanding between Germany and Britain and bring the two countries into a conflict which might plunge the whole world into war – 'a calamity without parallel in history'.

Hitler's reply to this was given to Sir Nevile Henderson on the evening of Tuesday the 29th. It noted with satisfaction His Majesty's Government's wish for Anglo-German friendship. It reiterated that the generous earlier German offer to Poland had been rejected through Polish intransigence and 'the barbaric actions . . . which cry to heaven' against people of German blood in Poland were quite unacceptable to a great power. This time, however, there was no reference to any British part in such intransigence.

Then came something that on the face of it seemed of importance. 'Though sceptical as to the prospects of a successful outcome', the German Government were prepared to accept the English proposal that direct negotiations should take place between Poland and Germany on the questions at issue. They insisted that a Polish representative with full powers to negotiate a settlement should arrive in Berlin by the end of 30 August, the next day.

Arrogant and peremptory as the demand was it was also clearly, if the negotiations were to continue to be regarded as serious, a matter of extreme urgency. But a strange hiatus now occurred. The offer was immediately conveyed to London and at two o'clock on the morning of the 30th, Sir Nevile Henderson was informed that careful consideration would be given to it but that it was unreasonable to expect a Polish representative to go to Berlin that day and that the German Government should not expect this. 'It might be well for you at once', went his instructions, '. . . to let this be known in proper quarters through appropriate channels.' He was told that a reply would be sent that afternoon. At 2.45 p.m. on the 30th Chamberlain sent Hitler a message through Henderson which was not in itself a reply but simply said that Hitler's note was being considered 'with all urgency'. It also said that His Majesty's Government was reminding Warsaw of how vital it was to reinforce all instructions to avoid frontier incidents. Evidence in the exchange of views of the desire for Anglo-German understanding was welcomed.

At 5.30 p.m. Henderson was sent another message from his Government to tell the Germans that the Polish Government could only exercise complete restraint on the borders if Germany did (there were reports of a sizeable sabotage operation by the Germans in Poland).

In other words it appeared, from a study of this White Paper at least, that nearly twenty-four hours had passed without the really important item in the last German message being attended to, namely the request – or insistence – that a Polish representative should go to Berlin within that twenty-four hours to take part in the direct negotiations which the British had recommended.

Only at 6.50 p.m. did Nevile Henderson receive the British Government's considered response to the German note of the night before. It read as if His Majesty's Government had been unconscious throughout the day. 'We understand', it said, 'that the German Government are insisting that a Polish representative with full powers must come to Berlin to receive German proposals.' It said His Majesty's Government could not advise the Polish Government to comply with this procedure because it was wholly unreasonable. 'Could you not suggest to the German Government', it went on, 'that they adopt the normal procedure, when their proposals are ready, of inviting the Polish Ambassador to call and handing proposals to him for transmission to Warsaw ...' The communication ended to the effect that His Majesty's Government could be counted on to do their best to facilitate negotiations in Warsaw if the German proposals offered a reasonable basis for them. These German proposals, which were those broadcast to the world on the night of 31 August, had been given to Nevile Henderson shortly before with notification of the fact that they were considered rejected because no Polish representative had come to Berlin.

But of course by the time Members of Parliament were able to peruse all this their minds were ill-disposed to look meticulously at events which had already begun to seem the academic detail of another era. For by now a million German troops had been driving into Poland for more than twelve hours and a score of Polish cities had been bombed.

When Parliament met the next day the mood was very different. It was now after 6 p.m. on 2 September and Neville Chamberlain was listened to in troubled silence as he told how, the evening before, the British Ambassador had been received by Ribbentrop and had delivered the ultimatum that was not quite an ultimatum. No reply had yet been received. 'It may be', said Chamberlain, 'that the delay is caused by consideration of a proposal which, meanwhile, had been put forward by the Italian Government, that hostilities should cease and that there should then immediately be a conference between the Five Powers. ... His Majesty's Government for their part would find it impossible to take part in a conference while Poland is being subjected to invasion, her towns are under bombardment and Danzig is being made the subject of a unilateral settlement by force.' He added that His Majesty's Government would, as stated yesterday, be bound to take action unless the German forces were withdrawn from Polish territory. They were in contact with the French as to the time necessary to know if the Germans were going to withdraw. 'If', he said, 'the German Government should agree to withdraw their forces then His Majesty's Government would be willing to regard the position as being the same as it was before the German forces crossed the Polish frontier. That is to say, the way would be open to discussion between the German and Polish Governments on the matters at issue between them, on the understanding that the settlement arrived at was one that safeguarded the vital interests of Poland and was secured by an international guarantee.' After the continual assertion of obligations and honour of the past few days this was strange talk and the House was seriously worried. When Arthur Greenwood for the Labour Opposition rose to speak, there were cries from all over the Chamber of 'What about Britain?', 'Speak for the working classes!', and Leo Amery was quoted by *The Times* as calling out: 'Speak for England!'

'I believe the whole House is perturbed by the Government's statement,' said Greenwood. 'There is a growing feeling, I believe, in all quarters of the House that this incessant strain must end sooner or later and in a sense, the sooner the better [there were cries of 'Now!'], but if we march, I hope we shall march in complete unity and march with France.'

At this moment the Independent Labour Party Member, James McGovern, called out: 'You people do not intend to march. Not a damned one of you!' Greenwood went on:

> I am speaking under very difficult circumstances and with no opportunity to think about what I should say, and I speak what is in my heart at this moment. I am gravely disturbed. An act of aggression took place thirty-eight hours ago. The moment that act of aggression took place one of the most important treaties of modern times automatically came into operation.... That delay might have been justifiable, but there are many of us on all sides of the House who view with the gravest concern the fact that hours have gone by and news came of bombing operations and news today of an intensification of it and I wonder how long we are prepared to vacillate at a time when Britain and all that Britain stands for and human civilization are in peril.... Every minute's delay now means a loss of life, imperilling our national interests – [here Robert Boothby, the Member for Aberdeen East, called out: 'Honour!'] – 'Well,' 'let me finish my sentence. I was about to say imperilling the very foundations of our national honour and I hope therefore that tomorrow morning – however hard it may be for the Rt Hon. Gentleman – and no-one would care to be in his shoes tonight – we shall know the mind of the British Government, that there shall be no more devices for dragging out what has been dragged out too long.

Sir Archibald Sinclair for the Liberals, trying not to allow the House's unease to turn into anything too divisive, said that at least the sitting would have demonstrated to the world that Britain's Parliament would not tolerate delay in fulfilment of 'our honourable obligations to Poland'. But of course what the world could not help noticing was that the delay, however intolerable, was there. And Sinclair went on to make an effective point against Chamberlain when he said that though the delay could possibly be explained by the Italian Government's proposal for a conference, it was noticeable that this had not delayed in any way the progress of the German army's advance into Poland.

Chamberlain made a second intervention to ask the House to recognize the 'difficult position' the Government found itself in, trying to synchronize action

with the French, and said that he thought he would have only one answer for the House the next day. He asked it meanwhile not to 'prolong the discussion which, perhaps, might make our position more embarrassing' than it was at the moment.

According to a Polish communiqué, there had already been fifteen hundred casualties including women and children from the bombing of over thirty Polish towns and cities.

When the House of Commons met twenty-one hours later on 3 September, the atmosphere had, as Arthur Greenwood himself immediately said, changed overnight. From being one of resentment, apprehension, and fear that delays might end in 'national dishonour and the sacrifice of the Polish people to German tyranny', the mood had been transformed into one of resolution and composure. Less than an hour before, Chamberlain, broadcasting to the nation, had told how a further communication had been given to the German Government that morning at 9 o'clock asking for an assurance that the German forces would, as requested before, suspend their advance into Poland; if a satisfactory assurance to this effect had not been received by eleven o'clock a state of war would exist between the two countries. Chamberlain broadcast at 11.15. No such satisfactory assurance had been received: 'Consequently this country is now at war with Germany.' For once he allowed some ideology to enter into his condemnation of Hitler, saying it was 'the evil things' that we should be fighting and mentioning injustice, oppression and persecution as well as brute force and diplomatic bad faith. There was an almost valedictory note to his speech in the House of Commons an hour later, as if he recognized that whatever might lie ahead, his own true part on the scene of public events had been eclipsed.

'This is a sad day for all of us,' he said, 'but to none is it sadder than to me. Everything that I have worked for, everything that I have hoped for, everything that I have believed in during my public life, has crashed into ruins.'

Certainly appeasement, in the sense the term had carried to date, was now over at last. And for those, particularly the young, who had had little but contempt for it, there was a simple sentence in the King's broadcast to the nation that evening, which did much to explain the almost bemused dedication with which Chamberlain and his supporters had sometimes seemed to pursue it.

Though himself only in early middle age, the King reminded his listeners that: 'For the second time in the lives of most of us we are at war.'

But it is not greatly in the power or inclination of youth to be ruled by an older generation's traumas. They even have a certain eagerness to meet their own. Not that it was only much of Britain's youth which felt a strange sense of relief, as well as other emotions, on the outbreak of war. Many people of an older generation too felt liberated from the creeping paralysis of appeasement, as Winston Churchill at last entered the Cabinet as First Lord of the Admiralty, and Anthony Eden (though, unlike Churchill, he was not to be in the inner War Cabinet) as Dominions Secretary.

In fact between the end of Chamberlain's broadcast and his speech to the

---

PREVIOUS PAGE Polish cavalry, 1939: 'Poles fight for their rights even when there is no chance of winning'.

House of Commons, Britain had already had its first experience of war. Chamberlain had just expressed certainty that against the 'evil things' the right would prevail. A series of short official announcements followed to the effect that the blowing of whistles or blaring of horns was now forbidden as these could be confused with air raid warnings, and that all theatres and cinemas were to be closed in order to minimize the chances of a large crowd being killed by a single bomb. 'Now,' came the voice, 'an announcement about food.' There was a long silence, interrupted only by a shuffling of papers and a low whisper. Then the National Anthem was played and in the middle came the scream of the air-raid sirens.

Two days before, the Lord Privy Seal's office had issued a pamphlet: 'What To Do In An Air-Raid'. It had been reassuring. The direct effects of a high explosive bomb, it said, extended over a limited range, generally a 30-foot circle round the bomb. If fifty large bombs fell in a square mile there was a hundred to one chance against an individual experiencing 'what may be called direct hits'. And it went on to say that the ordinary dwelling-house offered a good deal of protection: people should not be upset by pictures of what had happened to the poorly-built houses of Spain. So, remembering this but remembering also what they had often read in the newspapers during the past year of air-raids on Barcelona and Chungking and bearing in mind such pontifical statements as that of the *Manchester Guardian* that summer to the effect that the most devastating air-raids in a new war would almost certainly come at the very beginning, Londoners went calmly to their air-raid shelters and waited for the worst. Nothing happened. Twenty minutes later the first 'all clear' was sounded. Chamberlain picked up his gas mask in its new shiny black leather case and left Downing Street, where he had been waiting, for the House of Commons. Those Londoners who had not been among the 600,000 to be evacuated returned to what in all other respects was a normal Sunday morning, save that they were now 'at war with Germany'.

'We have heard the war begin in the precincts of this House,' said Arthur Greenwood dramatically when he spoke that morning.

But what exactly would 'war' now mean?

Churchill, who spoke for the first time as a member of the Government, made a characteristic contribution, hammering out his sentences, as the *New York Times* correspondent described it, so that they sounded 'like the barks of a field-gun'. He agreed with the Prime Minister that it was indeed a sad day but also wanted to add another note and that was 'the feeling of thankfulness that if these great trials were to come upon our island there is a generation of Britons here now ready to prove itself, not unworthy of the days of yore and not unworthy of those great men, the fathers of our land, who laid the foundations of our laws and shaped the greatness of our country'.

It was, he seemed to stress, principally a British occasion – almost as if Hitler had declared war on us rather than the other way round. But what about the country on whose behalf we had declared war? Churchill's next sentence contained a cold and even cruel truth in the rhetoric: 'This is not a question of fighting for Danzig or fighting for Poland. We are fighting to save the whole world from the pestilence of Nazi tyranny and in defence of all that is most sacred to man.'

Greenwood, for the Opposition, clearly found the realism embedded here difficult to bear but took comfort in some rhetoric of his own. 'For fifty-four hours', he said, 'Poland has stood alone at the portals of civilization, defending us and all free nations and all that we hold dear.' At this, there were cheers from all parts of the House. 'She has stood with unexampled bravery, with epic heroism before her hesitant friends have come to her aid. Poland we greet as a comrade we shall not desert.' (Once again there were loud cheers from all around the House.) 'To her we say, "Our hearts are with you and with our hearts all our power until the angel of peace returns to our midst."'

Now that hesitation had been removed it remained to be seen how 'all our power' – which was what the first clause of the Anglo-Polish treaty had pledged – could be sent 'at once' to Poland's aid. She was desperately in need of aid from somewhere. In the past fifty-four hours the Germans had driven deep into Polish territory, had virtually cut off the Corridor and were within fifty miles of Warsaw. The Germans' communiqué claimed that they now had 'unchallenged air domination over all Polish territory'.

Welcoming at last in London Britain's declaration of war, which was to be followed by that of France at 5 p.m., the Polish Ambassador in London, Count Raczynski, in view of this German claim to control Polish air space, expressed the hope 'that aerial activity on the part of Poland's allies in the West will help to redress the balance and put a stop to such attacks'.

What for the first two days of the war had been no more than Britain and France's benevolent neutrality was now formally at an end.

Meanwhile a number of foreign governments had hurried to declare themselves formally neutral, some having sympathy with Germany, others with Britain and France. Among the former was Italy, which had declared that it would take no initiative in military operations and was to consider itself in a position of non-belligerency rather than neutrality. Hitler had sent Mussolini a telegram approving of this stance, saying that he was convinced that with German military force he would be able to fulfil the mission 'destined for us. I think then that in these circumstances I will not have need of military aid from Italy.'

Spain, whose neutrality in the First World War had proved a source of considerable economic wealth, again declared herself neutral, an attitude easier to accept for many of General Franco's extreme right-wing supporters after the sense of shock and revulsion they had felt after the signing of the Nazi-Soviet Pact.

In Ireland's Free State, known since 1937 as Eire, Mr de Valera at once extracted from the neutrality which he proclaimed the advantageous nuances which that country's ambivalent past required. While indicating that many people in Ireland had their own sympathies (a statement which in itself allowed for two opposing views while apparently stressing whichever one the hearer wished to hear stressed) he used the opportunity to celebrate his own nationalistic tradition and make of neutrality not a negative attitude but a positive one of being against both sides at once. Ireland, of all nations, he said, had known what force used by a stronger nation against a weaker could mean. They had known the meaning of invasion and partition. They were not forgetful of their own history and so long as any portion of their country was subject to force by a stronger nation they ought to look to their own country first.

There could be no neutrality of any sort for the IRA, which spent the weekend of 1 to 3 September in Belfast attacking individual territorial soldiers and trying to strip them of their uniforms. One Private named McCullach was shot in the back in North Queen Street though the bullet was successfully extracted in hospital. In retaliation the Northern Ireland Government took a further forty-five IRA men 'into care', in the words of the Prime Minister, Lord Craigavon, as an added precaution against sedition and such attacks. They would remain there, he said, until the end of the war or until something happened to justify their release. All of which suggested that Churchill's famous remark in his book on the First World War about the dreary steeples of Tyrone and Fermanagh re-emerging afterwards from the receding floodwaters of great events as if nothing had happened might well prove equally true after the second.

In Washington there was no doubt about where most American sympathies lay. The *New York Herald Tribune* described 'an overwhelming sentiment for the French and British side of a sort which had not appeared last time until late 1915 or 1916'. This, it said, 'seems to rule out any course of policy founded on the futile assumption that the American people will be wholly indifferent to the outcome of a new European war'. On the other hand, the wish to keep out of that war was paramount and Roosevelt broadcast at once that 'this nation will remain a neutral nation' and that 'as long as it lies within my power there will be no blackout of peace in the United States'. He did, however, stress that even a neutral nation had a right to take account of the facts and could not be expected to ignore her conscience. And in a quite uncontroversial display of conscience he addressed an appeal to the five belligerent governments in Europe not to bomb civilians and open towns. More controversially, taking advantage of the technicality that Britain and France had not yet officially informed the United States of their decision, he postponed proclaiming the arms embargo made obligatory by the Neutrality Act but expected to do so within forty-eight hours. His broadcast was essentially an appeal for unity in the nation and an abandonment of partisan attitudes and he took care to include phrases to please isolationists like Senator Lodge of Boston, who had just been scoffing at another attempt to save the world for democracy, and recommending, 'We save democracy for the world.' 'We must act', said Roosevelt, 'to preserve the safety of our children in future years. . . . We seek to keep war from our firesides by keeping war from the Americas.'

But British and French firesides were now committed to war, and in Poland the news of this was welcomed enthusiastically in the streets of Warsaw between air-raids. The Government issued a statement to the effect that Poland's soldiers had 'for three days been shedding blood against a barbarian invasion which has violated the most primitive sense of justice. From today the alliance of Poland, the British Empire and France begins.'

What would that alliance now do for Poland? 'Within a day or two,' the *New York Times* correspondent in London had written, 'perhaps before twenty-four hours have elapsed, British and French troops will be fighting the Germans.'

PART III

3 SEPTEMBER – 31 DECEMBER 1939

23

The first real act of war for Britain – that is to say if the merciless assaults being suffered by the armies and civilian population of Poland were somehow to be regarded in a different category – took place in the afternoon of the day she declared it, at sea off the Hebrides and some 250 miles to the west of Donegal, but not on any British initiative. The Donaldson Atlantic liner *Athenia*, which had started out from Liverpool for the United States before the declaration of war, carrying, in addition to a crew of 315, 1,103 passengers, of whom 300 were United States citizens hoping to escape from the dangers of war, was torpedoed and sunk by a submarine, which afterwards came to the surface and shelled it on its way to the bottom. The *Athenia* had carried no guns.

A large number of survivors were picked up by two British destroyers and Norwegian and Swedish boats which were not far from the vicinity, but there were accidents to some of the lifeboats and 128 passengers were drowned. The Germans at first claimed to know nothing about the incident and the *Hamburger Fremdenblatt* even suggested that there was something suspicious about so many ships being suddenly on hand for the rescue and that Churchill, activated by his 'long ungovernable hatred of Germany', had sunk the ship himself. The submarine had, however, been seen by many of the US passengers, and the event seemed likely to provide a strong moral reinforcement for Roosevelt's position when he should come, as he inevitably would, to try once again to persuade Congress to repeal the Neutrality Act.

Britain suffered her first casualty on land early the next morning when in the course of an air-raid warning – which again turned out to be a false alarm – Police Constable George Southworth was killed falling from a third floor in Harley Street, London, after climbing up a drainpipe in an attempt to put out a light in one of the rooms there. He had been unable to get a reply when he knocked at the door.

'Poland's Stout Defence; Incessant Air Raids' – were the headlines in *The Times* that morning, and that afternoon the RAF went into action, carrying out a bombing raid on ships in Wilhelmshaven and Brunsbüttel at the entrance to the Kiel Canal. The raid was carried out in very poor visibility and the last stages of it in a blinding rainstorm, but the bombers came in at low altitude and claimed two hits on a pocket-battleship. The Germans named it as the *Gneisenau*, which it said had been bombed but not hit. They claimed at first that five bombers had been shot down and then twelve. American reports told of one unidentified bomber that afternoon dropping its bombs on the Danish town of Esbjerg and killing a civilian there. The Danes protested to the British Government against this infringement of their neutrality and received an apology saying that the aircraft had not been one of those that returned and explaining the hazardous conditions of the raid. The British newspapers, which were now under the tutelage of the new Ministry of Information, admitted that there had been casualties to the RAF but nothing like the figure claimed by the Germans. Later this statement was revised to say that the casualties had been nothing like the greater figure given by the Germans.

Those who were to think that this raid might be the beginning of a sustained air offensive to help the Poles were quickly disillusioned. Further RAF flights did indeed take place and over Germany too in the course of the week, but they were, in the words of an RAF communiqué, 'for the purpose of distributing a note to the German people'. There had been a number of such 'reconnaissance flights' by the end of the week and Chamberlain was proud to announce that ten million such 'notes' had been delivered.

Their content was a little curious. In arguing that the war was unnecessary because Germany was neither threatened nor deprived of justice, the leaflet implied that what Hitler had done at least up to 1939 had been no more than to obtain for Germany the justice that was her due. 'Was she not allowed', it asked, 'to re-enter the Rhineland, to achieve the Anschluss and to take back the Sudeten Germans in peace? Neither we nor any other nation would have sought to limit her advance so long as she did not violate the independence of non-German peoples.' The leaflet concluded by telling the German people that 'you do not have the means to sustain protracted warfare' and that 'you are on the verge of bankruptcy'.

The only known practical result of these leaflet raids was a protest from the Dutch Government to the British about the infringement of Dutch air-space in such flights. No resistance was met over Germany, and the *Manchester Guardian* pointed out that the German people might draw the obvious conclusion that, had Britain so wished, the leaflets could well have been bombs.

The Times in its headlines continued to chronicle what was happening in Poland: 'The Polish Struggle – Garden Cities Bombed' on 5 September and 'Poland's Gallant Fight Against Odds' on the 6th. On the 5th a correspondent to *The Times* had quoted Thucydides: 'As long as we have a particle of sense we shall not suffer our allies to be oppressed; nor shall we postpone our aid, as they cannot postpone their sufferings. No, we shall help them now and with all our might. We could not with honour deliberate longer.'

But the bombing of targets in Germany, though something which could be immediate and shown by the leaflet raids to be within Britain's power, was not, it seemed, to be undertaken even for the sake of honour. On 1 September President Roosevelt had issued an urgent appeal to all belligerents not to bomb civilians, and both Chamberlain and Hitler had expressed adherence to this humanitarian principle. Events in Poland, however, had quickly shown that the techniques of modern warfare made short work of chivalrous aspiration and

A Pole stands in his doorway dazed by German bombs: 'When is the help you promised coming?'

Last round-up in Warsaw, Poland, September 1939.

indeed the German High Command was, within a fortnight, to admit this with a published threat to 'employ all the means at its disposal to break resistance in open towns, markets and villages in battle areas'. Chamberlain nevertheless was to go out of his way to stress in the House of Commons that 'whatever may be the lengths to which others may go, His Majesty's Government will never resort to the deliberate attack on women, children and other civilians for purposes of mere terrorism'. The statement was greeted with loud cheers. Military targets in Germany were not, it seemed, to be bombed either (except in attacks on naval bases for the protection of British shipping) for fear presumably of encouraging reciprocal attacks against the British mainland.

The Times on 7 September reported that the Polish Government had moved to Lublin and that Cracow, a vital strategic point to the south, might be in German hands. There was, it said, a danger to Warsaw in the north. 'The Drive on Warsaw' on 8 September became 'The Fate of Warsaw' on the 9th.

Chamberlain's verbal support for the Poles was convincing enough when he gave the House of Commons his first review of the war on 7 September, praising their courageous and determined qualities and affirming that in spite of human and material losses their morale and courage remained unaffected. There was a cool, if sympathetic, detachment about his observation of what was happening to his allies, as if Britain's own war, which he had entered on their behalf, existed in a separate dimension from theirs.

> The Germans [he remarked] appear to be endeavouring to force a decision in this theatre [i.e. Poland] before they are compelled to transfer formations to the west to meet the threat of Allied intervention. With this object in view they have continued their relentless pressure on the Polish army, hoping thereby to break resistance and turn a hardly-contested withdrawal into a retreat.

But he did have a small bonus to offer the Poles: 'His Majesty's Government and the French Government have today signed an agreement with the Government of Poland for the provision of further financial assistance to enable her to replenish her resources.'

It was announced in Britain on 9 September that those theatres, football grounds and other places of entertainment closed in evacuation reception areas could now reopen. Those living in the danger zones were urged not to use their cars in order to travel into such safe areas for purposes of the said entertainment.

The streets of Warsaw were now reported to be filled with retreating Polish columns and the General in command of the garrison there issued an Order of the Day: 'We have occupied positions from which there is no retreat. At this outpost we must die to the last soldier.' And he ended: 'I am speaking from the Polish wireless station, which may be struck by the enemy's blows at any moment. If our aerial suddenly becomes silent it will be because it has been devastated.'

John Masefield, President of the National Book Council, had a letter in *The*

Times that day, in which he advised the laying-in of books against the long autumn and winter nights that lay ahead. 'The buying of books and the joining of libraries will certainly provide many helpful and forgetful hours and may possibly help to preface a peace in which the world may again bring forth some intellectual fruit.'

That weekend in Britain some macabre operations were taking place off the coast of Anglesey in North Wales, to which the sunken submarine *Thetis* had finally been successfully towed. Eighteen of the ninety-nine bodies had been recovered by Sunday the 10th. They were taken wrapped in canvas by tugs to the Moelfre lifeboat house, behind which waited a local contractor's grey lorry covered in tarpaulin. In this they were carried through the hedge-bordered Anglesey lanes to Holyhead, where a mass grave had been dug. The funeral, it was announced, was to be at public expense and relatives would be provided with a third-class rail return fare in order to attend it. The tribunal of enquiry which had concerned itself over many sittings with the most intricate details of human and mechanical behaviour – there having been some evident failure in both – stood adjourned for the time being. It was not to be concluded until December, and even then the President, Mr Justice Bucknill, could only say that in due course he would submit his report to the proper authorities. The Attorney-General in his own summing-up said a series of unconnected events seemed to have conspired together to produce the disaster. It was clear, he thought, that the disaster was not due to any failure of the structure (a view with which the attendant representative of Cammell Laird, the firm which had constructed it, was happy to concur), but to some mistake, the nature of which might never perhaps be completely clear. It seemed a fair enough judgment applicable also to the much greater number of victims the sea had been claiming since.

The Times began the second week of the war in a vein of admiration for Poland similar to Chamberlain's. 'Poland's Gallant Struggle' was the headline on Monday 11 September, followed on Tuesday by 'A Breathing-Space in Poland; Poland Stands Fast'. On both days there was a map showing the rapid drive of the Germans into Poland from north, west and south with a long eastwards-pointing nose-like Polish bulge round Warsaw. An assessment of the week's fighting by *The Times* military correspondent stressed not only the dogged fighting qualities of the Polish soldier but also the difficulties the Germans were likely to be having with their stretched communications after the destruction of so many bridges, culverts and railway lines. He explained that what the Poles were achieving was 'an orderly withdrawal'. Then, he said, there was the pressure being put on the Germans by the French in the west, which was 'obviously strong and increasing in strength', though 'it would be over-sanguine to expect quick large-scale results from operations against defences such as the Siegfried Line'.

The Times also imparted the information via a Mr Ray Bishop, writing from

'General Headquarters' in its letter columns, that the 'Tipperary' of this war was a song called 'Little Sir Echo'. In fact neither the tune nor the empty words of this momentarily popular ditty were a match for its famous forerunner. An attempt at something more relevant appeared from the hands of two song-writing anti-aircraft gunners. This ran:

> We're going to hang out the washing on the Siegfried Line,
> Have you any dirty washing, mother dear?
> We're going to hang out the washing on the Siegfried Line
> 'Cos washing day is here.
> Whether the weather is wet or fine
> We'll rub along without a care:
> We're going to hang out the washing on the Siegfried Line
> If the Siegfried Line's still there!

A German announcer on the Cologne–Hamburg radio station found this to be in very poor taste by contrast with 'Tipperary'. He refused to accept that it had been written by anti-aircraft gunners and said it was probably thought out by 'Jewish scribes in the BBC'.

The Siegfried Line was still there. The exact importance of the operations by the French army in front of it was difficult to determine from the short communiqués which had been published. The very first of these, on 4 September, had been laconic enough to have meant anything: 'Operations have been begun by the whole of the land, sea and air forces.' It was a sentence at the time capable of encouraging the embattled Poles and all who felt for them to believe that a major effort was about to be made by France and Britain to take German pressure off them. The RAF raid on Wilhelmshaven and the Kiel Canal that afternoon, though clearly not directly relevant to the Polish front, could be seen as confirmation of the intention to draw German forces away from Poland.

Subsequent French communiqués spoke of 'many local advances', and 'our first elements progressing beyond the frontier with an advance varying according to the different parts of the front'. There was still a possibility of serious action to be gleaned from this by those who so wished, although there were no further raids by the RAF. Even as late as Thursday 7 September *The Times* was talking of 'pending operations on a large scale' in the west which would reveal 'how unfounded is this persistent German presumption that Poland's allies will be as false as the Nazi Government itself'. However, the French communiqué of that date began to clarify what was happening. There were references to occupation of the no-man's-land between the Maginot and Siegfried lines. This varied in depth between three and thirteen miles. Here, it was announced, at some points French advances had actually extended to a short distance beyond the German frontier.

On 8 September the French General Staff announced that it was determined to avoid unnecessary losses while at the same time reporting 'fierce fighting' near

September: British soldiers leave for France again, but no casualties yet.
British Territorial Army reservists meet their sergeant-major.

Lauterbourg in the no-man's-land opposite Karlsruhe. And although at the weekend the French claimed they now held some 350 square miles of German territory, this was along a 120-mile front, giving an average depth therefore of about three miles; a large part of the forest of Warndt, west of Forbach, was in their hands. The Germans merely said that the French had left numerous dead behind on German territory and several prisoners including an officer – which suggested the limited scale of the fighting. Though the Germans were reported to have moved six divisions to the Siegfried Line as a result of such actions there seemed no evidence that these had been withdrawn from the seventy German divisions fighting the Poles, and there was certainly none to suggest that if they had, it had made any difference to the pace of their advance in Poland. In any case on Tuesday 12 September what the French in their communiqué were calling substantial progress on a twelve-mile front to the east of Saarbrücken was put into proportion by *The Times* Paris correspondent, who wrote that the wild reports which had been published in some quarters exaggerating these local advances into a piercing of the Siegfried Line were 'ridiculous. . . . All that is happening so far is that the French are feeling their way forward and testing out the enemy's strength everywhere with equal strength and determination.'

If there were to be a major offensive in the west there was presumably to be a major British contribution to it. On 11 September, the day before *The Times* Paris correspondent's sobering assessment, news of what had been rumoured for days had been finally confirmed: British troops were now in France. However, the Ministry of Information made clear that they were not in action. Some days later it was made to seem as if the arrival of the British Expeditionary Force in itself had been the action. It was announced that not a single man had been killed in the course of it. As to the French losses, the Paris paper *Excelsior* reported that in most French units the number of killed and wounded had been less than the normal number of casualties to be expected from transport accidents in the relevant period.

Although part of the Siegfried Line had undoubtedly been powerfully fortified and photographs of impressive rows of dragon's teeth to prevent the passage of tanks were to be seen in the British press, other parts were clearly vulnerable if not almost non-existent. A British reconnaissance pilot flew over it at 100 feet and described to the *Manchester Guardian* what he saw: 'I was impressed', he said, 'most of all by the unfinished state of the Siegfried Line.' He said it was absurdly easy to pick out because the grass had not had time to grow again over the scarred earth. 'In many places we saw mounds of freshly-thrown-up earth and white patches where they had been burrowing in the chalky soil. However, we saw no one actually at work on it.' He described how in one place he flew over a huge gun which a group of men were camouflaging. 'I could distinctly see them gaping up at us with their paint-brushes in their hands, apparently unable to move. Only when we were right past them did they seem to recover from their astonishment. Then some waved their hands while others went racing back to their huts.' Elsewhere they flew over a camp. 'Men came crowding out of the huts, and here it looked as though they were waving at us – though of course they might have been shaking their fists!'

By the middle of the second week of the war it was already becoming clear that the Poles were in the throes of one of the greatest military disasters in all history. *The Times* still proudly proclaimed 'Stiffer Polish Resistance' on the 13th, and on the 14th: 'Poles Resisting Strongly', while at the same time not disguising another reality: 'Devastation in Poland'. But that not everyone in Britain felt happy just to admire the Poles' courage was shown the same day when Hugh Dalton for the Labour Opposition rose in the House of Commons and said, 'May I ask whether the War Cabinet has constantly in mind the solemn obligation entered into in our Treaty of Alliance with Poland, whereby we undertook to render to Poland all the support and assistance in our power?'

'Yes, certainly, sir,' replied Chamberlain. And he left it at that.

'Ring Closing Round Warsaw' was *The Times* headline on Saturday 16 September and the Russian paper *Pravda* was already analysing the internal causes of Poland's military defeat. Such a total and overwhelming defeat, it said, was not to be explained merely by the superiority of German military equipment and 'by the lack of effective assistance to Poland on the part of Great Britain and France'. It was to be attributed to the internal instability of Polish society and the Polish State, in which insufficient attention had been paid to the large racial minorities, such as Ukrainians and White Russians, who had not been given autonomy on the Soviet model.

There were, coincidentally, increasing Soviet complaints of violation by Polish planes of Soviet air space and a number of Polish planes had been forced down. A Danish correspondent in Berlin reported that 'well-informed political circles are expecting very extensive military action by the Russians in a few days' time'.

Suddenly, on Monday the 18th, *The Times* made clear that what in Saturday's issue had been 'Poland's Desperate Fight' was all but over. 'Collapse In Poland', it revealed; 'Crushing German Attack'. The paper's correspondent in that country revealed that what only a few days before he had described as 'An Orderly Retreat' was something very different: 'The Polish front has collapsed completely.' But that was not all. There was a third headline in *The Times* that day: 'Red Army In Polish Territories', and the following day *The Times* reported 'The Rape Of Poland' with news that German and Russian troops had met at Brest-Litovsk, that the country was being partitioned and that the Polish Government had fled into Rumania. 'Meanwhile', wrote *The Times*, 'a shocked world watches the consummation of the dishonour by which they have been betrayed.' It meant the work of Ribbentrop and Stalin.

As usual, if words could have helped the Poles they would have been in no difficulties. The editor of *The Times* brought the full force of his resonance to their aid: 'In the agony of their martyred land', he wrote hopefully, 'the Poles will perhaps in some degree be consoled by the knowledge that they have the sympathy, and indeed the reverence, not only of their allies in Western Europe but of all civilized people throughout the globe. ... Poland now passes into Babylonian captivity.' In the House of Commons, Chamberlain stoutly averred that: 'nothing that has occurred can make any difference to the determination of His Majesty's Government, with the full support of the country, to fulfil their obligations to Poland and to prosecute the war with all energy until their objectives have been achieved'. And Churchill obliged with: 'The world which has watched the vain struggle of the Polish nation against overwhelming odds with profound sympathy admires their valour.'

Only Arthur Greenwood seemed to feel that such words were not quite enough, but his own words, though accompanied by the occasional 'hear, hear', and cheers from his Opposition supporters, did not seem to stir any very profound unease. He told the House:

> One thing I must say: it is a matter for very deep regret that once an understanding was reached with Poland, that she was not provided far more generously with sorely-needed assistance. ... It may be that what help we could have given Poland would not have enabled her to resist the terrible onslaught of both the Germans and the Russians. But it lies on my conscience and on that of other Members of the House that we did not do rather more for her before this terrible trial came upon her.

The trials of peace that now awaited the Polish people could only be guessed at, but there was evidence from Czechoslovakia, Austria and indeed Germany herself to suggest that they would be terrible indeed. Even the trials of war were not quite over. Warsaw, the capital, was still holding out under a merciless bombardment from the surrounding German artillery and from German bombers unchallenged at low altitudes.

It was to continue to do so for another forty-eight hours. Between 9 and 9.15 p.m. on Wednesday 20 September the BBC in London sent a message on its Polish news service to the city of Warsaw:

> All the world is admiring your courage. ... We, your allies, intend to continue the struggle for the restoration of your liberty. Please reply if you can to this message on SPZ 7170 kilocycles during to-night.

The Lord Mayor of Warsaw, Stefan Starzynski, replied thanking London for the message from the bottom of his heart and saying that the brutal bombardment of Warsaw was being carried out mercilessly.

'I feel therefore entitled to make a new appeal to you,' he concluded. 'When will the effective help of Great Britain and France come to relieve us from this terrible situation? We are waiting for it.'

24

A distinguished historian of the twentieth century described over twenty years ago the war which broke out in 1939 as 'a matter of historical curiosity'. He separated it from the real Second World War, which began when Hitler attacked Soviet Russia in June 1941, seeing the earlier phase as the last chapter in a European struggle which had begun in 1918 and ended with Hitler's greatest victory of all, the defeat of France, in 1940.

It could equally well be said that there was a separate war within that 'historical' war of 1939, namely the war in Poland. In the course of 1939 the governments of Britain and France had apparently abandoned the policy of appeasement with which the year had hopefully opened. In this there was a double paradox: not only did their inclinations remain to avoid war by appeasing Hitler but they were manoeuvred into abandoning the policy by Hitler himself, who would have preferred them to maintain it. Trapped somewhere within this double paradox were the unfortunate Poles. A British Government took one of the most fateful decisions in its country's history in the name of honour on behalf of a people for whom it did almost nothing to help save from destruction within a fortnight. Of course it is true that Britain and France had entered the war because they felt that something greater than the cause of Poland was ultimately at stake. But the fact remains that Britain had repeatedly pledged itself to go to the aid of Poland immediately it was attacked with 'all the support in its power'. Politicians on all sides had consistently attached Britain's honour to this pledge. Whether, if together with France she had honoured it regardless of the consequences to herself, this would have saved or in any way altered the martyrdom of Poland is a hypothetical question of the sort historians should refrain from considering. But to the purely moral question there can be only one answer. The honour, of which politicians had spoken so virtuously for so many months during 1939, faltered. Looking back nearly half a century later, it is difficult not to echo those words of Arthur Greenwood's in the House of Commons on Wednesday 20 September 1939: 'it lies on my conscience ... that we did not do rather more for her [Poland] before this terrible trial came upon her'.

The *Manchester Guardian* wrote: 'War was made on Germany but not war of a kind or a heat to compel her to bring back her airmen from Poland. This is a terrible episode in our history whatever the explanation may be.'

The explanation was never to be pursued very far.

It fairly soon became clear that the rest of 1939 was to be an anti-climax, and the people of Britain and France soon became accustomed to it. They were left with a war on their hands.

The prospect of this war had for the past eight months filled everyone in the West with the worst forebodings for the future of civilization and mankind. In Britain over 200,000 air-raid casualties had been anticipated in the first twenty-four hours. And yet, except to the Poles, virtually nothing had happened. The air-raid warning in Britain on the morning of 3 September, which seemed to fulfil all the direst expectations based on experience in China and Spain, had led only to the all-clear – an event symbolic, as things were to turn out, of the rest of the year.

In this the pattern of the last four months of 1939 was quite different from that of the first eight. The keynote of those first eight months had been their uncertainty and unpredictability. During that time no one could ever say what might or might not happen next, or indeed be wholly certain about what was happening at the moment. In the last four months of the year – or at least after the annihilation of Poland in the middle of September – the international scene was felt to be at least temporarily immobilized. Even the largest and most dramatic single event, the war which the Soviet Union launched against Finland on 30 November, was plainly a sideshow, even though one which, thanks to the spectacular military successes of the outnumbered Finns, was the cause of much cheering on the sidelines by the western democracies – bizarrely joined in this, though more discreetly, by Spain and Italy.

The Finnish refusal to accept the Soviet threat of satellite status, to which the Baltic States, Estonia, Lithuania and Latvia had been reduced a few weeks earlier by a bullying technique analogous to Hitler's, was a source of encouragement and inspiration to the democracies but plainly not central to whatever realities Hitler himself might have in store for them. For in this respect alone there was a similarity with the first two thirds of the year: it was the democracies who were waiting for Hitler to act. That they themselves did not consider taking any strong military initiative soon became publicly accepted. The *Observer* wrote on 8 October:

> In the air ... the position will remain one of waiting for Germany to move. And that she will move seems to be the opinion of those most qualified to judge. ... Both side are waiting. Great Britain is waiting for Germany to make a move ... Germany is waiting until everything is ready – possibly including the weather.

At the end of the month, on 29 October, the same paper wrote that Hitler's plan of action on the Western Front was 'shrouded in a veil of impenetrable mystery'.

By that date it did not need phrases in French communiqués to the effect that 'the first touches of winter' were hampering operations on the Western Front to make clear that the Allies themselves had no plan to extend operations in the foreseeable future if at all. Occasional newspaper phrases such as that Saarbücken was 'about to fall into our hands like a ripe plum' soon staled. The first British

The war in Finland: a Finnish soldier guards Russian corpses; the crouching
Russian on the left is dead, frozen rigid in that position. BELOW More Russian losses
in men and material.

troops, though announced as landing on 11 September, did not go into the Maginot Line effectively until the beginning of December and the first British soldier to be killed in action against the Germans was not killed until 9 December, Corporal Thomas William Priday leading a patrol there nearly three months after the defeat of Poland. Only three British soldiers had been killed in action by the end of the year.

More serious British casualties had occurred in the air and at sea. The heaviest were in the Royal Navy, largely as a result of German initiative. HMS *Courageous*, one of the earliest British aircraft carriers (a former cruiser launched in January 1917), had been sunk, by a submarine it was reported, as early as 18 September and of the crew of 1,100 there had been only 438 survivors. An even greater disaster shocked Britain on 14 October when HMS *Royal Oak* was torpedoed by a submarine which not only succeeded in penetrating right inside the defences of Scapa Flow but in getting out again undetected: 24 officers and 786 other ranks were lost.

In so far as there was a fighting war in these months it was fought, apart from skirmishes between the Maginot and Siegfried lines, at sea and in the air – and when in the air, largely as part of the war at sea. At sea it was a war fought against and on behalf of merchant shipping and the only encounter between orthodox naval units before the end of the year – a dramatic one which was to take place in December – was itself a consequence of this lethal game of catch-as-catch-can on and under the high seas.

It had been expected that Germany's most effective naval weapon, in view of her known inferiority in capital ships by contrast with the Royal Navy, would be her submarine fleet. And so it turned out to be. It became clear at once, and not only with the sinking of the *Athenia*, that a number of German submarines were already dispersed around the world ready to pick off British merchantmen wherever they were to be found. However, when Churchill, First Lord of the Admiralty, gave his first statement on the subject to the House of Commons on 26 September, admitting that nearly 100,000 tons of merchant shipping had been lost in the first three weeks and saying that further losses must be expected, he permitted himself on the whole an optimistic view for the future. By far the greater number of losses, he said, had occurred in the first week while our merchant ships were scattered and before it was possible to organize any sort of convoy system, and there had been considerable success both by the RAF and the Navy in destroying submarines. There were much greater advantages today in dealing with U-boats than in the campaign of twenty-five years before; and he estimated that one-tenth of all the U-boats afloat had already been destroyed by the end of this third week, and perhaps even as many as one-third of all those actively employed by the German Navy. Some German submarine commanders were behaving with extreme callousness, casting crews adrift with little hope of survival and even firing at them, while others behaved with chivalry. He cited among the latter one who had actually radioed him personally the exact position of the ship he had just sunk, signing his message 'German Submarine'. 'I was in doubt', said Churchill, 'at the time to what address I should direct the reply. However, he is now in our hands and being treated with every consideration.'

On 3 October came the ominous news, with the sinking of the 5,000-ton ship *Clement* of the Booth Line in the South Atlantic, that submarines were not the only risks to which our merchant ships were exposed. For the *Clement* had been sunk by 'an armed raider', a German cruiser or pocket battleship, of which more than one might well be at large. Indeed, the raid on Kiel on the very second day of the war may have been intended to keep as many such German ships in harbour as possible. Perhaps because the casualties on that daylight raid were higher than expected, there was no repetition until the end of the month, when on 29 September another daylight raid took place on the Heligoland Bight, from which 'some of our aircraft', said the RAF communiqué, 'have not yet returned'. The Germans said that six aircraft had taken part and that five had been shot down; also that the attack had been without result.

The RAF, however, remained preoccupied with the North Sea region between the Friesian islands and Heligoland as a target, particularly after the discovery that new magnetic mines dropped by parachute from sea-planes based in that area were adding seriously to the threat to our merchant shipping. Churchill said magnetic mines were 'the lowest form of warfare that can be imagined. It is the warfare of the IRA - leaving a bomb in the parcels office at railway stations.' More than half the British shipping losses in November were caused by magnetic mines.

The RAF raided Heligoland on 3 December again, claiming a hit on a cruiser, and again on 14 December when the principal consequence seemed to have been an air battle in which the RAF lost three aircraft and claimed to have shot down four Messerschmitts. On 18 December what was called 'the biggest air battle of the war' took place over Heligoland in which the RAF admitted the loss of seven aircraft but claimed that twelve German fighters had been shot down. The Germans claimed to have shot down thirty-four RAF machines - a number which the British Ministry of Information maintained was greater than the total number of aircraft on the mission.

That there were some doubts, however, about the value of these raids by Wellington and Blenheim bombers in daylight without the benefit of fighter escort was discreetly voiced by *The Times* air correspondent, hinting, as much as the Ministry of Information allowed him to, that the proportion of casualties was painfully high. 'The results must seem inadequate,' he wrote, 'when the courage of our aircraft crews and the skill with which they fought is taken into account.' However, he added, clearly there was an agreed RAF policy of under-taking no other type of bombing, for instance against land targets, for fear of inducing German retaliation.

The only other RAF activity, apart from the operations of Coastal Command against submarines, was the continuation of reconnaissance flights accompanied by leaflet-droppings over Germany (a night reconnaissance over Berlin and Potsdam was reported on 3 October) and the occasional skirmish in the air while reconnoitring the Siegfried Line.

Just as no bomb had been dropped on German soil (except at the naval bases), so no German bombs had been intentionally directed at British soil, though in the course of a raid on British naval bases, similar to those of the RAF against Germany, one bomb accidentally fell on the Shetlands on 13 November and was said to have killed a rabbit. The most spectacular such German raid had been carried out in the middle of October against Rosyth and the Firth of Forth, again in daylight on the afternoon on Monday the 16th. Though no air-raid warning was sounded in Edinburgh, its citizens were able to spot the swastikas on the bombers as they flew overhead. A dozen or so planes were thought to be involved. Some slight damage was caused to HMS *Southampton* on which three officers and thirteen ratings were killed. Another such raid took place on Scapa Flow the next day and on the 18th Chamberlain said that these air-raids on our naval bases seemed now to be a feature of the war, though they had been fully expected. The total number of German aircraft taking part had been forty. Britain claimed to have brought down twenty-five per cent of them; and certainly there was one Dornier brought down in open country near Edinburgh for all to see in the newspapers. There was, however, no German air action against land targets in Britain before the end of the year though reconnaissance was detected over both London and the Midlands.

Only twice during these months were there rumours or serious suggestions that Germany might be about to launch a real offensive on the Western Front and on neither occasion did they last long. On 14 October, General Gamelin, the Allied Commander-in-Chief in the west, issued an Order of the Day to the French army warning them to be prepared to face a general offensive. He cited this again in an Order of the Day to the British forces under General Gort two months later but only as a general exhortation on the need to be prepared. On 16 October, he said, the German preliminary action had actually started but 'our dispositions prevented any developments. Since then we have seen the Germans increase their preparations but up to now they have not dared to launch a general offensive.' He reminded the British of the need to await the issue with increased efforts.

Again early in the second week of November there was a short scare that the Germans were about to attack in the west through Holland. This reached its high point just after a mysterious attempt to kill Hitler in a beer cellar in Munich on 9 November had failed, owing to his departure from the hall earlier than expected. The Dutch were said to have manned their defences with all urgency, and a curious incident immediately followed in which two British officers, one of them attached to the Embassy at the Hague, were kidnapped by Germans at Venlo in Holland after a man had been shot; they were taken across the border

ABOVE LEFT Business as usual at the Kardomah coffee house. ABOVE RIGHT Gas masks for four-year-olds at Dr Barnardo's orphanage.

Labelled for the countryside, children are evacuated from London.

into Germany. The German press claimed that they were secret service agents who had somehow some responsibility for the bomb plot. The invasion scare, however, quickly died down and the Dutch Prime Minister, Jonkheer de Geer, specifically announced a few days later that there was 'no acute danger for the Netherlands ... not a single reason to be alarmed', and that the rumours had been caused by foreign press and radio reports.

Certainly it was known that the Germans now had some sixty-five to eighty divisions between the North Sea and Switzerland, and patrols in no-man's-land had been stepped up to sizes of between fifty and one hundred men. But most suggestions that the Germans might be about to launch an offensive against the Maginot Line seemed to emanate from the French, whereas in Berlin correspondents were reporting that any offensive was unlikely. Certainly by the end of the year nothing more had happened than that the Germans had recovered a good deal of the no-man's-land territory that had been gained from them in the preceding months. The *New York Times* summed up the four months' action:

> On September 1st, bringing an abrupt end to all efforts at appeasement, the fast motorized units of the German army plunged into Poland. Two days later Britain and France, pledged to help repel such an attack, finally entered the war on Poland's side. Last week with Poland in an advanced stage of German–Soviet digestion, the military situation on the Western Front stood pretty much as it had been on September 1st.

It was thought that the local German advances had been just enough to enable Hitler to boast that he had been able to spend part of his Christmas on French soil.

The editor of the *Observer*, J. L. Garvin, early began to show concern that the British people might be lulled into an apathetic sense of false security by the inaction to which they were becoming accustomed, and by the routine character of the home front. His film critic, C. A. Lejeune, had reported as early as the end of September that cinemas could now reopen and Clark Gable and Norma Shearer be seen in *Idiot's Delight*. Theatres could stay open until six o'clock and the non-stop Windmill show *Revuedeville* was beginning its 125th edition every day at noon. Towards the end of October Garvin was becoming quite seriously worried. 'The war', he said, 'was expected to be an apocalypse of terror from the outset. Instead, after seven weeks it looks to many like a dull and even boring enigma.' He then issued a warning against thinking of the war like this, as some inconclusive kind of struggle which would be indefinitely prolonged. That Britain and France had had 'seven full weeks without any serious interruption from the enemy is an advantage we never dreamt of enjoying. It is a gift from the gods – our people should be thankful for every minute instead of being dulled'. He did not make clear in what way the gift was to be turned to advantage, but, inferring that there must be one, said that the Allies had designed the postponement of what he called 'full grapple' for good reasons. 'The apparent dullness', he concluded, 'will be exploded soon enough, like a volcano bursting from quiescence into eruption.'

However, the year 1939 was to remain quiescent to the end. Nearly a month later Commander Stephen King-Hall, the newly-elected Independent Member of Parliament for Ormskirk, a man much vilified by Hitler for his firm anti-Nazi views though in reality no more than the author of an independent newsletter and a column in the *Sunday Pictorial*, wrote in that newspaper: 'The war remains in a state of suspended animation in which there is not much animation and a declining quantity of suspense.' A fortnight later the editor of the same paper, Hugh Cudlipp, faced up to what he called the fourth month of the war against aggression with the words: 'Our cities have not been bombed to destruction. Our proud race has not been defeated by death from the skies, by plague, starvation or by mustard gas. There have been no tremendous lists of casualties as we may have expected. The war indeed has turned out to be "a very queer business altogether".'

There had even been a moment quite soon after Hitler's subjugation of Poland when it had seemed just conceivable to some that the war might evaporate altogether. The Russian–German agreement settling the partition of conquered Poland was formalized in Moscow by Ribbentrop and Molotov on 29 September in a solemn German–Soviet Treaty of Friendship. Its first article included the statement that it would be in the real interest of all nations to end the state of war that existed and that Russia and Germany would make joint efforts, if necessary in agreement with other friendly powers, in order to attain this aim as soon as possible. The friendly powers clearly included Italy, where Chamberlain's old white hope of appeasement, Mussolini, had just made a speech at Bologna reflecting that it would be better for Great Britain and France to stop the war.

Mussolini's son-in-law Ciano went to Berlin to see Hitler on Sunday 1 October and two days later Chamberlain himself dealt with the suggestions in the German–Soviet Treaty of Friendship in the House of Commons, saying clearly that though he couldn't anticipate any proposals that might be made, no threat would ever make the country give up the reason for which it had entered the war, namely to put an end to successive acts of aggression by Germany, whose word in these affairs could not be trusted. But he added: 'If proposals are made we shall certainly examine them and we shall test them in the light of what I have just said.'

The debate which followed was notable chiefly for an intervention by Lloyd George who, having said that something better than the word of Hitler was certainly necessary as a guarantee for peace, also said that it was important that we should not come to too hurried conclusions about the proposals that were about to be made. Two neutral countries, he said, Italy and Russia, would be behind the peace proposals and the House should take time to consider them when they came. He asked for a secret session. Chamberlain, while disagreeing with the desirability of a secret session and saying that the offer might well be one which no self-respecting Government could accept, did agree with Lloyd George that they should not be in a hurry to give an answer to a proposal which really appeared to require serious consideration.

There was no uncertainty about the feelings of the House on that day. Lloyd George's speech caused a great deal of concern among Members, though there were those who congratulated him on his courage, and one in particular, George Buchanan, the Member for the Gorbals, said that he couldn't in fact find the so-called great unanimity for the war which was said to be behind the Government. Duff Cooper, deploring what he said amounted to consideration of surrender, made the best realistic point when he said he couldn't imagine the Germans now proposing terms which did not take into account the great victory they had just won.

Hitler's peace terms were in fact delivered to the world in a speech to the Reichstag on 6 October and they were both vague and, in the sense which Duff Cooper had indicated, sweepingly arrogant. A new Polish State was to be set up to be determined to the satisfaction of Germany and Russia; the only further revision of Versailles required was in connection with such colonial possessions 'as were due to the Reich'; the 'Jewish question' was to be 'solved'; there should be an international conference to discuss these things together with matters of general wider international concern such as disarmament and the economic ordering of markets and currencies.

If proffered with serious intent these proposals could only make sense on the basis that the British and French Governments were still at heart appeasement-minded and wished at almost any cost to get out of a war which they had hoped always to avoid, and for the nominal cause of which – the independence of Poland – they had displayed little endeavour. But such reasoning showed a lack of perception about what had happened in the democracies.

Though it had been a muddled process by which Britain and France had entered the war, their belief in their determination once the muddle was resolved had been all the stronger for their former uncertainty. And though new experiences of their own might well call the whole decision into question again, the most prominent feature of the war so far had been that they had had no new experiences of their own. Self-respect was something they still managed to hold onto after Poland, and Hitler's proposal was basically that they should surrender that too. As the *San Francisco Chronicle* wrote: 'The peace proposal boils down to the simple proposition that a burglar should be confirmed in his loot and given complete indemnity, in return for which he offers a conditional promise to cease housebreaking.'

Whether with intent or not Hitler had made it much too easy for Britain and France to say 'No'. As the *Manchester Guardian* had asked when the prospect of some such proposals was first considered:

How could any Englishman face the world if ... his country resigned itself to the extinction of Poland and settled down to its own life again as if nothing had happened? ... To what place should we sink in history after such a betrayal? And what notice would be taken of our Minister when he had crept shamefaced to his inglorious seat at the conference table?

It was reported from Berlin that those in close association with Hitler were 'serenely confident that his peace appeal would be heeded'. There was some talk of Roosevelt possibly offering mediation, should the Allies request it. The Soviet Government endorsed Hitler's terms, saying in *Izvestia* that they 'can serve as a real practical basis for negotiations for the early conclusion of peace'. But when Chamberlain, the man who would have had to take that seat at the conference table, gave the Government's formal reply on 12 October in the House of Commons his rejection was clear and unmistakable, even though the terms in which he expressed it bore his own singularly unemotive stamp. 'It would be impossible', he said, 'for Great Britain to accept any such basis without forfeiting her honour and abandoning her claim that international disputes should be settled by discussion and not by force.'

The only area of public divergence from this view – apart from the negligible British Union, or Fascist party – was to be found in a sort of intellectuals' coalition left of centre, which included up to a point Lloyd George, the weekly *New Statesman and Nation*, George Bernard Shaw and Stafford Cripps. Cripps, still an exile from his own (Labour) party, said in the House of Commons that the question was not whether we should accept these proposals but whether we ought to seize this opportunity to make a perfectly clear declaration of our own war aims and call for a world conference on the basis of such proposals. Comrades from the party from which he was temporarily expelled cheered him when he said this. He went on to say that the alternative was to proceed with a war that would mean the destruction of all the values of civilization ... the most terrible slaughter among soldiers and civilians. If in reality there were an honourable part which we could now take to diminish the likelihood of that catastrophe, he felt concerned that every responsible Member of the House would be only too anxious to take that alternative.

And this, though more specifically, and thus perhaps less realistically spelt out, was much the view of the editor of the influential weekly of the day, the *New Statesman and Nation*, Kingsley Martin. Martin had indeed begun the war in an idealistically pacific mood. 'To have begun the war by dropping leaflets instead of bombs on the towns of Germany is a right and imaginative stroke of good augury for the future,' he had written on 9 September as the Luftwaffe pounded the towns of Poland. Now, just over a month later, he counselled a reply to Hitler in terms which demanded 'a further answer from him. We should discuss his proposals in a blunter way than he may expect. ... Our reply to Hitler should be to turn his conference into our conference, open to him and to all who come. Our terms and our protocol should be on the table.'

An irritated correspondent, Princess Elizabeth Bibesco, wrote to the paper: 'There is a certain incoherence in our left-wing blackouts. All that is clear to the reader is: war was desirable until it occurred and peace is desirable since war has arrived.'

Lloyd George's sympathetic consideration of an immediate constructive approach to peace had seemed all the more disturbing to those who remembered the inspiration he had given the country as a Prime Minister in the First World War. In the popular Sunday newspaper, the *Sunday Pictorial*, he was taken severely to task for his 'surrender' speech in an article headed 'Twilight of a God' by the editor, Hugh Cudlipp. The week before, Cudlipp had even attacked Clement Attlee himself as being too timid and irresolute successfully to lead the Opposition, by contrast with Arthur Greenwood – 'the man who stopped the wobblers on the eve of war'. Attlee, of course, had not been well. 'In health', wrote Cudlipp, 'Clement Attlee was never a powerful leader, never a personality to reckon with. In sickness he is an impediment to the progress of vital national work. ... He is pathetically useless as the Leader of the Opposition. He is a miserable orator. And he is distinctly uninspired.'

It is however interesting to note, as an indication perhaps of the way in which the very stalemate in the war staled all attitudes, that for all the retribution meted out to Lloyd George in this issue of 15 October, in the *Sunday Pictorial*'s last issue of the year, Cudlipp literally gave Lloyd George his head: a large portrait of the former Prime Minister dominated the front page and he was there permitted to address himself in bold type to 'what he sees as the relevant question: "Will 1940 see the end of this strange and costly war?"' Lloyd George's analysis was that there were three possible contingencies ahead: (1) a sudden military victory of one side or the other; (2) the reduction of one side or the other by economic pressure and a blockade; and (3) 'that exhaustion and sheer boredom may make all nations revolt against the heavy taxation, flagging trade, ruined businesses, diminishing rations, blackouts and restrictions in every direction, and demand peace'. He ruled out the first contingency on the grounds that neither Britain nor France was 'contemplating offensive operations which would involve a repetition of the terrible carnage of the last war'. Britain, he pointed out, was not even taking steps to raise an army comparable in strength to last time. The Germans too, he felt, showed the same reluctance to repeat the last war's slaughter of its young manhood. The second contingency he ruled out on the grounds that Germany's alliance with Russia, in which the ties seemed to be becoming friendlier all the time rather than the reverse, made it impossible to conduct an effective blockade of the type which had helped to win the last war. Therefore only the third contingency remained and he spelled this out as follows:

As the war drags along, carrying increasing burdens on a weary world, the belligerents will begin to groan for a peaceable termination to their miseries. They will all be equally tired of the costly futility of a war which no one really wanted and which provides no spectacular appeals to national emotions, and they will insist that their rulers shall find some means of terminating so ruinous a conflict. Let us hope that in such a mood a just, satisfactory and workable peace can be obtained before the conflagration spreads to the whole of Europe and Asia.

But of course there were those whose groans and miseries would have remained unaffected by such rationally conceived relief. For them peace would have meant only perpetuation of that hell in which they lived. Their fate does not seem to have entered very prominently into the higher considerations of the world's statesmen.

On the last days of October, His Majesty's Government issued a White Paper giving details of the unimpeachable information it had been receiving throughout the year from its British Consuls-General in Germany about conditions in German concentration camps – principally about the torture and death inflicted with ever-increasing brutality and indifference on the inmates of Buchenwald and Dachau. The White Paper was issued with an explanation that such details had been withheld so long as there seemed a chance of peace being maintained, from fear of inflaming a delicate situation, and that it was only being published now because the Germans were indulging in an unprecedented propaganda campaign of hate against Britain. There were queues for the White Paper outside the Stationery Office in Kingsway, London, and between 8,000 and 9,000 people were reported to have bought it on the first day, but since it was known that governments at war with each other traditionally accuse each other of atrocities there was the danger that such revelations, known in fact to the Government since the beginning of the year, could be partially dismissed as mere counter-propaganda.

The next day, six distinguished barristers who had spent some time interviewing Jewish refugees living at the refugee camp at Richborough in Kent wrote to *The Times* to attest the same hideous details from the information which they had received there. This confirmed the worst of the White Paper's picture of German concentration-camp horrors, with accounts of men being made to crawl naked along paths of broken gravel, being hung from trees by their wrists tied behind their backs and receiving twenty-five strokes with steel-core whips, for such trivial offences as drinking water during working hours. 'Men were put to death', wrote the barristers, 'in circumstances so horrible as to be almost unbelievable ... for no other reason than that they were, by accident of birth, non-Aryan.'

Both sets of reports confirmed incidentally that the treatment had hitherto been used as a means of encouraging Jews to abandon everything they had in Germany and emigrate. 'Before leaving the camp', the British Consul-General at Munich had reported of Dachau on 5 January 1939, 'they are addressed by the Commandant, who advises them to leave Germany as soon as possible, since should they return to the camp they would never be released.' Once the war had closed Germany's frontiers and those frontiers had been extended to enclose the million and a half Jews in Poland, the outlook for all Jews within them acquired an even grimmer and more sinister aspect. It was an outlook the full horror of which it was perhaps still impossible for the mind of twentieth-century man, as he was in 1939, to grasp. On 4 September – four days after the German attack on Poland, when the German armies had already penetrated deep into the country – a revealing exchange took place in the House of Commons.

Colonel Josiah Wedgwood asked the Prime Minister whether His Majesty's Government 'will now review their request to the Rumanian Government to refuse passage of Jewish refugees over the Polish–Rumanian frontier, where 600 are now starving?'

R.A. Butler, the Parliamentary Under-Secretary at the Foreign Office, replied: 'His Majesty's Government are not prepared in the present circumstances to invite the Rumanian Government to modify their policy regarding the passage of Jewish refugees through Rumanian territory.'

Wedgwood: 'Is it not a fact that the Rumanian policy was initiated under pressure from His Majesty's Government and could we not cease this anti-semitism now that we are really at war with Hitler?'

Butler: 'We have left Rumanian policy to the discretion of the Rumanian Government. It is true that His Majesty's Government made a request through the Rumanian Government to this effect.'

Before long it became known from Jews who had managed to escape from Poland that the Germans were establishing there in the Lublin area a special 'Jewish Reservation' (*Judenreservat*) to which transports of Jews were being sent under SS guard and where they lived in camps which they had had to build themselves under SS supervision. From the SS camp at Tomaskov near Lublin it was reported that Jews, 'though apparently not physically ill-treated', were being 'starved to death'. There were increasing reports of such transports being sent to Poland from different parts of the Third Reich. Vienna was to be '*judenrein*' (free – literally 'clean' – of Jews) by February 1940. 'This scheme', wrote *The Times*, 'envisages a place for gradual extermination.' Precise numbers involved, it said, were not yet known but 'the size of the programme is very nearly irrelevant. It amounts to a mass massacre such as Nazi imagination can conceive but even Nazi practice can hardly carry through in full. Meanwhile it serves as a means of torture for many thousands and of terror for all the rest.' The *Manchester Guardian* reported at the end of December through its diplomatic correspondent that there was reliable and detailed information that Germany had been executing an average of 200 Polish Jews a day since the beginning of the war.

It was not of course only Jews in Poland who were being executed. There were continual reports of Poles being shot and hanged publicly by the Germans for the flimsiest of reasons or none at all. Towards the end of November it was reported that Stefan Starzynski, the Polish Mayor of Warsaw, who had addressed his city's desperate plea for help to the BBC, had been sent to Dachau.

Some of those who got away: Jewish refugees from Germany arrive in Palestine.

Some of those who did not: Jews rounded up by Germans at a camp in Poland, September 1939.

From Czechoslovakia too there came news of German brutality and national martyrdom, though on a more subdued scale, barely disguised by the message which Baron von Neurath, the Reich Protector, addressed to those in his keeping at the end of the year:

> Thanks to the wise decision of its State President to place itself under the protection of the Reich, the Czech people have been spared the fate of Poland. It can go about its work in quiet and peace, and all the essential conditions have been assured to open up for it a happy existence in the Greater German Reich. One condition for this is admittedly that the Czech people fit into this powerful community without after-thought.

Thus a dark night in which were to be concealed nightmares such as mankind had never before experienced descended on much of Europe and thus the year 1939, in which the great European powers had taken some of the most far-reaching decisions in their history, ended paradoxically with almost nothing happening on the international scene at all. Even what had already happened there in the course of the year, though dramatic, had been on a scale only to leave the dangers of a full-scale conflict and serious public injury to civilization still in the balance. Poland and Czechoslovakia had disappeared from the map but they had been off it before. Other things that had happened had happened before. Spain had ended a civil war; the Jewish people were in awful travail; Chinese peasants were subject to cruel vicissitudes ordained by distant warlords; Irishmen were killing and risking death in the belief that these things would free their country; Russia remained both part of Europe and not part of it and her peasants too were being mown down in a war which had little meaning for them, while those who fought them fought not them but the historic menace of the Russian bear. All these things had happened before. What possibly had not happened before was that the world had not waited for whatever was going to happen next with quite such a sense both of impending doom and ignorance as to the form that doom would take. There was even uncertainty as to whether it would materialize at all.

At such a time heroic actions beyond the humdrum tenor of the inconvenient but otherwise tolerable ways of life which passed for war (food rationing – and then only in a limited form – was not even introduced in Britain until after the end of 1939) were welcome not only as sources of human inspiration in themselves but also as some stabilizing reassurance that war was what it said it was. The David and Goliath aspect of the Finnish struggle did much to hearten people in this respect, though no one seriously expected it to end exactly in the form of the Bible story. Occasional naval episodes also stirred national spirits in a way which conformed agreeably with accepted conventions.

In the third week of December the British public received a Christmas present in the form of a small individual naval action in the seas of the South Atlantic, the exciting nature of which and its detailed reporting in newspapers all over the world again emphasized the strange isolation of the lives of most ordinary men and women and indeed of most soldiers, sailors and airmen from the war in which they were nominally involved.

That, in addition to the German submarine fleet, there were at least two or perhaps three German pocket-battleships on the high seas preying on Allied merchant shipping had been known for certain ever since survivors of the 5,000-ton Booth Line ship *Clement* had reported the sinking of their ship by an 'armed raider' in the South Atlantic on 5 October. Sinkings of other Allied merchant ships continued with unpleasant frequency in southern seas for the next two months. However, the first pocket-battleship to be encountered by the Royal Navy was found in quite different waters.

On Thursday afternoon, 23 November, the former P&O liner *Rawalpindi*, refitted as an armed merchant cruiser of the Royal Navy, painted grey and carrying 6-inch guns, was on contraband control enforcing the blockade of Germany, flying the White Ensign in the waters south-east of Iceland. Its Captain was Captain Edward Kennedy RN, who had retired in 1922 and in the meantime been among other things a Conservative political agent in Buckinghamshire. Most of the rest of the crew were Royal Naval reservists. At about 3.30 p.m. the *Rawalpindi* sighted an enemy ship on the horizon at a distance of about six miles. There was speculation as to whether it was the *Deutschland*. Captain Kennedy, examining it through his binoculars, declared: 'It's the *Deutschland*, all right', and immediately ordered his men to action stations.

The *Rawalpindi* was, of course, hopelessly outgunned in such a situation but smoke floats were put into the sea in the hope of evading the battleship, when a second enemy ship was sighted to starboard. The *Deutschland* signalled the *Rawalpindi* to stop and, when she refused to do so, sent a shot across her bows. This was equally ignored, and the first salvo came from the *Deutschland* at about 3.45 at a range of some 11,000 yards. The *Rawalpindi*, outranged, closed on her, firing with all four starboard guns. The third salvo from the *Deutschland* put out all her lights and destroyed the electric mechanisms of the ammunition supply. The fourth salvo shot away the bridge and wireless room. The second German ship had by now moved round behind her and was firing at close range. The *Rawalpindi* continued to fight until every gun was out of action and almost the whole ship ablaze. At about 4.20 the enemy ships stopped firing.

Three boats, one of them waterlogged, put off from the *Rawalpindi* and twenty-six survivors were picked up by the *Deutschland* before the approach of a British cruiser sent her off again into the fading light to follow her mysterious hunting-paths among the northern seas. Eleven more survivors, who had managed to swim to the waterlogged boat, were picked up by another British armed merchant cruiser, the P&O liner *Chitral*, and brought back to Britain to tell the heroic tale. At about eight o'clock that evening the *Rawalpindi* finally turned turtle to starboard and foundered with all remaining hands on board: 39 officers and 226 ratings were lost. Captain Kennedy went down with his ship.

Noble and heroic as the fight of the *Rawalpindi* had been – several commentators justly compared it with the fight of the *Revenge* under Sir Richard Grenville as described by the poet Tennyson – a victory at sea had so far eluded the greatest navy in the world. Indeed, with the loss of the capital ships HMS *Courageous* and HMS *Royal Oak* – though not the aircraft carrier *Ark Royal* in spite of persistent German claims – a naval victory was something of a pressing emotional requirement for the British people. Not long after the sinking of the *Rawalpindi* they were to have one. However, what the Germans at any rate were to claim as a further effective humiliation of the British Navy was to take place first.

On 28 August the queen of Germany's merchant navy, the liner *Bremen*, had arrived in New York and because of the apparent imminence of war had wanted to turn round and leave again as quickly as possible, but had been delayed for thirty-six hours by a United States contraband search. This was interpreted by the Germans as an unfriendly act intended to increase the risk of capture to the returning *Bremen* on the high seas should war break out. War did break out but the liner successfully reached the northern Russian port of Murmansk without interception on 6 September. There she spent fourteen weeks in safety before leaving for her home part on 10 December. The Germans proudly announced her arrival at Bremen on 12 December, claiming that a British submarine had tried to attack her in the North Sea *en route* but had been driven off by aircraft.

The British account was that the *Bremen* had been within torpedo range of the submarine but had been allowed to pass because the 1930 London Naval Treaty stipulated that belligerents should not sink merchant ships without warning and without allowing the crews and passengers to escape first. (The two versions were not incompatible: to have complied with the 1930 treaty regulations would presumably have exposed the submarine to a suicidal risk from the aircraft.) The British popular newspapers, however, voiced a sense of frustration, if not humiliation. 'Why didn't we sink the *Bremen*?' asked the *Daily Express* of 13 December, putting arguments both for and against action. 'Why wasn't she at least crippled?' asked the *Daily Mail*. There were those in Britain who felt some understanding for Germany's ridicule of the British statement as a face-saving exercise for a piece of naval incompetence.

A third leader in the *New York Times* of 13 December discussed the subject of German surface raiders and their actions against merchantmen on the high seas, on which they could outrun almost any ship in the British Navy. Such pocket-battleships were, it maintained, the backbone of the German Navy and the loss of one of them would be a tremendous blow to German morale.

That very evening at about six o'clock a Captain of the Uruguayan Navy, Captain Zapicán Rodríguez, was staring out to sea through his binoculars at Punta del Este at the mouth of the River Plate, having heard rumours all afternoon of a naval battle being fought some 200 miles to the north-east. Suddenly he spotted a warship some twelve miles away heading at full speed south-westwards towards land and flying the German flag in the evening sunlight. As this ship appeared over the horizon he spotted two other warships, a number of miles behind but apparently gaining on it. An hour later, at about 7 o'clock, firing began – first a batch of about twenty shells, followed by a short lull while the ships manoeuvred. This in turn was followed by a much fiercer gunnery battle in which about 120 shells were fired. By this time it had grown dark but the ships were closer inshore and he could see the flashes of their guns in the night. He was watching the closing stages of what was soon to be known as the Battle of the River Plate.

At dawn that day the British cruiser *Ajax* had been escorting the French passenger liner *Formosa* in those seas when she was attacked by the German pocket-battleship *Graf Spee* – though the first Admiralty report of the action was to describe her as the *Admiral Scheer*. Two more cruisers, HMS *Achilles* and the heavier HMS *Exeter*, arrived to help *Ajax* and immediately opened fire. *Exeter* in particular did great damage to the *Graf Spee* but was herself largely put out of action. The *Graf Spee* eventually turned and ran for the shelter of the River Plate, chased by the *Ajax* and *Achilles* which, though out-gunned by some 3,000 yards at first, having only six-inch guns compared with the 11-inch guns of the *Graf Spee*, were faster than the German ship. By making skilful use of smoke-screens and darting in and out of them to close the range, the two British ships inflicted further damage on the *Graf Spee*, which just before midnight limped into the neutral haven of Montevideo.

The British now demanded that she should leave within twenty-four hours but the Uruguayan Government said they would allow her to remain for repairs to make her seaworthy again. There was some dispute as to what repairs in fact were permissible in this context – the 1907 Hague Convention making clear that in such a situation a ship should not be allowed to improve her fighting capacity. Finally the Uruguayan President said he would give the *Graf Spee* seventy-two hours and ordered her to leave Montevideo at 6.30 p.m. on 17 December. Otherwise she would be interned, together with her more than 1,000-man crew, for the rest of the war. An interesting discovery was made while she was in harbour, to the effect that she had been carrying on board sixty-two British seamen, including five Masters from nine merchant ships intercepted and de-stroyed by her in the course of her predatory patrol of the South Atlantic. These survivors had been correctly treated, though they were still clad only in the clothes in which they had been shipwrecked. They sent a wreath to the funeral of the thirty-six members of the *Graf Spee* crew killed in the action. The funeral procession passed through Montevideo witnessed by some 100,000 citizens from the pavement including some Germans who dutifully raised their arms in the Nazi salute. 'To the brave men of the sea from their comrades of the British Merchant Service', ran the wreath's inscription. Seventy-two British sailors were killed in the battle, sixty-one of them in HMS *Exeter*.

The *New York Times* correspondent in London said that the news of what had happened had caused more rejoicing there than any event of the war to date. The mystery of so many ships lost in the South Atlantic was now cleared up, as also was the identity of the raider, thought to have been the *Admiral Scheer*. But, as his paper stated in a leader the next day: 'The end of an epic is still to be told.'

The *Graf Spee* was due to leave Montevideo at 6.30 p.m. on 17 December. At about 10.30 p.m. on the 16th lights on board, which had been burning brightly ever since nightfall while repairs continued, were put out to prevent the work being seen from the shore, but welders were still at work at 11.30 p.m. Local opinion was convinced that the *Graf Spee* would try to escape rather than accept internment for the duration of the war in Montevideo.

Half an hour after midnight the barges and launches which had been supplying her all day cleared from her side and she lay with bow pointed out towards the narrow opening in the breakwater that formed the entrance to the outer harbour. She would have half an hour's run before reaching the open sea and whatever might await her there. The reception committee, it was suggested, consisted probably of the cruiser *Cumberland*, her recent enemy the *Achilles*, and possibly the battleships *Barham* and *Renown* together with the French battleship *Dunkerque*. Many eyes were upon her as she lay at anchor throughout the night.

By 3 a.m. the moon had gone, the wind had died and a light fog had set in. At 3.30 Captain Hans Langsdorff, the *Graf Spee*'s captain, was seen to return to his ship after dining with the German Minister on shore. Diplomatic pressure for an extension of the ship's stay was known to be continuing.

All next day the *Graf Spee*'s crew worked busily further repairing the damage from the British shells and taking provisions on board. Hundreds of sailors were seen to be working all over the ship's superstructure and an observer described them, dressed in their brown and khaki overalls, as looking like brown ants scampering over an anthill. By 6.20 p.m., a bright sunny evening, almost the entire population of Montevideo was watching to see what would happen from docks, sea walls and rooftops.

The *Graf Spee* set off before her time limit expired towards the gap in the breakwater. If on passing this she were to turn west it was thought that she would be going to Buenos Aires, where internment might be more favourable than in Uruguay. If not, she could be heading for the open sea. She did turn west but it soon became clear that she was not necessarily going to Buenos Aires. The *Tacoma*, a German supply ship, followed her. It was reported that all the married men on the *Graf Spee* had been transferred to the *Tacoma*, suggesting that she might indeed be going to choose action. British warships could be seen on the horizon.

Just after seven o'clock the *Graf Spee* turned upstream to Buenos Aires but then anchored. It was difficult to see what was happening exactly because night was beginning to settle over the River Plate. Then at 7.55 there was a deep, dull explosion which was heard all over Montevideo. A great cloud of grey smoke

Captain Langsdorf (*left*) and officers of the *Graf Spee* with British merchant captains, held prisoner on the pocket battleship after she had sunk their ships in the south Atlantic, attend the funeral in Montevideo of thirty-six of her crew killed in the Battle of the River Plate.

The Wagnerian doom of the *Graf Spee* as she is scuttled by her captain on to the bed of the River Plate.

arose, followed by sheets of flame and further explosions. The entire ship's company had been taken off: the crew into waiting barges and launches and Captain Langsdorff and his officers into a separate launch from which, exactly as the sun went down over the horizon, Langsdorff had pressed an electric button which blew up a mine placed in the ship's magazine. The *Graf Spee* had been scuttled. Within three minutes she had settled on the river bottom and flames were soon roaring her entire length. The order for this Wagnerian doom was said to have been given by Hitler himself.

Langsdorff and his crew then set off up river to Buenos Aires, where they hoped to be treated as survivors of a sunken vessel, entitled to repatriation rather than as belligerents to be interned in a neutral country. In this they were to be disappointed. This may or may not have determined the final event in this dramatic story. On 19 December Captain Langsdorff killed himself with his own revolver in the naval arsenal in which the Argentines had interned him.

On 21 December the North German Lloyd liner *Columbus*, the third largest ship in Germany's merchant fleet, also scuttled herself some 300 miles off the coast of Virginia, where she had been intercepted by a British destroyer, which put a shot across her bows. She had hitherto been spending some time in the agreeably neutral company of American warships and one of these, the cruiser *Tuscaloosa*, now brought her crew, over 500 strong, safely into New York.

Britain's naval victory over the *Graf Spee* had, however, stirred American imagination. The *New York Herald Tribune* called the pocket-battleship's scuttling 'a spectacular admission of defeat'. In Walter Lippmann's words, the defeat of the *Graf Spee* was 'pleasing in all the Americas'. But sympathy with the Allied cause in the States, though warmed by such an event, coincided more strongly than ever with determination to refrain from joining it. The United States Ambassador in London, Joseph Kennedy, speaking in Boston on 10 December, had issued a call which, though it might be painful to some British ears, was a straight enough reflection of the way many Americans felt. 'As you love America,' he said, 'don't let anything that comes out of any country in the world make you believe that you can make a situation one whit better by getting into the war. There is no place in this fight for us. It is going to be bad enough as it is.'

Of course, from one important point of view the situation was very much better for the Allied cause than it had been when the war started. Roosevelt, in his broadcast of 3 September, while stressing his determination to keep the United States out of war, had also said that he could not ask every American to remain neutral in thought. 'Even a neutral', he said, 'has the right to take account of facts. . . . He cannot be asked to close his mind or conscience.' Two days later, however, he could delay no longer and had had to implement the existing Neutrality Act which officially proscribed the delivery of any arms to the war zone. But on 21 September he summoned Congress in extraordinary session to consider his proposals for revision of the Neutrality Act. These consisted, as anticipated, of removal of the arms embargo and at the same time the reinstate-

Then, life was natural, simple and full. To-day it is complicated exhausting and nerve-racking. Your body is fighting an unequa struggle. Luckily, as the article below shows, 'Sanatogen Nerve-Tonic Food can restore the balance.

How to win *your* 'war of nerves'

In warfare, every new offensive weapon is quickly met by an effective method of defence. Poison gas brings he gas mask, more perfect aero-lanes are countered by bigger and better anti-aircraft guns, and so on.

better of you, start a course of 'Sanatogen' Nerve-Tonic Food at once. But don't wait until the enemy's attack has weakened you. Start building your defence line *now*. By putting yourself and your family

HOW TO HAVE REAL WARMTH IN EVERY ROOM

ment of the old 'cash and carry' clause, by which other materials of use to a war economy could only be carried in foreign ships and after they had been paid for. Acceptance of the proposals was, however, by no means a foregone conclusion.

The Bill was debated both in the Senate and the House of Representatives for most of the following month. The arguments of both sides were very much what they had always been. Senator Pitman of Nevada, supporting Roosevelt, argued that if you thought an embargo was the way to preserve the peace of America, then you should apply it not only to arms but to all types of material that could possibly be used by belligerents, and this was plainly impossible. Senator Borah of Idaho sounded a familiar warning: 'Having changed our laws and our policies that we may send arms to the Allies, will we, can we in the hour of greater need refuse to send our armies? Whatever may be the philosophy of Nazism, however abhorrent we may write it down, it is not an issue in this conflict and its cure is not war.' The Bill was finally carried in the Senate on 28 October by 63 votes to 30 and in the House of Representatives on 2 November by 242 votes to 181. It received the President's signature on 4 November and within a month more than 130,000,000 dollars-worth of orders for aircraft engines, machine-guns, anti-aircraft equipment and other war material had poured into America from Britain and France. Chamberlain, in a speech which, because he was unwell at the time, was read for him by Sir John Simon at the Lord Mayor's Banquet, pronounced the revision of the Neutrality Act 'a momentous event. ... It reopens for the Allies the greatest storehouse of supplies in the world.'

It being the end of the year, it was in fact a time to take stock. As usual on such occasions, newspapers and their readers tried to look into the future, undaunted by the particularly opaque quality which 1940 seemed to present. The financial editor of the London *Observer*, in noting the firmness shown by prices on the London Stock Exchange, commented that it was 'indeed surprising in view of the obscurity in which the events of the coming year are shrouded'. Some things were of course quite normal. It had been a good Christmas for book sales – the Queen's *Book of the Red Cross* doing particularly well as also were James Agate's anthology *Speak for England*, Richard Llewellyn's *How Green Was My Valley*, Jan Struther's *Mrs Miniver* (said to be going like hot cakes), Vicki Baum's *Nanking Road* and – particularly at Harrods – Angela Thirkell's *Before Lunch*. A negligible demand for James Joyce's *Finnegan's Wake*, which had appeared in the course of the year, troubled few. 'London booksellers', wrote the *Observer*, in its traditional sonorous style, 'standing at the dead end of a testing year, facing a grim unknown one, take heart of grace too and sound the note of hope for the new year in spite of rises in book prices, in spite of war risks insurance, in spite of income tax, in spite of everything.' The editor of the *Observer* maintained his stance against national apathy. 'Nothing is more fallacious', wrote Garvin, 'than to call this a dull war. You might as well blame a remarkable overture for not being the whole of a grand opera whose motive it suggests.'

The *Observer*'s rival, the *Sunday Times*, while also warning of 'stern ordeals' ahead and the possibility of a German land offensive 'exceeding in weight and severity even the greatest in 1914 to 1918', contrived a certain backwards looking complacency in doing so. 'The war', it said, 'has now lasted four months and we have certainly no reason for dissatisfaction for the measure of success that 1939 has given us. It has banished, as far at any rate as one can see ahead, the horrible nightmare of the slaughter of Ypres, Verdun, the Somme and Passchendaele in the last war.'

There were even those who, with similar complacency, were prepared to go much further. The writer St John Ervine, in a letter to *The Times*, compared Britain's position at the end of the first year of the present war with that of the end of the first year in the previous world war and found it incomparably better. His assessment of the present situation was as follows:

The German people are disunited and, compared with 1914, inefficient and under-nourished. Their will to victory is virtually impaired by neurosis. Never at any time a race able to suffer adversity with fortitude, they are now so little able to bear misfortune that they manifest a strong tendency to suicide and despair. . . . By contrast we have again subdued their submarines and mastered their airmen. We have a great army in France and a great army in training. The French are on the top of their form and we are in the pink. But the most significant fact of all, sir, is this. Belgium is uninvaded and the only Germans on the soil of France this day are prisoners.

The *Daily Mail* prided itself on its realism. Resolution was required, it said. Britain's enemies believed they were winning, and 'an excellent case can be made to support their belief'. Britain should copy some of the

hard-headed thinking of the French. . . . Happily we have made a good start. One illusion of which we have recently divested ourselves is that the United States is likely to give us anything more than sympathy or goods for cash. There has been far too much moral and mental leaning on America during the past two decades. Not the least of the victories which we should win from this war is that of standing firmly on our own feet. . . . Appealing eyes must not be turned westwards again as they were in 1917 before the United States finally declared for our side. Sympathy is a charming quality but not much practical use when the gloves are off.

In Rome the air of inaction seemed perhaps more ominous than in London, where a Gallup poll revealed that the British newspapers' lack of anxiety more or less reflected the opinion of their public – sixty-one per cent of all Britons being satisfied with the way in which the war was being run, eighteen per cent dissatisfied, one per cent against it and ten per cent 'no view'. Even the German broadcaster in English from Hamburg had been comfortably integrated into the British scene as 'Lord Haw Haw' – 'a brightener of the blackout' a correspondent to *The Times* named Harold Hobson called him, pointing out that he was the subject of a popular song and revue sketch, and with 'that ineffable voice of his by Cholmondeley-Paget out of Christ Church an irresistible fascination'. But from Rome the *New York Times* correspondent, Anne O'Hare McCormick, reported that the atmosphere was 'heavier than last Spring, the general mood grimmer and more fatalistic but it is still the mood of atmosphere and suspense. While the great military offensive is postponed, Europe is still waiting for the decisive blow to fall.'

In any case, as Christmas approached, talk of peace and goodwill tended to modify such tension as there was. The Pope made an appeal for peace and there was some talk of his being joined in a move for mediation with President Roosevelt who, though the United States had had no official diplomat at the Vatican since 1870, now sent Myron C. Taylor, formerly of the United States Steel Corporation, to be his personal representative there. The partisan quality of the President's neutrality was discreetly veiled in the message he sent with him. The theme was an extension of John Donne's maxim that no man is an island unto himself. 'Because', wrote Roosevelt, 'the people of this nation have come to the realization that time and distance no longer exist in the older sense, they understand that that which harms one segment of humanity harms all the rest. They know that only by friendly association between the seekers of light and the seekers of peace everywhere can evil be overcome.'

Yet there were indications among the American public that the inaction of this strange war that was only spasmodically a war at all was dulling the edge of enthusiasm for the Allied cause. Though opinion polls showed that eighty-seven per cent of those questioned wanted the Allies to win there was a distinct shift by the end of the year in favour of keeping the United States out of the war at all costs.

In India, Gandhi declared his own complementary position for the millions who followed him: 'Show no enthusiasm for the war in Europe and refrain from stabbing Britain in the back.'

From Germany there now came few sounds of peace though still no acts of war. Hitler too had a message, principally for the Almighty, who in the past year had taken Germany under his protection and was asked to give his blessing to it again in the coming one. '. . . For before us lies the hardest battle for the existence or non-existence of the German people.' Goering sounded a more straight-forward stirring call to his Luftwaffe: '. . . You showed the claws of the German eagle to the enemy. The eagle will swoop and strike when the Führer gives the order. The password for the German Air Force for 1940 is Victory!' And General von Brauchitsch, Commander-in-Chief of the German army, also declared confidently that 'the spirit and strength of the troops will give us the certainty of final victory.'

General Franco, who already had his final victory, was in no mood to be generous with it in his New Year Message. True, he stressed the need to unite Spain and to liquidate the hate and passions caused by the Civil War. But this, he said, 'must not be done in the old liberal manner of wholesale amnesties, but by true repentance through toil.' One of those in Spain being accorded such an

King George VI with General Gamelin, French Commander-in-Chief Allied Forces
in France on the 'western front', December 1939. 'The future will be what we want
it to be.'

opportunity was Julián Besteiro, the moderate Socialist member of the last Republican Junta in Madrid, who had done much to ensure a bloodless handover to Franco when all was lost. The prosecutor at his trial had demanded the death sentence. But the court martial had been merciful and sentenced him to thirty years' imprisonment.

Jean Giraudoux, the playwright and now French Commissioner-General of Information, issued a message to Britain for 1940 which contained – perhaps in some subconscious vein of prophecy – references to Joan of Arc, Wellington, the Black Prince and other aspects of the two nations' ancient rivalry, though intended merely to illustrate the noble fighting qualities of each. He ended by proclaiming unexceptionably that each should 'rise on the first day of the year with an ally who shall be worthy of her'.

In Britain on the whole the static nature of the war seemed to have infected the spirit of prophecy itself. Even where the forecasts looked at the possibilities of action they were somehow lifeless and subdued. This was true of different reaches in the political spectrum. The *New Statesman* on 30 December wrote:

> Four months of the strangest war in history now lie behind us. Poland is crushed. . . . On land with uneventful monotony the youth of three nations faces each other across impregnable fortifications and the war tends to become an interminable siege. One risks any prediction about this war with diffidence but the impression grows that even if the Germans contemplated a mass offensive on the French front they have lost their moment and the longer they wait the less likely it is to recur. . . . From this siege warfare in the West with its suggestion of stalemate one side or both is bound to consider the chances of an escape as the New Year runs on. One escape would be to patch up a peace. Failing that, the escape must be a sortie from the siege.

Commander Stephen King-Hall, in the *Sunday Pictorial* at the year's end, looked at evidence of warfare so far and commented particularly on the way in which both sides – whether rightly or wrongly – had decided to confine bombing to warships either at sea or in port – though even this use of the bomber had led to very negligible results. He too went on to make his predictions: 'Hitler will sit tight. . . . We shall not see a spectacular offensive on the Western Front in 1940. . . . There will be no fighting on a big scale and the casualties on the road from the blackout may continue to equal those for the guerrilla war on land, air and sea.'

His paper's editorial prediction was the safest and, indeed, turned out of course to be completely correct.

'And now, in parting,' it said to its readers, 'please accept our greetings for 1940. Remembering this – that 1940 will bring Peace one year nearer.'

General Gamelin, Commander-in-Chief of the Allied forces, also had the soothsayer's knack after a fashion. 'The future', he said in his last message of the year, 'will be what we want it to be.'

Adolf Hitler: 'The British Empire has 40 million square kilometres . . . Germany
600,000. It is quite clear who desires to conquer the world.'

SOURCE NOTES

Many sources are self-explanatory in the text; that is to say, the name and date of the newspaper in which they occur are there stated. Others can be traced by obvious association of events and their dates with *The Times* and the *New York Times* and their indexes, or, where applicable, with *Hansard*. Where I have thought the source was not so obvious or the reader might have a particular wish to confirm it quickly or explore it further I have given a specific reference below.

SYMBOLS:

T	*The Times*	SP	*Sunday Pictorial*
NYT	*New York Times*	DM	*Daily Mail*
OB	*Observer*	DE	*Daily Express*
NC	*News Chronicle*	KCA	*Keesings Contemporary Archives*
MG	*Manchester Guardian*	CDT	*Chicago Daily Tribune*
DT	*Daily Telegraph*	ST	*Sunday Times*

CHAPTER 1
Philadelphia Quakers: NYT, 3/1
New York New Year: NYT, 1/1, 2/1
American coffee: NYT, 29/1
Lejeune: OB, 7/1
Television: T, 10/1, 3/1; OB, 1/1, 8/1; MG,
    3/1; NYT, 30/1
Air Services: NYT, 3/1
NKVD: NYT, T, 3/1
Mussolini: NYT, 3/1
Niekisch: NYT, 3/1
Mooney: NYT, 8/1
British police: T, 2/1
Flogging, Sir R. Coventry: T, 3/1; Lady
    Baldwin T, 10/2
Archbishop: T, 2/1

CHAPTER 2
Barcelona: NC, 2/1; T, 6/1; NYT, 6/1
Madrid: T, 2/1
Manchester Guardian: MG, 2/1
Bartlett, Forrest, *La Stampa*: NC, 2/1
S. Cripps & others: MG, 4/1

CHAPTER 3
Republicans: NYT, 4/1
Taft, Townsend: NYT, 5/1
Morrison: T, 7/1

Chamberlain: NYT, 5/1; T, 7/1
Castle: NYT, 11/1
Eden: NYT, 11/1
Mooney: NYT, 8/1
Al Capone: NYT, 8/1

CHAPTER 4
Spain: NYT, NC, T, DT, 4-11/1
Chamberlain: T, NC, MG, 10-17/1; OB, 8/1,
    15/1; NYT, 13-16/1
Daladier: T, 3/1; NYT, 6/1
Heath: T, 6/1
Italian casualties: T, 13/1
Congress for AFF Cttee: NYT, 11/1

CHAPTER 5
Rublee visit to Germany: NYT, 11/1
Mussolini: NYT, 5/1
Manchurian Jewish settlement: T, 11/1
Jews stranded in Uruguay: NYT, 16/1, 17/1
Jewish children in Britain: T, 12/1
Baldwin Fund: T, NYT, 11/1
Fascists: NYT, 15/1; OB, 15/1
NYT Correspondent: NYT, 15/1
Rosenberg: NYT, 16/1
Goldman: NYT, 17/1
Ben-Gurion: NYT, 17/1
War Office statement: T, 10/1

CHAPTER 6
Matthews: *NYT*, 15/1
Franco: *NYT*, 17/1
Barcelona: *NYT*, *T*, *NC*, 15–17/1

CHAPTER 7
Dunn, Robey: *T*, 12/1
Vivien Leigh: *NYT*, 14/1
Northamptonshire: *T*, 16/1
Wells: *T*, 7/1
Germany & music: *NYT*, 8/1; *T*, 17/1
Niekisch: *NYT*, 11/1
Niemöller: *NYT*, 15/1; *T*, 16/1
Germany, internal: *T*, 2/1
NYT correspondent: *NYT*, 8/1
Scharnhorst: *NYT*, 8/1
The Times: *T*, 4/1

CHAPTER 8
Churchill: *OB*, 8/1
Anderson: *T*, 10/1
Air-raid sirens: *T*, 21/1
Barcelona: *T*, 13/1
Strauss: *T*, 13/1
Geddes: *T*, 18/1
Albert Hall: *T*, 25/1

CHAPTER 9
New York Times: NYT, 21–24/1
Stimson: *NYT*, 24/1
Eden: *T*, 25/1
NYT correspondent: *NYT*, 25/1
Italy: *NYT*, 27/1
New York Times: NYT, 25–27/1
Comboy: *NYT*, 26/1
Hopkins debate: *NYT*, 24/1
Barcelona: *NYT*, 28/1
Pyrenees: *NYT*, *T*, 29/1
Douglas: *T*, 30/1
Barcelona: *T*, 30/1
New York Times: NYT, 29/1
Yeats: *NYT*, 30/1
Nye: *NYT*, 29/1

CHAPTER 10
Beck-Ribbentrop: *T*, 27/1
The Times Mussolini: *T*, 16/1
Hoare: *NYT*, 29/1
Baldwin: *T*, 30/1

New York Times: NYT, 25/1
Lewis-Louis: *NYT*, 26-1
Evelyn Waugh: *T*, 20/2

CHAPTER 11
Senate Mil. Affairs Cttee: *NYT*, 2/1
Johnson, Hoover: *NYT*, 2/1
Ickes: *NYT*, 3/1
IRA: *MG*, *DE*, 7/2, 11/2, 15/2
De Valera: *MG*, *DE*, 8/2
Hornchurch Murder: *Romford Times*
 (weekly), March, April
Key: *T*, 18–19/1, *NC*, 16–17/2
Spain, Figueras: *NYT*, 2/2
Puigcerda: *NYT*, 12/2
Cripps: *T*, 27/1
Enrique Lister Brigade: *NYT*, 8/2
Prisoners: *NYT*, 26/2; *T*, 28/2
Bishop: *NYT*, 26/2
Argelès-sur-mer: *NC*, 9/2, 21/2
Lister Brigade: *NYT*, 16/2
Álvarez del Vayo: *MG*, 6/2
Miaja: *NYT*, 8/2
Matthews: *NYT*, 5/2
Liverpool: *MG*, 1/2
International Brigade: *NYT*, 5/2
Franco: *MG*, 23/2
Trafalgar Square: *T*, 27/2
News Chronicle: *NC* 18/2

CHAPTER 12
Weizmann: *T*, 14/2
The Times: *T*, 9/7/38
Jewish refugee figures: *NYT*, 8/2
Goebbels: *T*, 21/11/38
Cazalet, Winterton: *T*, 30/7/38
Hoare: *T*, 22/11/38
Daily Express: DE, 7/2
Rosenberg: *NYT*, 8/2
Concentration camp releases: *NYT*, 22/1
Zeitlin: *NYT*, 22/1
Goldmann: *NYT*, 17/1
Zionist Congress resolution: *T*, 18/1
Beersheba: *T*, 13/1
Weizmann: *T*, 23/1
Sykes: *T*, 25/1
Refugee figures: *NYT*, 5/2
Masaryk: *NYT*, 16/1
Rublee, etc.: *NYT*, 14/2, 19/2
Queen's Gate: *T*, 14/3
Goering: *NYT*, 24/2

CHAPTER 13
MacCormick: *NYT*, 6/3
Churchill: *DT*, 9/3
Czechoslovakia: *MG*, 13/2, 15/2; *NYT*, 23/2
Commons debate: *T*, 8/2
Tiso: *NYT*, 23/2
Chvalkovski: *NYT*, 23/2, 24/2
Hacha in Berlin: *NYT*, 15/3; *DT* 15/3
Inskip: *T*, 5/10/38
Chamberlain, Attlee: *DT*, *T*, 15/3
Eden, Chamberlain, Grenfell: *DT*, *T*, 16/3
Churchill: *DT*, 15/3
Soviet Embassy official: *NYT*, 21/3

CHAPTER 14
Richardson trial: *Romford Times*, March,
    April
Butler: *DE*, 29/5
Weidman: *OB*, 18/6
USSR: *NYT*, 1/3
Halifax: *T*, 21/3

CHAPTER 15
Eden: *NYT*, 24/3
Danzig: *NYT*, 25/3
Cripps: *T*, 3/4
Bryant: *T*, 3/4
Boon, Danahar: *T*, *DE*, 17/2, 23–24/2
Albania: *T*, 8/4, 21/4
Dutch Government, Roosevelt: *T*, 12/4
Roosevelt: *T*, 15/4
Mussolini, Goering, *Diario*: *T*, 21/4
Hitler: *T*, 29/4

CHAPTER 16
The Times: *T*, 29/4
Moscow, Soviet flyers: *NYT*, 2/5
Chamberlain, Attlee: *T*, 3/5
Mosley, Morrison: *T*, 8/5
Rushcliffe, Shulbrede, Elton: *T*, 3–5/5
Appeasement: *MG*, 6/5
Chamberlain, Attlee, Noel-Baker: *MG*, 6/5
M. Guardian: *MG*, 20/5
Churchill: *MG*, 27/5
M. Guardian: *MG*, 27/5
Squalus: *NYT*, 24–26/5
MacCormick: *NYT*, 19/5
Johnson: *NYT*, 3/5
Landon: *NYT*, 4/5
Gallup: *NYT*, 7/5

Cardus: *MG*, 13/5, 29/5
Thetis: *T*, 2–5/6; *NYT*, 2–4/6
Spain: *NYT*, 27/5
Franco parade: *NYT*, *MG*, 20/5
Kondor Legion: *MG*, 19/5

CHAPTER 17
Wedgwood: *MG*, *DE*, 26/5; *NC*, *DE*, 14/6
The Times: *T*, 20/4
Guardian: *MG*, 1/6
New York Times: *NYT*, 18/5
Ben-Gurion: *NYT*, 14/5
Rabbi: *NYT*, 18/5
Jerusalem: *NYT*, 19/5
The Times: *T*, 3/4
Sachsenhausen: *NC*, 15/6

CHAPTER 18
Chicago Daily Tribune: *CDT*, 3/6
La Guardia: *NYT*, 11/6

CHAPTER 19
Mrs Clarke: *NYT*, 28/6
IRA: *MG*, *T*, 1/7
IRA: *T*, 12/7
China air-raids: *NYT*, 16/1, 4/5, 26/5; *T*, 12/5
Chinese casualties: *KCA* 3410/1939
Tientsin: *NYT*, 25–6/6
Chamberlain, Noel-Baker: *T*, 25/6
Moseley, etc.: *NYT*, 19–21/5, 1–4/6
Bloom, Fish: *NYT*, 28/6
Borah: *CDT*, 14/6

CHAPTER 20
Opinion poll: *NC*, 21/6
Snell: *T*, *MG*, 9/6
Halifax: *T*, *MG*, 9/6
News Chronicle, *NC*, 10/6
Mosicki: *NYT*, 30/6

CHAPTER 21
Zhdanov: *NYT*, 30/6
Chamberlain: *OB*, 30/7
Pravda: *T*, 1/8
Parliament: *T*, 1/8
A.P. Herbert: *T*, 3/8
The Times: *T*, 15/8
Roosevelt, Berkeley: *T*, 15/8

The Times: T, 3/8
Parliament: *T*, 25/8

CHAPTER 22
Lord Privy Seal: *T*, 25/8
Insurance: *NC*, 25/8
France: *T*, 26/8, 28/8
Japan, press: *T*, 25/8
U.S. press: *T*, 25/8
Forrest: *NC*, 30/8
Izvestia, Pravda: T, 28/8
Tourists: *T*, 28/8
France, press: *DT*, 31/8
Diplomatic notes: *T*, 2/9
Chamberlain broadcast: *NYT*, 4/9
Pamphlet: *T*, 1/9
Racynski: *T*, 4/9
de Valera: *T*, 4/9
IRA: *T*, 5/9
Roosevelt: *T*, *NYT*, 4/9
New York Times: NYT, 2/9

CHAPTER 23
Athenia, Hamburger Fremdenblatt: T, 7/9;
    MG, 11/10
Southworth: *T*, 5/9
Esjberg: *NYT*, 5/9; *T*, 5/9, 7/9, 12/9
Leaflets: *MG*, 8/9
Chamberlain, bombing: *T*, 15/9
Thetis: T, 11/9
Songs: *T*, 8/9
Pilot's report: *MG*, 7/10
Excelsior: MG, 30/9

Danish correspondent: *T*, 16/9
Times leader: *T*, 19/9
Greenwood: *T*, 21/9
Warsaw message: *T*, 20/9

CHAPTER 24
Historian: A.J.P. Taylor, *Origins of The
    Second World War*, p.278
Guardian: MG, 25–9
Anticipated casualties: *T*, 24/11
British Army casualties: *T*, *DM*, 27/12; *SP*,
    31/12
Magnetic mines, Churchill: *T*, 7/12
Times air correspondent: *T*, 21/12
Dutch Prime Minister: *T*, 14/11
Garvin: *OB*, 22/10
King-Hall: *SP*, 19/11
Cudlipp: *SP*, 3/12
Izvestia: T, 10/10
Cudlipp, Attlee: *SP*, 8/10
White Paper: HMSO Cmd 6120; *T*, 31/10;
    KCA 3861/1939
Jews in Poland: *T*, 8/11; *MG*, 28/12
von Neurath: *T*, 1/1/40
Books: *OB*, 31/12
Sunday Times: ST, 24/12
Ervine: *T*, 8/11
D. Mail: DM, 13/12
Haw-Haw: *T*, 13/12
Lloyd George: *SP*, 31/12
Gandhi, Franco: *NYT*, 11/12
Giraudox: *OB*, 31/12
King-Hall: *SP*, 31/12
Gamelin: *OB*, 24/12

INDEX

Numbers in *italic* type refer to illustrations in the text.

ILLUSTRATION
ACKNOWLEDGEMENTS

The author and publishers are grateful to the staff of the *Daily Telegraph* picture library for their
help and to the following for permission to reproduce copyright photographs from the
following sources:

John Hillelson/Magnum: ii (Cornell Capa), 31 below (Robert Capa)
Illustrated London News Library: 6 below, 149, 161, 199 above, 253, 339

Mander & Mitchenson Theatre Collection/Angus McBean: 13 above and below

BBC Hulton Picture Library: 41 below, 67 above and below, 111 above, 115, 143 below left and
right, 147 above, 157, 165 below, 179 above left and below, 185 above and below, 199 below,
207 all, 259 below, 269 below, 277 above and below, 288 above, 289 above and below, 313
below, 323 above left, 345

Kobal Collection: 59 below

Rizzoli Editore: 37 below

British Library (Colindale): 41 above, 46, 47 below, 91, 152, 179 above right

Popperfoto: 47 above, 59 above, 75 below right, 129 below, 143 above, 147 below, 165 above,
209 above and below, 231 above, 235 above and below, 239 above, 245, 249 below, 259 above,
288 below, 298-9, 309 below, 313 above, 319 above and below, 323 above right and below,
331 above, 337 above and below, 343

Mansell Collection: 31 above, 75 below left, 129 above

Keystone Press: 11 below, 157 below, 233 below, 309 above, 331 below

Associated Press: 233 above, 269 above

Sport and General Press Agency: 306

Central Press: 249 above

Chicago Daily Tribune: 231 below, 237 below

The Trustees and Estate of David Low: 237 above

Picture research by Linda Poley